MW01259817

TALL TALES AND SHORT SHORTS

Sports Icons and Issues in Popular Culture

Series Editors
Bob Batchelor and Norma Jones

In an age when sports icons cross over into everyday lives and popular culture, the time is ripe for assessing, reassessing, and refocusing our gaze on the significance of athletes in the contemporary world. The Sports Icons and Issues in Popular Culture series engages with star athletes and significant sports issues to examine how they have influenced not just the sporting world, but also popular culture and society. By looking beyond the on-field stats and figures, this series helps readers further understand sports icons both as individuals and as cultural phenomena.

Titles in the Series

TALL TALES AND SHORT SHORTS

Dr. J, Pistol Pete, and the Birth of the Modern NBA

Adam J. Criblez

ROWMAN & LITTLEFIELD
Lanham • Boulder • New York • London

Published by Rowman & Littlefield
A wholly owned subsidiary of The Rowman & Littlefield Publishing Group,
Inc.
4501 Forbes Boulevard, Suite 200, Lanham, Maryland 20706
www.rowman.com

Unit A, Whitacre Mews, 26-34 Stannary Street, London SE11 4AB

British Library Cataloguing in Publication Information Available

Library of Congress Cataloging-in-Publication Data

Name: Criblez, Adam, author.
Title: Tall tales and short shorts : Dr. J, Pistol Pete, and the birth of the modern NBA / Adam J.
    Criblez.
Description: Lanham : ROWMAN & LITTLEFIELD, [2017] | Series: Sports Icons and Issues in
    Popular Culture | Includes bibliographical references and index. | Description based on print
    version record and CIP data provided by publisher; resource not viewed.
Identifiers: LCCN 2016041918 (print) | LCCN 2017011541 (ebook) | ISBN 9781442277687 (elec-
    tronic) | ISBN 9781442277670 (hardcover : alk. paper)
Subjects: LCSH: National Basketball Association—History. | Basketball players—United States—
    Anecdotes. | Basketball—United States—History.
Classification: LCC GV885.515.N37 (ebook) | LCC GV885.515.N37 C75 2017 (print) | DDC
    796.323/64—dc23
LC record available at https://lccn.loc.gov/2016041918

Printed in the United States of America

All images © Larry Berman

CONTENTS

ACKNOWLEDGMENTS

Writing is a solitary process. But despite spending many hours alone at my computer composing, editing, and rewriting, I am also incredibly fortunate to have had tremendous support along the way.

First, I have to thank my editor at Rowman & Littlefield, Christen Karniski, and the series editors, Bob Batchelor and Norma Jones. Their feedback has helped me focus on important topics and themes, and my book is much better because of their input.

This project began three years ago when I took a trip to Springfield, Massachusetts, the home of the Naismith Memorial Basketball Hall of Fame. During my visit, I had the opportunity to meet Matt Zeysing, the curator and historian. Matt and his crew provided some great ideas and helped me shape this book at an early stage.

A big thanks to my colleagues at Southeast Missouri State University. In particular, my department chair, Wayne Bowen, has supported my work on this book and helped me develop a course on sports history as a result of my research. And Susan Welker, from Southeast's Kent Library, has gone above and beyond to track down hard-to-find books, magazines, and microfilm.

Although my Ph.D. work was in nineteenth-century social and cultural history, I have found sports historians unbelievably welcoming as I invaded their turf. In particular, Aram Goudsouzian, Aaron Haberman, and Johnny Smith have given me fantastic advice and become good friends along the way.

The Internet has made connecting with other hoop-o-philes easier than ever. I have not met Shawn Fury, Jason Mann, Rich Kraetsch, or Todd Spehr in person, but all are passionate about basketball history and have helped my research and writing. Matt Love, another Internet connection, hooked me up with terrific audio files from the Trail Blazers' 1977 championship run, and Stanley Radzicki provided dozens of videos so I could watch a little fabulous footage from the era.

I was fortunate to stumble onto Larry Berman's photography website (bermansports.com) through a random Internet search, and he graciously agreed to provide the images for both the cover and the interior of this book. His photographs are top notch and truly bring this story to life.

And finally, my biggest thank you goes out to my family, especially my wonderful wife Jennie and our three daughters: Avery, Eliza, and Charlotte. Thank you for tolerating hours of vintage NBA video marathons. Thank you for understanding why I had to spend many evenings and weekends researching and writing. And thank you, most of all, for your love.

PREGAME

The 1969 Finals

In January 1970, Americans flocked to theaters to watch the dark comedy *M*A*S*H*, starring Donald Sutherland as Captain Benjamin "Hawkeye" Pierce; they swayed in time to B. J. Thomas's "Raindrops Keep Fallin' on My Head"; they cheered for the Kansas City Chiefs (or the Minnesota Vikings, poor saps) in Super Bowl IV; and some even watched professional basketball. In the first NBA game played in the 1970s, Chet "the Jet" Walker and the visiting Chicago Bulls outscored the Seattle SuperSonics by eight points in the final minute to escape with a 114–111 win.

Most Americans celebrated the beginning of the new decade on the first of January. But by the time of the Bulls comeback win in Seattle, basketball fans were already in midseason form. In fact, August 4, 1969 (just two weeks after Neil Armstrong took his famous giant leap for mankind), was the real start of the seventies in the NBA. That day, a new issue of *Sports Illustrated* hit newsstands carrying a surprising headline: Bill Russell was retiring as the player-coach of the Boston Celtics. "Since 1943, when I first saw a basketball," Russell explained in the exclusive interview, "I've played approximately 3,000 games, organized and otherwise. I think that's enough." Russell's announcement shocked the basketball world. Celtics president Red Auerbach tried to convince him to reconsider, but the eleven-time champ had made up his mind. He was done.[1]

For thirteen years, Bill Russell and the Boston Celtics were synonymous with professional basketball. When Russell entered the league in 1956, most teams played a below-the-rim, slow-paced game relying on patterned ball movement and plodding centers like Minneapolis Lakers star George Mikan. Russell's incredible athleticism allowed the Celtics to employ a fast-breaking style that revolutionized the game. Auerbach, the stogie-smoking architect of those Celtics teams, surrounded Russell with exceptionally skilled role players. Bob Cousy (and later K. C. Jones) handled the ball and ran the offense while Bill Sharman (and then Sam Jones) served as designated shooters. In the forward slots— called "cornermen" in the '60s and '70s—the Celtics trotted out Tom "Satch" Sanders as the defensive stopper and Tom "Tommy Gun" Heinsohn as another scoring threat. The Celtics also benefitted from tremendous depth as, for most of Russell's career, the team employed their second-best forward as a "sixth man," with future Hall of Famers Frank Ramsey and John Havlicek thriving as substitutes.

Surrounded by these talented teammates, Russell led Boston to an unprecedented eleven NBA titles. But the last was perhaps the most dramatic and unlikely. In the 1969 finals, Russell's 48–34 Celtics squared off against the heavily favored 55–27 Los Angeles Lakers led by the high-scoring trio of Elgin Baylor, Wilt Chamberlain, and Jerry West. This marked the sixth time in eight seasons that Boston and Los Angeles had met for the league title, and the Celtics were 5–0. But despite his team's poor track record against Boston, West was confident of a Los Angeles victory. "Most of the years we played they were better than we were," West later admitted. "But in '69 they were not better. Period. I don't care how many times we played, they weren't better. We were better."[2]

In the first game of their best-of-seven series, West scored fifty-three points and handed out ten assists to lead Los Angeles to a 120–118 victory in what Bill Russell called "the greatest clutch performance ever against the Celtics." For an encore, West added forty-one in game two and Los Angeles pulled to a commanding 2–0 series lead. In the third game, a nearly blinded Havlicek, who inadvertently had taken a finger to the eye, hit a pair of key free throws to help the Celtics hold on to a 111–105 victory. The following contest also came down to the wire; a miraculous off-balance eighteen footer from the notoriously clutch Sam Jones with just three seconds left on the clock provided the margin of victory: Celtics 89, Lakers 88.[3]

The teams split games five and six to set up the deciding seventh game in the Lakers' palatial Forum in Inglewood. Inexplicably, Lakers owner Jack Kent Cooke ordered hundreds of balloons secured in the rafters to be dropped after his team beat the Celtics. As if Boston needed any more motivation. Heading into the fourth quarter, Boston led by fifteen and seemed to be pulling away. But the Lakers began to slowly cut into the Celtics' lead, inching to within nine points halfway through the fourth quarter. Then the unthinkable occurred—Chamberlain suffered a knee injury after leaping for a rebound. As the Lakers trainer sprayed Freon on Chamberlain's injured leg, hoping to numb it enough to allow the big man to continue, the crowd at the "Fabulous Forum" deflated. But even without Chamberlain, Los Angeles cut the lead to a single point in the final minutes. With the Lakers edging closer, Chamberlain pled with Coach Butch Van Breda Kolff to put him back into the game. "I told him," Van Breda Kolff said later, "that we're doing well enough without you" and left the future Hall of Famer seething on the bench.[4]

As the clock ticked under a minute, West poked the ball away from Havlicek and the Celtics' title hopes hung in the balance. But the loose ball bounced right into the waiting hands of potbellied Celtics forward Don Nelson. Nelson's rushed jump shot hit the rim, bounced several feet in the air, and dropped right through the net. Final score: Celtics 108, Lakers 106. Chamberlain was livid, certain that Van Breda Kolff's decision to keep him on the bench had "not only humiliated me," but "had deprived me and my teammates and the Lakers fans of an NBA championship." At least one of his teammates was just as angry as Chamberlain. Sportswriters named West the first-ever finals MVP (the only time a player on the losing team won the award). His prize? A car painted a lovely shade of Celtics green. Not surprisingly, West said he "felt like putting a stick of dynamite in it and blowing it up right there."[5]

Two months later, with the greatest winner in NBA history hanging up his sneakers, the league suddenly had a vacancy at the top. Even before Jack Kent Cooke could send the balloons from the rafters of the Forum to a local children's hospital, fans and media members debated potential successors to the Celtics dynasty. Could the Lakers' big three of Baylor, Chamberlain, and West make one more run at the title?

What about Walt Frazier and Willis Reed? Could they bring champion-ship basketball back to the Big Apple for the New York Knicks? Might "the Kangaroo Kid" Billy Cunningham jump-start the Philadelphia 76ers? Or would a dark horse emerge? Maybe Earl "the Pearl" Monroe and the Baltimore Bullets or "Sweet" Lou Hudson's Atlanta Hawks?

Regardless of who succeeded the Celtics as the team of the decade, the NBA was on the cusp of a great transformation. In the ten years following Russell's retirement, eight different franchises took home championship rings; salaries skyrocketed as players gained the right to free agency; the NBA merged with the rival ABA; and a culture of violence and drugs pervaded pro basketball locker rooms. In the 1970s, fans witnessed the rise of "Doctor J" Julius Erving, the brilliance of "Pistol Pete" Maravich, and the birth of the modern NBA.

1

1969 TO 1970

Bill Russell's retirement in the summer of 1969 ended the greatest dynasty in pro sports history. But even before Russell made his historic announcement, a new era in the NBA was dawning, launched by a conference call. On March 19, 1969, via teleconference Commissioner Walter Kennedy met with representatives from the Phoenix Suns and Milwaukee Bucks for a coin toss to determine the first pick in the upcoming draft. Depending on the outcome of the flipped coin, either Phoenix or Milwaukee could draft the biggest prize to enter the league in at least a decade: Lew Alcindor.[1]

Alcindor was a household name even among casual basketball fans. In three college seasons at UCLA, he led the Bruins to back-to-back-to-back NCAA titles. Scouts considered Alcindor a surefire superstar, a seven footer with a deft shooting touch who could handle the basketball like a guard. In fact, the NCAA changed their rules to limit his success, outlawing the dunk from 1967 to 1976 in what became known as the "Alcindor Rule." Alcindor was also a terror on the defensive end, blocking countless shots in an era before that statistic was even recorded.

Lew Alcindor was almost perfect. Almost. Detractors charged Alcindor with occasionally giving less than one hundred percent on the court and, even more damning, participating in a boycott of the 1968 Olympic Games. As the best-known black college ballplayer in the country, the normally reserved Alcindor made it abundantly clear that he would not shy away from controversial issues pertaining to civil rights. News also leaked that Alcindor converted to Islam while at UCLA. For Americans torn over the recent refusal of Muhammad Ali to fight in Vietnam, Alcindor's stance as an outspoken African American Muslim seemed somewhat troubling, especially for the legions of white men who dominated the NBA's fan base. Despite the seriousness of these concerns, Alcindor was (ironically) a slam dunk for whoever won the coin flip.

From his New York City office, Kennedy dialed the team owners. "Gentlemen," Kennedy began, "I am going to put the receiver down on my desk" (no hands-free receivers in 1969) "then I will flip this coin in the air, catch it in my right hand, and put it on the back of my left." The Bucks let the Suns make the call of heads or tails. Phoenix chose heads. Kennedy laid down the telephone, tossed the coin in the air, and turned it onto his left hand. Tails. Listening in from Milwaukee, Bucks owner Wes Pavalon cheered, grabbing the team's general manager in such a tight bear hug that he jammed a lit cigarette into his employee's ear. Suns owner Dick Bloch was gracious in defeat but obviously distraught over missing out on a potential superstar.[2]

Drafting Alcindor was only the first step to getting him in a green and white Bucks uniform. Alcindor was born and raised in New York City and attended college in California; he hated the idea of moving to the Midwest. "They were glad to have me in Milwaukee," he later wrote, "but I wasn't the happiest guy in the world to be there." Milwaukee, according to Alcindor, "looked to me like a whole lot of red-necked farmers getting drunk." Given a choice, he would have preferred to play on a coast, and Kennedy feared that Milwaukee's good fortune might cost the NBA their young star. He might, Kennedy reasoned, sign with an ambitious rival league that would happily let Alcindor play wherever he chose.[3]

That rival league, the American Basketball Association (ABA), did make a huge push to sign Alcindor. "If he wants to play in Oshkosh or on the moon, or anywhere between, we'll establish franchises there," boasted ABA commissioner (and former Minneapolis Lakers great) George Mikan. "We want Lew and we'll give him anything he wants." ABA owners did their due diligence and decided to try and wow Alcindor by handing him a $1 million bonus check. But during the league's pitch, Commissioner Mikan inexplicably left the check in his pocket, offering instead a four-year, $1 million deal to play for the league's New York Nets. Alcindor, in an exclusive interview with *Sports Illustrated* a few months later, revealed that "the ABA had the inside track on me."

He wanted to play for the Nets, but decided that he and his advisers would hear just one offer from each league. He wanted no part of a prolonged bidding war. When Mikan failed to offer the $1 million bonus, Alcindor assumed he had heard the ABA's best pitch. It fell short of the Bucks' five-year, $1.4 million offer, so he signed with Milwaukee. Several ABA owners tried to convince Lew to reconsider, this time with checkbooks in hand. But Alcindor said, "as much as I wanted to make a deal with the Nets, my father and I agreed that we had given our word. . . . The ABA had had the inside track, but they had blown it."[4]

In his first game for Milwaukee, Alcindor squared off against the Detroit Pistons and their all-star center Walt Bellamy. Alcindor started quickly, sinking his first shot on a short turnaround jumper over Bellamy from the left block. This basket marked Alcindor's first in what would become a record-breaking career; he retired in 1989 after scoring 38,387 points. Ironically, Alcindor's final points came nearly two decades later against those same Pistons when Alcindor, then known as Kareem Abdul-Jabbar, scored from almost the exact same spot on the floor. Abdul-Jabbar's team lost his last game but won his first as the rookie Alcindor scored a game-high twenty-nine points to go along with twelve rebounds and six assists. It was the dawn of a new era, with Alcindor leading the charge. As a rookie, he led the Bucks to fifty-six wins, a twenty-nine game improvement, while averaging 28.8 points (second in the league to Jerry West), and nearly fifteen rebounds per game (trailing only Elvin Hayes and Wes Unseld).

Alcindor's arrival also made Topps reconsider its stance on printing basketball cards. In 1969, more than a decade after abandoning the basketball card market, Topps featured Alcindor in their ninety-nine card release. His '69 Topps tallboy became the most valuable basketball card ever printed in a set that also included "rookie" cards for many NBA vets, including Willis Reed, John Havlicek, and Bill Bradley. The cards stood out from their baseball and football counterparts because they, much like the players they pictured, were larger than average. Standing more than an inch taller than standard sports cards, they were too big to be hooked to bicycle spokes, a trick that made a run-of-the-mill Schwinn sound like a revving Harley.

Unlike Alcindor and the Bucks, on their way to the top, the once-mighty Boston Celtics had fallen on hard times. The retirements of Russell and Sam Jones decimated their team. "The Celtics seemed disorganized," one opponent observed, "almost as if they didn't know what to do without Russell." To fill Russell's vacant slot in the starting lineup, the Celtics traded for seven-foot stiff Henry Finkel, who, in the words of *Boston Globe* reporter Bob Ryan, only remained in the league because of "a pituitary accident." The combination of Finkel and hold-over Jim "Bad News" Barnes (dubbed "Bad News Finkel-Barnes" by legendary Celtics broadcaster Johnny Most) clearly could not replace the departed legend, but the Celtics did have some talented young players, led by rookie guard Jo Jo White. Several teams passed on White in the 1969 NBA draft because he had already been drafted: by the U.S. Army. But after signing with Boston, Commissioner Kennedy helped broker a deal allowing White to enlist as a Marine Corps reservist and, instead of losing two full seasons to the armed forces, White missed only a handful of games in the fall of '69. Adding White certainly bolstered Boston's backcourt, but forward John Havlicek remained the Celtics' best player. Havlicek excelled in his usual sixth-man role, averaging around twenty-four points, eight rebounds, and seven assists per game. But his Celtics won just thirty-four games under new head coach Tom Heinsohn, and there were rumblings that the team might move—maybe to Long Island, where the new Nassau Coliseum put to shame the antiquated parquet of the old Boston Garden.[5]

Boston was rebuilding and Milwaukee was too inexperienced, so the Eastern Division came down to a battle between two bitter rivals: the Baltimore Bullets and the New York Knicks.

Baltimore featured the highest-scoring guard tandem in the league, with Earl Monroe and Kevin Loughery combining for forty-five points per game. Loughery was a solid veteran, but Monroe was a revelation, a Philadelphia playground legend known as "Magic" or "Black Jesus" (and by the media as the more alliterative "Earl the Pearl"). Alongside Loughery and Monroe, the Bullets started two top-notch forwards, Jack Marin, one of the league's most eligible bachelors and best long-range marksmen, and Gus "Honeycomb" Johnson. Johnson was an excellent defender and scorer but was best known for his rim-rattling dunks. One evening, when Johnson was in college, the owner of a local nightclub asked Honeycomb to show off his impressive leaping ability. From a standing start, Johnson touched a spot on a beam later measured at 11.5 feet off the floor. The proud owner hammered a nail into that spot and promised free drinks to anyone who could duplicate Johnson's feat—

the record stood for more than twenty years. Johnson was not only an exceptional leaper, he was also one of the strongest players in the league, described by Walt Frazier as "a rocket with muscles." In January 1971, Honeycomb's Bullets were down by forty points to the Bucks when he stole the ball and dribbled it the length of the court. Johnson rose into the air and, using his six-foot-six-inch, 230-pound frame, viciously dunked the ball. The ball went through the hoop and the rim pulled away in Johnson's hands, shattering the backboard into a million tiny pieces. "I want respect," Johnson explained. "When I come to the hoop, get out of my way, or I'll break your hand."[6]

Playing the pivot for the Bullets was Wes Unseld. At six-foot-seven, Unseld was a good four or five inches shorter than almost every other center in the league. He could barely jump and was, by any measure, one of the league's slowest players. But, as one journalist explained, he was also "wide enough to set a pick on the sun" and threw pinpoint outlet passes igniting the Baltimore fast break. Opposing players also quickly realized that Unseld's greatest assets did not show up on any stat sheet and often used the term "unselfish" to describe the Afroed intimidator. Even as a rookie, Unseld shot the Bullets up the standings, becoming just the second player in league history to be named both rookie of the year and the league's most valuable player. The only other player to accomplish the feat, Wilt Chamberlain in 1960, recorded an otherworldly thirty-eight points and twenty-seven rebounds per game; Unseld took home both awards in 1969 after averaging just fourteen points and eighteen rebounds.[7]

The Bullets ended the season with fifty wins, but their archrivals from the Big Apple fared even better. The 1969–1970 New York Knicks might be the most extensively covered basketball team of all time. Dozens of journalists and historians, and even several of the players themselves, have published books recalling that storied season. Part of the appeal of those Knicks is that they won a title in New York City. But fans and sportswriters also fell in love with the eccentric personalities of larger-than-life players nicknamed "the Captain," "Clyde," "the Butcher," "Dollar Bill," "Fall Back, Baby," and "Muscles."

The on- and off-court leader of the Knicks was undoubtedly "the Captain" Willis Reed, New York's six-eight center who represented "the hub around which the New York attack spins." Reed, born and raised on a cotton farm in rural Louisiana, played with fierce determination.

"If just one thing was to be written about me," Reed wrote in his second early-1970s autobiography, "I'd like it to be, 'Willis Reed gave 100 percent of what he had all the time.'" Reed was a hulking warrior, famously battling the entire Lakers team on opening night in October 1966. One veteran sportswriter called it "the most unbelievable fight I ever saw in basketball," and future teammate Phil Jackson described it as "a massacre" with Reed "shrugging 230 pounders off of him like a bear shaking off the rain." Reed, a second-round draft pick out of Grambling, quickly established himself as an elite player as well as a fearsome enforcer. In fact, sportswriters named Reed the league MVP in 1970 after he averaged nearly twenty-two points and fourteen rebounds per game with a soft left-handed jump shot and stout interior defense that fit perfectly into coach Red Holzman's scheme, allowing his teammates to find openings on offense and gamble for steals defensively.[8]

If Reed was the Knicks' heart, its soul was flamboyant guard Walt Frazier. Frazier, nicknamed "Clyde" after once buying a hat reminding the team's trainer of one worn in the 1967 hit film "Bonnie and Clyde," ranked among the most popular players of his era. In 1974, Frazier coauthored *Rockin' Steady: A Guide to Basketball and Cool*, in which he devoted six full pages to what he called "Clyde's wardrobe stats." Among the articles of clothing hanging in his closet at the time were maroon corduroy pants with a UFO patch on the back and a pair of pink and blue shoes with two-inch heels purchased specifically to coordinate with a baby blue lambskin suit. At times, the off-court persona of "Clyde the Glide" overshadowed Walt's considerable on-court ability. If his sense of style drew comparisons to stylistic luminaries like footballer Frenchy Fuqua or fellow New Yorker "Broadway" Joe Namath, journalists most often compared his on-court play to Oscar Robertson and Jerry West, placing him among the league's elite at his position. Frazier played cerebral offense. He mastered both a deadly jump shot from the high post and a knack for backing down defenders and scoring close to the basket. But it was his defense that drew the most attention and fueled the Knicks' fast-break attack. Frazier possessed such quick hands that stories about his ability skirted the line between fact and fiction. Clyde famously snatched flies out of the air until, as he claimed, "the flies know about me, so they don't come around." Unsurprisingly, the fly-catching, nattily dressed Frazier made the All-Star team, the league's All-Defensive team, and first-team All-NBA during the 1969–1970 season.[9]

Reed and Frazier drew the most attention as the team's center and lead guard, respectively, but the Knicks' other three starters were equally important to the team's success. Crafty thirty-year-old Dick Barnett started alongside Frazier in the New York backcourt. His specialty was an unorthodox left-handed jump shot in which he kicked both legs out behind him. He dubbed it the "Fall Back, Baby" jumper because, whenever he took it, his teammates could "fall back" on defense, baby: the shot was going in. Power forward Dave "the Butcher" De-Busschere played with a blue-collar ferocity. He started his career in Detroit, where he became a twenty-four-year-old player-coach in 1964, moonlighting as a pitcher for the Chicago White Sox in the offseason. In 1968, DeBusschere joined the Knicks in a trade for center Walt Bellamy and guard Howard Komives, transforming the Knicks. The deal allowed Reed to slide over to Bellamy's spot in the pivot after spending his first four years at forward and moved Frazier into the starting lineup, replacing Komives. With DeBusschere on board, the Knicks had four of their starters set. Just one question remained: who fit in best at small forward?

New York opened the 1969–1970 season with an intense competition between Cazzie Russell and Bill Bradley for the final starting spot. Russell was the top pick in the 1966 draft out of Michigan and, as a pro, earned the nickname "Muscles"—both for its alliteration and because it was a fitting description of his chiseled frame. Fully recovered from an ankle injury suffered in January 1969, "Muscles" Russell hoped to regain his spot in the starting lineup.

Bill Bradley was the opposite of Russell in almost every way. Russell was black and had played in the Big Ten; Bradley was fair skinned and attended Princeton on an academic scholarship. Ironically, the two met in the 1965 NCAA tournament when Russell's Wolverines knocked Bradley's Tigers out of the Final Four. But it was Bradley, a two-time consensus All-American, who became the poster boy for the student-athlete ideal. In an era when many fans and media members increasingly viewed professional basketball as becoming "too black," Bradley was a "Great White Hope," celebrated for his on- and off-court demeanor. Unable to find a real-life equivalent, journalists compared him to Clark Kent and Jack Armstrong. He was everybody's All-American: the Golden Boy. The Knicks drafted Bradley the year before selecting Russell, but "Dollar Bill" spent a year as a Rhodes Scholar and enlisted in the Air Force Reserves before finally reporting to New York midway through the 1967–1968 season.

Bradley struggled in his transition to pro ball, as his collegiate success and massive $125,000-per-year contract raised expectations. Russell's broken ankle in January 1969 gave Bradley an opportunity that the future U.S. senator seized like a pit bull. Unlike Russell, who excelled at scoring, Bradley did not need the ball in his hands to help the Knicks. Instead, Bradley dodged and darted around the court and constantly moved without the basketball, creating open layups for himself and his teammates. Dr. Jack Ramsay, then Philadelphia's coach, said Bradley's ability "to run the floor, run the baseline, move without the ball, keep the ball moving, knock down the open shot . . . opened up everybody's game." However, Bradley and the Knicks had an uncertain relationship, as "Dollar Bill" had more career options than most of his contemporaries. He could walk away at any time and run for public office (which he eventually did, becoming Senator Bradley in 1979). The Knicks knew this and quietly signed him to a series of one-year deals that led, in the mid-seventies, to Bradley becoming one of the highest paid players in the league.[10]

Sportswriters celebrated the Knicks for their diversity: their captain was an undersized soft-spoken Louisianan center; their lead guard a publicly flamboyant but privately reserved fashion plate; their small forward a "Great White Hope" Rhodes Scholar; their power forward a beer-guzzling, blue-collar Detroit kid; and their shooting guard an aging, unconventional left-handed playground legend who went on to earn a doctorate in education. During the season, two other Knicks players, Cazzie Russell and Mike Riordan, missed a few days of practice after their National Guard units were called up to deliver mail as a result of a postal workers strike. All of the Knicks, as the legend goes, sacrificed individual accolades for team success. "It's not a new game we've invented," Bradley explained, "but a practical application of how basketball should be played." Their selfless play seamlessly wove five very good (if perhaps not great) basketball players into an excellent team finishing with a league-best sixty wins. Maybe more importantly, the Knicks came to symbolize all that was right with America in the early seventies, an era plagued by failing foreign policy in Vietnam and contentious race relations.[11]

Although the Knicks gained national media attention for their stellar play and fascinating personalities, the Cincinnati Royals made headlines for entirely different reasons. The Royals (who would, after several relocations, eventually become the Sacramento Kings) entered the 1969–1970 season with both excitement and trepidation. Just days before the season started, the team traded their second-biggest star, forward Jerry Lucas, to the San Francisco Warriors. Lucas, beloved in Cincinnati, found himself at odds with new head coach and hall-of-fame point guard Bob Cousy. "Lucas did not fit into our offense, which is now built on speed," Cousy explained. Cousy wanted a young team built from the ground up through the draft, just as his title-winning Celtics teams had been in the 1950s and 1960s. Trading Lucas was the first step in that process. A much bigger hurdle was convincing legendary point guard Oscar Robertson to buy in. But Cousy and Oscar never saw eye-to-eye and Robertson requested a trade early in the season. "I didn't have any role in the team Cousy wanted," Robertson said. "We were a team in flux, a mishmash of veterans and young guys without any cohesion or identity." With the Royals shopping their superstar guard, Cousy further infuriated Robertson and provided basketball fans with a dose of unintentional comedy by activating himself for seven regular-season games.[12]

In November 1969, news of the My Lai Massacre dominated national headlines; *Sesame Street* debuted, introducing kids to Big Bird, Bert, and Ernie; Apollo 12 astronauts landed on the moon; and forty-one-year-old Bob Cousy checked into a game against the New York Knicks, seeking their then-league-record eighteenth consecutive victory. According to Walt Frazier, Cousy "walked onto the court in such an arrogant way, like he was still the king of basketball." Entering the game with less than two minutes left and the Royals clinging precariously to a three-point lead, Cousy calmly sank two free throws to put Cincinnati up five. But six quick points by the Knicks, most egregiously on a poor pass by Cousy leading to the go-ahead score, gave New York the win (and the record streak). Opposing coaches designed offensive strategies to take advantage of the overmatched player-coach, and his comeback ended after just seven games and thirty-four total minutes played. But despite its brevity, Cousy's untimely activation was the last straw for

Robertson. "One month into the season, Bob Cousy, age forty-one, completed our youth movement," Robertson quipped. "He put himself in because he didn't trust anyone else, like he was trying to make a point: 'I'll show you how it's done.'" After months of testy negotiations and following Cousy's re-retirement, the Royals finalized a trade that would have sent Robertson to the Bullets. But Baltimore balked at Robertson's exorbitant salary demands (three years, $700,000) and the deal fell through. The final months of the Royals' season were forgettable; their star player wanted out and Cousy's squad limped to a 36–46 record, fifth best in the seven-team East.[13]

The Philadelphia 76ers and Detroit Pistons rounded out the Eastern Division. The Sixers were just three years removed from their historic 1967 championship team led by Wilt Chamberlain, Hal Greer, Chet Walker, and Billy Cunningham. But after trading Chamberlain in 1968 and Walker the following year, the team stalled, finishing fourth in the East during the 1969–1970 season despite strong seasons from Greer and Cunningham. The Pistons also featured a high-scoring duo as guards Dave Bing and Jimmy Walker combined for forty-four points per game. At least on paper, Detroit looked to be a good team. But as would be the case throughout most of the decade, the Pistons underachieved and finished dead last in the East, winning just thirty-one times and guaranteeing themselves, for the third time in five seasons, a chance to participate in a coin flip for the top overall pick in the upcoming collegiate draft.

The Western Division race came down to two very different teams. The Los Angeles Lakers, who finished second, relied on three superstars: Elgin Baylor, Wilt Chamberlain, and Jerry West. The division-winning Atlanta Hawks, on the other hand, used a much more balanced, team-based approach.

The Lakers' "big three" were the most celebrated threesome in the NBA. Baylor had been around the longest, drafted first overall by the then–Minneapolis Lakers in 1958. Baylor revolutionized the sport as a bull-strong, high-flying, high-scoring African American forward and became, according to longtime *Sports Illustrated* writer Frank Deford, the first player ever called a "superstar." After drafting West out of West Virginia in 1960, the Lakers moved to L.A. In the sixties, the names Baylor and West became synonymous with finishing second. The duo faced the Celtics in the 1962, 1963, 1965, 1966, and 1968 NBA finals. They lost each time. After falling in '68, the Lakers traded three players to Philadelphia for Chamberlain, making them the clear favorites in '69. One journalist, in fact, called them the "fearsome threesome," and almost everyone predicted that they would breeze to a title. Even Chamberlain bought into the hype, claiming before the trio had ever played a game together that "we'll simply have the best team in basketball history." One Philadelphia newspaperman decided that "with Wilt Chamberlain joining Elgin Baylor and Jerry West, Ronald Reagan and Doris Day could play the other two positions for the Lakers." Had the L.A. threesome remained healthier and had a few shots bounce their way, perhaps the two Hollywood icons could have suited up in the team's trademark gold and Forum blue to bring an NBA title to L.A. But as usual, Bill Russell and the Celtics got in the way in the spring of 1969.[14]

Losing the '69 finals was heartbreaking, but the following season was just as difficult for the Lakers. Injuries limited Chamberlain to just twelve games and one Lakers beat writer recalled that "you could almost see Elgin fade before your eyes." Fortunately for Lakers fans, West was still one of the NBA's best, pouring in a league-leading 31.2 points per game and dishing out better than seven assists per contest. But the real revelation was the play of Harold "Happy" Hairston, the Lakers starting power forward. In Chamberlain's absence, Hairston chipped in better than twenty points and twelve rebounds per game. When Happy suffered a season-ending injury in March, however, the Lakers window seemed to be closing and the era of the "big three" fading rapidly. Frank Deford candidly wrote in April 1970 that "the Laker geriatric cases are running out of time and wonder drugs."[15]

Unlike Los Angeles, the division-winning Hawks did not have even one superstar (let alone three) on their roster. "The Hawks are almost all somebody else's rejects," Deford wrote. "They seldom receive individual acclaim [and] tend to blur in the public mind since none was a fantabulous super-duper in college." Prophetically, Deford added that "there is not a white hope among them." Instead, the Hawks started five very good, if not great, African American players led by swingman Lou Hudson. Hudson, favorably compared to West by more than one contemporary, averaged more than twenty-five points per game, tops on the team. But Hudson was an introverted, articulate, and composed man, not prone to self-promotion. He just quietly went about his business. In a November game played in Auburn, Alabama, Hudson had his best performance as a pro, pouring in fifty-seven points in a win over the Chicago Bulls. But Hudson also had to experience the racial realities of living in the civil rights–era South when he witnessed several African American Bulls players refused service at a local restaurant. Chicago management reported the incident to the Justice Department, but it quietly went away. It was a fitting metaphor for the civil rights movement during this tumultuous era: some athletes, like Bill Russell, Muhammad Ali, or Jim Brown, might have used this incident to fan the flames of civil rights. Other ballplayers, like Hudson, chose to remain silent, unconvinced that the nation needed more disharmony.[16]

If "Sweet Lou" seemed to be quietly headed for stardom, teammate Joe Caldwell was far more outspoken and might have been the league's most underrated player. Caldwell, nicknamed "Pogo" or "Jumpin' Joe" for his amazing leaping ability and stifling defense, scored more than twenty-one points per game. In fact, all five starters averaged at least fifteen points per game and exhibited balanced rebounding and assist numbers. Winners of their last six regular season games, Atlanta seemed to be peaking at just the right time and, despite a rather pedestrian 48–34 regular-season record, gained the top seed in the Western Division.

Even as Hawks fans celebrated the team's on-court success, Atlanta's front office unintentionally sowed the seeds of future discontent. Head coach and general manager Richie Guerin orchestrated a complicated mid-season trade. The rights to former Hawks center Zelmo Beaty, mulling a jump back to the NBA from the ABA's Los Angeles Stars, went to the San Francisco Warriors for a player to be named later and a first-round draft choice. Following a late-season collapse by San Francisco, that pick became the third overall selection in the 1970 draft, positioning the Hawks perfectly to select fair-skinned college superstar "Pistol Pete" Maravich from Louisiana State.

The Hawks' fortunes were about to turn on a trade, but Phoenix had already experienced a franchise-altering shift when they missed out on Lew Alcindor. Fortunately, Suns fans did have some cause for celebration due to a newly acquired twenty-seven-year-old rookie forward nicknamed "the Hawk."

Connie "the Hawk" Hawkins was a New York City playground legend in the late fifties and early sixties. Despite being barely literate and scoring poorly on college entrance exams, Hawkins received dozens of scholarship offers. He chose Iowa because, in his words, "they seemed like nice people, and they offered me the most money." Unsurprisingly, Hawkins lasted just one season in Iowa City after rumors of his involvement in a highly publicized New York City gambling and point-shaving scandal swirled around the six-foot-eight young black man. Although never arrested or indicted for any criminal activity (and apparently guilty only of accepting a $200 loan and a $10 "appearance fee" from renowned gambler Jack Molinas), the court of public opinion had already decided the fate of the semiliterate eighteen year old. In 1961, both the NCAA and NBA passed down lifetime bans on Connie and, for much of the next decade, Hawkins survived as a basketball-playing mercenary. In his first professional season, as a precocious nineteen year old, Hawkins earned the MVP award in the fledgling American Basketball League. In 1966, after barnstorming with the Harlem Globetrotters for two seasons, Hawkins filed a $6 million lawsuit in federal court seeking punitive damages related to his NBA banishment. While awaiting resolution, he signed with the Pittsburgh Pipers of the newly formed ABA and, once again, earned MVP honors, leading the league in scoring and his Pipers to the championship. Despite winning the league title, the Pipers moved to Minnesota (as the Muskies) and then back to Pittsburgh (rechristened the Condors) in consecutive seasons, with Hawkins as the face of their nomadic franchise. In 1969, "the Hawk" was able to parlay that success (and the popularity of an article in *Life* magazine advocating his innocence in the gambling scandal) into an opportunity to finally play in the NBA.[17]

Hawkins and the NBA agreed to an out-of-court settlement and the league awarded his rights to the Suns, who this time won the coin flip. But even before Hawkins suited up for Phoenix, the hype machine was in full gear. Indeed, stories of his playground accomplishments circulated well in advance of his first NBA game. One contemporary publication tagged him as "a phantom immortal," legendarily ephemeral, while another claimed that "since he has played in exile for so long, he has the same effect upon the observer that a lost Rembrandt discovered in an attic has upon an art hunter." His peers also heaped praise on the Suns' new forward. Lew Alcindor said, "I've seen the best in the NBA, but I've never seen anybody better than Hawkins"; Celtics guard Em Bryant called Hawkins "better than Baylor"; Wilt Chamberlain ranked

him as "one of the three best players I ever saw"; and Oscar Robertson
called Hawkins "a prelude to Dr. J and Michael Jordan." But Hawkins's
showmanship went beyond rim-shaking dunks. His signature move was
to receive the basketball with his back to the basket and wave it around
in one giant hand, waiting to pass to a cutting teammate or to quickly
drive to the rim, where he often finished with a graceful hook shot or
long-limbed finger roll.[18]

Although the Hawkins who joined the Suns was not the same player
he had been a decade earlier—knee problems sapped his legendary
athleticism—"the Hawk" soared as a twenty-seven-year-old rookie in
Phoenix, averaging better than twenty-four points and ten rebounds per
game. But perhaps more importantly for a fledgling Suns franchise still
reeling from the coin-tossed loss of Alcindor, "the Hawk" gave Phoenix
a bona fide superstar and box-office draw.

The remaining Western Division squads—the Chicago Bulls, Seattle
SuperSonics, San Francisco Warriors, and San Diego Rockets—each
ended the 1969–1970 season with a losing record. The Bulls finished a
distant third in the division under second-year head coach Dick Motta
but had, through savvy trades, acquired forwards Chet "the Jet" Walker
and Bob "Butterbean" Love, creating the foundation of some excellent
Bulls squads later in the decade. After losing to Chicago on January 1,
Seattle fell to fifth in the West. Most notably, though, on Halloween
night, the 0–6 Sonics won their first game under rookie coach and star
point guard Lenny Wilkens. Wilkens, who led the team that night with
thirty-eight points, would go on to win a record 1,332 games as an NBA
coach for six different teams before his retirement in 2005. Although
Wilkens has since been surpassed for coaching victories by Don Nelson
(in 1969 still an important player for the post-Russell Celtics), he remains the league's all-time leader in games coached with 2,487.

In San Francisco, the biggest news involved two trades in which the
Warriors acquired Jerry Lucas from the Royals and sent the draft pick
that would become Pistol Pete Maravich to the Hawks. The Warriors'
star player, Nate Thurmond, remained among the league's top centers
and paired with Lucas to form one of the best inside tandems in the
NBA, but the squad's shaky perimeter play kept them in the bottom
half of the West. The San Diego Rockets posted the worst record in the
Western Division, despite the outstanding play of second-year center
Elvin Hayes. The Rockets selected "the Big E" with the first overall

pick in 1968, and convinced him to join them in San Diego rather than sign with the ABA's Houston Mavericks, who bet their franchise on signing Elvin. Hayes went to Southern California; disappointed Mavericks owners folded their team. Such was the star power of a young Elvin Hayes. One pro scout argued that Hayes, who had grown up in rural Louisiana picking cotton since the age of eight, was "the sort of player you can build a team around, like Bill Russell, Wilt Chamberlain, Rick Barry or Elgin Baylor." Hayes paid immediate dividends for the Rockets, leading the NBA in scoring as a rookie (although he lost out on rookie of the year voting to Wes Unseld). As an NBA sophomore, Hayes upped his game. His patented turnaround jump shot helped him average better than twenty-seven points per game, while his athleticism allowed him to lead the league in rebounding (16.9 rebounds per game). But Hayes was basically a one-man team and, by virtue of finishing 27–55, the Rockets could look to the 1970 draft (and a coin flip against Detroit for the top overall pick) for hope in building a better team around their star big man. [19]

Halfway through the season, the NBA made two big announcements. First, they publicized the next phase of their ambitious expansion program intended to combat the rise of the rival ABA. Having added the Suns and Bucks in 1968, the league announced the addition of four new teams for the 1970–1971 campaign: Buffalo, Cleveland, Portland, and Houston. After the Houston deal fell through when they failed to pay their $3.7 million expansion fee, the three new squads brought the total number of teams to seventeen. The NBA also announced a new television contract with ABC, a three-year, $16.5 million deal that would increase the number of nationally televised games from eighteen to twenty-eight per season. Clearly, this was a league on the rise.

As the regular season came to a close, the league prepared to enter its second season: the NBA playoffs. The 1970 postseason included eight of the league's fourteen teams matched in best-of-seven series. Even the 39–43 Suns and equally mediocre Bulls found themselves playoff bound. In one Eastern Division semifinal, Lew Alcindor's Bucks squashed the Philadelphia 76ers in just five games. The other Eastern Division semifinal unsurprisingly pitted New York against their archrivals from Baltimore. The Knicks ultimately prevailed in seven hard-fought games, setting up a showdown between the towering rookie

Alcindor and the Knicks' team of destiny. The Knicks took only five games to dash the young Bucks' championship dreams. In the West, the Bulls faced off against the Hawks and the Suns met the Lakers. Atlanta won in five games and L.A. in seven to set up their highly anticipated Western Division Final. The over-the-hill, superstar-led Lakers surprisingly swept the balanced Hawks, leading to the first New York–Los Angeles playoffs matchup in NBA history.

League officials would have been hard-pressed to script a better championship series for the spring of 1970 than Knicks-Lakers. New York and Los Angeles were two of the nation's largest media markets and the storylines were sure to attract casual fans. The sun-soaked celebrity superstars from Southern California seeking to shed the label of "noble losers" against the diverse menagerie of great but not exceptional players trying to deliver the Big Apple its first league title. Ratings gold.

Oddsmakers favored the Knicks, and the first game in the series seemed to follow that script when New York opened a double-digit lead in rowdy Madison Square Garden. Willis Reed, after battling Wes Unseld and Lew Alcindor in the first two rounds of the playoffs, outplayed Wilt Chamberlain, still recovering from a knee injury that had cost him most of the regular season. Jerry West and Elgin Baylor, determined not to lose for the seventh time in their seventh finals appearance, led a furious game-one comeback and briefly put the Lakers ahead in the fourth quarter. But the Knicks regained the lead and pulled away, winning 124–112 thanks to a game-high thirty-seven points from Reed.

L.A. quieted the New York crowd in game two. Chamberlain played tighter defense on Reed, forcing the Knicks captain into shooting twelve for twenty-nine from the field and blocking a potential go-ahead shot with less than a minute left on the clock. West calmly sank two free throws to ice the game and tie the series at one game apiece.

If not for the final game of this legendary series, fans might remember game three of the 1970 finals as one of the greatest in NBA history. Returning to Los Angeles, the Lakers appeared to have the momentum after stealing game two. At halftime during the third game, L.A. led comfortably, headed for an easy win. But the Knicks stormed back and tied the game late in the fourth quarter. With three seconds left, the ball ended up in the hands of DeBusschere, who launched an off-balance, contested, fifteen-foot jump shot that somehow found the bottom of the net to give the Knicks a two-point lead. The Lakers, out of timeouts, deflated. Chamberlain lazily inbounded the ball to West, who took three quick dribbles to avoid Reed and heaved the ball the length of the court as time expired. West's shot flew sixty feet in the air . . . and went in. DeBusschere, the hero just moments before, fell to the ground, later calling West's Hail Mary "the single most incredible shot I'd ever seen in my life." Yet despite the sudden shift in momentum, the Lakers could not capitalize in overtime and fell by three points. "Jerry West made a sixty-three-foot shot at the buzzer, and the Lakers still lost. This is like surrendering after Hiroshima—to the Japanese," quipped Frank Deford, adding that "the team has finished second so often that Tom Dewey and William Jennings Bryan [two noted presidential bridesmaids] could open in the backcourt." In the locker room after the game, the Lakers were inconsolable. "I'm positive that one game cost us the championship," West recalled years later, "[it] haunts me. . . . I'll never forget it as long as I live."[20]

Despite their heartbreaking loss, the Lakers rebounded quickly, evening up the series at two games apiece by winning game four. As usual, West was brilliant, leading L.A. with thirty-seven points despite gutting out two painfully swollen hands. But it was the play of Baylor that made the difference. After all but disappearing in the first three games, Baylor looked like the Elgin of old out on the floor of the Forum, scoring thirty points and keeping DeBusschere and Bradley on the bench with foul trouble, setting the stage for the pivotal fifth game.

But on May 4, 1970, national attention turned far from Madison Square Garden and instead focused on a small town in northeastern Ohio.

NBA players generally insulated themselves from political and social causes taking place during the season. Players spent countless hours folded into small airplane seats, relaxing in hotel rooms or clubs, or in basketball arenas preparing for the next game. But on May 4, even NBA players stopped to take notice of the world coming down around their shoulders. The Vietnam War was exceedingly unpopular nationally but was particularly so on college campuses. Student rallies against American involvement in southeastern Asia had by 1970 grown increasingly violent. But no one could have foreseen the shooting that took place at Kent State University, leaving, in the immortal lyrics of Crosby, Stills, Nash, and Young, "four dead in Ohio." National Guardsmen fired into a crowd of protesting students, capturing the attention of, among others, gangly Knicks forward Phil Jackson. "Up until Kent State, you had to worry about long hair and being against the war," Jackson explained. "Then it turned and people were asking, 'How can this be happening, and all for a war that most people don't know why we're in? You had to be paying attention to what was going on." Jackson's teammate Bill Bradley was definitely sensitive to these social issues. The previous October, when antiwar activists assembled on college campuses for what was dubbed Vietnam Moratorium Day, Bradley joined the fray, offering his support for the protestors. Having grown up in what one historian describes as "an idealistic world of infinite possibility . . . [possessing] a special sensitivity to the terror of extinction," young men and women similar in age to the athletes playing professional basketball saw in national politics an inauthenticity and possessed a growing dissatisfaction with America's foreign and domestic policies.[21]

In Madison Square Garden on the night of May 5, the atmosphere was surreal. Harvey Araton, a longtime New York journalist, recalled that "there was a feeling of restlessness in the crowd, an air of pessimism and fear that came close to resignation." Despite the national focus rightfully shifting to college campuses and antiwar protests, the Knicks and Lakers decided to go ahead and play the fifth game as scheduled.[22]

Los Angeles came out hot in game five, pulling ahead by ten points in the first quarter. New York, forcing the action, funneled the ball to their captain, Willis Reed. Reed drove past Chamberlain and suddenly crumpled to the floor, holding his right thigh in agonizing pain. Reed limped to the sidelines as his teammates watched their title hopes evaporate. "I could see our championship lying on the floor," DeBusschere remembered. "I could see the whole year crumbling with Willis' right knee." Years later, Frazier wrote about Reed's injury. "The papers were filled with stories about the four students who had been killed at Kent State a few days before, and about the protests over it," Frazier explained. "There were articles about expanding the Vietnam War into Cambodia and about demonstrations calling for America to get out. But today, I just couldn't concentrate on those things. All I cared about was Willis." DeBusschere, Frazier, and their Knicks teammates did not give up. Instead, the absence of Reed forced both teams to adjust. The Lakers stopped moving as much on offense, forcing the ball inside to

Chamberlain rather than also relying on West and Baylor. Chamberlain towered over his Knicks opponents: one sportswriter compared six-six DeBusschere guarding seven-two Chamberlain to "a tourist leaning on the Empire State Building." But the Knicks also shifted strategies, playing five perimeter-oriented players to force Chamberlain away from the basket defensively. Frazier led six Knicks players in double figures and New York came away with an unlikely 107–100 win before L.A. evened up the series by taking game six.[23]

College campuses throughout the nation closed their doors and cancelled exams after the Kent State massacre. But the Knicks and Lakers battled on to a decisive seventh game. All signs pointed to Reed watching from the sidelines, which terrified Knicks fans. Against Willis's undersized replacements in game six, Chamberlain exploded for forty-five points and twenty-seven rebounds. New Yorkers, now down to their last hope for winning a long-awaited title, held their collective breath, awaiting word of their captain's health. Not even Reed knew if he could play in game seven. "There was never any doubt in my mind that I was going to try to play that seventh game," Reed remembered, "the doubt in my mind was whether or not I was going to be able to do it." In the early afternoon, Reed underwent more than an hour of treatment to loosen the muscles in his right thigh. A few hours before tipoff, Reed warmed up, testing out his leg. The pain was almost unbearable. Reluctantly, Reed allowed the team doctor to inject a numbing agent into his thigh as his teammates took the court for pregame warmup. Sitting for a few minutes on the trainer's table, Reed suddenly hoisted himself up and, grimacing, made his way toward the court.[24]

As Reed came into sight, the crowd erupted. Frazier likened the sound to "a thunderstorm moving slowly through a valley," and Jack Twyman, announcing the game on television for ABC, excitedly exclaimed in a voice that became increasingly higher in pitch, "I think we see Willis coming out!" Reed trotted (he did not limp) over to the other Knick players warming up, took a pass from a teammate, and calmly sank a practice shot from just inside the foul line. No problem. All eyes turned to the Knicks captain—even those belonging to the visiting team. "The Lakers were absolutely mesmerized," Frazier said. "Watch those guys," DeBusschere told Cazzie Russell, nodding toward the L.A. players. "We got 'em."[25]

As the national anthem played, some of the young people sitting in Madison Square Garden refused to rise, demonstrating that antiwar activism had not died down since May 4. With the anthem and the announcement of the starting lineups out of the way, the game tipped off. Only Wilt Chamberlain tried for the jump ball; Willis Reed hopped a bit. But it was Reed who struck first, knocking down a foul-line jump shot as the home crowd roared. He dragged his right leg back down court like a foreign appendage. But when Reed hit another shot from the wing a few moments later after not bothering to run back on defense, the crowd reached a fever pitch. Reed went scoreless the rest of the way, but it didn't matter. To start out the second half, the Knicks backup center stood ready to jump for possession (until 1975, each quarter began with a center jump), but Reed came out at the last moment and waved him off. Up big at halftime, the Knicks coasted to a 113–99 win in one of the most famous games in NBA history. Reed's four points and three rebounds look inconsequential, but stats tell only part of the story here. In game seven, Reed held Chamberlain in check and, more importantly, gave his teammates a huge psychological boost. Frazier, in particular, was amazing, recording thirty-six points, nineteen assists, and seven rebounds in the title-clinching contest.

Jerry West, playing through such pain in both hands that he took multiple injections before the game to reduce swelling, scored a team-high twenty-eight but once again had to deal with the stigma of the Lakers being losers. "We played poor, very poor basketball," West admitted afterward. "We were just terrible on defense." Chamberlain had a different take. Frazier "whipped Jerry's ass that night," he recalled, "but the papers somehow forgot to mention who won that particular duel; all they talked about was how poor, crippled Willis Reed 'beat' Wilt Chamberlain."[26]

Sportswriters named "crippled" Willis Reed the finals MVP, despite playing just twenty-seven minutes in the last two games combined and in spite of Frazier's brilliant series. During the course of seven games, Reed scored more than twenty-three points per game and played stifling defense on Chamberlain. But perhaps most importantly, his mere presence in game seven deflated the Lakers and inspired his Knicks teammates to greatness.

In the spring of 1970, it would have been easy to anoint the Knicks as the obvious successor to the Celtics dynasty of the sixties. Like Boston a decade earlier, New York had a young and talented team featuring an MVP-winning center and a flashy All-Star point guard. But in 1971, the Knicks did not raise another championship banner to the rafters of Madison Square Garden. In fact, they failed to even make the finals. Instead, the 1970–1971 season would be dominated by Milwaukee, thanks to that historic 1969 coin flip and the arrival of an electrifying rookie guard from Louisiana everyone called "the Pistol."

Statistics for 1969–1970

Eastern Division	W	L	Western Division	W	L
New York Knicks	60	22	Atlanta Hawks	48	34
Milwaukee Bucks	56	26	Los Angeles Lakers	46	36
Baltimore Bullets	50	32	Chicago Bulls	39	43
Philadelphia 76ers	42	40	Phoenix Suns	39	43
Cincinnati Royals	36	46	Seattle SuperSonics	36	46
Boston Celtics	34	48	San Francisco Warriors	30	52
Detroit Pistons	31	51	San Diego Rockets	27	55

Playoffs

Eastern Division Semifinals	Milwaukee d. Philadelphia (4–1)
	New York d. Baltimore (4–3)
Western Division Semifinals	Atlanta d. Chicago (4–1)
	Los Angeles d. Phoenix (4–3)
Eastern Division Finals	New York d. Milwaukee (4–1)
Western Division Finals	Los Angeles d. Atlanta (4–0)
NBA Finals	New York d. Los Angeles (4–3)

All-NBA Teams

First Team	Second Team
F—Billy Cunningham (Philadelphia)	F—John Havlicek (Boston)
F—Connie Hawkins (Phoenix)	F—Gus Johnson (Baltimore)
C—Willis Reed (New York)	C—Lew Alcindor (Milwaukee)

G—Walt Frazier (New York) G—Lou Hudson (Atlanta)

G—Jerry West (Los Angeles) G—Oscar Robertson (Cincinnati)

League Leaders

Points per Game (31.2)	Jerry West (Los Angeles)
Rebounds per Game (16.9)	Elvin Hayes (San Diego)
Assists per Game (9.1)	Lenny Wilkens (Seattle)
Most Valuable Player	Willis Reed (New York)
Rookie of the Year	Lew Alcindor (Milwaukee)

Time-Out

The Pistol

He was something to see—mop of brown hair, floppy socks—the
holy terror of the basketball world—high flyin'—magician of the
court. The night I saw him he dribbled the ball with his head, scored
a behind the back, no look basket—dribbled the length of the court,
threw the ball up off the glass and caught his own pass. He was
fantastic. Scored something like thirty-eight points. He could have
played blind.[1]
—Bob Dylan

The crowd roared as the rail-thin ballplayer stood up and pulled off his
blue and green pinstriped warmups to check in for the Atlanta Hawks
in their season-opening game against the Milwaukee Bucks. Most people expected the Bucks to compete for an NBA title, but it was not the
men from Milwaukee (or even their hometown Hawks) who fans had
come to see. Instead, the excitement revolved around the thin Atlanta
guard, "Pistol Pete" Maravich. Hawks coach Richie Guerin had hol-
stered the Pistol in the game's first twelve minutes, keeping him on the
bench while Atlanta's starting five, all veteran African American players,
staked out a six-point lead. But when twenty-three-year-old Maravich
tucked his number 44 jersey into his short shorts and jogged out onto
the court, the crowd screamed like the Beatles were in town. Photogra-
phers quickly swung into motion, bulbs flashing rapidly to capture the
image. At long last, the legendary Pistol Pete was in the NBA.

Maravich was a national celebrity long before taking the court against the Bucks in October 1970. In fact, the legend of Pistol Pete started nearly a decade earlier when, as a five-foot-six, 100-pound eighth grader, Maravich played for the varsity team at Daniel High School in Central, South Carolina. Although barely strong enough to reach the rim with a two-handed set shot hoisted from his right hip—which one sportswriter likened to a gunfighter about to unholster a pistol—Maravich quickly became a local celebrity. Fans loved his diminutive size and cocksure attitude; Pete reveled in the adulation. "When I threw a behind-the-back pass the applause began," Pete said. And so he continued to throw them. He added passes thrown between the legs, around the neck, and the length of the court (underhanded) to his repertoire and beamed as his legend grew. University of Maryland coach Lefty Driesell informed Pete that "I have never once seen Oscar Robertson throw a pass behind his back or between his legs. All he ever throws are two-handed passes and chest passes." Pete looked Driesell straight in the face and said truthfully, "Coach, I want to be a millionaire some day and they don't pay a million dollars for two-hand chest passes."[2]

Pete's father, Press Maravich, was tough on his youngest son, even as the Pistol demonstrated an uncanny understanding of the game. Press poured his heart and soul into training Pete and preparing him to play professionally, as Press himself had done in the 1940s. "Some people are born to paint and some people are born to write music," Press once explained. "Pete was born to play basketball." Aware that he was raising a basketball prodigy, Press drove Pete relentlessly both on and off the court, and Pete alternated between trying to please his demanding father and resisting Press's domineering ways.[3]

Press devised creative drills to hone Pete's reflexes and improve his ball-handling ability. Press called the maneuvers "homework basketball," and gave each exercise a descriptive name. One was called "ricochet," in which Pete tossed the ball between his legs at a forty-five-degree angle off the floor and caught it behind his back, then repeated the process in reverse. Then there was the potentially groin injury–inducing variation called "bullet ricochet," wherein Pete put the ball in both hands high over his head and whipped it downward, catching it behind his back after it bounced hard between his legs. "I knew one kid who did the bullet ricochet once and ended up in the hospital," Pete later recalled with a laugh. Another maneuver was "pretzel," named for the contortions Pete performed with his thin body, the ball seemingly attached by an invisible cord to either of young Maravich's hands as he whipped it around his neck and between his spindly legs. Pete dribbled blindfolded, while wearing gloves, while riding a bicycle, while walking the two miles between home and school, at the movie theater, and even out of the passenger door of a moving car. Once a classmate bet Pete five dollars that he could not spin a ball on his finger for an entire hour. Maravich took the bet and, for sixty long minutes, spun that ball while a crowd cheered him on. Pete's right index finger began to bleed from the friction, so he switched fingers, then hands, eventually spinning the ball on all ten digits plus his knuckles and thumbs. He won the five bucks.[4]

Besides training his own son, Press Maravich also coached college basketball. While Pete was in junior high, Press coached the Clemson Tigers. As the head coach at an Atlantic Coast Conference school, the older Maravich could test his skinny son's skills against Division I talent. This clearly improved Pete's game and also gave him immeasurable confidence—some might say cockiness—in his blossoming talents. If he could compete against top college players, he knew he could destroy his high school competition.

Pete ultimately attended three different high schools and never demonstrated much interest in academics, clearly intending to ride his basketball talent to an athletic scholarship. Initially, Press fueled Pete's academic laziness. One teacher expressed her concerns about Pete's in-class performance, to which Press responded, "I'll see to it that he gets into college and gets to be a basketball star." Grades did, however, become a major concern in the Maravich home once Pete began narrowing down his college choices. Press desperately wanted Pete at North Carolina State (where he was currently coaching), but the younger Maravich lacked the necessary grades and test scores to enroll. Pete decided instead to follow in the footsteps of Lakers superstar Jerry West by attending West Virginia (which did not have an entrance exam requirement at the time). But when Louisiana State University offered Press their vacant head coaching job and a significant pay bump, Press worked to convince his son to join him in the bayou. While Press was in Baton Rouge signing his contract with LSU, Pete was in the Pittsburgh airport headed to Morgantown, West Virginia. Press had a friend stop

Pete from boarding the plane and then flew to Pittsburgh himself to make a final pitch to his son in person. The two argued, as they often did. Pete called LSU a "doggone football school" and stubbornly insisted that he was going to be a Mountaineer unless Press bought him a car. Ultimately, both Maraviches got what they wanted. Press convinced Pete to enroll at LSU and Pete drove around Baton Rouge in a new Volkswagen.[5]

In three varsity seasons, Pistol Pete rewrote the NCAA record books. He averaged better than forty-four points per game over his three years, including a sixty-nine point performance against Alabama as a senior. Even the pregame layup lines at LSU became a must-see event, as Pete stationed himself at the foul line, whipping basketballs to cutting teammates while the LSU band played "Sweet Georgia Brown." The Maraviches put LSU basketball on the map. The $11.5 million Assembly Center, completed in 1971, became known as "the house that Pete built," providing an arena in which Shaquille O'Neal, among others, would eventually play their college home games. Amazingly, despite playing only three seasons (freshmen could not yet play varsity basketball) in an era without a three-point line, Maravich remains the NCAA all-time scoring leader; his career total of 3,667 points is hundreds more than his nearest competitor. Sportswriters unanimously voted Maravich a first-team All-American in all three seasons and, in 1970, named him the winner of the Naismith Award, given annually to the nation's top collegiate player.[6]

Even as Pete and Press brought great notoriety to LSU, their relationship remained tense, a product of two driven personalities both hell-bent on making Pete the best basketball player the world had ever seen. But it was Pete's relationship with his mother Helen that was perhaps the most stressful for the Pistol. Helen became increasingly withdrawn after the family moved to Baton Rouge and was obsessively protective of her granddaughter, Pete's niece Diana. Helen turned to drinking, hiding her alcoholism from even her family. Eventually Helen's illness forced Press to assume the responsibilities of homemaker as well as head basketball coach. Once, as a college senior, Pete returned home to find his mom drunk and obstinate. Pete punched through a wall in frustration and stormed out.

Despite problems at home, Pete's collegiate career still seemed headed for a storybook ending. In the spring of 1970, the New York

Knicks were rolling toward their first NBA title; journalist Pete Ax-thelm's recently published book, *The City Game*, brought tremendous media attention to New York's famed playground basketball scene; and Pistol Pete Maravich led the LSU Tigers into the postseason National Invitational Tournament (NIT) held annually at historic Madison Square Garden. But unlike the Knicks in May, Pete could not will his team to a title. The Tigers won their first-round game over George-town, but Maravich scored only twenty points in his Garden debut. In the second round, Pete scored thirty-seven to lead LSU over Oklaho-ma, but the Tigers ran into a buzz saw in the NIT's final four and were crushed by Marquette 101–79. Pete was again held to just twenty points in the loss.

By the time his Tigers fell to Marquette, Pete was accustomed to the pressure accompanying the nation's most popular college athlete. De-spite his father's continual lectures and his mother's alcoholism, Pete turned to booze to deal with the stress, racking up several DUIs during his time in Baton Rouge. In New York, when he should have been buckling down to win an important postseason tournament, he was out on the town, partying to escape the pressure of the big stage. The night before the semifinal game against Marquette, Maravich drank heavily. "The party continued into the night and I got totally wasted," Pete later admitted. "I drank to feel good and forget." Maravich did not even suit up for the consolation game and watched helplessly as his Tigers fell to Army, earning LSU a fourth-place NIT finish.[7]

Amazingly, the hype surrounding Pistol Pete *increased* after the tournament, because now Maravich was going pro. Three organizations considered themselves contenders in the Maravich sweepstakes: the NBA, ABA, and the Harlem Globetrotters. The Globetrotters, an exclu-sively African American traveling troupe, reportedly offered Pete $1 million to become a white Globetrotter. Although Pete's showmanship clearly would have fit well with the princes of the parquet (who were preparing to launch an animated Saturday morning cartoon series), the Pistol was not interested in playing comedy basketball against the Globetrotters' hapless foils. Instead, the race to sign Maravich would come down to the NBA's Atlanta Hawks and the ABA's Carolina Cou-gars.

As with Lew Alcindor the previous spring, officials from both leagues desperately tried to sign "Pistol Pete." Like Alcindor, Pete wanted to play in a particular market. But where Alcindor preferred a large city on the East or West Coast, Pete had, in the words of his father Press, "a strong preference for playing in the South." Although not as athletically gifted as Alcindor (and standing a good nine inches shorter than the Bucks' big man), both leagues recognized the marketing potential of a white-skinned basketball wizard playing his home games south of the Mason-Dixon Line. One journalist wrote that, by the summer of 1970, "only Muhammad Ali and Joe Namath [were] names with more box-office magic" than Pistol Pete Maravich.[8]

Once word leaked out that Pete was not going to become a Globe-trotter, ABA owners plotted the best strategy to land Maravich. They collectively determined that the Cougars, owned by Hardee's hamburger magnate Jim Gardner, possessed the best chance to sign Maravich. Gardner bid aggressively, offering a five-year, $2.5 million contract with a life insurance policy, an annuity for his post-playing career, and rumors of both a movie deal with MGM and a hamburger franchise dubbed "Pistol Pete's Hamburger Courts." Perhaps most tempting for the Maraviches was the ABA's offer to pay Press nearly three times his LSU salary to coach the league's Pittsburgh Pipers.

As Pete (and Press) mulled over the Cougars' offer, NBA teams met in March 1970 to conduct their annual draft. By virtue of posting the worst records in their respective conferences, a coin toss between the Detroit Pistons and San Diego Rockets determined the top overall pick. The Pistons won the toss and the right to select first. Maravich never considered Detroit in the running for his services: cold winters did not appeal to Pete and the Pistons already employed two ball-dominant guards in Jimmy Walker and Dave Bing. Unsurprisingly, Detroit passed on Maravich and selected St. Bonaventure center Bob Lanier. But the Rockets, picking second, were an intriguing option. They also revolved around a player who liked to score. But Elvin Hayes played center, not guard, and would have potentially drawn enough attention inside the paint to open up room for Maravich to perform his acts of wizardry from the perimeter. Plus San Diego, though not a southern city in the usual sense, boasted a much more temperate climate than Detroit. But the Rockets, scared off by the price Maravich was sure to command, passed on Pistol Pete to select rugged forward Rudy Tomjanovich.

Thanks to a midseason trade with the San Francisco Warriors, the Atlanta Hawks, despite finishing the 1969–1970 season with the best record in the Western Division, suddenly had the opportunity to select the NCAA all-time scoring leader with pick number three. At the time of the trade, the Warriors' record was 24–32. But San Francisco nose-dived after the deal, dropping twenty of their final twenty-six games to finish with the third-worst record in the NBA. Thus, it was the Hawks—and not the Warriors—who announced, via conference call, the selection of Pistol Pete Maravich with the third overall pick in the 1970 NBA draft.

Whether or not the Hawks could successfully counter the Cougars' offer quickly became the hottest topic of basketball's off-season. Gard-ner informed the *Atlanta Constitution* that the Hawks "will think Quan-trill's Raiders were a bunch of amateurs if Atlanta lucks out and signs Pete Maravich. If we don't get the kid," Carolina's owner threatened, "we're going to take the money and call [Hawks players] Lou Hudson or Walt Hazzard." Monetarily, the Hawks' offer to Maravich was lower than the contract tendered by the Cougars: a $1.5 million salary spread over five years, plus perks including a no-cut, no-trade clause, a country club membership, a furnished apartment, a personal secretary, and a brand-new dark green Plymouth GTX with a telephone and alligator skin roof. In total, the deal was worth about $1.9 million, roughly $500,000 more than Alcindor had signed for the previous spring. Pete signed with Atlanta.[9]

Even as a rookie, Maravich supplemented his basketball salary with lucrative sponsorship contracts. It seemed like everyone wanted a piece of the Pistol. In his rookie year alone, Pete signed endorsement deals with Uniroyal (manufacturers of Pro Keds shoes), the United States Hosiery Corporation (for his trademark floppy gray socks), and the Seamless Company (basketball makers). But it was Pete's $150,000 deal with Vitalis that drew the most off-court attention. In a series of com-mercials hawking Dry Control hairspray, Pete dribbled around players on a basketball court while his hair remained perfectly coifed. "Ball control by Maravich; Dry Control by Vitalis," the narrator pitched, re-minding listeners that "that's just got to be the best hair in the league!"

Perhaps emboldened by Maravich's popularity, the Hawks made a controversial decision in their preseason publicity push. Rather than promote multiple players and focus on past (and hopefully continued) team success, their new marketing campaign revolved around their Dry Control hairspray–wearing rookie. Advertised as the "New Hawks," the team replaced its red, white, and baby blue uniforms with a mod lime green, blue, and white number and added cheerleaders and a mascot, infuriating Hawks veterans who wondered what was so wrong with the division-winning "Old Hawks."

Pete and the "New Hawks" faced problems from the get-go. High NBA draft choices typically end up on bad teams as selections are made in inverse order of regular-season win-loss records. But Pistol Pete was not joining a bottom-feeder. He was headed to the Western Division champions who were already starting five talented, veteran players who fit perfectly into head coach Richie Guerin's team-oriented, ball-control, slow-it-down system. Fittingly, Guerin had the phrase "Hawks Team" engraved on the team's most valuable player trophy after their division-winning season, declaring that he had "never seen a more close-knit team." The Hawks boasted a well-rounded core, but the heart and soul of the team was Joe Caldwell, nicknamed "Jumpin' Joe" after once leaping over a 1955 Ford Mercury. *Sports Illustrated* writer Frank Deford called Caldwell "the league's most versatile defensive property—perhaps the best—and the steward of the team's fast-break game." Caldwell, more than any other Hawks player, could expect to benefit from the up-tempo, fast-breaking style Maravich was sure to bring to Atlanta.[10]

Instead, Maravich's arrival threw the team into turmoil. His race and contract were two big problems. As one journalist predicted, "the veterans on the club are a close knit group. They are all black and they are all well out of Maravich's tax bracket. There has to be some resentment." The journalist was wrong: there was a lot of resentment. Pete expected to play significant minutes, just as he had done since his days as an eighth grader at Daniel High. "I don't like to sit on the bench," Pete told a reporter, "[and] I don't intend to." But neither did any of the Hawks starters plan to make it easy on the team's rookie phenom. That the incumbents were all African American made Pete's task doubly daunting. Not only would he have to try to fit into an already cohesive team playing an established system that had achieved considerable success, but he would have to do so with the pressure of being a fair-skinned player in a southern city struggling with race relations. As teammate Lou Hudson later recalled, "Pistol Pete was the Great White Hope. Not just for Atlanta, [but] for the NBA." Fellow Hawks player Bill Bridges agreed, at least initially. "A white player of his ability is what Atlanta and the NBA need." But soon he, too, would be singing a different tune.[11]

In fact, it was Bridges who first broached the topic of salary inequity with Hawks management. During the 1969–1970 season, Bridges led the team in minutes played and pulled down more than fourteen rebounds per game. But he made just $50,000 per year, less than 10 percent of what Maravich would earn as an untested rookie and one-third of Pete's hairspray deal. "I'm not asking for a million," Bridges said to Hawks owner Tom Cousins, "but I do expect some compensation for what I've meant to the Hawks." Cousins told Bridges no. Next up was "Jumpin' Joe" Caldwell. Caldwell made approximately the same salary as Bridges but, unlike his teammate, went into the owner's office with a specific dollar figure in mind: he wanted exactly one dollar more per season than Maravich. And unlike Bridges, he was willing to hold out to force Cousins's hand.[12]

Atlanta played poorly during the preseason, finishing with a 3–9 record as Pete recorded more than twice as many turnovers as assists. Clearly, the team missed Caldwell's athleticism and defensive ability. And at times Maravich appeared to be moving out of sync with his teammates like a record playing at the wrong speed. He was used to having the ball in his hands constantly, and his running-and-gunning style was at odds with the patterned play preferred by his veteran teammates and Coach Guerin. During one preseason game, center Walt Bellamy ran up and down the court several times while Pete hogged the ball. Bellamy turned to a Boston player and asked, "How's the game going?" Later, Bellamy reflected that "it was conveyed to the team by management that in order for the Hawks to win, Pete has to shoot the ball. . . . Mr. Maravich had confidence in his shot. He thought it'd go in from whatever distance. . . . We got away from the traditional things that made the team a success." In practices, Pete threw the ball away while trying to showboat and demonstrated poor shot selection, frustrating his teammates and coaches to no end. "I thought Richie Guerin was going to hang himself," recalled Herb White, Pete's closest friend on the team. Also vexing the veterans was that Pete appeared immune to the more trivial aspects of being an NBA rookie. "We had been doing things to rookies that most rookies had to go through, and they no longer applied to Pete," Hudson recalled. "Rookies were supposed to carry the clocks in exhibition season, and he didn't have to do that. Pete could do whatever he wanted to do and if we had a problem with that then we were punished or threatened."[13]

For his part, Maravich was well aware of how his arrival had upset team chemistry. He tried to overcome this with generous gestures like paying for teammates' meals and drinks when out at a restaurant, but they resented that Pete was, in White's words, "subconsciously rubbing it in, letting them know who had all the money." If he didn't offer to pay, he was a cheapskate: damned if he did, damned if he didn't. Beat reporters for the Hawks considered him "an intruder," a showboating outsider breaking up the team they loved, lampooning Pistol Pete as "the Peachtree Popgun."[14]

As the Hawks prepared to open their regular season against Milwaukee, Maravich became increasingly nervous about the upcoming game. "I didn't get much sleep the night before. . . . I was totally psyched out," he said. "My legs felt like spaghetti, my hands like ping-pong paddles." Trying to capitalize on Maravich's popularity, ABC bid for the broadcast rights to the game, ensuring the NBA a tidy $75,000 payday, but only if Maravich actually played. If he sat out for any reason, ABC retained the right to cancel their broadcast and completely recover their fee.[15]

More than 7,000 fans packed into Alexander Memorial Coliseum to watch the Hawks square off against the Bucks that October evening. Despite Caldwell's contract dispute sidelining "Jumpin' Joe," Maravich started the game on the bench. So when Pistol Pete finally entered the game to kick off the second quarter, the crowd's loud reaction was understandable. Sure, they had come to root for their hometown Hawks, but they were far more interested in Pete's NBA debut. Maravich's impact on the game was immediate and obvious; the Hawks flew up and down the court at a breakneck pace, and the announcers raved about the team's improved movement. Pete scored his first professional basket after stealing the ball on defense and then dribbling the length of the court before stopping on a dime and swishing a picture-perfect jump shot. For all his nervousness, "the Pistol" played with pizzazz, throwing behind-the-back passes and leading the fast break with aplomb while the crowd oohed and aahed their approval.

But mixed with the good—as always seemed to be the case with Pistol Pete Maravich—was the bad. He committed several out-of-control turnovers while the announcers repeatedly reminded viewers of both his record-setting collegiate career and record-setting pro contract. Pete finished his first NBA game with just seven points, and his Hawks surrendered their early lead, losing to the Bucks by nine. After the game, Maravich was despondent, sitting with his head bowed for half an hour while his teammates showered and left the arena. He finally pulled the towel off his head and told a reporter, "what I played, it's called Bad Ball. . . . I wasn't ready emotionally. I was totally flushed." It was only one game, the first of many for Pistol Pete Maravich in the NBA. But in some ways, his first game as a pro symbolized his entire career: clouds of personal turmoil and team failure punctuated by shining rays of transcendent on-court brilliance and awe-inspiring showmanship.[16]

2

1970 TO 1971

One of the most iconic images in basketball history shows University of Cincinnati guard Oscar Robertson leaping to snatch a rebound, his legs splayed out into a midair split. For more than a decade, Robertson was synonymous with Cincinnati basketball, first leading his Bearcats to back-to-back Final Four appearances in 1959 and 1960 and then signing with the NBA's Cincinnati Royals. During the 1960–1961 season, his first year as a pro, Robertson averaged 30.5 points, 10.1 rebounds, and 9.7 assists per game for the Royals. Robertson was even better in year two, when he became the only player in NBA history to average a triple-double (more than ten each of points, rebounds, and assists per game) for an entire season. Amazingly, Oscar finished a distant third in the MVP race that season behind runner-up Wilt Chamberlain (who averaged fifty points and scored one hundred in a single game against the Knicks) and winner Bill Russell (who led the Celtics to their fourth consecutive title). If there was a knock against Robertson during his ten years as a Royal, it was that he never won a title. In fact, Cincinnati never even advanced to the finals.

By the early seventies, Oscar Robertson was firmly entrenched as one of the top players in NBA history and was the only non-center to win the league's most valuable player award in the two decades after 1960 (during the 1963–1964 season, when he averaged 31.4 points, 9.9 rebounds, and 11 assists per game). He revolutionized guard play in the NBA. Standing six-five and weighing 200 pounds, he was built more like a linebacker than a point guard, and he played with exceeding patience and deliberation, using his strength and exceptional court awareness to grind down his opponents. Early in games, he would often defer to teammates to get them involved, using his tremendous court vision to pass off for easy assists. Once his teammates felt comfortable, Oscar took over. Robertson rarely wasted any motion; his game relied on efficiency, not flash. Robertson himself said, "I learned to take a good shot, to get as close to the basket as possible before you shoot, and that each possession was important." His future teammate Lew Alcindor agreed. "Oscar does everything exactly the way it should be done," he said, "with as few frills and flairs as possible." For Robertson, basketball was a game of inches. One of his go-to moves, in fact, was to back his defender from the top of the key toward the basket, usually reaching the foul line area before launching a quick turnaround jump shot, released just above a defender's outstretched hand. Robertson's shot appeared easy to block but was rarely touched. He was amazingly athletic (as the iconic photo from his college days attests) but Robertson never dunked in an NBA game. Never. Dunking was just wasted energy. And Oscar never wasted energy.[1]

Robertson also overcame tremendous adversity as an African American man in an era ruled by segregation. After his all-black Crispus Attucks high school team won the Indiana state championship in 1955, city officials forced them to celebrate in the predominantly African American section of Indianapolis rather than downtown, as the all-white team from Milan (glorified in the film *Hoosiers*) had done the year before. More than once, Robertson heard racial slurs from opposing fans. Like Bill Russell, Elgin Baylor, and other black pioneers in professional basketball, he had to remain silent, because if he responded, it was the player, not the heckler, rebuked by the predominantly white media. But Oscar, like Russell and Baylor, did take those discriminatory actions to heart and used them to fuel his notorious competitiveness. "Oscar was so ahead of the rest of us humans that you could never come up to his level," remembered one teammate. "But because of his greatness, you hated to fail him."[2]

In 1969, the Cincinnati Royals introduced legendary Boston Celtic Bob Cousy as their new head coach. The pairing of Cousy and Robertson seemed perfect: the best guard of the 1950s and the best of the 1960s. But the relationship quickly soured, and before the 1970–1971 season the Royals traded Robertson to the Milwaukee Bucks, receiving forward Charlie Paulk (mocked by Robertson as "a Marine who hadn't played ball in two years") and All-Star guard Flynn Robinson. It was a steal for Milwaukee.[3]

With Oscar Robertson penciled in at point guard and reigning rookie of the year Lew Alcindor roaming the paint, the Bucks boasted the best one-two punch in the league. Fueled by "the Big O" and "the Big A," the 1970–1971 Bucks registered the most dominant season to that point in league history. Their sixty-six wins was the second-highest total of all time (trailing only the sixty-eight-win 1966–1967 76ers), and they ranked first in points per game and third in points allowed. To this day, their average margin of victory (12.3 points per game) remains an NBA record.

Naysayers may claim that Milwaukee's amazing record deserves an asterisk. After all, 1970–1971 was an expansion season, as the league welcome three new teams to the fold: the Buffalo Braves, Cleveland Cavaliers, and Portland Trail Blazers. To accommodate the newcomers, the league realigned and moved the Bucks and Detroit Pistons to the Western Conference (renamed from the Western Division) and the Atlanta Hawks to the Eastern Conference. Now there were four divisions—the Atlantic and Central in the Eastern Conference and the Midwest and Pacific in the Western Conference—each with four or five teams. As part of this restructuring, the playoffs changed to include the top two teams in each division, regardless of record.

Despite being newcomers in the Western Conference, Milwaukee all but sewed up a playoff spot in November, opening the season 17–1. But the Bucks were not the only exceptional team in the Midwest, as the Chicago Bulls finished 51–31, the third-best mark in the league. Chicago played a distinctly different style than their rivals in Milwaukee. The Bucks led the league in offense by scoring more than 118 points per game while the Bulls had the second-best scoring defense, limiting opponents to just over 105. Milwaukee also relied on two superstars with swinging nicknames—"the Big O" and "the Big A"; Chicago countered with a group of castoffs playing a hardnosed style of basketball described by one sportswriter as "boring and goring."[4]

The "boring and goring" Bulls played with a tenacity reflecting the temperament of their head coach, Dick Motta. Standing only five-feet-nine-inches, Motta never played a single minute of high school, college, or professional basketball but was incredibly knowledgeable about the game and a fierce competitor. In 1968, following a 29–53 season from the Bulls, Chicago execs tapped Motta as their next coach. Through savvy trades, Motta shaped the team into a slow-it-down, defensively oriented squad of good but not great players. "We're disciplined and we stress team play over individual play," Motta explained. "I believe in having the type of player who puts the team above himself, who has the character to do that." Much like the New York Knicks 1970 title team, the Bulls of the early seventies put together a core group who bought into Motta's selfless system—at least for the time being.[5]

Jerry Sloan, for one, was a perfect fit for Motta. After his playing days ended, Sloan racked up more than 2,000 career wins in twenty-six seasons as a coach (including twenty-three with Karl Malone, John Stockton, and the Utah Jazz). But before moving to the bench, Sloan was a scrappy guard who joined the Bulls in the 1966 expansion draft and gained the nickname "the Original Bull" for his long-standing ties to the team. Fans and opponents alike knew Sloan as a hard-nosed (some said dirty) player willing to sacrifice his body diving for loose balls and taking charges. For his efforts, sportswriters named Sloan to the All-Defensive first or second team for six straight seasons. But perhaps most importantly, Sloan became an extension of Motta: an on-court coach who set the tone for the tough-minded Bulls.

Sloan was the team's heart and soul, but the Bulls' best two offensive players were forwards Bob "Butterbean" Love and Chet "the Jet" Walker. To be successful, Motta's system required a center with exceptional high-post passing skills, two defensively oriented guards, and a pair of high-scoring forwards. Love and Walker fit the bill perfectly. Like "the Original Bull," "the Jet" and "Butterbean" both came to the Bulls as castoffs.

Walker moved to Chicago from Philadelphia, where he was a three-time All-Star and invaluable cog in their 1967 championship team. The trade to the Windy City devastated Walker, who briefly considered retirement. After deciding to give Chicago a chance, Walker provided the Bulls with something they desperately needed: a scorer. When the Bulls' half-court offense stalled, Walker would, in his own words, "go to work." Fans knew "Chet the Jet" as one of the top one-on-one players in the league; opponents knew him as unguardable. "He does pretty much what he wants on a basketball court, getting a good shot at his whim," one player admitted. Walker finished second on the Bulls in scoring (twenty-two points per game), trailing only his fellow cornerman, Bob Love.[6]

Love came to Chicago with far less fanfare and history of success than Walker. Frank Deford, in a *Sports Illustrated* article, wrote that Love "epitomizes today's Bull player. Originally cut from the NBA after he got out of Southern U. in 1965, Love fell to the Eastern League and came back as an obscure substitute. He was shuffled along in the expansion draft, and then became a throw-in on a trade." Chicago was Love's third team in three seasons, and he had never averaged even seven points per game. In fact, the Bulls nearly cut Love in 1969. But when "Butterbean" (so named because of his love for that particular legume) suffered injuries in an off-season auto accident, the Bulls stashed him on the injured reserve list. By the time Love recovered, the Bulls needed him to replace other injured players, and he never gave up his spot. By the 1970–1971 season, Love was firmly entrenched as a starter, pouring in a team-high 25.2 points per game.[7]

Along with Milwaukee and Chicago, the Phoenix Suns and Detroit Pistons rounded out the geographically ill-conceived Midwest Division. Both Phoenix (48–34) and Detroit (45–37) improved from the previous season and both featured star players. The Suns relied on multitalented forward Connie "the Hawk" Hawkins, the Pistons on rookie center Bob Lanier. Lanier, the top overall pick in the 1970 draft, came to the NBA fresh off tearing a knee ligament in the NCAA Final Four. Now fully healed, Lanier and his size 22 sneakers—the largest in NBA history— gave the Pistons something they had long lacked: in the words of a contemporary journalist, "that gooooood big man." Despite his big feet, Lanier was a quick and mobile center who led the Pistons to a 12–1 record to begin the season. Unfortunately for Detroit fans, the team cooled off and finished dead-last in the ultra-competitive Midwest.[8]

Atop the Pacific Division—although finishing with an identical record as the Suns—sat the Los Angeles Lakers. Los Angeles finished the 1969–1970 season within a heroic Willis Reed hobble of the NBA title. But their "big three" of Elgin Baylor, Wilt Chamberlain, and Jerry West were now thirty-six, thirty-four, and thirty-two years old respectively, and when Baylor suffered a season-ending torn Achilles tendon in just the second game of the year, the Lakers finished 48–34 and fired their coach. In L.A., it was championship or bust, injuries or not.

   Trailing the Lakers in the Pacific were the San Francisco Warriors and San Diego Rockets. Forward Jerry Lucas and center Nate Thurmond gave the Warriors a stellar frontcourt duo, but mediocre guard play resulted in a .500 record. The Rockets were equally strong on the inside, with Elvin Hayes finishing third in the league in both points (28.7 points per game) and rebounds (16.6 rebounds per game). Alongside Hayes, San Diego added two top-notch rookies: Rudy Tomjanovich and Calvin Murphy. Murphy stood just five-foot-nine, earning him the poetic nickname "the Pocket Rocket." But he quickly gained a reputation as a tough guy whose background in (of all things) baton-twirling prepared him physically for the rigors of the NBA. Using his strong wrists and arms, the Pocket Rocket soared down the lane, scoring on much taller players and earned a spot on the All-Rookie team. Tomjanovich, Murphy's fellow first-year Rocket, struggled as a rookie and averaged only five points per game. But the pair of Rudy T and the Pocket Rocket soon became cornerstones of the Rockets franchise.

   The thirty-eight-win Seattle SuperSonics finished two games behind San Diego in the standings. But Seattle also featured the league's most talented newcomer. Spencer Haywood grew up in rural Mississippi and spent his childhood picking cotton to help his mother, a washerwoman raising eleven kids on her own. At age fifteen, Haywood moved to Detroit and shot up college recruiters' boards after growing into a six-foot-eight, 230-pound basketball prodigy. In his own estimation, Haywood received "serious offers from 339 colleges." He decided on Tennessee, where he was set to become the first African American basketball player in Southeastern Conference history. "Somebody had to integrate college basketball in the South," Haywood later wrote, "and Mama always told me I was special." Raised in abject poverty, Haywood had no qualms about taking money from recruiters, asking "who was I cheating? I would be working hard to fill their field house and make millions of dollars for the school, so what was the harm if I had a nice set of wheels and didn't have to wear the same pair of pants every day?" Tennessee head coach Ray Mears disagreed and pressured his precocious recruit to attend a junior college after Haywood failed the University of Tennessee entrance exam. Haywood tried to leave Knoxville and enroll elsewhere, but university administrators refused to release him from his scholarship. And so, in the middle of the night, Haywood bolted for Trinidad State Junior College in Colorado.[9]

After one spectacular season at Trinidad, U.S. Olympic officials asked Haywood to try out for the 1968 Olympic men's basketball team. Haywood easily made the squad and became the youngest American basketball player in Olympic history. Far more attention, though, was paid to the players who did not play for the United States in '68. Most famously, Lew Alcindor and his UCLA teammates Mike Warren and Lucius Allen boycotted the games as part of the Olympic Project for Human Rights, intended to raise awareness of civil rights and institutionalized segregation. A handful of other top college players bowed out for personal reasons—some cited exhaustion after playing a full college season and others feared injuries that might harm future earnings. Despite calls for all African American athletes to boycott the games, Haywood and his Olympic teammates proudly represented their country in international competition. Jo Jo White, then entering his senior season at Kansas, summed up the opinions of those who played when telling *Sports Illustrated*'s Curry Kirkpatrick, "I make up my own mind, and I've decided to play. I don't care if I'm the only one. They can go ahead and boycott; I'm playing." In Mexico City, White and Haywood were brilliant, leading the United States to an emotional gold-medal finish. But even in Mexico City, their efforts were overshadowed by the black-gloved salutes of sprinters Tommie Smith and John Carlos and the Tlatelolco massacre taking place even before the opening ceremonies.[10]

After returning from Mexico City, Haywood transferred to the University of Detroit for the 1968–1969 season, convinced—at least in part—because administrators promised to bring his former high school coach to their school. Haywood earned first-team All-American honors for the Titans and expected to return to Detroit for his junior year. But the university reneged on their agreement to bring in his high school coach, and Haywood reconsidered his decision to stay. "I was making $15 a month in school, and when suddenly someone says you can make $100,000 a year, you start listening," Haywood said. At the time, the NBA prohibited players from joining the league before their academic class graduated from college.[11]

But the rival American Basketball Association had no such restriction and was open to bending the rules to compete for the once-in-a-lifetime talent. In order to justify signing Haywood, the renegade league created what became known as the "hardship rule." As one ABA general manager remembered, "there was no legal research or anything, we just invented the term. So we came out and said that Spencer was a special case." Haywood signed a lucrative contract with the Denver Rockets and left Detroit.[12]

Haywood led the ABA in nearly every statistical category as a rookie and won the MVP award by a landslide. But Haywood's brief stay in Denver was—like much of his career would be—controversial. He led the Rockets to the finals and brought about what one local sportswriter later called "the brightest [time] in our basketball history." He also lasted just one season in the Mile High City after accusing the team owners of racism. "The Ringsbys [Denver's owners] treat me like a nigger," Haywood wrote in an early autobiography, "they call me a 'black nigger' and the ABA, the commissioner . . . he just laughs."[13]

The racial bigotry Haywood faced in Denver became increasingly mainstream in the early seventies, exemplified by Carroll O'Connor's portrayal of Archie Bunker in the hit television show *All in the Family*, which debuted in January 1971—a few short months after Haywood left Denver. Fred Ferretti, reviewing the show for the *New York Times*, admitted the "pot-bellied, church-going, cigar-smoking son of Middle America, Archie Bunker," was funny enough, but argued that the show was also tasteless in perpetuating racial, ethnic, and gender stereotypes for a laugh. Maybe the Ringsbys and ABA commissioner Jack Dolph became, like President Nixon and millions of other Americans, Archie Bunker fans. But Haywood certainly did not. And he wanted out of Denver.[14]

Angry at the Rockets front office, Haywood jumped leagues in 1970 to join the SuperSonics, claiming that Denver broke his contract. Seattle's renegade owner, Sam Schulman, defied the other NBA team owners in signing "Hardship" Haywood and threatened to move the Sonics from the NBA to the ABA—maybe to Los Angeles where he could woo UCLA freshman sensation Bill Walton—if the league refused to allow Haywood to play for Seattle. Since Haywood's six-year, $1.5 million contract was with Schulman personally and not with the Sonics, league officials had to take the threats seriously. Soon Haywood, Schulman, and the two competing leagues were suing and countersuing each other. NBA and ABA officials vilified Haywood; the former for challenging their established four-year rule and the latter for jumping leagues. "I am being made to look like the worst man since Hitler," Haywood complained. Haywood also suffered in the court of public opinion. Fans called him spoiled and teammates viewed him as a mercenary. Haywood once wondered how, as an Olympic gold medal winner, "in the space of one year and without committing a major felony, [I could] be downgraded from great American hero to greedy, subversive malcontent?"[15]

Court cases kept basketball's Benedict Arnold from donning SuperSonics green and gold until finally, on December 30, 1970, a federal district court judge allowed Haywood to suit up for a game against the Bulls. Although he never even checked into the game, Chicago filed an official protest with the league, citing a "distractive and disruptive atmosphere which was a direct cause of an injury to our player, Chet Walker." Commissioner Kennedy dismissed the Bulls' protest, but Haywood remained on the Sonics bench.[16]

In early January 1971, the English rock band Led Zeppelin released their third album, *Led Zeppelin III*; the U.S. banned radio and television advertisements for cigarettes; the Baltimore Colts defeated the Dallas Cowboys in Super Bowl V; and Spencer Haywood finally played in an NBA game. On January 4, Haywood scored fourteen points to lift Seattle to a victory over the Portland Trail Blazers. After the game, Portland argued that Seattle should forfeit their win, citing their use of "an 'illegal' player." In fact, the opposing team filed a protest in each of Haywood's first eight games, and the Royals listed Haywood in their game program simply as "No. 24—Ineligible Player."[17]

Haywood's case finally reached the Supreme Court in March 1971 where, in a landmark 7–2 decision, the court determined the NBA's four-year rule violated the Sherman Antitrust Act. In the short term, Haywood and the NBA settled and Kennedy duly dismissed team protests filed against the Sonics. But in the long term, the ruling opened the floodgates for early entrants to join the NBA. In the fall of 1971, the league held a special "hardship draft," open only to underclassmen previously barred because of the four-year rule. Phil Chenier, from the University of California, Berkeley, ended up in Baltimore, giving the Bullets one of the league's best young backcourt men. Even more importantly, the Haywood decision allowed high school players to jump directly to the pro ranks. In the 1970s, only two players made the leap (Darryl Dawkins and Bill Willoughby in 1975). But decades later, the fortunes of the Minnesota Timberwolves, Los Angeles Lakers, and

Cleveland Cavaliers turned when Kevin Garnett, Kobe Bryant, and LeBron James arrived on the scene fresh out of high school.

While Seattle worked through its off-court issues during the 1970–1971 season, their neighbors to the south, in Portland, struggled on the court. The first-year Blazers were a mix of has-beens and never-weres, but they gained a catchy nickname when, after a clutch basket late in a game against the Lakers, announcer Bill Schonely spontaneously yelled "Rip City!" In the team's first season, most "Rip City" cheers came because of rookie guard Geoff Petrie. Petrie entered the league from Princeton as a relative unknown—headlines in the Portland newspapers asked "Geoff Who?" when the team drafted him eighth overall—but he drew immediate comparisons to a young Jerry West. Unsurprisingly, Petrie modeled his game after the Lakers star, noticing that West took one "real hard dribble" just as he rose to shoot his jump shot. So Petrie did the same. Petrie led the team in scoring, averaging nearly twenty-five points per game, and after the season shared the rookie of the year title with Boston's Dave Cowens, ahead of far more heralded players like "Pistol Pete" Maravich, Calvin Murphy, and Bob Lanier.[18]

Petrie and the Blazers managed just twenty-nine wins on the season. But that nearly doubled the Cleveland Cavaliers' output. The Cavaliers (a nickname that won out over the Towers, Jays, Presidents, and Foresters in a fan poll) set records for futility in their first season. Their fifteen wins tied them with the 1967–1968 San Diego Rockets for the fewest over an eighty-two game season in NBA history. Some teams in the 1970s had a bad offense, others a bad defense. Cleveland had both. The Cavaliers started the season 0–15 and stood at 4–37 at the halfway point; only a strong stretch in December saved them from finishing with single-digit wins. The 1970–1971 season was, however, a memorable one for the team, and it started even before they had any players. As the Cavaliers prepped for the expansion draft, they lacked scouting reports (or scouts), so team officials purchased dozens of packs of NBA trading cards and, according to one assistant coach, studied the statistics printed on the back of the cards "extensively to make our draft picks." To lead this ragtag bunch, Cleveland tapped former collegiate coach Bill Fitch; if nothing else, Fitch brought spirited gallows humor to the role. On the day he was hired, Fitch reminded reporters to "remember, the name is Fitch, not Houdini," and declared "war is hell and expansion is worse." Fitch was well aware of his team's shortcomings: one player was cut because he stood in line at the concession stand in his warmups to buy and eat a hot dog; another opened the second half in a game against Portland by scoring in the wrong basket. "We've got a bunch of backup players," Fitch said. "We'd probably make somebody a hell of a farm club."[19]

The other three teams in the Central Division finished with better records than the hapless Cavaliers but were also far less entertaining. At 42–40, the Baltimore Bullets won the division, finishing ahead of the 36–46 Atlanta Hawks and 33–49 Cincinnati Royals. Cincinnati, under second-year coach Bob Cousy, featured an electric backcourt pairing of Norm Van Lier (also in his second season) and rookie Nate "Tiny" Archibald. Van Lier led the league in assists (10.1 per game) while Archibald, a second-round pick out of the University of Texas at El Paso, exhibited a fearlessness that belied his short stature. The duo fit perfectly into Cousy's fast-breaking offensive system, and the Royals seemed likely to compete for a division title in the near future.

In Atlanta, Hawks fans assumed that adding Pistol Pete Maravich to a team that had posted the best record in the West would make their Hawks instant title contenders. But Atlanta got off to a rocky start: after opening the 1969–1970 season 21–9, they stood at 9–21 thirty games into the 1970–1971 campaign. Maravich received most of the blame. "A three-on-one fastbreak should be an easy layup," coach Richie Guerin complained of his rookie guard. "If you go behind your back or through your legs, and it backfires, the fans boo and your teammates get annoyed." Forward Bill Bridges agreed. "I certainly didn't understand Pete's creativity, didn't understand it at all. We'd been doing all these nice, safe things and here comes this rookie with the new stuff." As the team struggled, the press quickly turned on the player that they had anointed the team's fair-skinned savior just months earlier. One Hawks beat reporter later said, "a lot of people deep down resented him coming into a good ballclub and fucking it up."[20]

After the Hawks signed Maravich to a record-setting contract making him the league's highest paid player, Bridges and "Jumpin' Joe" Caldwell demanded more money. Both were turned down. Bridges returned to the team, but Caldwell held out and in October signed with the ABA's Carolina Cougars. Guerin was outraged. "We're telling Joe we can't afford to pay . . . but we can afford to pay this white superstar college player. I would be offended myself." In this era of civil rights activism, even an old-school ex-Marine like Guerin recognized the cultural shift taking place around him. The NBA was becoming increasingly populated by African American players (about half the league was black in 1970; by the end of the decade, it was closer to three out of four), and the hype surrounding Maravich, the greatest of the white hopes, wore on the team and coaching staff, even as Pete developed into an All-Star-caliber player.[21]

"Pistol Pete" started his rookie season coming off the bench as Guerin tried to reign in Maravich's showboating style. But by the end of November, Guerin was starting the hotshot rookie and Maravich made an immediate impact. In his first six games as a starter, Pete averaged better than thirty points, including his first forty-point game as a professional, against the Knicks in Madison Square Garden, the site of his forgettable National Invitational Tournament performance a year earlier. With Pistol emerging as one of the league's top scorers, the Hawks soared into the playoffs, posting a 9–2 record in their last eleven games. Maravich also made his mark at the box office as home attendance increased by 20 percent and gate receipts jumped by almost 50 percent. Also, the "New Hawks" appeared on national television five times and sold out eighteen home games—up from two televised appearances and three sellouts for the more successful pre-Maravich "Old Hawks."

Baltimore beat out Atlanta to win the Atlantic Division with a balanced offensive attack featuring six players who averaged double figures in points for the season. One of these, Jack Marin, scored both nineteen points per game and a lot of phone numbers after the game. Marin was a well-known NBA bachelor who parlayed his movie-star good looks into both a guest appearance on the hit television show *Mod Squad* and numerous postgame one-night stands. In a 1971 interview, Marin explained that "being single is one of the beauties of traveling as a basketball player." "It keeps life interesting," he said, "our schedule is so demanding, if we didn't have the night life in the cities we visited, we'd be schizophrenics." Marin rated each of the seventeen NBA cities by its social scene, reviewing each in a sentence or two. Chicago ranked near the top because of O'Hare Airport, providing Marin a number of stewardesses he could perhaps meet for a late-night rendezvous. "A typical date for me in Chicago," Marin said, "would be dinner, maybe at the Sheraton Chicago where we stay, a few stops at nearby clubs and then back to the hotel for . . . well, never mind." Ironically, Marin met his future wife in his hometown of Houston. "She wasn't into basketball," Marin quipped. "I told her I was with the Rockets. She thought I worked at the space center."[22]

Marin ranked Beantown right in the middle of his scoresheet, joking that "I used to know a Playboy Bunny who lived in Boston. That was a hare raising experience." Visiting teams like Marin's Bullets celebrated the first Celtics losing record in twenty years when, in 1969–1970, the once mighty Bostonians dropped to 34–48. Their elation was short-lived as the Celtics bounced back above .500 with a talented core led by former sixth-man extraordinaire John Havlicek. Havlicek scored a career-high 28.9 points per game in his ninth season, good for second in the league behind MVP Lew Alcindor.[23]

But the real revelation in Boston was the play of rookie center Dave Cowens. The Celtics selected Cowens fourth overall in the 1970 draft, just one spot after the Hawks took Pistol Pete Maravich. Cowens had attended Florida State and remained out of the national spotlight as the Seminoles faced NCAA sanctions barring them from postseason play. Although he flew under the radar, Celtics team president Red Auerbach certainly knew about Cowens and loved the fiery redhead. In fact, Auerbach was so nervous that other teams would draft Cowens just to spite Boston that Red feigned disinterest during a college All-Star game featuring the feisty Florida State big man. "I only stayed five minutes," Auerbach recalled, "and I made a big scene when I left so people would think I was disgusted." After the Hawks picked Maravich, Auerbach jumped up and screamed Cowens's name for the Celtics. Not everyone was as enthusiastic as Red about the former Florida State star. He was not a traditional center, standing barely six-foot-nine, and many critics (including Cowens himself, who "didn't like the idea of being the smallest pivot in the league") suggested Boston move him to forward. But Auerbach and head coach Tommy Heinsohn were adamant that Cowens was a center and were richly rewarded almost immediately for their stubbornness. In his first season, Cowens averaged seventeen points and fifteen rebounds per game and was named rookie of the year alongside Blazers guard Geoff Petrie. Although comparatively short, Cowens fit perfectly into Celtics culture; Willis Reed described Cowens as possessing "the competitive fire of a Havlicek with possibly more natural ability." His competitiveness spilled over into the Celtics locker room

where the rookie invented a game called "butting heads." As the name
suggests, two men playing "butting heads" would stand next to one
another and, as teammate Don Nelson recalled, "conk each other's
noggins until someone gives up." No one beat Cowens. Dave was also
an eccentric outside the game. By the end of his rookie year, he main-
tained "a working interest in vegetable gardening, the Boston Sympho-
ny, homemade soup, archery, the Bible with emphasis on the Old Tes-
tament, marketing, auto repairs and the bass violin." Part Renaissance
man, part Neanderthalic warrior, Cowens vaulted the Celtics into the
NBA's upper echelon in his rookie season and helped the team rebound
from Russell's retirement far sooner than most expected.[24]

The Celtics were also well-represented on the NBA's "Silver Anniversary Team," revealed by the league as part of its twenty-fifth anniversary celebration held over the midseason All-Star break. Only retired
players were considered, and some of the names on the list might be
unfamiliar to modern readers: panelists named Celtics stars Bob Cousy,
Sam Jones, Bill Russell, and Bill Sharman along with Paul Arizin, Bob
Davies, Joe Fulks, George Mikan, Bob Pettit, and Dolph Schayes as
players while Celtics boss Red Auerbach earned the coaching honors.

Boston was clearly the team of the past, and possibly of the future.
But in the spring of 1971, as the playoffs neared, it was very clear that
Milwaukee and New York were the teams of the present. Twice during
the regular season, the Knicks had ended long Bucks winning streaks:
one sixteen games long and the other a league-record twenty. In fact,
New York took four out of their five regular season matches against
Milwaukee after knocking them out of the playoffs the year before. But
unlike in 1970, when the Knicks knocked the Bucks out of the Eastern
Division postseason, the two titans could not meet up until the NBA
finals. Hoops fans prayed for a Bucks-Knicks championship series.

Milwaukee did its part, surviving three series to handily win the
Western Conference. In the opening round, Alcindor dominated the
Warriors, and the Bucks won the best-of-seven series in five. After
slipping by the Bulls in seven grueling games, the injury-riddled Lakers
(missing both Baylor and West) were easy pickings for the healthy
Bucks, who won that series four games to one. The Bucks' side of the
bracket was complete. Bring on the Knicks.

New York hoped to have just as easy a time in the East as Milwaukee
did in the West. In the first round, the Knicks knocked out Pistol Pete

Maravich and the Atlanta Hawks in five games, while their archrivals from Baltimore took seven to eliminate the 76ers, setting up, for the third straight season, a New York–Baltimore playoffs matchup. In both '69 and '70, the Knicks eliminated the Bullets and hoped to make it three straight in '71. "Baltimore and New York always produce close games," wrote *Sports Illustrated*'s Peter Carry, "their starters match up strength on strength—Unseld-Reed, Johnson-DeBusschere, Monroe-Frazier." And the Bullets were hyped up. "You want to punch, we can punch," boasted Bullets forward Gus "Honeycomb" Johnson, channeling his inner Muhammad Ali. "You want to dance, we can dance, baby." Fittingly, Madison Square Garden had hosted, less than a month earlier, an Ali fight dubbed "the fight of the century" against heavyweight boxing champion Joe Frazier that ended in a fifteen-round decision for Frazier.[25]

Knee injuries kept Honeycomb Johnson from boxing, dancing, or even playing in the first five games of the Eastern Conference finals. Reeling from the loss of their star forward, the Bullets dropped the first two games to the Knicks in New York. But after the Bullets won the next two games at home, the series returned to even. The Knicks took game five in New York, but in game six, Johnson had his own Willis Reed moment, limping out onto the court to lead his teammates to an emotional victory. He scored just ten points in limited action, but the inspired Bullets coasted to a 113–96 victory to send the series to a decisive seventh game.

On April 19, 1971, Los Angeles Superior Court Judge Charles Order handed down death sentences to four of Charles Manson's brainwashed Manson Family members. Three thousand miles away, on a court of a different sort, Madison Square Garden was packed to the rafters with fans far more worried about beating the despised Baltimore Bullets than with Manson's Helter Skelter. Before game seven, Bullets owner Abe Pollin delivered what guard Kevin Loughery later described as "the greatest pregame speech by an owner in the history of sports," promising the players his share of the gate receipts if Baltimore won. Perhaps motivated by their owners' offer, Baltimore came out strong, and, although the game was close throughout, the Bullets' biggest stars outplayed their Knick counterparts to a man. Wide-bodied Wes Unseld pulled down a game-high twenty rebounds and fended off New York's once-again-gimpy center Willis Reed while Honeycomb Johnson gamely battled Knicks strongman Dave DeBusschere to a standstill. Most glaringly, Baltimore's Earl "the Pearl" Monroe flashed through the lane at will and popped in twenty-six points, exactly double what Walt "Clyde" Frazier managed for New York. Appropriately for such an intense rivalry, the game boiled down to the final seconds. As the clock ticked toward zero, the ball ended up in the hands of Knicks forward Bill Bradley. The future U.S. senator launched a shot that would have sent the contest into overtime. But Unseld stretched his six-foot-seven frame to its fullest and managed to get a fingertip on the ball, which fell harmlessly into Honeycomb's waiting hands. The Knicks were shocked. "The game's over, the season's over, and it's like death—you can't change it. You can't go out and say add up the score again," said coach Red Holzman somberly after the game. Just like that, the promised Knicks dynasty had ended. They would not match Russell's historic streak of eight straight titles, and they failed to win even back-to-back banners. The highly anticipated Bucks-Knicks series would also have to wait. Instead, the Baltimore Bullets would be the ones to face one of the greatest basketball teams of all time for the NBA title.[26]

"We honestly didn't think Baltimore would beat the Knicks," recalled Oscar Robertson years later, "they weren't who we'd been gunning for." Robertson and his Bucks teammates were surprised, and maybe even a little disappointed, that the Bullets advanced past the Knicks. "I want to play New York," Milwaukee coach Larry Costello complained. "If it's Baltimore, they'll always be able to say, 'But you didn't beat the Knicks.'" Lew Alcindor agreed. The Knicks, he said, were "the defending champions, and we wanted to take the crown from the king." The indestructible Bucks suddenly appeared ripe for an upset and fans wondered if Milwaukee might overlook the Bullets. Baltimore already had two championship teams: the Orioles and Colts were the reigning World Series and Super Bowl champions, respectively. A Bullets win would be the perfect storybook ending, giving Baltimore a sweep of the three major American sports in a single year. As Bullets guard Kevin Loughery boasted, "We feel that this is our year, that we're supposed to win."[27]

Milwaukee breezed to a ten-point win in game one, sending a clear message that the Bullets might not, in fact, be a team of destiny. Three Bucks wins later, and the sweep was complete as Milwaukee joined the '59 Celtics as the only teams in league history to win every game in the finals. "Finally," was the first word out of Oscar Robertson's mouth as the clock ticked down to zero at the end of the fourth game. "Finally," he repeated. "It's been a long time coming." Robertson had played a nearly perfect series, averaging 23.5 points, 5 rebounds, and 9.5 assists per game. Teammate Lew Alcindor was even better, winning the finals MVP award to match his regular season trophy after posting 27 points and 18.5 rebounds per game in dominating the Bullets' undersized Unseld.[28]

As quickly as fans and journalists had declared the New York Knicks the team of the seventies, they now scrambled to back the Bucks. "It is too early to talk about a dynasty in Milwaukee," one sportswriter admitted, "but the Bucks have all the ingredients necessary." *Sports Illustrated*'s Peter Carry called the squad "the best team—ever," writing that "none of today's professional basketball teams can approach the Bucks, and if one recognizes a steamroller when it comes down the road, probably few teams of the past could match them, either." The Bucks won the 1971 NBA title after posting a combined record of 88–18, including the regular season, playoffs, and undefeated exhibition campaign. Looking forward, Milwaukee had all the necessary components to create a dynasty: a steady veteran guard able to control the pace of the game (Robertson), a cast of one- or two-dimensional players willingly embracing their roles (shooter Jon McGlocklin, athletic defender Bob Dandridge, scrappy Greg Smith, and flashy scoring guard Lucius Allen), and—most importantly—a center able to dominate the game on the offensive and defensive end in regular season and finals, MVP Lew Alcindor.[29]

After a decade of frustration in Cincinnati, Oscar Robertson finally had his championship ring. But while the Reds of his old hometown went on to win back-to-back World Series titles in the mid-seventies, "the Big O" could not match that feat in the NBA. In fact, just one year after the Bucks made the claim that they were the best team in league history, sportswriters would identify a new "best team ever" as Milwaukee failed to even return to the finals.

Statistics for 1970–1971

Eastern Conference	W	L	Western Conference	W	L
Atlantic Division			*Midwest Division*		
New York Knicks	52	30	Milwaukee Bucks	66	16
Philadelphia 76ers	47	35	Chicago Bulls	51	31

Boston Celtics	44	38	Phoenix Suns	48	34
Buffalo Braves	22	60	Detroit Pistons	45	37
Central Division			*Pacific Division*		
Baltimore Bullets	42	40	Los Angeles Lakers	48	34
Atlanta Hawks	36	46	San Francisco Warriors	41	41
Cincinnati Royals	33	49	San Diego Rockets	40	42
Cleveland Cavaliers	15	67	Seattle SuperSonics	38	44
			Portland Trail Blazers	29	53

Playoffs

Eastern Conference Semifinals	Baltimore d. Philadelphia (4–3)
	New York d. Atlanta (4–1)
Western Conference Semifinals	Milwaukee d. San Francisco (4–1)
	Los Angeles d. Chicago (4–3)
Eastern Conference Finals	Baltimore d. New York (4–3)
Western Conference Finals	Milwaukee d. Los Angeles (4–1)
NBA Finals	Milwaukee d. Baltimore (4–0)

All-NBA Teams

First Team

F—Billy Cunningham (Philadelphia)

F—John Havlicek (Boston)

C—Lew Alcindor (Milwaukee)

G—Dave Bing (Detroit)

G—Jerry West (Los Angeles)

Second Team

F—Bob Love (Chicago)

F—Gus Johnson (Baltimore)

C—Willis Reed (New York)

G—Walt Frazier (New York)

G—Oscar Robertson (Cincinnati)

League Leaders

Points per Game (31.7)   Lew Alcindor (Milwaukee)

Rebounds per Game (18.2)   Wilt Chamberlain (Los Angeles)

Assists per Game (10.1)	Norm Van Lier (Cincinnati)
Most Valuable Player	Lew Alcindor (Milwaukee)
Rookie of the Year	Dave Cowens (Boston) and Geoff Petrie (Portland)

3

1971 TO 1972

In the 1960s, any list of top American athletes would include Baltimore Colts quarterback Johnny Unitas, New York/San Francisco Giants outfielder Willie Mays, and the Los Angeles Lakers trio of Elgin Baylor, Wilt Chamberlain, and Jerry West. But by the fall of 1971, all five were rapidly approaching retirement. Thirty-eight-year-old Unitas split time at quarterback for the Colts and threw nine interceptions against just three touchdown passes. Mays, now forty, made the All-Star team and batted a respectable .271; the next year he was shipped to the New York Mets where he struggled mightily, retiring probably two seasons too late.

The Lakers stars, too, seemed to be past their primes. Baylor was thirty-seven, trying to return from a torn Achilles tendon that cost him most of the 1970–1971 season; Chamberlain was thirty-six and fresh off his worst year as a pro (although, to be fair, this still meant more than twenty points and eighteen rebounds per game); and the thirty-three-year-old West remained the league's most famous bridesmaid: seemingly destined to finish second. Baylor and West entered the season with seven NBA finals appearances: they were 0–7. Chamberlain was not much better, winning just one of four. Rather than getting better, L.A. seemed on the verge of dropping off. Compounding problems, the team would begin the season with a new coach, their third in four years, who, as a player in the sixties, had helped ruin Lakers title hopes repeatedly as a member of the hated Boston Celtics.

Much of the uncertainty in Lakers land revolved around Baylor. In his prime, Baylor was among the best forwards of all time. He joined the Lakers in 1958 (when they still called Minneapolis home) and earned rookie of the year honors after averaging twenty-five points and fifteen rebounds per game. Even as a rookie, Baylor revolutionized the game. Standing six-foot-five with 225 pounds of chiseled muscle, Baylor possessed remarkable body control and the ability to hang in midair seemingly forever, making near-impossible shots appear routine. Thanks to Wilt Chamberlain's jaw-dropping statistical brilliance, Baylor never led the league in scoring or rebounding despite pulling down almost twenty rebounds per contest during the 1960–1961 season and tossing in thirty-eight points per game the following season. But in the 1960s, no one could match the Lakers duo of Baylor and West. Baylor (L.A.'s "Mr. Inside") posted up smaller defenders and scored on swooping drives to the hoop while West ("Mr. Outside") tossed in long jump shots and played lockdown defense. Chamberlain's arrival in 1968 forced every Laker to adjust, but none more than Baylor. Offensively, their skill sets seemed to overlap; both liked to camp near the basket to overpower opponents. Neither had an above-average jump shot and so, with Baylor and Chamberlain playing at the same time, the lane clogged up and both players grew frustrated. They also clashed off the court. Baylor "didn't want to have to play second-fiddle to me on the Lakers," Chamberlain said, insisting that Baylor was "almost exclusively an offensive player" and that "defense was something Elg did only to help pass the time between shots."[1]

By opening night, it was clear that Baylor's career was coming to an end and that only his past accomplishments justified his position on the Lakers starting five. One *Sports Illustrated* writer claimed "Elgin Baylor simply should not be playing anymore," admitting that although this might sound "shockingly heretical," "Baylor's scarred legs no longer provide the thrust needed to shoot his jumper or the agility that playing defense requires." Baylor himself realized that retirement was an approaching inevitability. In a preseason interview, he announced that this would be his final season, putting Lakers management in a difficult position. Should they stick by their aging superstar, even if it hurt the team? Or should they bench one of the league's all-time greats and risk alienating Lakers fans and Baylor's teammates?[2]

One Laker who probably opposed benching Baylor was Elgin's long-time running mate, Jerry West. West joined the Lakers in 1960, two years after Baylor, when the team moved from Minneapolis to L.A. By the time the Lakers broke training camp for the 1971–1972 season, West already had eleven All-Star games and eight All-NBA first teams under his belt. He was also a dogged defender with an eighty-one-inch wingspan, allowing him to close down passing lanes almost single-handedly.

West was such an important player in the NBA that in 1969 the league unveiled a new logo depicting a man dribbling a basketball silhouetted on a field of blue and red. Today, this image can be found on nearly all league-related merchandise, generating more than $5 billion in annual revenue. Although the NBA refuses to identify the inspiration behind the popular logo, its designer happily spilled the beans. "It's Jerry West," Alan Siegel insists. Siegel based the logo on a design he sold to Major League Baseball in 1968. Baseball was America's most popular sport in the late sixties and establishing a brand with a strong resemblance to it appealed to NBA commissioner Walter Kennedy.[3]

Using West as the league's All-American poster boy also appealed to Kennedy, since West had come to symbolize all that was right—and white—in the league during the fight over civil rights. The racial make-up of the league changed dramatically during West's tenure with the Lakers, and by the time of his retirement in 1974, African Americans outnumbered white players in the league. Yet despite this on-court transition, most NBA fans were white, and, well aware of their primary audience, league officials catered to the group that propelled Richard Nixon to the presidency in 1968: the silent majority.

There was just one blemish on the otherwise spotless resume of Jerry "the Logo" West: his lack of an NBA championship ring. By 1971, West had become, "in essence, the great, great loser"—a Robert E. Lee of the hardwood. Even West recognized his closing window of opportunity. "Let's face it," he admitted before the season, "our chances for an NBA championship this year are not the best. Our key players are older now and it would be foolish for me to think that we can play as well as we played a few years ago." West was clearly a fantastic player; one of the best in NBA history, in fact. But Lakers fans—and even West himself—began to question how far an injury-riddled thirty-three-year-old guard could carry an aging team.[4]

Another Laker whose name was synonymous with losing had ironically already won an NBA title before coming to L.A. Despite leading the 1966–1967 Philadelphia 76ers to the championship, critics still called Wilt Chamberlain a loser. No one doubted his talent. Hall of famer Dolph Schayes called Chamberlain "the most perfect instrument made by God to play basketball." Wilt stood more than seven feet tall with a wingspan estimated at between seven-and-a-half and eight feet in length. He could nearly touch the rim flat-footed. Chamberlain's physical exploits became the stuff of legend. "He is," one journalist wrote, "Paul Bunyan, Davy Crockett, Billy the Kid and Big Foot all rolled into one. He is modern American folklore." Could he palm and lift a bowling ball one-handed? Did his long strides allow him to cover the distance between the foul lines in just five steps? Did he actually work out with Arnold Schwarzenegger and out-lift Olympic weightlifters? Did he possess a fifty-inch vertical leap? Did he sleep with 20,000 women during his lifetime? Was there a contract for him to box against Muhammad Ali? The answer to each of the questions is yes—if you believed Wilt Chamberlain.[5]

Despite his superhuman physicality, or maybe because of it, Chamberlain could not shake charges that he was a loser, more interested in individual accomplishments than in team success. In 1962, "the Dipper" (his preferred nickname) *averaged* better than fifty points per game and recorded one hundred points one night against the Knicks. But his productivity dipped in the playoffs, and he never averaged as many points per game during the postseason as he did during the regular season. He also struggled mightily at the free throw line, a condition he blamed on knee problems forcing him to tweak his technique. He connected on barely half of his free throw attempts and regularly changed his approach, hopeful that something might click. Sometimes, he launched free throws underhanded. Other times, he stood at the top of the circle—a full four feet behind the free throw line—to hoist line drives at the rim. But mostly he seemed frustrated and perplexed at his inability to make such easy shots. For "Dipper" (he hated being called "Wilt the Stilt") basketball always came easy—except for those damned free throws.

The Dipper's biggest problem, though, was the comparison to Bill Russell. Chamberlain dominated statistically, but Russell had eleven rings and Wilt just one. Did that make Russell a winner and Wilt a loser? Many sportswriters and NBA fans sure thought so. Critics even latched onto some of Chamberlain's own statements to prove their points. Of Russell, Chamberlain wrote "to Bill, every game—particularly every championship game—was a challenge, a test of manhood." But to Wilt, basketball was "a game, not a life-and-death struggle," and he remained insistent that "I don't need scoring titles or NBA championships to prove that I'm a man." So the popular perception persisted: Russell was a winner and Chamberlain a loser.[6]

The Lakers legion of losers welcomed a new coach for the 1971–1972 season by the name of Bill Sharman. Sharman starred alongside Bob Cousy in the Boston backcourt from 1951 to 1961, winning four NBA titles in the process. As a coach, Sharman led the George Steinbrenner–owned Cleveland Pipers of the short-lived American Basketball League to a title before jumping to the ABA's Los Angeles Stars. In 1971, after the Stars relocated to Utah, Sharman took them to a title as well. A few months later, Lakers owner Jack Kent Cooke tried to persuade UCLA's John Wooden to become the team's head coach. When Wooden passed, Cooke offered the gig to Sharman, who jumped at the opportunity to test his mettle in the NBA.

Sharman, as much as any player, set a standard of excellence motivating an aged, ailing team to excel. First, he insisted the Lakers would play a more up-tempo game. Critics mocked the idea of the league's oldest team laboring up and down the court, joking that broken hips might sideline any or all of L.A.'s "big three." But run they did. Before Sharman's arrival, the Lakers averaged 115 points per game, seventh in the seventeen-team league. Under Sharman, they led the NBA with 121 per contest—nearly five points more than their nearest competitor. The key to the Lakers' offense was the fast break, often started with a rebound from Wilt Chamberlain. Wilt had a well-deserved reputation as a me-first stat-stuffer, priding himself on having led the league in every major statistical category without ever once fouling out of a game. Sharman convinced the Dipper that he needed to emulate Chamberlain's nemesis (and Sharman's teammate in Boston), Bill Russell. Chamberlain responded by scoring less than fifteen points (half his career average), pulling down nearly twenty rebounds per game, and, most importantly, providing a menacing defense. His performance against the hated Celtics in a mid-November game was especially Russell-esque. That night, Wilt scored three points, pulled down thirty-one rebounds, handed out ten assists, and blocked thirteen shots. During the season, he also reached the 30,000-point plateau (the first player in league history to accomplish the feat) and became the NBA's all-time rebounding leader after pulling down number 21,621.

Even more questionable than increasing their pace of play or convincing Chamberlain to channel his inner Bill Russell were some of Sharman's newfangled training techniques. The new Lakers boss held mandatory film sessions with reel-to-reel movies compiled laboriously by a team scout who, to ensure players paid attention, occasionally spliced in a photo of a Playboy Bunny. Sharman also forced his players to attend a morning shoot-around on game day, a foreign concept at the time. Demanding that NBA players, especially veterans like those on the Lakers, wake up early and practice on game day could have spelled disaster. In particular Chamberlain, a well-known night owl, initially bristled at the idea. "It doesn't do anything for me except interrupt my sleep," Chamberlain groused. But he agreed to give the morning shoot-arounds a chance. "If it helps the team, I'll go along. If not . . . then we'll see what happens," the Dipper told his coach. The Lakers won. The shoot-arounds stayed.[7]

As the team adjusted to Sharman's style, the Lakers started off mildly, winning just six of their first nine games. But on November 5, 1971, the 6–3 Lakers began a historic streak launching them into the record books and, in the minds of some observers, into the debate over the best team in NBA history. The streak started with little fanfare—a ho-hum four-point victory over the Bullets in Inglewood's "Fabulous Forum" followed by a double-digit win in Oakland against Golden State and then a win over the Knicks back in L.A. Suddenly, Los Angeles had three straight wins. Then they won thirty more. For more than two months, the Lakers were undefeated, smashing the old league record by a baker's dozen. In fact, their thirty-three game winning streak set the all-time American sports record, passing the twenty-six straight ballgames reeled off by baseball's New York Giants in 1916.

On January 9, 1972, the Bucks had a chance to end the streak when the teams met in a suddenly important midseason game broadcast live on ABC. Bucks fans packed the stands to watch the battle, cheering every Oscar Robertson drive and booing each Jerry West jumper. Coach Sharman, always known as a yeller, was in rare form, hollering to be heard over the rowdy crowd. But his Lakers lost, 120–104, and the streak was over. Sharman had screamed himself hoarse and defied doctor's orders to rest his throat for a week or so after the game. Instead, he continued to yell (sometimes accompanied by a handheld microphone and amplifier) and suffered permanent vocal cord damage, which forced him out of coaching a few years later.

Looking back on the historic thirty-three-game winning streak, it is unfortunately easy to pinpoint the precise moment the Lakers transformed from being a good team into a historically great one. On November 4, Baylor announced his retirement from professional basketball: one day later, the streak began. The exact circumstances of Baylor's retirement are somewhat hazy. Sports Illustrated's Peter Carry reported that Baylor was "nudged into retirement by the Los Angeles management" while historian Charley Rosen argued that Baylor had been given a "split or sit" ultimatum and, not wanting to come off the bench, decided to hang up his sneakers. Baylor claimed his retirement was voluntary and helped out younger Lakers mired in backup roles. "By retiring it made it a lot easier for myself, too," Baylor added, "because I don't know how much I would have played" coming off the bench. Lakers owner Jack Kent Cooke immediately retired Baylor's trademark number 22 jersey and transitioned him into a role as a scout and public relations personality to finish out his contract. Whether voluntary or involuntary, with or without pressure from above, Baylor's retirement shook up the Lakers. Although L.A. lost their veteran captain and franchise leader in points and rebounds, they somehow became a better team.[8]

The Baylor-less Lakers coasted to the Pacific Division title after winning an NBA record sixty-nine games. But Lakers fans knew their season would not be complete without an NBA title. And to win the title, they would have to get past Milwaukee, which returned most of the players from their '71 title team. Oscar Robertson, now entering his twelfth NBA season, remained a rock-solid point guard while third-year forward Bob Dandridge, emerging as a superstar, paired with newcomer Curtis Perry on an improving frontline for a sixty-three win Bucks team.

The focal point of the Bucks' attack remained their dominant center, although many fans suddenly had a hard time remembering his name. In 1969, when Lew Alcindor entered the league, it was widely known that he practiced Islam and had a Muslim name—much like Muhammad Ali had once been known as Cassius Clay. In an interview during his rookie campaign, Alcindor said "call me Kareem; call me Lew. I'm not going to get uptight about it." But in 1971, Alcindor informed the press that he wanted to be known as Kareem Abdul-Jabbar. "I had lived two lives too long," Abdul-Jabbar later explained. As he increasingly focused on his religion, he turned even more inward, and Kareem Abdul-Jabbar became even less relatable for the predominantly white, middle-class NBA fan base than had Lew Alcindor. He was, he admitted, "a black man first and an American somewhere down the line." Chamberlain, who was used to being the bad guy, said "with Lew Alcindor becoming Kareem Abdul-Jabbar, the fans had a new villain to jeer."[9]

In 1972, Kareem also portrayed a villain of another sort. That year, he appeared in the kung fu flick *Game of Death*. In what would be the last film for martial arts star Bruce Lee (who died before filming wrapped), Abdul-Jabbar played a character named Mantis defending a mystical pagoda. In one scene, Abdul-Jabbar, wearing a pair of cool shades, kicked Lee's ass before the astute martial artist discovered Mantis's light sensitivity and choked out the lanky seven-foot bad guy.

Somehow, between his rigorous religious schedule and budding acting career, Abdul-Jabbar managed to become the first NBA player to endorse a particular brand of basketball shoe. In the fifties and sixties, most players wore canvas and rubber sneakers—primarily the Converse Chuck Taylor All Stars and the Pro-Keds Royals. In the fall of '71, Abdul-Jabbar signed a contract with Adidas, which introduced the Abdul-Jabbar footwear line. The Jabbar was white leather with navy stripes and included a small graphic of Abdul-Jabbar's face and a copy of his signature on the tongue. The shoe was a big hit and sold well to the public and among pro athletes, leading shoe companies to sign big-name stars to lucrative shoe deals to compete with Adidas and the Jabbar.

Decked out in a pair of his trademark sneakers, Abdul-Jabbar again led the league in scoring and was second in both rebounding and field goal percentage (trailing only Chamberlain in those two categories). He took home his second consecutive MVP award, joining Chamberlain and Bill Russell as the only players in NBA history to win it in back-to-back seasons. His per-game averages were remarkable. Abdul-Jabbar put up 34.8 points, 16.6 rebounds, and 4.6 assists per contest and blocked countless shots in an era before the statistic was officially recorded.

Hot on the heels of Milwaukee and Abdul-Jabbar were their Central Division rivals from Chicago. Dick Motta's "boring and goring" Bulls kept pace with the Bucks for much of the season and finished with fifty-seven wins by relying on a stingy defense forcing teams toward the baseline to cut off ball reversal. During the 1971–1972 season, they added a new point guard in reigning assist leader Norm Van Lier, stealing him from Cincinnati in exchange for a backup center. It was probably the second biggest heist of 1971, trailing only D. B. Cooper's daring skyjacking in the skies above rural Washington State.

In Chicago, Van Lier paired perfectly with Jerry Sloan, forming a scrappy defensive duo. "When Van Lier was traded to Chicago," one opponent recalled, "he and Jerry Sloan became the two dirtiest, cheap-shoting-est teammates in the NBA." Unsurprisingly, Sloan earned first-team All-Defense recognition while Van Lier made the second team. But most importantly, the Bulls personified a team-based approach; no Bulls player even made the All-Star team. "We had an image of a scrappy, aggressive, physical, battling team," coach Dick Motta explained, "with no big name superstars." Their offense was tightly patterned and highly regimented. "Their self-discipline is beautiful to watch," admitted Knicks coach Red Holzman. Chicago fans embraced their squad as attendance, which had once been under 4,000 fans per game, now topped 10,000.[10]

Despite remarkable on-court success, there were problems on the horizon in the Windy City. In the 1971 draft, the Bulls found gems in third-round selection Clifford Ray and seventh rounder Artis Gilmore. But in the second round, they chose talented Villanova forward Howard Porter. To get Porter, the Bulls orchestrated the only cross-league trade in ABA-NBA history, sending cash and a player to the Pittsburgh Condors in return for the rights to Porter. Coach Motta initially saw the rookie as a Gus Johnson–type player, a big, strong warrior who could eventually succeed Chet Walker in the Bulls starting lineup. But soon after training camp opened, Motta realized the Bulls had made a mistake: Porter was a bust. Unfortunately, Porter had a huge guaranteed contract, and suddenly an unproven (and likely overrated) rookie was the highest paid player on a veteran team gunning for a title. As Jerry Sloan said, "I don't know if I deserve any more money, yet, considering

Porter's contract, this certainly might be a good time to think about it." Forward Bob "Butterbean" Love, who had already renegotiated his contract in 1969 and 1971, again asked for a raise. During the 1971–1972 season, the Bulls were able to harness the discord, using it as motivation for an us-against-the-world mentality. But the team would not be so fortunate in the coming years.[11]

Two Western Conference teams relocated before the 1971–1972 season. The Golden State (formerly San Francisco) Warriors moved across the bay to Oakland and added high-scoring forward Cazzie "Muscles" Russell to pair with veteran center Nate Thurmond, creating a potent inside-outside combo. The other team to move, the Houston Rockets (recently of San Diego), featured center Elvin Hayes, a legend at the nearby University of Houston, where he led the Cougars to a win over UCLA and Lew Alcindor in the 1968 "game of the century." Hayes responded to the relocation with what had become a typical year for him: twenty-five points and fifteen rebounds per game playing for a really bad team.

Finishing between Golden State and Houston in the Pacific Division, Seattle's SuperSonics were a much improved squad thanks to another season of development from much-maligned superstar forward Spencer Haywood. Haywood's arrival in the NBA in 1970 ended the antiquated "four-year rule" and opened the door for high school players to jump directly to the league. Now, with his legal issues finally resolved, Haywood was free to focus on basketball, where contemporaries compared the six-eight phenom to a young Elgin Baylor. After finishing fourth in the league in points (26.2 per game) and leading the team in rebounding (12.7 rebounds per game), only a late-season knee injury Haywood suffered after slipping on water leaking from the Seattle Coliseum roof kept the Sonics from making the playoffs.

Like Seattle, the Phoenix Suns also featured a multitalented, controversial forward as Connie "the Hawk" Hawkins put together a superb campaign during the 1971–1972 season, averaging twenty-one points and eight rebounds per game. In March 1972, the Suns gave him some help, convincing reigning ABA scoring champ Charlie Scott to jump from the Virginia Squires. Merger talks between the NBA and ABA continued in fits and starts between 1967 and 1976. Signing Scott ignited another round of interleague warfare and ABA commissioner Jack Dolph immediately fired off telegrams to the other eleven Phoenix

Suns players trying to even the score. Scott quickly demonstrated a level of talent on par with any guard in the NBA, including Walt Frazier, Oscar Robertson, or Jerry West. Scott was fast and strong and wasn't shy about his on-court ability. "I have the most potential to do more things than any of the other guards," he boasted. "I'm six-six and I've been given quickness by the Creator. I can drive. I can shoot outside. I can play defense." Even given his great promise, Phoenix fans feared what Scott might cost the Suns as the Boston Celtics actually controlled his draft rights. Celtics president Red Auerbach knew he had Phoenix in a tight spot but agreed to let the Suns' signing stand in exchange for a player to be named later. Auerbach wanted Paul Silas, the Suns' hard-working, blue-collar power forward. But when the Suns refused, Red remained patient, knowing he still held the upper hand. The Suns finished 49–33 but still missed the playoffs, and to this day forty-nine wins remains the record for a team failing to make the postseason. Despite the setback, the future looked appropriately sunny in the Arizona desert.[12]

The remaining Western Conference teams struggled during the 1971–1972 season. The Detroit Pistons won only twenty-six games under three head coaches. The third of those coaches, Earl Lloyd, was no stranger to struggle or controversy. In 1950, Lloyd broke basketball's color barrier, becoming the first African American to play in an NBA game when he suited up for the old Washington Capitols. In 1968, Lloyd became the league's first black assistant coach and, in 1971, its second black head coach, following in the footsteps of Celtics player-coach Bill Russell. In this, the NBA was ahead of its time: Frank Robinson skippered the Cleveland Indians as Major League Baseball's first African American manager in 1974 and Art Shell became the first black head coach in the modern era of the National Football League fifteen years later.

Finishing behind even the miserable Pistons during the 1971–1972 season were the bottom-feeding Portland Trail Blazers, who entered the season with a new big man to pair with sharpshooting guard—and reigning co–rookie of the year—Geoff Petrie. With the second pick of the 1971 draft, and after paying the Cavaliers $250,000 to pass on their guy, the Trail Blazers selected two-time All-American power forward Sidney Wicks out of UCLA to create an offensively potent one-two punch. Wicks lived up to the hype and took home rookie of the year honors after averaging almost twenty-four points and eleven rebounds per game. But even with their own version of "Mr. Inside" and "Mr. Outside," the Blazers struggled, finishing a league-worst 18–64.

The Western Conference included three elite teams—the Bucks, Bulls, and Lakers—each with at least fifty-seven wins, and half a dozen mediocre squads. The Eastern Conference, on the other hand, had a little more balance, and just one team ended the season with more than fifty wins: the resurgent Boston Celtics. For those who had rejoiced in the Celtics' post-Russell struggles, their elation was short-lived. After plucking All-Stars Jo Jo White and Dave Cowens from back-to-back drafts, the Celtics fluidly blended youth and experience in their return to the top. Cowens (who critics still claimed was better suited to forward than center) and White paired with veteran John Havlicek to create a Boston "Big Three." With the possible exception of Abdul-Jabbar, no player meant more to his team than Havlicek. He switched effortlessly between forward and guard and led the league in minutes played, earning a spot on both the All-Defense and All-NBA first teams in the process. All that the Celtics lacked to become a truly dominant team was a strong inside presence to pair with the undersized Cowens, who, at six-foot-nine, liked to play on the perimeter offensively to take advantage of his quickness and shooting touch. Maybe Auerbach could still pry Silas from the Suns.

Boston's toughest competition in the East came from the forty-eight win New York Knicks. After shockingly falling to the Baltimore Bullets in the 1971 playoffs, the Knicks front office decided to shake up their roster by adding two veteran superstars to an already talented team. New York's top off-season priorities targets included a backup for oft-injured center Willis Reed and clearing the team's logjam at small forward. They managed both in one fell swoop. In May, just weeks after their season's disappointing end, the Knicks dealt backup forward Cazzie "Muscles" Russell to Golden State for Jerry Lucas. Lucas was both an above-average defensive center and, according to longtime teammate Oscar Robertson, "a relentless . . . rebounding demon." Offensively, Lucas was an adept passer and long-distance shooter who could space the floor (much like Reed) allowing for teammates to cut through the lane or drive to the basket.[13]

As an undergraduate at Ohio State, Lucas ranked among the best players in NCAA history, a three-time All-American who Bill Bradley described as "handsome, with thick black hair and perfectly formed teeth, he was every mother's hope and every coed's dream." Lucas was also a very good pro basketball player, earning seven All-Star bids and five All-NBA team selections in his first eight seasons. With the Cincinnati Royals, Lucas teamed with Robertson to form a high-scoring duo who could not bring a title home to the Queen City. After Cousy took over as the team's head coach, management, looking to begin a youth movement, shipped both stars out. Robertson went to Milwaukee and won a championship while Lucas struggled through one-and-a-half seasons with the Warriors before being moved to the Big Apple where he was "overjoyed" to join the title-contending Knicks.[14]

Lucas was not only an excellent player, but also a world-class eccentric. Nicknamed "the Computer" by his Knick teammates, Lucas once memorized portions of the New York City phone book just to pass the time. He also committed to memory Mario Puzo's 1969 book, *The Godfather.* Francis Ford Coppola released a film based on the novel starring Marlon Brando as the iconic Don Corleone, and *The Godfather* won multiple Academy Awards and set box-office records. Lucas preferred the book. After all, memorizing it gave him something to do on monotonous road trips as his teammates played cards. "They won't let me play with them," Lucas explained, "all they let me do is keep score. I'm known as the computer. I keep the score in my head." Lucas's eccentricity carried over onto the basketball court as well. At any point during the game, Lucas could rattle off exactly how many points, rebounds, and assists he had accumulated. When questioned about this practice and the implication that he was obsessed with his statistics, Lucas simply replied, "I like to count things, remember?"[15]

Adding Lucas was supposed to let the Knicks rest Willis Reed more often. As it turned out, Lucas had to play much more than expected, as knee tendinitis limited the Knicks captain to just eleven games. The Lucas trade also helped Bill Bradley: unloading Russell made Bradley the undisputed starting small forward. The future U.S. senator responded with one of his best seasons as a pro, increasing his scoring output from twelve to fifteen points per game and using his constant motion to drive the Knicks' patterned offense.

New Yorkers generally supported trading Russell for Lucas. But the team's other major off-season move divided Knicks fans. For years, the Knicks and Bullets were archenemies, meeting three straight times in

hard-fought playoff series. But in November 1971, just weeks into the
season, the rivals agreed to a trade: New York sent two bench players
and cash to Baltimore for All-Star guard Earl Monroe. Monroe gained a
well-deserved reputation as a flashy scorer with a playground game and
cool nicknames to match: "Black Jesus," "the Lord's Prayer," and the
more poetic "Earl the Pearl." Monroe was content playing for Baltimore but believed he was woefully underpaid, earning just $20,000 per
season while the ABA-NBA war sent player salaries skyrocketing. The
Bullets refused to renegotiate his contract, citing multiple surgeries on
the Pearl's chronically injured knees. Monroe wanted paid and, three
games into the season, went on strike. Baltimore suspended their unhappy star before, shockingly, the Knicks stepped in and traded for Earl
the Pearl, shaky knees and all.

Adding Monroe to an already star-studded lineup doubtlessly excited many New York fans. Others, though, had to wonder if he would be,
in the words of teammate Walt Frazier, "the complete opposite of
everything we stood for—teamwork, patience, [and] control." In fact,
rumors began to circulate around the Big Apple that Frazier would be
the next Knick sent packing, maybe to Houston for Elvin Hayes. "I'm
taking that sort of for true," Frazier admitted. "That's the only way the
trade for Monroe makes sense. They don't need both him and me in the
backcourt." Whether or not the Knicks ever intended to deal Frazier, a
trade never materialized. Instead, the pairing of "Clyde the Glide" Frazier and "Earl the Pearl" Monroe picked up another nickname: the
"Rolls Royce Backcourt," driving the Knicks toward a deep playoff
run.[16]

Walt Frazier also set the mark for fashion in the early seventies, both
on and off the court. In the 1970 finals, Frazier wore white Chuck
Taylor All-Stars sneakers with blue shoelaces on one foot and orange on
the other. Unsurprisingly, Puma approached Frazier a few years later
and offered him a $25,000 contract (plus 25 cents for each pair of
sneakers sold) to wear their newly released "Clyde" basketball shoes.
"The Puma Clyde, just like its namesake, was the perfect mix of style
and substance," one journalist later wrote, "the first sneaker also designed to make a fashion statement." It was a low-cut shoe in suede, at a
time when most sneakers were canvas or leather, perfectly matching
Frazier's personality and cross-over appeal.[17]

Soon kids everywhere were sporting the Clydes, making them the hippest shoe on the market. Near Frazier's home in New York City, shoes became a form of self-individualization and could be modified (using markers or paint) to create a unique style. "Sneakers were how you defined yourself," one New York City resident said, "how you claimed an identity amidst an overpopulated city full of adversity." Even NBA players took to personalizing their kicks. Swen Nater wore his wedding ring on his shoes during games, and Darnell Hillman, sporting a huge Afro hairstyle and out-of-the-gym leaping ability, had "Dunk" inscribed on the back of his sneakers.[18]

Puma and Adidas were probably not interested in any players on the 30–52 Philadelphia 76ers. More troubling than a lack of sneaker sponsors, though, was the uncertainty surrounding star forward Billy Cunningham. Cunningham was a blue-collar, under-the-radar superstar as beloved in Philadelphia as Flyers hockey enforcer Dave "the Hammer" Schultz. Cunningham was the heart and soul of the Sixers, challenging every jump shot, chasing down each rebound, earning dozens of technical fouls for his emotional outbursts, and willing Philadelphia to hard-fought victories. But in August 1969, Cunningham—an alumnus of the University of North Carolina—signed a contract with the ABA's Carolina Cougars to begin in the 1972–1973 season. Many fans interpreted the signing as another step toward an ABA-NBA merger; for Cunningham, it was a chance to cash in on his NBA success, although his partnership with Cougars owner Jim Gardner in a series of surf-and-turf restaurants named "Lob-Steer" spectacularly crashed and burned. Naturally, the Sixers sued the Cougars for Cunningham's rights, but a federal appeals court upheld Cunningham's ABA contract. Although the 1971–1972 season was disappointing for Sixers fans, the team was nowhere near as bad as they would be the next season, when they set NBA records for futility.

While the Sixers were in free fall, the Buffalo Braves built a team to compete with the NBA's best. It began with their top selection in the 1971 draft, Kentucky center Elmore Smith. Winning an NBA title in the sixties and seventies required a defensively dominant center and scouts compared Smith to a young Bill Russell while a teammate christened him the "best defensive center to come into the league since Kareem." Although statisticians did not record blocked shot totals until 1973, Smith was certainly among the league leaders in his first year and earned a spot on the All-Rookie team. But the surprise of the draft (ten rounds that required just seventy minutes to complete) was another Smith drafted by the Braves: seventh rounder Randy Smith of nearby Buffalo State. Buffalo picked Smith solely to mollify local fans who were still upset that the team passed on Niagara's Calvin Murphy a year earlier. Even the Braves' general manager admitted he was trying to "give a local kid a chance." But Randy was more than an afterthought and surprised everyone by moving into the starting lineup early in the season. Despite winning only twenty-two games (for the second straight season), the combo of Smith and Smith gave Braves fans a lot of hope for the future.[19]

The Atlantic was clearly the dominant division in the East, despite Buffalo and Philadelphia's mediocrity. The Central Division, on the other hand, had no teams with winning records, and the 38–44 Bullets and 36–46 Hawks backed into the postseason thanks to the new playoff format rewarding the winners and runners-up of each of the league's four divisions.

The two Ohio-based, bottom-feeding teams in the Central—the Cleveland Cavaliers and Cincinnati Royals—ranked among the worst in the league. Cleveland added top overall pick Austin Carr, giving them their franchise's first star player. Carr, described by one journalist as "the Black Messiah of Cleveland," and "the Second (and shorter) Coming of Lew Alcindor," was a smooth six-foot-four shooting guard twice named a consensus All-American at Notre Dame. Unfortunately, Carr easily led the team in scoring (21.2 points per game) and the rest of the Cavaliers struggled. Across the state, Coach Bob Cousy continued to mold his Cincinnati Royals into an up-tempo, fast-breaking squad behind the play of shifty second-year guard Nate "Tiny" Archibald. Archibald responded by averaging more than twenty-eight points and nine assists per game, but the Royals won only thirty games, and whispers of the team leaving Cincinnati grew louder as attendance and local fan interest waned.[20]

In Baltimore, the Central's top team dealt with tremendous roster turnover, particularly in their backcourt. Before sending Earl Monroe to the Knicks, the Bullets picked up Archie Clark in a trade with Philadelphia. Clark took a circuitous route to the NBA. He left high school with few offers to play college ball and instead joined the Air Force and served in Korea while most of his peers signed ABA or NBA contracts.

After leaving the service, Clark caught on with the Lakers in 1966. But despite making the All-Star team in 1968, the Lakers shipped Clark to Philly in the Wilt Chamberlain trade. As a Sixer, Clark perfected the "shake and bake" move, a quick crossover dribble ending in an almost-impossible-to-block jump shot, and during the 1971–1972 season, now with Baltimore, Clark shaked and baked his way to twenty-five points per game. Clark helped Baltimore far more than the team's top draft pick, Stan Love. Love came from a talented family: his brother Mike was one of the Beach Boys and his son, Kevin, became an All-Star forward for the Minnesota Timberwolves. Unfortunately for Bullets fans, Stan was the least talented of the trio: not as strong a vocalist as Mike, whose pop hits in the sixties included "Wouldn't It Be Nice" and "Sloop John B," or as accomplished a basketball player as Kevin. Instead, Stan struggled to replace former All-Star Gus "Honeycomb" Johnson, now a shell of his former rim-rocking self, and the team was definitely worse than the 1971 NBA runners-up.

Like Baltimore, Atlanta backed into a playoff spot thanks to weak competition in the Central Division. The Hawks expected to contend for the title, shaping their roster around Pistol Pete Maravich. But in training camp, Maravich developed a high fever and sore throat. Diagnosed first as tonsillitis, then as strep throat or scarlet fever, doctors eventually decided Pete had mononucleosis. Mono sapped Pete's strength. He dropped almost forty pounds and thought a lot about his future. "I love basketball, but it's not worth my life," he told the *Atlanta Journal*. "Maybe I should sit it out a year." Fortunately for the Hawks, Maravich returned to the lineup in November. But post-mono Maravich was not the same Pistol Pete who finished the 1970–1971 season as one of the league's best players. It took months for Maravich to regain lost strength and endurance, and by season's end he remained twenty pounds underweight. Atlanta made the playoffs, with Maravich amazingly suiting up for sixty-six games, but critics openly questioned whether Pistol Pete could be the best player on a title-winning team—mono or no mono.[21]

Despite his illness, Maravich remained one of the league's top scorers, and during the season he joined thirty-one other players in the NBA's first-ever one-one-one basketball tournament sponsored by Vitalis (Pete's go-to hairspray manufacturers). Two players from each team took part in the competition, taped by ABC for the network's "Game of the Week" broadcast. Unfortunately, many of the top stars were absent. Some, like Chamberlain and Abdul-Jabbar, decided against competing, while others, like Robertson, Monroe, Cowens, and Havlicek, lost to teammates in intrasquad qualifiers. Those making the field of thirty-two took part in a tournament in which the first player to score twenty points (leading by at least five points) advanced. Maravich lost a first-round marathon to Pistons center Bob Lanier; each player scored more than forty points before Lanier eliminated Pete. In fact, Lanier ended up winning the tournament, eliminating Boston guard Jo Jo White in an underwhelming finale in which Lanier, who stood a foot taller, simply dribbled in close to the basket where he could score at will over White. Each participant earned a cash prize for his involvement, ranging from $500 for losing in the play-in round to $7,500 for making it to the finals. Lanier earned $15,000—paid out in one-dollar bills (it was, after all, a *one*-on-*one* tournament)—stuffed into a suitcase and delivered by a cackling Bill Russell during halftime of the fifth game of the NBA finals.

As the playoffs neared (and the one-on-one contest came to a merciful end), it was obvious the Lakers and Bucks were head and shoulders above any other Western Conference teams, and the Celtics and Knicks were the best in the East. Not surprisingly, then, these four teams all made the conference finals.

Basketball fans eagerly anticipated the 1972 Final Four pitting the Knicks against the Celtics and the Bucks against the Lakers. New York shocked Boston in their series, winning in five games. The "Rolls-Royce Backcourt," which had taken some time to gel, helped a lot. But, as was usually the case with the early seventies Knicks, it was truly a team effort—all five starters averaged at least thirteen points per game in the series.

If fans were excited for the Boston–New York series, they were nearly apoplectic over the Bucks–Lakers matchup. During the regular season, Milwaukee boasted a 63–19 record, the fourth-best season of all time behind only the 1966–1967 76ers, their own team the previous season, and their rivals from Los Angeles. The Lakers, for their part, won sixty-nine games, a record that stood for twenty-five years before the Michael Jordan–led Chicago Bulls won seventy-two during the 1995–1996 season. During the regular season, the Lakers won four of five from Milwaukee, but their one loss ended the historic thirty-three game winning streak. Both teams had a score to settle in the playoffs—as if the matchup needed any more drama.

In game one, the Bucks shocked the Lakers in Los Angeles, winning by twenty-one and holding the high-scoring Lakers to just seventy-two points—by far their lowest output of the season. Several Lakers, led by guard Gail Goodrich, complained about the lighting used by ABC for their television production, and with newly situated lighting displays L.A. eked out a game two win, 135–134, overcoming a forty-point performance by Kareem Abdul-Jabbar to even the series 1–1. After splitting games three and four, the series appeared to be bouncing back and forth like the tiny white ball in an intense game of Pong, the highly addictive arcade title released by Atari in the fall of '72.

In game five, the Lakers finished on the right side of a lopsided score when they won by twenty-five. Milwaukee fans, expecting to send the series to a decisive seventh game, left Milwaukee Arena disappointed as L.A. won game six (104–100) to move on to the finals. Chamberlain, who scored twenty points and pulled in twenty-four rebounds in the clinching game, said, "I feel as happy right now as I ever have after any one particular game." West, though pleased to advance, felt the Lakers had overcome his poor play to rally to victory. He knew that reaching the finals was not enough; they had to win the title to exorcise the ghosts of seven second-place finishes.[22]

New York and L.A. had met in the 1970 finals, but their matchup two years later featured far different personnel. Now the Lakers matched high-scoring guards Jerry West and Gail Goodrich against New York's Rolls-Royce Backcourt of Walt Frazier and Earl Monroe. At the forward slots, Ivy League grads Jim McMillian (Columbia) and Bill Bradley (Princeton) squared off while blue-collar big men Happy Hairston and Dave DeBusschere prepared for a fierce battle inside. Winning the series seemed to boil down to the center matchup. Los Angeles counted on Wilt Chamberlain to be both a defensive anchor, staying inside the paint to keep opponents from driving into the lane, and an offensive force, bulling his way inside for short finger rolls and fadeaway jump shots. In 1970, the Knicks had countered with Willis Reed, whose gutsy game-seven performance became one for the ages. With Reed sidelined, the Knicks turned to Jerry Lucas, a slimmer player who preferred to pop in long-range jump shots rather than wrestle inside. Since Lucas could clearly not match up physically, fans wondered whether Chamberlain would bully the smaller Lucas, who gave up at least four inches and seventy pounds, or whether Lucas could pull Chamberlain away from the basket to open the inside for the passing-and-cutting offense preferred by coach Red Holzman's Knicks.

The first half of game one in Los Angeles seemed to favor Lucas. Already wary of being too optimistic (seven finals losses in a decade will do that to you), Lakers fans began filing out at halftime with their team down by eighteen. The Knicks shot 72 percent from the field in the first half, including a nine-for-eleven performance from Lucas. The Lakers were only marginally better in the second half than they had been in the first as Knicks defenders held L.A.'s two highest scorers, Goodrich and West, to zero field goals in the last twenty-four minutes. But even the victorious Knicks knew that the series was not close to being over, despite their easy 114–92 win. "All our shots were going in," Lucas said afterward. "But that doesn't mean they always will. The Lakers have a great team and we haven't won anything yet." Lucas's words seemed prophetic when the Lakers rallied to beat the Knicks in game two. Even more disastrous to the Knicks' cause was an injury to DeBusschere limiting him to just a few minutes of playing time in games two and three. Without DeBusschere on the court, Happy Hairston and Wilt Chamberlain dominated play inside, relentlessly rebounding and scoring over Lucas and Phil Jackson, DeBusschere's rail-thin, bearded, hippy backup who was still almost two decades away from becoming the legendary coach of the Chicago Bulls and Los Angeles Lakers. Game three also marked a relatively easy win for the Lakers, who pulled away in the second quarter and coasted to a double-digit victory behind a game-high twenty rebounds and twenty-six points (on just ten shots) from Chamberlain.[23]

Pivotal game four was far closer, as Frazier tapped in a missed shot to force overtime. With 1:35 left in the extra period, the game was knotted at 111 and Chamberlain, who had never fouled out of an NBA game (a statistic he was proud to have kept intact), was saddled with five personal fouls, one away from being disqualified. Rather than avoid contact, Chamberlain played like a man possessed, swatting away shots and rebounding like a demon, silencing critics who assumed he would play tentatively to protect his precious record. West hit two free throws to give the Lakers the lead for good, and Goodrich drove in for a twisting layup providing the game's final score. With a 115–111 victory, the Lakers held a 3–1 series lead. But no one, especially Lakers owner Jack Kent Cooke, was ready to put balloons in the rafters of the Fabulous Forum just yet.

Two years earlier, Willis Reed hobbled onto the court to help the Knicks win the 1970 title. Now Chamberlain did the same, receiving anti-inflammatory shots in both hands (injured in a fall earlier in the series) before having them heavily padded and taped. Sportswriters deified Reed but glossed over Chamberlain's gutsiness; sometimes his oft-repeated phrase "nobody roots for Goliath" was spot-on. Swollen hands and all, Chamberlain helped the Lakers jump out to an early 10–0 lead before DeBusschere connected on a seventeen footer to put the Knicks on the board. Wilt answered with a powerful dunk and the rout was on. Final score: Los Angeles 114, New York 100. As the clocked ticked off the final seconds, the Forum faithful stood on their feet and chanted together "We're number one!" For the first time since George Mikan carried the 1954 Minneapolis team to a title, Lakers fans were right; they were number one.

For Jerry West, the victory was bittersweet. Of course, he was glad to win a ring and get the two-ton gorilla off his back. But the Lakers won in spite of his play, not because of it. "I played terrible basketball in the finals," West said. "And we won. And that didn't seem to be justice for me personally, because I had contributed so much in other years when we lost. And now, when we won, I was just another piece of the machinery." West did understand the importance of his teammates in the Lakers success; despite his spotty play, he admitted "maybe that's what the team is all about."[24]

The 1971–1972 Los Angeles Lakers were one of the greatest teams in NBA history. They won sixty-nine games, including an NBA-record thirty-three straight. But the Lakers' historic season also had long-term ramifications. Los Angeles's "Showtime" Lakers of the 1980s, led by Earvin "Magic" Johnson, James Worthy, and, yes, Kareem Abdul-Jabbar, modeled themselves after the 1971–1972 squad. As one historian notes, "the true architect of Hollywood showtime was Bill Sharman and the blueprint was the 1972 championship Lakers."[25]

Before the season, most fans dismissed the Lakers as being too old to win the NBA title. Going forward, would Chamberlain and West end up like Johnny Unitas and Willie Mays, spending the twilight of their careers as shells of their former selves? Or could they make one last run

and hold off the pesky Bucks, up-and-coming Celtics, and star-studded
Knicks? By 1972, it was clear the league was wide open and any number
of franchises could still lay claim to being the team of the seventies.

Statistics for 1971–1972

Eastern Conference	W	L	Western Conference	W	L
Atlantic Division			*Midwest Division*		
Boston Celtics	56	26	Milwaukee Bucks	63	19
New York Knicks	48	34	Chicago Bulls	57	25
Philadelphia 76ers	30	52	Phoenix Suns	49	33
Buffalo Braves	22	60	Detroit Pistons	26	56
Central Division			*Pacific Division*		
Baltimore Bullets	38	44	Los Angeles Lakers	69	13
Atlanta Hawks	36	46	Golden State Warriors	51	31
Cincinnati Royals	30	52	Seattle SuperSonics	47	35
Cleveland Cavaliers	23	59	Houston Rockets	34	48
			Portland Trail Blazers	18	64

Playoffs

Eastern Conference Semifinals	New York d. Baltimore (4–2)
	Boston d. Atlanta (4–2)
Western Conference Semifinals	Milwaukee d. Golden State (4–1)
	Los Angeles d. Chicago (4–0)
Eastern Conference Finals	New York d. Boston (4–1)
Western Conference Finals	Los Angeles d. Milwaukee (4–2)
NBA Finals	Los Angeles d. New York (4–1)

All-NBA Teams

First Team	Second Team
F—Spencer Haywood (Seattle)	F—Bob Love (Chicago)
F—John Havlicek (Boston)	F—Billy Cunningham (Philadelphia)
C—Kareem Abdul-Jabbar (Milwaukee)	C—Wilt Chamberlain (Los Angeles)
G—Walt Frazier (New York)	G—Nate "Tiny" Archibald (Cincinnati)

G—Jerry West (Los Angeles)	G—Archie Clark (Philadelphia/Baltimore)

League Leaders

Points per Game (34.8)	Kareem Abdul-Jabbar (Milwaukee)
Rebounds per Game (19.2)	Wilt Chamberlain (Los Angeles)
Assists per Game (9.7)	Jerry West (Los Angeles)
Most Valuable Player	Lew Alcindor (Milwaukee)
Rookie of the Year	Sidney Wicks (Portland)

4

1972 TO 1973

The year 1972 is probably best remembered for the reelection of Richard Nixon to the presidency, widespread antiwar protests on college campuses, Don McLean crooning "American Pie," and the passage of Title IX (an act fighting discrimination in higher education). But it was also a time of crisis for many American workers struggling to maintain strong unions in the face of increasing automation, jobs moving overseas, and the onset of economic stagflation. Though professional athletes certainly made more money than most other Americans, they too campaigned in the early seventies for better working conditions and higher wages.

In April 1972, Major League Baseball players went on strike over their pension fund, delaying opening day by two weeks. Football players, furious at the so-called Rozelle Rule barring free agency in their sport, followed two years later. Professional basketball could trace its labor efforts to the mid-1950s when Bob Cousy organized the National Basketball Players Association. For its first fifteen years of existence, the union worked tirelessly to raise minimum player salaries, limit exhibition games, improve health benefits, and fund pensions for retired athletes.

In 1970, the union took a huge step forward: suing the National Basketball Association for violating the Sherman Antitrust Act. The so-called Robertson Suit (named for union president Oscar Robertson) worked its way through the court system without resolution, delaying a merger between the NBA and American Basketball Association (ABA) for half a dozen years. But in September 1972, just weeks before the start of the 1972–1973 season, the U.S. Senate Antitrust Subcommittee approved the merger if the NBA agreed to get rid of the reserve clause, an age-old tactic used by all major American sports to tie players to teams in perpetuity. Faced with the specter of free agency, NBA owners backed out of a merger deal. "The NBA didn't like the changes," said Dick Tinkham of the ABA's Indiana Pacers, "so it was back to square one. We went back to suing each other and trying to bankrupt each other to sign players, and no one was making any money. Now and then," Tinkham recalled, "we'd have more merger meetings, then we'd break up and declare war on each other."[1]

Disagreements about the reserve clause prevented a merger, but the NBA and its players association did come to terms on a collective bargaining agreement. In March 1973, the two sides hammered out a three-year contract setting minimum player salaries at $20,000 (then the highest of any American sport). But the league was adamant in defending the reserve clause and the Robertson Suit remained an insurmountable obstacle to a merger between the NBA and ABA.

Several teams in the NBA had more than merger problems on their minds as the 1972–1973 season approached. In 1972, Daryl and John Oates released *Whole Oats*, their debut studio album including the song "Fall in Philadelphia." Although the ballad described autumn in the City of Brotherly Love, it could just as easily have expressed the decline of the city's pro basketball franchise. In the late sixties, the Sixers ranked among the NBA's best, featuring star players like Wilt Chamberlain, Billy Cunningham, Hal Greer, and Chet Walker. Philly traded Chamberlain and Walker, but Greer and Cunningham soldiered on and kept the team competitive into the early seventies. During the 1972–1973 season, however, the Sixers bottomed out, producing the worst team in NBA history.

In April 1972, as baseball players refused to report to spring training, Dr. Jack Ramsay decided he no longer wanted to coach the down-and-out Sixers, leaving Philadelphia for Buffalo to coach the up-and-coming Braves. "We had a lot of veteran players who were at the ends of their careers," Ramsay explained. "We didn't have an influx of young, quality players. And I just didn't want to be a part of it." Philadelphia's first call was to John Wooden. But the legendary UCLA coach passed. So did Marquette's Al McGuire. And longtime Kentucky coach Adolph Rupp.

Growing desperate, the Sixers posted a "coach wanted" ad in a local newspaper. Still no luck. They finally convinced Roy Rubin, a successful high school and college coach from Long Island, to take the gig. Unfortunately, the team Rubin inherited was, as Ramsay predicted, terrible. All told, Rubin's 76ers suited up nineteen players and pulled off eight substantive trades during the season, but, if anything, the team got worse through the constant shuffling.[2]

With a revolving door of veteran players and a series of poor draft picks depleting their roster, the Sixers had few young players worth developing. Emblematic of this problem was 1970 top choice Al Henry out of Wisconsin. In drafting Henry, the Sixers' front office relied on a new form of technology—the computer—to help make their pick more scientifically. Keep in mind that this was still five years before Bill Gates dropped out of Harvard to create Microsoft and six years before Steve Jobs and Steve Wozniak formed Apple Computer. In the early seventies, computer technology was still in its infancy; and so, after hours spent poring over film and personally attending countless games, team scouts fed their reports into a computer programmed to rank available college seniors. When Philadelphia's turn came up in the 1970 draft, future stars like Calvin Murphy and Nate "Tiny" Archibald were still available. But the computer calculated that the Sixers should take Al Henry, a marginal collegian at best. Philly called Henry and told him he was their twelfth pick; Henry assumed they meant the twelfth round and was shocked when told he was the twelfth *overall* selection. Henry lasted just two seasons in the NBA, and the Sixers mercifully cut him before their horrible 1972–1973 season.

Philadelphia started off poorly under Rubin, dropping a league-record fifteen games to open the season. Months later, they broke their own record by losing twenty straight. Other teams looked forward to playing the Sixers. "It was like [management] played a dirty trick on us," guard Fred "Mad Dog" Carter—the self-proclaimed inventor of the fist bump—said, "deliberately putting together the worst team and the worst coach ever! I mean we were a universal health spa, healing everything that was wrong with all the other teams in the league."[3]

In mid-December the players staged a coup, meeting secretly in a hotel room and deciding that guard Kevin Loughery would be their de facto coach. After losing to Baltimore in mid-January to drop to 4–47, the Sixers fired Rubin and Loughery officially took over the team. Rubin opened an International House of Pancakes restaurant in Florida and never coached again. Maybe Loughery should have done the same; the Sixers were not much better on his watch, dropping eleven straight to run their losing streak to twenty. But then the team rallied slightly and pulled to 9–60 before dropping their last thirteen to end with a league-record seventy-three losses. All but forgotten in this dreadfulness was the sad end of a Hall of Fame career. In mid-March, Hal Greer scored one basket in a loss to the Knicks; it was his last two points in a career spanning a then-record 1,122 NBA games spread over fourteen professional seasons. He retired as the fifth-highest scorer in league history playing on the worst team NBA fans had ever seen.

As Philly careened to the finish line with Greer watching from the bench, most of the players were ready for the nightmare to end. Before the last game of the season, the trainer told the team, "don't anybody get hurt tonight and for godsake don't call any time-outs. Let's get this over with as quickly as possible." Despite their horrific season, there was a ray of hope for Philly fans. After all, by posting the worst record in the Eastern Conference, the Sixers had a fifty-fifty chance at earning the top pick in the 1973 draft. The prize, they hoped, would be UCLA standout center Bill Walton—if the tall redhead declared as a "hardship case." The team clearly bottomed out—dare we say tanked?—during the 1972–1973 season, but Sixers fans hoped that, as Jimmy Cliff sang in his upbeat 1973 hit of the same name, "better days are coming."[4]

After the Sixers, the second-worst team in the league might well have been Dr. Jack Ramsay's new squad, the Buffalo Braves, winners of just twenty-one games (after back-to-back twenty-two-win seasons). But, unlike Philadelphia, the Braves had a lot of young talent, and one journalist declared them "the team of the future." The Smith boys—guard Randy and center Elmore—looked like future stars, as did rookie Bob McAdoo, a six-foot-nine jump-shooting big man who won the Rookie of the Year award. With McAdoo and the Smiths sporting groovy powder blue uniforms, Buffalo lacked only a top-flight point guard to become the franchise of the present, rather than the team of the future.[5]

The Atlantic Division included the two worst Eastern Conference teams (Philadelphia and Buffalo) as well as the two best (Boston and New York). The Celtics won sixty-eight games, tops in the league and the third-highest total in NBA history. The biggest addition to Boston's lineup was Paul Silas, the player-to-be-named sent from Phoenix for Charlie Scott a year earlier. Basketball insiders loved Silas; one called him a "ferocious rebounder who played every moment in swirls of dripping sweat and crashing bodies." Silas's arrival in Boston, much like that of Dave DeBusschere in New York a few seasons earlier, added toughness and smarts to an already elite squad. Rather than start, Silas slid effortlessly into the Celtics' famed sixth-man role. Coming off the bench, Silas averaged thirteen points and thirteen rebounds and perfectly complemented center Dave Cowens's more perimeter-oriented offensive game. Paired with Silas, Cowens earned league MVP honors after averaging 20.5 points, 16.2 rebounds, and 4.1 assists per game (although he only made the second-team All-NBA behind Kareem Abdul-Jabbar). With Silas, Cowens, forward John Havlicek, and guards Jo Jo White and Don Chaney, Boston boasted All-Star caliber players at every position. On any given night, the Celtics could win with stifling defense (led by Havlicek and Chaney) or a high-octane offense (relying on Cowens and White).[6]

Only the Knicks challenged the Celtics in the East. Like Boston, New York got off to a sizzling start, taking ten of their first eleven and fifteen of their first eighteen en route to a fifty-seven-win season. A season earlier, the Knicks had overhauled their roster by bringing in Earl "the Pearl" Monroe and Jerry "the Computer" Lucas. During the 1972–1973 season, Willis Reed's improved health had the same effect, improving a team that had advanced to the 1972 finals even without their captain. In his prime, the Knicks could count on Reed for twenty points and a dozen rebounds per night. Now Reed managed roughly half that but also contributed in intangible ways. He played punishing defense and set brutal picks, freeing the team's guards to gamble more defensively and popping them open for mid-range jump shots on offense. Reed's resurgence also allowed the eccentric Lucas to play a little less, keeping them both fresh and reasonably healthy for a postseason push. Besides Reed's revival, the other major improvement in the Big Apple was at the guard spot opposite Walt "Clyde" Frazier. Dick Barnett had started at shooting guard for seven straight years, but Barnett, now at age thirty-six, was no longer the "Fall Back, Baby" playground legend he had once been. As Barnett's playing time dwindled, Monroe stepped effortlessly into the starting lineup, revving up the "Rolls Royce Backcourt" of "Clyde the Glide" and "Earl the Pearl." The most popular change to the Knicks rotation, though, was reserve forward Harthorne Wingo. Wingo (Harthorne, not Hawthorne, as it is sometimes misspelled) was a New York City playground legend signed by the Knicks out of the semipro Eastern League. Wingo played sparingly but became a fan favorite—Madison Square Garden crowds chanted "WIN-go, WIN-go, WIN-go" when the Knicks held a commanding late-game lead. New York's bench, Wingo included, was particularly strong during the 1972–1973 season. "We were not a five-man team, nor even an eight-man squad," Reed said, "we were and are a twelve-man ball club and everyone earns his salary. I can't stress that too much."[7]

Among the players no longer contributing to the Knicks' depth was Baltimore Bullets forward Mike Riordan. Riordan, included in the trade that sent Earl the Pearl to the Big Apple, emerged as an unlikely star in his second season with the Bullets. Sportswriters described Riordan—a former eleventh-round pick from Providence—as "a special kind of pro who cared more about fast breaks than investment reports" and a "gym rat" who "approaches every game as if it was a street fight." Frazier called Riordan "probably the player with the least amount of natural talent who ever made it in the league." In the seventies, these terms were universally applied to white men like Riordan or Dave Cowens or "Pistol Pete" Maravich. White players were hard-working, scrappy, and intelligent. African Americans relied on pure athleticism and natural abilities.[8]

If Riordan was the perfect white ballplayer in the seventies, his newest teammate on the 1972–1973 Bullets fit the stereotype of black athlete to a tee. Before the season, Baltimore traded playboy forward Jack Marin to Houston for mercurial big man Elvin Hayes. On the surface, trading Marin for Hayes seems incredibly one-sided; Hayes was a physical specimen and already a four-time All-Star coming off a season in which he averaged twenty-five points and nearly fifteen rebounds per game. Marin was one year older, two inches shorter, not half as good a rebounder as Hayes, and attended law school in his spare time. But Hayes was an enigma. For all his statistical brilliance, he had been unable to lead the Rockets to respectability. In his four seasons, the team never won more games than they lost. Hayes also had a reputation as a coach killer, a player unwilling to sacrifice individual statistics for team success. Fans called him the "Big E," but former coaches referred to him as "the world's worst human being" and "the most despicable athlete I have ever been associated with." *Sports Illustrated*'s Peter Carry claimed "most coaches admitted they would rather take arsenic than Elvin Hayes," adding that "his reputation was that of a man with a fragile ego who alternately stormed and sulked at criticism . . . who would cause dissension in the Partridge Family."[9]

Whether or not Hayes would have clashed with Shirley, Keith, Laurie, Danny, and the rest of the Partridges, he fit in perfectly with the Bullets. Hayes paired particularly well with center Wes Unseld. The Bullets twin big men dominated the boards, combining for more than thirty rebounds per game as Unseld remained the league's premier outlet passer and pick setter, the essence of unselfishness. With Riordan, Hayes, Unseld, and guard Phil Chenier (who scored a season-high fifty-three points against the Trail Blazers one December night), the Bullets easily won the Central Division and, once again, looked to challenge for the Eastern Conference title.

In Atlanta, the 46–36 Hawks again finished behind Baltimore. But they are also an all-time "what-if?" In the spring of 1972, the Hawks convinced "Dr. J" Julius Erving to leave the ABA's Virginia Squires and sign a five-year, $1 million deal to play in Atlanta. After secretly agreeing to the contract, Atlanta tried to quietly trade for a first-round draft pick in order to select Dr. J. Instead, the Bucks, who owned two first-round choices, took a flyer on Erving before the Hawks could swoop in, kicking off a barrage of interleague litigation. Erving sued his former agent, alleging that he had been in cahoots with the ABA; the Squires sued the Hawks for stealing Erving; the Bucks sued the Hawks for signing a player they had drafted; and Erving sued the NBA, claiming the draft violated the Sherman Antitrust Act (this was separate from the Robertson Suit, although the arguments were almost identical). As lawyers and judges sifted through piles of paperwork, Erving suited up for the Hawks in the preseason and played in three games. Dr. J and Hawks star Pistol Pete Maravich developed instant on-court chemistry. "Those two played like they had been teammates forever," recalled future NBA star David Thompson, who saw an exhibition game in person. "With Pete," Erving said, "after just a few days, we [had] a sort of telepathy between us . . . it's a clinic in transition basketball." But the dream pairing was short-lived; a federal judge issued an injunction preventing Erving from playing for the Hawks and, in October, Erving rejoined Virginia, delaying his regular-season NBA debut until 1976.

"We could have been some team," Erving wistfully remembered. "I would have been a Hawk for the rest of my career."[10]

On top of losing Erving, Maravich struggled with medical problems. After weathering mononucleosis the previous season, Pistol Pete came into training camp in fantastic physical condition. In the offseason, he had become a karate fanatic, spending as many as eight hours a day honing his body—one of millions of Americans participating in a martial arts craze stemming from Bruce Lee's portrayal of the character Kato in the *Green Hornet* television series. But on the morning of November 9, 1972, Maravich woke to the realization that the right side of his face was numb. A neurologist diagnosed Maravich with Bell's palsy, an inflammation of facial nerves resulting in paralysis, and recommended that Pete sit out until the condition cleared—whether it took days, months, or even years. Maravich ignored the doctor's advice and missed just six games, taping his paralyzed right eye shut so he could sleep at night. After a month, Maravich started to regain feeling in his face and began playing like the Pistol Pete of old, earning his first All-Star game nod. By the end of the season, Maravich ranked fifth in the league in scoring (26.1 points per game) and his career-high 6.9 assists per contest was good for sixth in the NBA. Although with Erving, Maravich and the Hawks would have been instant title contenders, their ten-game improvement under coach Cotton Fitzsimmons indicated that at least Atlanta was headed in the right direction.

Headed in the right direction was not a phrase usually associated with the Central Division's two cellar dwellers. The thirty-three win Houston Rockets underwent a roster overhaul in the offseason, sending Elvin Hayes to Baltimore for playboy Jack Marin and flipping point guards with Detroit, as Stu Lantz headed to Motown for 1967 top overall pick Jimmy Walker. Walker, whose son Jalen Rose starred with the "Fab Five" at Michigan in the early 1990s and played thirteen seasons in the NBA, teamed with Marin, Rudy Tomjanovich, and Calvin Murphy to form the league's highest-scoring (112.8 points per game) and fastest-paced team. Unfortunately, they also gave up points in bunches, ranking next to last in the league defensively and allowing opposing players to top fifty points on four separate occasions. The Cleveland Cavaliers played a much different style as thirty-five-year-old point guard Lenny Wilkens favored a slow and deliberate pace. Unsurprisingly, the Cavaliers finished last in the league in scoring and 32–50 on the season.

Despite their poor record, the Cavaliers were the best pro hoops team in Ohio. Of course, they were also the only pro hoops team in the state. After the departure of Oscar Robertson in 1970, the Cincinnati Royals struggled to attract fans, drawing a league-worst 3,557 per game during the 1971–1972 season. The local baseball team had no such problems; in 1973, the Reds finished second in Major League Baseball in attendance as over two million fans (roughly 25,000 per game) packed into beautiful new Riverfront Stadium. The NFL's Cincinnati Bengals also drew well—averaging more than 50,000 fans in their eight home contests. Only the Royals struggled. "We have tried every promotion under the sun," the team's general manager complained, but "Cincinnati is not a great basketball city, in fact, not even a good one." In January 1972, Sargent Shriver (John F. Kennedy's brother-in-law and father of Maria Shriver) linked Royals owners Max and Jeremy Jacobs to an organized crime syndicate. Shriver and the NBA pressured the Jacobs brothers to sell the team to a conglomerate that moved them to Kansas City—sort of. The newly named Kings (to avoid confusion with baseball's Kansas City Royals) played half their home games in Kansas City and the rest in Omaha or St. Louis, making the Kings the NBA's first regional franchise. In a nod to its regional appeal, the team took on the cumbersome name of the Kansas City–Omaha Kings.[11]

Cincinnati or Kansas City–Omaha? Royals or Kings? Did it matter? Not really. The team was still terrible. "Except for Tiny Archibald," Coach Bob Cousy later recalled, "we had nothing. For example, our center, Sam Lacey, was afraid of French poodles, the dark, and water. I'm still surprised that we weren't the team that only won nine games that season." As Cousy admitted, Archibald was the team's undisputed star. Although generously listed at six-one (he was closer to five-ten), Archibald was not content hanging around the perimeter. He made his money on daring drives to the basket and an instinctive fearlessness. In 1972, sportswriters overlooked him in naming the league's All-Stars. Stung by the slight, Archibald averaged nearly thirty-four points per game over the rest of the season and carried that momentum over into the 1972–1973 season, becoming, in the words of one journalist, "the most exciting player in the league . . . a David dominating a sea of Goliaths." That season, Archibald became the only player in NBA history to lead the league in both scoring and assists, averaging an eye-popping 34 points and 11.4 assists per game. For good measure, Archibald also paced the league in minutes played, field goals attempted, field goals made, field goals missed, free throws attempted, and free throws made. Archibald topped fifty points three times during the 1972–1973 season and either scored or assisted on more than half the Kings' points on the season. Tiny played basketball much like future 76ers star Allen Iverson. Fittingly, the two remain the shortest players to lead the NBA in scoring, more than thirty years apart. Unsurprisingly, sportswriters not only voted Archibald to appear in the 1973 All-Star game, but also named him to the starting lineup.[12]

Archibald and the Kings relied on efficient offense to win games because their defense ranked among the worst in the league. The second-place Bulls played exactly the opposite style and won fifty-one games (twenty-five more than Kansas City–Omaha) using a grind-it-out, defensive-oriented game plan. Guards "Stormin' Norman" Norm Van Lier and "the Original Bull" Jerry Sloan continued to abuse opposing backcourts through their gritty play and hard-nosed defense while forwards Bob "Butterbean" Love and Chet "the Jet" Walker provided the scoring punch. It was the center position that again ultimately limited the Bulls' effectiveness as incumbent Tom Boerwinkle played in just eight games due to injuries. Second-year man Clifford Ray filled in admirably and contributed double-digit rebounds and stiff defense, but the Bulls' offense, never its strong suit, suffered without Boerwinkle's elite passing ability from the high post. Meanwhile, Howard Porter—whose exorbitant contract remained a touchy subject for several relatively underpaid Bulls vets—continued to collect splinters and big paychecks while sitting on the Chicago bench, playing less than ten minutes a game. Coach and general manager Dick Motta knew the Bulls' window of opportunity was closing: how long could he keep the team winning with increasingly unhappy veterans?

The class of the Midwest Division was, once again, the Milwaukee Bucks. But the Bucks, like the Hawks, are a great historical "what-if?" Like Atlanta, Milwaukee believed they could convince Julius Erving to jump leagues after selecting him in the 1972 draft. Erving, if signed, would have created an all-time great trio alongside Kareem Abdul-Jabbar and Oscar Robertson. In fact, Bulls coach Dick Motta admitted that if Erving became a Buck, "we would all be smart to forfeit the eighty-two games and avoid the frustration." Even without Erving, the Bucks rolled through the regular season with a 60–22 record. Their star, Abdul-Jabbar, became the league's highest-paid player after he signed a four-year, $2 million deal. Kareem was worth every dime, and his accomplishments are even more remarkable considering the personal tragedy he dealt with during the season.[13]

In October 1972, police pulled over Abdul-Jabbar and teammate Lucius Allen and found drugs in the car. Both players professed their innocence and Abdul-Jabbar faced no criminal charges. Just four months later, members of Philadelphia's Black Mafia—an African American–Muslim organized crime syndicate—invaded Abdul-Jabbar's home in Washington, D.C., while he was in Milwaukee. The attackers killed seven acquaintances, including Abdul-Jabbar's spiritual leader, in a dispute stemming from religious differences between the Black Mafia and Abdul-Jabbar's Hanafi Muslim friends. It was not the only religiously motivated crime perpetrated during the mid-seventies as, months later, news of the "Zebra" killings rocked the nation when a gang of Black Muslims in San Francisco calling themselves the "Death Angels" claimed at least fifteen murders (although the total death toll may have exceeded seventy). Frustration with stalling civil rights activity and continued American involvement in Vietnam fed a new radicalism, especially prominent among young African Americans.

Two thousand miles southwest of Milwaukee (but only a few hours down the Pacific Coast Highway from the Zebra murders), the Bucks' biggest rivals played their home games in the Fabulous Forum of Inglewood, California. The 1971–1972 Los Angeles Lakers put together one of the greatest seasons in NBA history, winning sixty-nine games (including thirty-three straight) before defeating the Knicks to win the championship. Defending their title proved far more difficult. L.A. won sixty games during the 1972–1973 season and were a deeper squad than their title team, adding Keith Erickson—lost for much of the previous season due to two knee surgeries—and Bill Bridges—rescued from the Sixers in midseason. In fact, in the three weeks after adding Bridges, the Lakers won seventeen of eighteen games. "We were playing so well it was almost scary," remembered reserve guard and future NBA coaching legend Pat Riley. "It was beautiful." Jerry West believed "it was the best team we've ever had," topping even the sixty-nine win champs. Unfortunately, injuries finally caught up with the aging Lakers. For-

ward Happy Hairston played in just twenty-eight games, and West
missed a baker's dozen with various bumps and bruises. But even without their full roster, the Lakers ran away from the pack in the Pacific
Division, as the backcourt duo of West (22.8 points per game) and Gail
Goodrich (23.9 points per game) led the offensive attack while Wilt
Chamberlain again paced the circuit in rebounding (18.6 per game) and
field goal percentage (an amazing 72.7 percent).[14]

For the third straight season, the forty-seven-win Golden State Warriors finished behind the Lakers in the division race. But the biggest
story out of Oakland in 1972 was not another second-place finish for the
Warriors or the first winning season for baseball's Oakland Athletics
since the early fifties. Instead, newspaper headlines trumpeted the return of Rick Barry to the Bay Area. In 1967, Barry jumped from the
Warriors to the Oakland Oaks of the ABA. Now, after five years of
lawsuits and countersuits, he was back with Golden State. In his return,
Barry scored twenty-two points per game (including fifty-one against
the defensively challenged Rockets) to earn a spot on the All-NBA
second team. But in Barry's absence, and even after the return of Gold-
en State's golden boy, teammate Nate Thurmond remained the heart
and soul of those Warriors.

"Nate the Great" Thurmond was a six-foot-eleven, 225-pound center
who looked like he was chiseled from marble, all lean muscle and
sinewy strength. He played his entire career out of the spotlight. In high
school, he was overshadowed by teammate Gus "Honeycomb" Johnson;
few scouts ventured to watch his college career at Bowling Green State;
and Wilt Chamberlain dominated the Warriors that Thurmond joined
in 1963. Wilt went to Philadelphia in 1965, but Barry joined the Warriors that summer and became the team's big box-office draw. But night
in and night out, Thurmond simply did his job; he was a blue-collar,
lunch-pail player in a league rewarding flash and dash. "I guess you've
got to have some kind of flair and I don't," said Thurmond. "I don't
dunk unless I have to. About the only fancy thing I do is block a few
shots in every game." In an era before statisticians recorded blocked
shots, statistics failed to measure Thurmond's impact. At his peak,
Thurmond was better defensively than Chamberlain and better offensively than Bill Russell: two of his more celebrated contemporaries.
Only four players in NBA history ever averaged more than twenty
points and twenty rebounds per game for an entire season: Wilt Cham-

berlain, Jerry Lucas, Bob Pettit—and Nate Thurmond. Fittingly, during the 1972–1973 season, Thurmond scored 1,349 points and pulled down 1,349 rebounds (good for second in the league), averaging 17.1 of each per game.[15]

The Phoenix Suns (38–44), Seattle SuperSonics (26–56), and Portland Trail Blazers (21–61), rounded out the top-heavy Pacific Division, and all would have loved to pencil in Thurmond at center. Charlie Scott, who cost the Suns veteran forward Paul Silas, lived up to his lofty billing and high price tag as he finished sixth in the league in scoring while handing out a team-high six assists per game. But knee injuries sustained over decades of playing basketball on asphalt playgrounds and second-rate semiprofessional gymnasiums were finally catching up with the other Suns superstar, Connie "the Hawk" Hawkins. Seattle also featured a superstar forward, but theirs, Spencer Haywood, seemed to be on his way up, not down, and averaged 29.2 points (third in the league) and 12.9 rebounds per game. The Sonics, though, had a hard time finding a coach who fit, and Seattle owner Sam Schulman started pestering legendary Celtic Bill Russell, hoping to woo him to the West Coast to tutor the precocious Haywood.

Russell, pushing forty, would have been a serious upgrade for the underachieving Portland Trail Blazers. For the third consecutive season (in their three years of existence), the Blazers finished dead last in their division. Portland should have been better than they were; back-to-back rookies of the year Geoff Petrie and Sidney Wicks put up outstanding individual statistics, and Petrie even won the league's second annual one-on-one tournament, besting Cavaliers reserve forward and Ohio Wesleyan product Barry Clemens in the tourney finals to earn a cool $15,000. In January 1970, Petrie exploded for fifty-one points against— no surprise here—the Rockets. After the game, Houston guard Mike Newlin promised "he'll never do that again." Two months later, Petrie duplicated the feat—against Newlin and the Rockets. Alongside Petrie, Wicks emerged as a star in his own right, averaging twenty-four points, eleven rebounds, and five assists per game as an NBA sophomore. But the newest Blazers rookie sensation was a complete disaster and possibly the biggest bust in basketball history.[16]

Picking first in the 1972 draft, Portland selected Loyola University of Chicago center LaRue Martin. Teams with dominant, defensive-oriented centers always seemed to win the NBA title, and the Blazers hoped

Petrie, Wicks, and Martin could form the core of a championship-contending team—their own West, Baylor, and Chamberlain. "We took Martin because we thought he is the best center in the draft," explained Blazers general manager Stu Inman at the time. But, as Pulitzer Prize–winning author David Halberstam wrote, "Martin was not by nature aggressive, nor strong or agile. His early years in Portland," Halberstam decided, "were murderous. The fans had expected a savior and he had signed for a savior's salary. He became almost immediately an object of scorn, from the fans, from the media." Inman had spent hours scouting the nation's top college players and watched as Martin held his own against Bill Walton of UCLA and Marquette's Jim Chones, considered two of the NCAA's best big men. Unfortunately for Inman and the Blazers, those were the best two games of Martin's otherwise undistinguished college career.[17]

Blaming Inman and Martin for all of Portland's problems would be easy. But it was also becoming increasingly apparent that Wicks and Petrie simply could not coexist, with or without a dominant center. "By the end of the season I hated Sidney," Petrie admitted. "Sidney didn't think I gave up the ball enough and I thought Sidney took too many bad twenty-five-foot jumpers." Wicks also clashed with rookie head coach Jack McCloskey, who later brought the Detroit Pistons multiple titles as the team's general manager. Early in the season, McCloskey corrected Wicks on the court and the second-year forward erupted. "I've checked you out," Wicks yelled at McCloskey, "and you're nothing but a loser! You've been a loser every place you've coached, and I've been a *winner* every place I've played." Wicks claimed he was an All-Star caliber player; McCloskey disagreed. "All-Star?" McCloskey scoffed, "Sidney Wicks an All-Star? The only team you could make is the all-*dog* team." In an era of escalating player salaries (Wicks made $300,000 per year), it was the coach sent packing.[18]

In January 1973, President Richard Nixon declared a ceasefire in Vietnam, signing the Paris Peace Accords to bring about an end to the Vietnam War. Two years later, North Vietnam captured Saigon to complete their unification of the nation under communism. It was a stunning setback for the United States in their ongoing Cold War with the Soviet Union. But despite the defeat, most Americans celebrated the end of American involvement in Vietnam, glad to be done with a war halfway across the world spanning two decades and costing more than 58,000 American lives.

Even as Nixon worked to pull troops out of Vietnam, a new story emerged to dominate the national news: the Watergate scandal. In June 1972, five men broke into the Democratic National Committee head-quarters staffed by future NBA commissioner Larry O'Brien. Over the following months, FBI agents traced clues eventually leading investigators to the Oval Office and President Richard Nixon, actively trying to cover up any connection to the burglars. By the spring of 1973, the NBA playoff season, Nixon was fighting a war of attrition, and just days after the start of the NBA finals, he announced the resignations of several top White House aides. In October 1973, Vice President Spiro Agnew resigned, and Nixon himself resigned under mounting pressure in August 1974.

As usual, professional sports distracted from the grim news of the day. And so, as the 1973 NBA playoffs approached, basketball fans could focus on the eight squads preparing for postseason play rather than the end of the Vietnam War or the Watergate cover-up. This season, rather than including the top two teams in each of the league's four divisions, the playoffs featured the four division winners plus the next two best teams in each conference regardless of division.

Despite the change in playoff structure, there were few surprises in the Eastern Conference race and the Knicks and Celtics both advanced, New York besting their archrivals from Baltimore, and Boston eliminating Pete Maravich and Atlanta. The conference finals between the Knicks and Celtics might have been the best series of the playoffs. After losing in game one, the Knicks dominated the Celtics in game two (129–96) and eked out a seven-point win in Boston in game three. In that game, Celtics star forward John Havlicek sustained a serious shoulder injury that sidelined him for a classic game four. With Havlicek and Knicks guard Earl "the Pearl" Monroe out with injuries, the Knicks trailed by as many as sixteen late in the game, and it looked like the Celtics would even the series at two games apiece. But questionable refereeing apparently favoring New York—a Philadelphia newspaperman called it "the rape of Madison Square"—sent the game into overtime. After one extra period, the score remained tied: 101–101. During the second OT, Cowens fouled out and unsung Knicks rookies Henry Bibby and John Gianelli (who scored all ten of his points in the second overtime) led New York to a thrilling 117–110 victory that Knicks reserve guard Dean Meminger called "the greatest game I've either participated in or seen." [19]

Now holding a commanding 3–1 lead in the best-of-seven series, the Knicks looked to close out the Celtics in game five. But Havlicek had other ideas. Like Willis Reed in 1970 and Wilt Chamberlain in 1972, Havlicek battled through the pain. Although he could barely raise his shooting arm, Havlicek managed eighteen points in leading his Celtics to a nail-biting 98–97 win. Boston remained alive by winning game six, as well—in hostile Madison Square Garden, no less—to set up a decisive seventh game in an already thrilling series.

Boston Garden was electric on April 29, 1973, as the crowd cheered the unlikely Celtics comeback to force a game seven. Boston backers, though, left the Garden sorely disappointed. The Knicks defense stifled the Celtics high-octane scoring attack, holding the injured Havlicek to just four points. Final score: Knicks 94, Celtics 78. New York head coach Red Holzman was ecstatic: "This was their year and we got 'em," he crowed. The series was as dramatic as any in the decade. But it paled in comparison to the events shaking up the Western Conference race. [20]

The Los Angeles Lakers defeated the pesky Chicago Bulls in seven grueling games in their opening-round meeting. But shockingly, L.A. would not meet their archrivals from Milwaukee in the Western Conference finals, as Golden State eliminated Milwaukee utilizing a very balanced attack, a strategy that would prove useful in the coming seasons for the Bay Area boys. Six Warriors averaged double figures—led by Rick Barry's 16.5 points per game—and Nate Thurmond played stifling defense on Kareem Abdul-Jabbar to score the unlikely upset. Unfortunately for Warriors fans, the clock struck midnight on their Cinderella run as the mighty Lakers dismantled Golden State to send L.A. back to the NBA finals, where they would once again meet the Knicks for the title.

With news from Washington, D.C., hogging headlines, the Knicks and Lakers set to meet for the third time in four seasons for the NBA title. In 1970, the Knicks won in seven games, and, two years later, L.A. took just five to dispose of New York, setting up a rubber match in 1973. For the most part, the cast of characters was much as it had been a season earlier: the Knicks counted on their "Rolls-Royce backcourt" of Walt Frazier and Earl Monroe, along with a frontcourt including Bill

Bradley, Dave DeBusschere, Jerry Lucas, Willis Reed, and Phil Jackson. Los Angeles countered with their own high-scoring backcourt, Gail Goodrich and Jerry West, alongside Wilt Chamberlain, Jim McMillian, "Happy" Hairston, and reserve Pat Riley (yes, Pat Riley and Phil Jackson shared the court many times in the early seventies).

On paper, at least, it was a pick 'em: two evenly matched veteran squads with championship experience. If anything, the Lakers held a slight edge as they enjoyed an extra four days of rest while the Knicks battled the Celtics in their grueling seven-game marathon.

Game one followed that script to a tee. Chamberlain swatted away seven shots and the left-handed Goodrich shot, drove, and twisted his way to thirty points. Final score: Los Angeles 115, New York 112. "My worst playoff game that I can remember," Frazier admitted afterward. Unfortunately for Lakers fans, game one would be their only victory in the series. Just as Los Angeles had done in 1972, New York took four straight games after dropping the opener to win the NBA title. Chamberlain, the '72 finals MVP, was a non-factor in '73; when the Dipper received the ball close to the basket, Reed and Lucas fouled him, and Wilt connected on an abysmal 37 percent from the foul line as the Lakers lost several close games.[21]

The 1973 Knicks championship season is often overshadowed by the preceding title teams. In '72, the Lakers set a league record for victories and Jerry West shed the label "loveable loser." In '71, the Bucks got Oscar Robertson his elusive ring, and second-year sensation Lew Alcindor led Milwaukee to the title. In '70, New Yorkers reveled in the Knicks' glorious and emotional title run, as the reams of paper dedicated to singing the praises of that particular Knicks team can attest. In fact, as Frazier later admitted, "the 1973 title was just basketball, nothing more." There was no emotionally charged Willis Reed–limping-out-to-the-court moment that season. The better team simply won. "The '73 team was a better playoff team," Reed said later. "It was a good team to watch in terms of the style of basketball. Good shooting. Good passing. Good technique." In fact, Reed believed that the '73 club was better than the more famous 1970 squad, although he admitted that "a lot of people don't even remember that we won a second championship." Still, the 1972–1973 Knicks provided New Yorkers with their last NBA title and would forever be part of a significant era of basketball history. At season's end, the question on everyone's mind was the same as it had been since the retirement of Bill Russell: would the champs repeat? In a word—no.[22]

Statistics for 1972–1973

Eastern Conference	W	L	Western Conference	W	L
Atlantic Division			*Midwest Division*		
Boston Celtics	68	14	Milwaukee Bucks	60	22
New York Knicks	57	25	Chicago Bulls	51	31
Buffalo Braves	21	61	Detroit Pistons	40	42
Philadelphia 76ers	9	73	Kansas City–Omaha Kings	36	46
Central Division			*Pacific Division*		
Baltimore Bullets	52	30	Los Angeles Lakers	60	22
Atlanta Hawks	46	36	Golden State Warriors	47	35
Houston Rockets	33	49	Phoenix Suns	38	44
Cleveland Cavaliers	32	50	Seattle SuperSonics	26	56
			Portland Trail Blazers	21	61

Playoffs

Eastern Conference Semifinals	New York d. Baltimore (4–1)
	Boston d. Atlanta (4–2)
Western Conference Semifinals	Golden State d. Milwaukee (4–2)
	Los Angeles d. Chicago (4–3)
Eastern Conference Finals	New York d. Boston (4–3)
Western Conference Finals	Los Angeles d. Golden State (4–1)
NBA Finals	New York d. Los Angeles (4–1)

All-NBA Teams

First Team	**Second Team**
F—Spencer Haywood (Seattle)	F—Rick Barry (Golden State)
F—John Havlicek (Boston)	F—Elvin Hayes (Baltimore)
C—Kareem Abdul-Jabbar (Milwaukee)	C—Dave Cowens (Boston)

G—Nate "Tiny" Archibald   G—Walt Frazier (New York)
(KC–Omaha)

G—Jerry West (Los Angeles)   G—Pete Maravich (Atlanta)

League Leaders

Points per Game (34.0)   Nate "Tiny" Archibald
                                 (KC–Omaha)

Rebounds per Game (18.6)   Wilt Chamberlain (Los Angeles)

Assists per Game (11.4)   Nate "Tiny" Archibald
                                 (KC–Omaha)

Most Valuable Player   Dave Cowens (Boston)

Rookie of the Year   Bob McAdoo (Buffalo)

5

1973 TO 1974

Fans watching game five of the 1973 finals unwittingly witnessed the end of an era. Just months after the Lakers loss, their legendary center Wilt Chamberlain defected to the ABA to coach and play for the San Diego Conquistadors. Since legal entanglements ultimately prevented Chamberlain from ever actually playing for the Q's, his dunk in the final meaningless moments of that fifth game became the last points he scored in a record-breaking career.

Chamberlain retired as the most individually dominant player in NBA history. He made thirteen All-Star teams, earned a spot on seven All-NBA first teams and three second teams, and collected four MVP awards. Chamberlain left as the all-time leader in points (31,419), rebounds (23,924), field goal attempts (23,497), free throw attempts (11,862), and minutes played (47,859), and although many of his career records have since been broken, several of his single-season and single-game records might as well be set in stone. During the 1960–1961 season, for example, Chamberlain pulled down 27.2 rebounds per game, including one Herculean 55-rebound effort. The next season, Chamberlain *averaged* more than fifty points per game, including both a historic one-hundred-point outburst against the Knicks and a stretch in which he scored at least fifty in seven straight games.

Chamberlain's retirement (which he never formally announced, leading to rumors of a potential comeback for more than a decade) made the Pacific Division race much more competitive than it had been in half a dozen years. With Chamberlain, the Lakers were title contenders; without him, LA barely beat out the other four teams in the Pacific. Although the Lakers again led their division, winning just forty-seven games after posting a 60–22 record the year before worried even the most diehard fans like up-and-coming actor (and Lakers season ticket holder) Jack Nicholson.

To replace Chamberlain, the Lakers pulled off a major trade with the Buffalo Braves, sending high-scoring forward Jim McMillian to Buffalo for defensive-oriented center Elmore Smith. Smith admirably filled Chamberlain's role in Coach Bill Sharman's system, leading the NBA in a new statistical category: blocked shots. For more than a decade, Smith's 393 blocks (4.9 per game) remained the highest single-season total in league history, and his single-game mark of seventeen remains the most of all time. The other Lakers newcomer, acquired to replace both McMillian on the court and Chamberlain at the box office, was former Phoenix Suns forward Connie "the Hawk" Hawkins. Hawkins was clearly not the player he once was, leading one journalist to quip that "everybody agrees the Hawk is a work of art. Some nights . . . poetry in motion. Other nights . . . still life." But even without his former explosiveness, the New York City playground legend remained as flashy as ever, daringly waving the ball around in one huge hand while setting himself up for short jump shots or passes to cutting teammates. The Lakers' frontcourt play was solid, but the team's backcourt—once a strength—struggled as a groin injury sidelined Jerry West for all but thirty-one games and limited his effectiveness; his 20.3 points-per-game scoring average was his lowest output in more than a decade.[1]

Although finishing three games behind the sliding Lakers, the Golden State Warriors were much improved, building on their surprising '73 playoff run (where they upset the sixty-win Bucks) to finish 44–38. Behind All-Star forward Rick Barry, the Warriors led the division with just ten days remaining in the season. But the Bay Area boys dropped six of their last seven and barely missed the playoffs. Next year, fans said. Next year.

Trailing Los Angeles and Golden State, the Seattle SuperSonics were, as Stealers Wheel's 1973 hit song told listeners, "Stuck in the Middle," finishing third in the five-team Pacific with a 36–46 record. But like Golden State, there was reason for optimism in the Emerald City. Most importantly, the Sonics had hired legendary Boston Celtic

Bill Russell as their new head coach. Sonics owner Sam Schulman brought in Russell, also the team's general manager—a rare double-duty in those days—to instill discipline in the high-priced Sonics, whose $6 million payroll was second highest in the league. Sonics fans expected Russell to create a "Boston West" in Seattle, convinced that he could build a championship team around superstar forward Spencer Haywood. At first, the marriage of Russell and Haywood seemed like a match made in hoops heaven: the wizened teacher and his star pupil. Russell immediately named the six-foot-eight Haywood his starting center, reasoning that "he takes those big people out where they can't breathe. They have to come out after him or he'll hit that 15–20 foot shot all night." Haywood embraced both the new role and the new boss, insisting that "now that Russell is here as the coach, I'm certainly satisfied with Seattle and the Sonics. He was," Haywood said, "the last link in the chain. I want to do the things Russell did in his time to produce winners." Spencer even likened Russell to the biblical Moses, sure to "show us the way out of the wilderness" into the promised land of the NBA playoffs.[2]

Coach Russell was also eminently quotable. One reporter asked him to discuss the parts of the game his team needed to work on the most. Russell deadpanned "offense, defense and teamwork. Other than that, we're in pretty good shape." To instill mental discipline and a sense of pride in team defense, Russell made the Sonics run laps equal to the number of points surrendered in losses. Losing a game while giving up one hundred points, for example, meant one hundred laps around the gym. "I tell them that if they intend to lose, they better do it by the lowest score possible," Russell cackled. "That's what's called emphasizing defense."[3]

Russell clearly built the Sonics around the talented Spencer Haywood, while the Pacific Division doormats in Phoenix and Portland struggled to find an identity. Connie Hawkins was the only star in the short history of the Phoenix Suns franchise. But in his four seasons in the desert, "the Hawk" only led the team to one winning record and a single playoff appearance. Now, the Suns were Charlie Scott's team. But injuries cut Scott's season short and he struggled to shed the perception that he was a talented shoot-first (and second . . . and third . . .) point guard who could not lead a team to a title (or even to the playoffs) as Phoenix finished 33–49. Portland also appeared directionless, and it was becoming increasingly evident that the pairing of Sidney Wicks and Geoff Petrie was a spectacular failure; despite their individual statistical brilliance (both averaged better than twenty-two points per game and made the All-Star team), the Blazers finished 27–55, and 1973 top overall pick LaRue Martin proved to be a complete bust who rarely left the bench.

In the strong Midwest Division (three teams had at least fifty wins), the fourth-place Kansas City–Omaha Kings were the lone disappointment and Coach Bob Cousy lasted just twenty games into the 1973–1974 season before being fired. Kings fans expected the Cooz to bring to Kansas City the same success he had enjoyed as a player with Boston in the '50s and '60s where he won six league titles. Cousy failed. Part of the problem, at least during the 1973–1974 season, was that Nate "Tiny" Archibald, who led the league in both points and assists a year earlier, tore his Achilles tendon and missed most of the season. Instead of leading Kansas City–Omaha, Archibald watched helplessly from the sideline as his Kings ended the Cousy era with a record of 36–46.

Like George and Louise Jefferson, whose hit show *The Jeffersons* debuted on CBS the following year, the 1973–1974 Detroit Pistons and Chicago Bulls were "movin' on up." Detroit set a franchise record with fifty-two wins, a dozen more than the year before. There was no single reason for their sudden turnaround: no high draft choice, new coach, or big trade vaulted the Pistons up the standings. They simply played better together. "We're an intelligent team that gets along now," guard Dave Bing explained. "We don't care anymore who shoots or who scores. And you better believe that wasn't the case around here before." Bing and center Bob Lanier gave Detroit a pair of All-Stars and one of the league's best one-two punches as Bing tossed in long jump shots while Lanier scored at will in the post on soft left-handed hook shots and, a capable defender, averaged three blocks and a steal per game. The Pistons won more games than the division leaders in both the Pacific and Central Divisions, but 1952 placed them in third place in the Midwest, two behind second-place Chicago. The Bulls remained the league's premier defensive team as guards Norm Van Lier and Jerry Sloan attacked opposing ball handlers, taking full advantage of lax rules regarding hand checking, while forwards Bob Love and Chet Walker provided the offensive punch, and center Tom "the Building" Boerwinkle once again proved to be the best passing big man in the league, zipping pinpoint passes to cutting teammates after lumbering into position at the high post. With a solid starting five, the Bulls finished 54–28 on the season, their third-straight fifty-win campaign. Unfortunately for Chicagoans, the next time they won fifty would be during the 1987–1988 season, when a fourth-year guard named Michael Jordan led the charge.[4]

Try as they might, Chicago always seemed to play second fiddle to the Milwaukee Bucks. During the off-season, Bucks management sent a memo to their all-world guard Oscar Robertson, requesting that he "lose some weight." After a few months of training, "the Big O" became the "Not-Quite-As-Big O," dropping five or six pounds to satisfy the team. But despite the weight loss, his on-court play continued to decline; he became, as one journalist wrote, "a ghost of what he was." As Robertson slipped, the other Bucks top star, center Kareem Abdul-Jabbar, was growing increasingly dissatisfied in Wisconsin. "I don't want to get down on Milwaukee," he insisted in an interview, "they're nice and not nice and that's wherever you go. But the atmosphere is not what I'm used to—big city. Milwaukee is middle America, and things that are for me and what I am have nothing to do with middle America." Abdul-Jabbar grew up in New York and attended college at UCLA—he wanted to move to a major media market and rumors began to circulate that Kareem wanted out of Milwaukee. Even with these distractions, the twenty-seven-year-old Abdul-Jabbar finished third in the league in scoring (27 points per game), fourth in rebounding (14.5), and second in both blocked shots (3.5) and field goal percentage (54 percent). For good measure, sportswriters named him to the All-Defensive and All-NBA first teams and to his third MVP award in four seasons. It might have been Kareem's greatest season as a pro.[5]

Abdul-Jabbar was the best-known athlete in Milwaukee, topping any of the hometown Brewers. But a decade earlier, another African American sports pioneer called Brew City home. Henry "Hank" Aaron joined baseball's Milwaukee Braves in 1954. For the next twenty seasons, he rewrote the history books, hammering home runs at a record-setting pace. In April 1974, Aaron broke Babe Ruth's historic home run mark, smacking his 715th long ball off Dodgers pitcher Al Downing.

By the time of Aaron's record-breaking blast, the Braves had relocated to Atlanta, where the hometown Hawks season had already ended with a disappointing 35–47 record under second-year head coach Cotton Fitzsimmons. Before the season, Atlanta's marketing department declared the Hawks ready "to soar in 1974." But on- and off-court problems proved insurmountable. In an early February loss to the Rockets, superstar guard "Pistol Pete" Maravich was thrown out of the game for arguing a call. Pete stormed into the locker room and cracked open a beer. And then another. And another. Coach Fitzsimmons discovered Pete after the game, surrounded by empty beer cans, and suspended his drunk star. Maravich, once hailed as the Hawks' fair-skinned savior, was dangerously close to being labeled a problem child. Trading the league's Great White Hope out of Atlanta seemed like an impossibility before the season. But now? An injury to the other Hawks star, "Sweet Lou" Hudson only exacerbated problems as Maravich reverted to playing selfishly in the absence of his high-scoring wingman.

Atlanta's division rivals from Baltimore moved the franchise fifteen miles east to Landover, Maryland, and renamed themselves the Capital Bullets. Their new arena, the Capital Centre, was state of the art, featuring luxury boxes and a unique $1.25 million "Telscreen" on which fans could watch instant replays of on-court action. It was also a popular concert venue; on December 4 and 6, 1973 (while the Bullets were in Houston to play the Rockets), the Allman Brothers and The Who performed in Landover, drawing huge crowds to the new arena. Despite their new digs, the roster looked much as it had the year before, revolving around their talented big man duo of Wes Unseld and Elvin Hayes. Hayes led the league in both rebounding (18.1 per game) and minutes played (44.5 per game) and finished fifth in blocked shots (3.0 per game), helping Capital to a 47–35 record.

The Bullets easily won the Central Division while the Atlantic once again boiled down to the Boston Celtics and New York Knicks. Boston finished 56–26 (a dozen games worse than the season before) but remained dangerous. On defense, the Celtics played a switching man-to-man style that (although technically against the rules) allowed the center to roam the paint playing a one-man zone. Once a shot was taken, Boston went for rebounds with a ferocity one sportswriter compared to "a subway station scene in New York during the rush hour." Forward Paul Silas and center Dave Cowens were Boston's best inside players. Silas dominated the offensive glass while Cowens tore around the court like a man possessed, flying after loose balls and slamming his six-eight body into opponents to gain more leverage. Strong rebounding and stout interior defense allowed for long outlet passes igniting the team's vaunted fast-break offense.[6]

Silas and Cowens were important to Boston's success, but the man who really made the Celtics' attack go was do-everything forward John Havlicek. In his sixteen-year career, Havlicek never once led the league in scoring, rebounding, or assists, and as Cowens explained, "fans couldn't focus on one aspect of his game and identify with it." He was never a flashy passer, and his scoring mostly came from short jump shots or layups, not explosive dunks or long-range bombs. Havlicek simply did all of the little things to make Boston a better team. "Havlicek's value does not always show in the box score," one reporter wrote. But diehard basketball fans and sportswriters knew his value. Havlicek made eleven All-NBA teams, eight All-Defensive teams, and thirteen straight All-Star teams. He even had a cool nickname—Hondo—given to him by a high school classmate who thought Havlicek looked like movie star John Wayne.[7]

Hondo was an outstanding player and the poster boy for the NBA ideal: a humble family man who hustled his way to superstardom. "He's apple pie, hot dogs and all that stuff," Pistons center Bob Lanier said. "His greatest contribution is as a model for our kids." Havlicek was not only an outstanding person, but a world-class athlete as well. At six-foot-five, his long arms and strong hands perfectly complemented his tremendous ability to anticipate the actions of opposing players, leading to numerous steals and tipped passes on defense. In college at Ohio State, Havlicek teamed with Jerry Lucas and future Indiana University coach Bobby Knight to lead the Buckeyes to the 1960 NCAA title. At Ohio State, Havlicek's athletic exploits bordered on the fantastical. Woody Hayes, the school's legendary football coach, introduced Havlicek as "the best quarterback in the Big Ten" even though Hondo never played for Hayes. Schoolmates knew him as the best in his class at tennis, swimming, and fencing; he batted .400 as a freshman for the baseball team but gave it up because it interfered with basketball. After graduating from Ohio State in 1962, both the Celtics and the NFL's Cleveland Browns drafted him, and Havlicek initially chose football, attending training camp as a wide receiver before switching to hoops.[8]

As a young player, Havlicek replaced Frank Ramsey on the Boston bench and became possibly the greatest sixth man in NBA history, winning league titles in six of his first seven seasons playing alongside Sam Jones and Bill Russell. Most famously, he preserved a Boston win in the 1965 Eastern Division finals by stepping in front of a pass intended for 76ers forward Chet Walker, immortalized by Celtics radio broadcaster Johnny Most's call of *"Havlicek stole the ball!"* After Jones and Russell retired in 1969, Boston became Hondo's team, and now with an entirely different supporting cast, Havlicek again had his Celtics in the title hunt.

Trailing the Celtics in the Atlantic were the defending champion New York Knicks, unknowingly entering the last season of their short-lived dynasty. Dave DeBusschere, Jerry Lucas, and Willis Reed all called it quits after the season and struggled through their final year as players. DeBusschere still played solid defense and scored in double figures, but Reed, just thirty-one years old, was a shell of his former MVP-winning self and only suited up for nineteen games, while Lucas, now thirty-four, contributed only a handful of points and rebounds each game. Reed's absence and Lucas's struggles opened up playing time for Phil Jackson. Jackson was a gangly six-nine power forward, all arms and legs, whose hustle kept him on the court. The future Zen master of the Chicago Bulls and Los Angeles Lakers possessed an ugly jump shot but was able to score in double digits for the first time in his career in '74, providing hope for Knicks fans that the bearded youngster from North Dakota could step into a starting role the following season.

Jackson's aging Knicks desperately needed something to stay ahead of Buffalo because there was no hotter team in pro basketball than the Braves. Buffalo's best player was reigning rookie of the year Bob McAdoo, moved to center after the team traded Elmore Smith to Los Angeles. McAdoo had no problem transitioning to center and became just the sixth player in league history to average at least thirty points and fifteen rebounds per game, joining Kareem Abdul-Jabbar, Wilt Chamberlain, Elgin Baylor, Bob Pettit, and Walt Bellamy. No player has joined the list since, although both Moses Malone and Shaquille O'Neal barely fell short in the eighties and nineties respectively. Not only did McAdoo put up amazing individual statistics, but he did so in a unique way—as a tall jump shooter. In the seventies, basketball coaches demanded that tall players remain close to the hoop while shorter ones could shoot the ball from farther out. But the six-foot-nine McAdoo roamed outside the painted area and was probably the best shooter in the league. Baltimore center Wes Unseld explained that McAdoo "has a variety of shots—inside, out and way out." Sonics coach Bill Russell agreed. "You try to get him out of range," Russell said, "but he never is." "You've got to pick him up at half court," an opposing player insisted. "He can hit, man." McAdoo was decades ahead of players like Dirk Nowitzki and Kevin Durant in revolutionizing the game as a near-seven-foot-tall jump shooter, but he was also a trendsetter in college, where he attended the University of North Carolina as Coach Dean Smith's first junior college transfer. He played just one season at UNC before also becoming the first player to leave the Tar Heels early, paving the way, in his own words, for "[Michael] Jordan and [James] Worthy doing it. I guess I helped clear the way for those guys because I caught hell for leaving."[9]

Between February and March 1974, Bob McAdoo scored at least twenty-five points in fifteen straight games, the most impressive scoring streak of the season. But McAdoo was far behind the nation's most well-known streaker, Robert Opel. During the forty-sixth Academy Awards, Opel jogged onto the stage—buck naked—and flashed a peace sign at the camera while actor David Niven made a joke about the streaker's "shortcomings." Streaking became especially prevalent on college campuses and at sporting events (although more so in Europe than in the United States) and even inspired Ray Stevens to write a popular novelty song, released in March 1974, called "The Streak." So, although no team during the 1973–1974 season was in danger of breaking the Lakers' long winning streak or any of Wilt Chamberlain's ridiculous individual scoring streaks, the nation was still fixated on the streaking fad.

An important part of Bob McAdoo's scoring streak was his new teammate, rookie point guard Ernie DiGregorio. "Ernie D" first attracted attention in an exhibition game between American collegians and the Soviet national team. DiGregorio put on a show that night, dribbling circles around the flabbergasted Russians and effortlessly flipping behind-the-back passes to cutting teammates (and, of course, demonstrating American chutzpah in the midst of the seemingly endless Cold War). Unsurprisingly, scouts compared the young Italian American wunderkind to Bob Cousy, another undersized ethnic (French American) guard, who, as luck would have it, coached DiGregorio in the exhibition. The ABA and NBA engaged in a fierce bidding war when DiGregorio decided to leave Providence College for the pros;

Ernie D called three press conferences because of eleventh-hour negotiations before agreeing to a deal with the Braves, who outbid the Kentucky Colonels with a $400,000 annual contract, making the young
guard among the NBA's best-paid players. Braves owner Paul Snyder
shrugged off concerns about the high salary, reasoning that "Ernie is
going to give us the product to sell—a legitimate contender." It helped
that Ernie D was a good Italian boy in a city with a strong Italian
identity and heritage.[10]

Standing barely six feet tall, sporting an impish grin, DiGregorio
seemed to be just a regular guy, easily relatable in a sport usually featuring more imposing men. But his unassuming appearance was a ruse;
DiGregorio brought a brashness and swagger to the Braves that they
lacked in their first three seasons. Coach Dr. Jack Ramsay, for one, was
a big fan of his young leader. "Not since Oscar Robertson came into the
league," Ramsay said, "has any rookie guard been asked to do so much
and has done it so well as Ernie has." DiGregorio easily won rookie of
the year honors, leading the league in assists (8.2 per game) and free
throw percentage, sinking more than 90 percent of his attempts from
the charity stripe. In Portland, on New Year's night, DiGregorio set an
NBA record that still stands for assists by a rookie, dropping twenty-five
dimes against the Blazers in a 120–119 victory. With Ernie D passing
the ball and McAdoo scoring it, the Braves were a team on the rise. "It
could almost be a catchy jingle," mused one sportswriter, "McAdoo in
'72, Ernie D in '73, playoff lore starts in '74." In fact, the forty-two win
Braves did qualify for the postseason in the spring of 1974, a first in
franchise history.[11]

Another team on the rise, almost by default, was the Philadelphia
76ers. Philly lost an NBA-record seventy-three games during the
1972–1973 season but missed out on UCLA big man Bill Walton, who
decided to return to college for his senior season. Instead, the 76ers
used the top overall pick in the 1973 draft on Illinois State guard Doug
Collins. Collins, like Buffalo's DiGregorio, was best known for his play
in international competition, having led the 1972 U.S. Olympic men's
team to a silver-medal finish. It should have been a gold. In the final
game against the Soviet Union, Collins put the Americans ahead 50–49.
Clinging to a one-point lead, the referees twice replayed the final seconds of the game before, on their third try, the Soviets scored a layup to
hand the United States its first loss in Olympic history. As an NBA

rookie, Collins was unable to build on his short-lived Olympic stardom, spending much of his first season injured, and the 25–57 Sixers remained the worst team in the East, giving them another shot at a top-two pick in 1974. This time, however, the winner of the coin flip *would* land Bill Walton.

With the Sixers long eliminated from postseason contention, the 1974 NBA playoffs closely resembled those of seasons past as the Bucks, Lakers, Celtics, and Knicks remained the top four teams in the league. For the sixth straight season, the Knicks and Bullets squared off in the playoffs, and, unsurprisingly, the bitter rivalry stretched to seven games before the Knicks eked out a 91–81 win in Madison Square Garden to advance to the Eastern Conference finals.

The other Eastern Conference semifinal, Celtics versus Braves, was also a barn burner. Behind twenty points in the fourth quarter, Boston took game one thanks to Dave Cowens, who scored at will over Bob McAdoo. After trading wins in games two and three, Buffalo evened the series when McAdoo took his revenge, pouring in forty-four points in a nail-biting game-four overtime win. The Celtics won game five, sending the series back to Buffalo for a must-win game six. Clinging to a two-point lead with just ten seconds left, Boston inbounded the ball at midcourt. McAdoo intercepted the pass and dribbled in for an uncontested layup to tie the game. Now with just seven seconds remaining, the Celtics worked the ball to Havlicek. McAdoo again came up big, blocking Hondo's jumper. But the rebound caromed to Jo Jo White, and, as time expired, White took a last-second shot. McAdoo deflected the ball and the crowd roared. Overtime! But no—wait. There was a whistle. Foul on McAdoo. With no time left on the clock in a tie game and with the Braves season on the line, White calmly sank both free throws. Final score: Boston 106, Buffalo 104. The upstart Braves were headed home while the Celtics were Big Apple bound.

The Bulls-Pistons Western Conference semifinal was almost as dramatic as the Braves-Celtics series. Chicago held home-court advantage but quickly lost it by dropping game one. The series seesawed back and forth, with Detroit matching Chicago at every turn, sending it to a decisive game seven in the Windy City. The hometown Bulls jumped out to a nineteen-point third-quarter lead, headed for an easy win. The Pistons fired back and, with three seconds left, cut the lead to two and had possession of the ball before a turnover cost them the game and the series.

Chicago's "reward" for defeating Detroit was to face the winner of Milwaukee–Los Angeles. With Wilt Chamberlain retired and Jerry West struggling through injuries, the Bucks rolled past the Lakers in just five games. West managed just one ineffective appearance in the series, scoring four points in what would prove to be his final NBA game. He retired as only the third player in league history to surpass 25,000 career points (Chamberlain and Oscar Robertson did it first). In his career, "the Logo" also appeared in fourteen All-Star games, made the All-NBA first-team ten times and the second-team twice, and won the NBA title in '72, finally breaking through after a league-record eight runner-up finishes.

Jerry West was one of the all-time greats, a player known as "Mr. Clutch" for his late-game heroics. Unfortunately for NBA fans, there were few nail-biters in the conference finals series. The Celtics beat the Knicks in five games and Milwaukee swept Chicago. Despite lasting just four games, the Bucks-Bulls matchup was hard fought. Game three was particularly prickly. Having already received one technical foul for arguing a call with referee Earl Strom, Bulls coach Dick Motta rolled up his sport coat and threw it, hitting Strom. Strom called another technical and tossed Motta from the game. Chicago's bovine mascot, Benny the Bull, rushed the court in Motta's defense and made obscene gestures toward the referees, so Strom ejected Benny as well—the first, and to date only, time a mascot has been thrown out of an NBA game. Despite the obvious passion with which the Bucks and Bulls played (and coached, and, umm, mascoted), Milwaukee easily advanced to the finals.

Despite two relatively uninspired conference finals matchups, the Bucks-Celtics tilt for the league title proved one for the ages. Before the series began, *Sports Illustrated* writer Peter Carry declared that "not since 1969, the last time Boston was in the finals, had the NBA offered such an enticing matchup, such a sweet juxtaposition of styles and stature. It was," he wrote, "the small Celtics against the big Bucks, Boston's pressure against Milwaukee's patience, 7'2" Abdul-Jabbar, the pros' best center, against 6'9" Dave Cowens, the pros' next best." For others, the series took on added racial significance. It "hooked right into classic racial stereotyping," Harvey Araton argues in his book *When the*

Garden Was Eden, "the 'tough, hungry' white against the 'talented, lazy' black." These racial implications weighed especially heavily because Boston was in the midst of desegregating its public school system. In 1974, U.S. District Courts controlled the schools, using busing to provide racial balance in Boston public education. Violent protests followed these actions, leading to white flight to nearby suburbs and a steep drop in public school enrollment.[12]

Despite the stereotype described by Araton, Abdul-Jabbar was anything but lazy, sitting out only six minutes in the entire seven-game series while putting up an otherworldly thirty-three points, twelve rebounds, and five assists nightly. Injuries, not slovenliness, were the Bucks' downfall. Starting guard Lucius Allen's season ended with torn knee cartilage in a mid-March game against the Pistons, and without Allen the Bucks relied too heavily on thirty-five-year-old Oscar Robertson and Jon McGlocklin, who also missed several games in the series. As the Bucks' top ball handlers dropped like flies, the pressing Celtics' defense ramped into high gear, forcing numerous turnovers and converting Milwaukee mistakes into easy transition baskets. Using this pressing-and-running strategy, the Celtics took games one and three, but the slower-paced Bucks managed to squeak out wins in games two and four, sending the series to Milwaukee for game five. Despite a game-high thirty-seven points from Abdul-Jabbar, Boston won the fifth game 96–87, taking advantage of twenty-seven Bucks turnovers, and seemed a lock to clinch the title as the series returned to Boston Garden for game six.

Game six of the 1974 NBA finals ranks among the greatest in league history. Thirty-nine million Americans (about 70 percent of the number watching the Super Bowl in the mid-seventies) tuned in to watch a game sportswriter Bob Ryan of the *Boston Globe* later claimed "may very well have been the single most important basketball game in NBA history." Bucks coach Larry Costello started six-foot-seven reserve forward Mickey Davis in the backcourt in a desperate attempt to break the Celtics' vaunted pressing defense. Davis, who Bucks general manager Wayne Embry later called "the closest thing I had ever seen to a hippie basketball player," flew up and down the court, "his shoulder-length blond hair flapping in the breeze" as he connected on five out of his six shots to keep Milwaukee's hopes alive. But Davis's effort was overshadowed by the play of the teams' starting centers. Late in the game,

Cowens switched onto Robertson and poked the ball away from "the Big O" as the shot clock ticked down to zero. Cowens stumbled and tripped after the ball, diving headlong in a desperate attempt to gain possession, sliding across the famous parquet floor for several feet on his stomach. Boston fans jumped to their feet and gave him a standing ovation. But it was the other center, Abdul-Jabbar, who ultimately decided game six. [13]

With the score knotted at eighty-six, the game went into overtime. John Havlicek sent it into a second extra period after following his own miss with a short jumper to tie the game: 90–90. In double-overtime with Cowens watching from the bench after fouling out, the Celtics took a one-point lead on a wild, high-arching Havlicek jump shot from the baseline, setting the stage for the game's most memorable moment. With just three seconds left and the Celtics clinging to a precarious one-point lead in double OT, Milwaukee inbounded the ball to Abdul-Jabbar, who was supposed to pass off to Bob Dandridge for the last shot. But Boston blanketed the Bucks forward, forcing Kareem to improvise and hoist an off-balance skyhook out of a Celtics double-team. Reserve center Henry Finkel (of the old "Bad News Finkel-Barnes" combo) stretched his seven-foot frame to its fullest, but Abdul-Jabbar's fifteen footer dropped through the hoop, giving the Bucks an unlikely victory and sending Celtics fans home unhappy in a series stretched to a decisive seventh game.

For all the buildup, game seven of the finals proved anticlimactic. Boston jumped out to a 53–40 halftime lead by double- and even triple-teaming Abdul-Jabbar and held on despite a furious Bucks run, cutting the lead to just five. Final score: Boston 102, Milwaukee 87. Havlicek, the finals MVP, called the win "one of the greatest thrills of my life," admitting that "doing it without anyone of the stature of Bill Russell made it sweeter," silencing critics insistent the Celtics' success in the sixties was solely because of Russell. In fact, Havlicek said "this one means the most. I was with them from scratch. It was," he said, "a rebirth." For players like Jo Jo White, Paul Silas, and Dave Cowens, this was their first taste of NBA gold. After winning the game in Milwaukee, the Celtics flew back home to the racially charged city of Boston. Cowens, too keyed up to sleep, went out on the town and woke up the next morning on a park bench in Boston Public Garden, a conquering hero surrounded by a legion of pigeon friends. [14]

As Celtics fans and players rejoiced in the team's first post-Russell title, Bucks backers mourned an opportunity lost. "We had the better ball club," insisted Milwaukee general manager Wayne Embry. "I kept saying to myself '*Jesus, if we were playing anybody but the Celtics.*'" Months after the season, Robertson retired to become an analyst for CBS, leaving behind a tremendous legacy. Robertson left as the league's all-time assist leader and the second-highest scorer in NBA history, setting a precedent for bigger guards as, at six-five, 200 pounds, Oscar dwarfed most of his opponents. Most famously, "the Big O" remains the only player to average a triple-double for a single season. His retirement severely hurt Milwaukee, already struggling to surround an increasingly unhappy Kareem Abdul-Jabbar with competent teammates. During the finals, reporters hounded Abdul-Jabbar to candidly discuss his teammates' shortcomings. Finally, Abdul-Jabbar said, "You're trying to get me to say that my teammates aren't any good." The reporter said "I guess so." Kareem's dismissive, "I have no comment on that," certainly did little to endear him to his teammates or to alleviate fears that the Bucks' championship window was rapidly closing. In fact, not only would Robertson retire before the 1974–1975 season, but that campaign would mark Kareem's last in Milwaukee green.[15]

In the spring and summer of 1974, Americans pondered the Vietnam War, read news of Richard Nixon's Watergate cover-up, and laughed at Mel Brooks's satirical *Blazing Saddles*. But it was also a pivotal time in the NBA as the league weathered the retirements of five all-time greats: Oscar Robertson, Dave DeBusschere, Jerry Lucas, Willis Reed, and Jerry West. Coupled with the recent departures of Wilt Chamberlain, Elgin Baylor, and Hal Greer, the NBA was very clearly in a period of transition. Led by up-and-coming stars like Bob McAdoo, Pistol Pete Maravich, Kareem Abdul-Jabbar, and Bill Walton, the mid-seventies bridged the Celtics dynasties of the sixties and the golden age of the eighties. But the question remained: would there be a signature team of the decade?

Statistics for 1973–1974

Eastern Conference	W	L	Western Conference	W	L
Atlantic Division			*Midwest Division*		
Boston Celtics	56	26	Milwaukee Bucks	59	23
New York Knicks	49	33	Chicago Bulls	54	28

Buffalo Braves	42	40	Detroit Pistons	52	30
Philadelphia 76ers	25	57	Kansas City–Omaha Kings	33	49
Central Division			*Pacific Division*		
Capital Bullets	47	35	Los Angeles Lakers	47	35
Atlanta Hawks	35	47	Golden State Warriors	44	38
Houston Rockets	32	50	Seattle SuperSonics	36	46
Cleveland Cavaliers	29	53	Phoenix Suns	30	52
			Portland Trail Blazers	27	55

Playoffs

Eastern Conference Semifinals	New York d. Capital (4–3)
	Boston d. Buffalo (4–2)
Western Conference Semifinals	Chicago d. Detroit (4–3)
	Milwaukee d. Los Angeles (4–1)
Eastern Conference Finals	Boston d. New York (4–1)
Western Conference Finals	Milwaukee d. Chicago (4–0)
NBA Finals	Boston d. Milwaukee (4–3)

All-NBA Teams

First Team

F—Rick Barry (Golden State)

F—John Havlicek (Boston)

C—Kareem Abdul-Jabbar
(Milwaukee)

G—Walt Frazier (New York)

G—Gail Goodrich (Los Angeles)

Second Team

F—Spencer Haywood (Seattle)

F—Elvin Hayes (Capital)

C—Bob McAdoo (Buffalo)

G—Norm Van Lier (Chicago)

G—Dave Bing (Detroit)

League Leaders

Points per Game (30.6)	Bob McAdoo (Buffalo)
Rebounds per Game (18.1)	Elvin Hayes (Capital)

Assists per Game (8.2)	Ernie DiGregorio (Buffalo)
Steals per Game (2.7)	Larry Steele (Portland)
Blocks per Game (4.9)	Elmore Smith (Los Angeles)
Most Valuable Player	Kareem Abdul-Jabbar (Milwaukee)
Rookie of the Year	Ernie DiGregorio (Buffalo)

6

1974 TO 1975

National politics dominated newspaper headlines in the summer and fall of 1974. President Richard Nixon resigned in August but was pardoned by his successor, Gerald Ford, just weeks later. Within days of Ford's decision, thousands of Americans sent telegrams and letters to the White House; some supported Ford in the name of national healing while others were livid that "Tricky Dick" avoided prosecution.

Pro basketball fans tired of Watergate argued instead about the competition between the NBA and its upstart rival, the American Basketball Association. Formed in 1967, ABA rosters initially featured a bunch of has-beens and never-weres. But by 1974, many ABA teams were just as good as their NBA counterparts. In fact, there were even whispers that "Dr. J" Julius Erving and the ABA-champion New York Nets could beat John "Hondo" Havlicek and the NBA-champion Boston Celtics.

Not only could Erving and the Nets compete, ABA supporters insisted, but Artis Gilmore and the Kentucky Colonels or George McGinnis and the Indiana Pacers could as well. This talent gap narrowed even further with the off-season retirements of NBA stars Dave DeBusschere, Jerry Lucas, Willis Reed, Oscar Robertson, and Jerry West. Fans in Los Angeles and New York, in particular, began to lose interest in their teams—despite a league-wide attendance increase—and fewer and fewer fans made the trek to the Fabulous Forum of Inglewood or Madison Square Garden.

In the spring of 1973, the New York Knicks stood on top of the basketball world, celebrating their second title in four seasons behind a deep, veteran team. Just eighteen months later, the Knicks were in shambles. After a disappointing loss to Boston in the 1974 Eastern Conference finals, New York suffered three bigger losses: DeBusschere, Lucas, and Reed. "Right now it feels like the end of an era," new starting forward Phil Jackson admitted, "like everything is disintegrating. It's a shame." Even with their "Rolls Royce Backcourt" of "Clyde the Glide" Frazier and "Earl the Pearl" Monroe earning All-Star nods, the team finished with a losing record (40–42) for the first time since 1967. Only another terrible season from the Philadelphia 76ers (34–48, a twenty-five game improvement over the 1973–1974 season) kept the Knicks out of the Atlantic Division cellar.[1]

Boston ran away with the Atlantic Division crown, posting a 60–22 record behind their All-Star trio of John Havlicek, Jo Jo White, and Dave Cowens. Each of these Celtics earned a spot on the All-NBA second team and helped Boston to the third-highest scoring mark in the league, 106 points per game. Besides being an offensive juggernaut, the Celtics also played lights-out defense, finishing near the top of the league in that category as well. In fact, the Celtics defense was so good that four of their five starters (Cowens, Havlicek, Paul Silas, and Don Chaney) earned spots on the All-Defensive first or second team.

Hot on the heels of the Celtics was the "team of the future" from Buffalo. "The Braves," one journalist wrote, "are Buffaloaded." At guard, flashy Ernie DiGregorio whipped behind-the-back passes and wowed his legions of Italian American fans with jaw-dropping plays while backcourt mate Randy Smith continued to rank among the most athletic players in the league. But the star of the Braves remained third-year center Bob McAdoo, who took home league MVP honors after leading the league in points per game (34.5) and finishing fourth in rebounds (14.1). Not everything was rosy, though, in Buffalo. For one, McAdoo, already frustrated at his lack of public notoriety *before* his MVP campaign, became increasingly upset *after* winning the trophy. "I don't think anyone pays much attention to what I've been doing," McAdoo complained. Of more immediate concern, the Braves suffered on the court when DiGregorio, the pilot of the team's high-flying attack, suffered a serious knee injury in October, costing Ernie D three months of the regular season and much of his quickness. To help the Braves' playoff push, DiGregorio returned to the lineup too soon, lacking the mobility to slip quick passes to teammates or dart into the lane for short jump shots. Ernie's defensive shortcomings became even more obvious as opposing teams began running plays designed to take advantage of his lack of quickness. Despite all this, the Braves won a franchise-record forty-nine games, the third-highest total in the league, and with McAdoo on board, it looked like they would remain in the title hunt for the rest of the decade.[2]

Boston ruled the Atlantic, winning the division by eleven games, but the renamed Washington (formerly Capital) Bullets were even more dominant in the Central, ending the season nineteen games ahead of the second-place Houston Rockets. Washington was a balanced team, the only one in the league to finish in the top five in both points scored and points allowed per game. A big reason for their dominance was Elvin Hayes, the star forward who was labelled a coach killer before being traded to the Bullets in 1972. During the 1974–1975 season, Hayes was at the top of his game, hitting his deadly turnaround jump shot almost at will and drawing rave reviews for his defense. In fact, Washington Coach K. C. Jones compared Hayes favorably to Bill Russell, and while it might seem laughable to compare Hayes to the best defensive player in league history, Jones and Russell were teammates for nine seasons in Boston. If anybody could make the comparison, it was K. C. With Hayes, Afroed center Wes Unseld, and young guards Kevin Porter and Phil Chenier leading the way, the Bullets breezed to sixty wins and expectations of meeting the Celtics in the Eastern Conference finals.

An unlikely off-season trade linked two other teams in the Central, who immediately shared more than just a struggle to win ball games. On May 3, 1974, the day before Cannonade won the one hundredth Kentucky Derby, the Atlanta Hawks did the unthinkable, trading "Pistol Pete" Maravich to an expansion franchise located in New Orleans. To obtain Maravich, New Orleans—which lacked a nickname, coach, or any other players—gave up a king's ransom: two first-round picks, two players, and an agreement to take washed-up center Walt Bellamy off Atlanta's hands. Basketball experts panned the five-for-one deal as a "Hawk heist," and "little short of highway robbery." Bob Wolf joked in a *Chicago Tribune* column that Atlanta should be "investigated along with the conspirators at Watergate," for the theft.[3]

Without Maravich and "Sweet" Lou Hudson, sidelined with an elbow injury, Atlanta won only thirty-one games. But they did find a gem in rookie John Drew. Drew came out of nowhere as a second-round pick out of tiny Gardner-Webb University and earned All-Rookie first team honors after leading the league in offensive rebounding and scoring almost twenty points per game. "He's one of the best offensive machines I've ever seen in pro basketball," gushed teammate Dean Meminger. "He's incredible now and he's going to be unbelievable." With two selections in the top three picks of the 1975 draft headed their way thanks to the Maravich trade (could they get North Carolina State guard David "Skywalker" Thompson *and* Morgan State center Marvin "the Human Eraser" Webster?), the future seemed bright in Atlanta.[4]

Maravich's new team, New Orleans (later named the Jazz) believed they could compete for a title right away. "We will have all the elements of a playoff-caliber team, if not a championship team, by 1975," the owner boasted after acquiring Pistol Pete. On the court, Maravich was as good as advertised, scoring twenty-one points per game even though the team went through three coaches and had a 23–59 record. But off the floor, Pete continued to battle alcoholism and the pressure of being the league's Great White Hope and, in particular, the death of his mother, Helen, who committed suicide during the season.[5]

Maravich's New Orleans Jazz was one of the worst teams in the entire NBA, joining Philadelphia and Atlanta as the doormats in the Eastern Conference. Unlike in the East, the Western Conference was wide open; all nine teams won between thirty and forty-eight games. Sensing an opportunity to vault to the top of the heap, the Chicago Bulls went all in to make a title run in 1975 and swapped centers with Golden State, dealing Clifford Ray for Nate Thurmond. The addition of the future Hall of Famer made the Bulls prohibitive championship favorites, giving them potential All-Stars at all five positions. General manager and head coach Dick Motta called the trade "the best in the club's history," and Thurmond "the best defensive center in the NBA." Unfortunately for Bulls fans, the season did not finish with a storybook ending, and even before opening night, there were signs of distress. High-scoring forward Bob "Butterbean" Love again asked for a pay raise (his third in four seasons) and, joined by guard Norm Van Lier (also seeking a raise), held out. With two starters frustrated with their coach/general manager sitting on the sidelines, the Bulls started 3–7. Thurmond, at least, lived up to the hype, recording the first "quadruple-double" in NBA history in a mid-October game against the Hawks, scoring twenty-two points, hauling down fourteen rebounds, handing out thirteen assists, and blocking twelve shots. In January, with Love and Van Lier back in the fold, the team made a late-season run and won a franchise-record twelve straight home games to take the Midwest Division crown, finally passing their archrivals from Milwaukee.[6]

After four straight division titles and a pair of NBA finals appearances, the Milwaukee Bucks plummeted to the bottom of the Midwest. As the season neared, Bucks fans wondered if legendary guard Oscar Robertson would return for a fifteenth season. In September, Robertson decided against it, announcing both his retirement and his agreement to share a booth with play-by-play man Brent Musberger at CBS. He lasted just one season as an announcer and then disappeared from the national spotlight, effectively blackballed from the league and all NBA front offices because of his role in the Oscar Robertson lawsuit. More on that later.

No more "Big O" left a gaping hole in the Bucks backcourt. "They lack direction since they lost Oscar," explained Celtics guard Jo Jo White. "He moved the ball, made everybody work on offense and they were better off." Even without Robertson, the Bucks expected to contend for the conference title. After all, they still had Kareem Abdul-Jabbar, the best player on the planet. But Abdul-Jabbar missed the first month of the season with a broken hand, injured when he punched the basket support in a preseason game after being gouged in the eye. "I was furious," Kareem said afterward, blaming referees for his injury. "They let [Dave] Cowens and all those guys climb all over me . . . and now because of their stupidity, I might be severely injured." Abdul-Jabbar returned wearing goggles to protect his eyes, an accessory that would become as synonymous with Kareem as the skyhook. The 1974 version of his goggles was not the sleek pair he sported as the bald, elder statesman of the 1980s Showtime Lakers. Instead, they looked like chemistry lab rejects: huge black-framed monstrosities. With Abdul-Jabbar recovering from his hand injury and adjusting to his new eyewear, the Bucks faltered. Milwaukee started 3–13 and finished just 38–44, missing the playoffs for the first time since Kareem's arrival in 1969.[7]

Just as in Milwaukee, where the Bucks struggled with life after Oscar, the Lakers had to learn to cope without Jerry West, the league's logo and arguably one of the top ten players of all time. West initially announced that he would retire *after* the 1974–1975 season. But a contract dispute with team owner Jack Kent Cooke ended in a dizzying array of lawsuits and countersuits forcing West to the sidelines earlier than he or Lakers fans had hoped. Cooke publicly excoriated West, blaming him for the team's dismal performance. And to some extent, Cooke was right; the Lakers *were* miserable without "the Logo." Emblematic of their struggles, Connie "the Hawk" Hawkins contributed just eight points per game, and his most memorable moment came when he guest starred on the second-ever episode of *Saturday Night Live*, appearing in a cameo to play one-on-one against tiny Paul Simon. Fortunately for Lakers fans, the team was stockpiling talented young players and draft choices. Besides twenty-five-year-old center Elmore Smith (who finished second in the league with almost three blocked shots per game), Los Angeles added All-Rookie guard Brian Winters and a future first round pick in a trade with Cleveland. In the spring of 1975, the Lakers pushed all these chips into the middle of the table, going all in to change the future of their franchise. But during the 1974–1975 season, L.A. was a hodgepodge of veterans like Hawkins and Gail Goodrich awkwardly paired with up-and-comers like Smith and Winters.

Even with West's untimely retirement, the biggest transformation in the Pacific Division took place in Portland, not Los Angeles. A 27–55 record during the 1973–1974 season and a coin flip that came up tails "earned" the Blazers the first pick in the 1974 draft, which was used to select UCLA center Bill Walton. Even before Portland's selection, there was a rush to sign Walton. The ABA struck first, desperately trying to lure the UCLA big man to their league. "Bill could have played for any ABA team he wanted," ABA commissioner Mike Storen admitted. "There even was some talk of putting an ABA team in L.A. and calling them the L.A. Bruins or something and trying to get all the old UCLA stars together." In the ABA, as one executive explained, "it isn't who you draft. It's who you sign. The draft is really just a formality." Fortunately for Blazers fans, Walton decided he wanted to face the best big men in the business, turning down the ABA and signing with Rip City.[8]

Coaches and scouts unanimously agreed Walton was a once-in-a-generation talent. "I was with the Boston Celtics when Bill Russell came into the league," Lakers coach Bill Sharman recalled. "Walton is the same type of player." Lenny Wilkens, the Blazers player-coach, also heaped praise on his redheaded center. "He reminds me of Oscar Robertson," Wilkens said. "And in time, I think he may become what Oscar was—the most complete player in the game." Even as a rookie, Walton possessed all the skills NBA scouts looked for. Listed at six-foot-eleven (Walton refused to be typecast as a seven footer, even though he was probably seven-foot-two or -three), he towered over most opponents. He released his jump shot with a feathery soft touch and intimidated opponents with phenomenal timing to block countless shots. And perhaps most importantly, Walton was an excellent—and willing—passer, throwing long outlet passes rivaling those unleashed by Bullets center Wes Unseld. Walton flashed amazing potential in averaging twelve points, twelve rebounds, five assists, and three blocks per game as a rookie. Unfortunately, he also struggled with a litany of back and leg problems, and although fans expected Walton to walk away with the Rookie of the Year award, injuries kept him from walking much at all. Without Walton on the court, the Blazers had to rely on the combustible tandem of Geoff Petrie and Sidney Wicks. Wicks led the team in scoring and rebounding (earning a spot in the All-Star game), while Petrie chipped in with eighteen points per game. Unbeknownst to Portland fans at the time, their team was on the cusp of greatness; unfortunately, Blazermaniacs had a few more years of the Wicks-Petrie era left before reaching the promised land.[9]

Walton made headlines for both his on-court play and off-court radicalism. He was one of only a handful of athletes willing to speak out against the war in Vietnam and the endemic racism plaguing the United States in the early seventies. In some ways, though, Walton was following a trail blazed a decade earlier when Celtics center Bill Russell railed against racial injustice and inequity, joining well-known black athletes Jim Brown and Muhammad Ali as leaders in the civil rights struggle. Russell retired in 1969 but resurfaced as a head coach in 1973, serving as a mentor for young Seattle superstar Spencer Haywood.

In their second season under Coach Russell, the SuperSonics showed definite improvement, winning forty-three games and making the playoffs for the first time in franchise history. Spencer Haywood remained the Sonics' star, starting in the All-Star game and earning a spot on the All-NBA second team. Haywood was also able to move back to his more natural position of forward after the Sonics drafted seven-foot-two Tom Burleson from North Carolina State. Burleson, nick-named "the Needle" after the famous Space Needle highlighting the Seattle skyline, earned All-Rookie honors while guard "Downtown" Freddie Brown, in his fourth season, finished second on the team in scoring. At the time, the link between Russell and Haywood appeared strong. "I've learned a lot from him," Haywood said. "He kind of looks at me as a son, too." But their relationship was on the brink of break-down and neither man was long for the Pacific Northwest.[10]

All signs pointed to the Golden State Warriors dropping below the Sonics in the standings; after four straight years of finishing second in the division, the team waved good-bye to two of their top three players: Nate Thurmond and high-scoring forward Cazzie Russell. To make matters worse, the Warriors also lost starting forward Clyde Lee to the Hawks because of a clerical error. Journalists picked the Warriors, sud-denly down two starters and a valuable sixth man, to finish anywhere from second to fourth in the division. "The future," one preseason pub-lication surmised, "is bleak." At best, the new Warriors acquisitions, former Bulls center Clifford Ray and draft choices Keith Wilkes and Phil Smith, had big shoes to fill if they hoped to replace Thurmond, Russell, and Lee.[11]

Keith (later Jamaal) Wilkes was a smooth, six-foot-six, 190-pound forward given the nickname "Silk" for his on-court gracefulness. "An effortless player with loads of talent," was how one publication de-scribed his play coming out of UCLA, where he twice helped the Bruins to the NCAA title and earned All-American honors. Wilkes also made a splash before even playing an NBA game, starring as "Corn-bread" in the dramatic film *Cornbread, Earl and Me*. In *Cornbread*, Wilkes's character is determined to leave the ghetto to attend college on an athletic scholarship but becomes the victim of mistaken identity and is gunned down by police. The only witness, Wilford Robinson (played by fourteen-year-old Laurence Fishburne), becomes the true star of the movie, refusing to be intimidated by white police and telling his story on the witness stand. Filming kept Wilkes from training and he came into camp in poor condition. But Silk quickly worked himself into shape and joined the starting lineup as an undersized power forward.[12]

Wilkes started for the Warriors while Phil Smith joined a loaded backcourt, splitting time with Butch Beard, Charles Johnson, and Jeff Mullins. This foursome gave the Warriors enviable depth; they could create matchup problems and ride a hot hand like few other teams in the league. Golden State also boasted depth at center, despite losing Thurmond, as Clifford Ray and George Johnson formed a potent inside tandem. According to Wilkes, Ray was "the power guy" with a more refined offensive game while Johnson was "the finesse type" who was an exceptional shot blocker, using his rail-thin six-foot-eleven frame to average two blocks in less than twenty minutes of playing time per game.[13]

Wilkes, the center duo, and the guard quartet created an excellent supporting cast for superstar forward Rick Barry. In 1967, Barry turned the sports world on its ear when he became the first player to jump from the NBA to the ABA, leaving the then–San Francisco Warriors for the Oakland Oaks, coached by his father-in-law Bruce Hale. After just two years, the team folded, fired Hale, and was reborn as the Washington Capitols. Barry refused to report to Washington and re-signed with the NBA's Warriors. As the court system worked through Barry's sticky legal situation, ABA officials forced him to join the Capitols, who, in 1970, relocated to Virginia as the Squires. Barry was incensed. "My son Scooter is supposed to go to nursery school this year," Barry complained in a *Sports Illustrated* interview. "I hate to think of the complications that'll cause in Virginia. I don't want him to go down there to school and learn to speak with a Southern accent. He'll come home from school saying, 'Hi yall, Daad.' I sure don't want that." Shortly after *Sports Illustrated* hit the newsstands, the Squires traded Barry to the New York Nets. Coincidence? Probably not. Barry was happy; the Nets played in New York City and were fresh off an ABA finals appearance. Now Barry regretted signing his Warriors contract and hoped to stay with the Nets. But once again Barry lost his case, and in October 1972, a U.S. District Court judge ruled that he had to play for Golden State and Barry reluctantly rejoined the Warriors.[14]

In the mid-seventies, Barry was the best all-around forward in professional basketball. "His shooting borders on eagle eye perfect," one journalist wrote, "his passing always deft and flawless, and playmaking, well, it was always beautiful, graceful and crowd pleasing." Barry played basketball like it was chess and he was always one move ahead of his opponent. He often caught passes in midair, as if already in motion for a layup before even receiving the ball, and fired off brilliant passes that sometimes surprised even his teammates, passing it to where they *should* be rather than where they were. On defense Barry admittedly took some plays off but still managed to lead the league in steals, setting a new NBA record with 228 (2.9 per game), using his long arms and incredible instincts to tip away passes and errant dribbles. On a team of great role players like the Warriors, Barry stood out as one of the NBA's top scorers, finishing second in the league, behind Bob McAdoo, with 30.6 points per game. In fact, his fifty-five-point outburst against Philadelphia in January was the highest total of any player during the season. The six-foot-seven Barry shot well from long range and, perhaps more than any of his contemporaries, would have benefitted from an NBA three-point line. But Barry was at his best attacking the basket. Not only could he score with an assortment of twisting layups, but opponents often fouled him, sending him to the free throw line, where he led the league by making better than 90 percent of his attempts.[15]

Rick Barry is probably most well-known today for his free throw technique. Barry, unlike the vast majority of players then or since, shot free throws underhanded—"granny style." For Barry, free throw shooting was not simply a means to score points: it was affirmation of his superiority. "Free-throw percentages," Barry explained, "are the only statistics in basketball that can't possibly be questioned." Free throws are the only truly individual measurement in the sport; assists rely on teammates' scoring ability, rebounds can only occur after missed shots, and even scoring points depends on many variables including the opponent's defensive ability. So why shoot free throws underhanded? As Barry explained, keeping your arms below your waist reduced the variable of tired arms. A simple two-handed flick of the wrist elevates the ball from between the shooter's legs into the waiting hoop. Simple. In fact, teammate George Johnson took Barry's advice and began learning at the knee of the free throw master. After a month or two of practice, Johnson nearly doubled his percentage, sinking 80 percent of his shots after a 41 percent average as a rookie. But the technique never caught on. Maybe it was the ungainly appearance of a grown man flinging shots at the hoop "granny style." Or maybe it was just that Rick Barry was so damned unlikeable.[16]

For all his on-court ability and free throw–shooting mastery, Barry might have been the most universally despised player in the league in the 1970s. Barry should have been hailed as a pioneer by his fellow players. After all, he was the NBA's answer to Curt Flood, challenging

the reserve clause and indirectly bringing about free agency in professional basketball. Instead, players, fans, and owners generally disdained
the man. Barry believed fans saw him as "a rotten, no-good SOB who
raped owners and teams for every cent he could." More bluntly, Bill
Simmons, a modern journalist, called Barry "a prick . . . the Association's most despised player, someone who whined about every call, sold
out teammates with a variety of eye rolls and 'why the hell did you drop
that' shrugs and shamelessly postured for a TV career." Barry did, in
fact, spend his off-seasons as an analyst for NBA playoff games and, on
camera, was smart but condescending, bordering on arrogant as an on-
air commentator. That brashness clearly carried over from his off-came-
ra personality. Barry was a perfectionist and a horrible loser. Journalists
called him "Mighty Mouth," "Hollywood, "League Jumper," and "Crybaby." He flopped to draw fouls, reacting as if a freight train had hit him
after even the slightest contact. His statistics were clearly good enough
to warrant MVP consideration, but since that award was voted on by his
peers, Barry finished a distant fourth during the 1974–1975 season.
Tellingly, Barry's broadcast career came to an abrupt end during the
1981 playoffs when he made a racist remark to Bill Russell. CBS decided not to renew his contract.[17]

Despite all this, Barry was the model teammate during the
1974–1975 season, and Coach Al Attles even named him team captain.
Barry's unique skill set coupled with the Warriors' enviable depth and
positional flexibility propelled them to a conference-best forty-eight
wins and the top seed in the Western Conference.

Commissioner Walter Kennedy introduced a new playoff structure
for the 1975 postseason: ten teams, five per conference. Once again, the
four best regular-season squads advanced into the conference finals as
Boston and Washington, both sixty-game winners, matched up in the
East while Chicago and Golden State prepared for a Wild West showdown.

In many ways, the Boston-Washington Eastern Conference finals
matchup looked like the "real" championship during the 1974–1975
season: a battle between the NBA's two best teams. Washington
shocked Boston in game one thanks to a Herculean thirty-four-point
effort from Elvin Hayes, who also led the Bullets to a game two win at
home, pouring in twenty-nine. The Celtics won game three, but Washington took game four to give the Bullets a 3–1 edge. Boston fans had

reason for optimism: this was, after all, the eleven-time champion Celtics. And in game five, the luck of the Irish rang true; Boston won by four. But in game six, back in Washington, the Bullets closed out the series with a six-point win, giving them tremendous momentum going into the NBA finals where the Bullets would be heavy favorites no matter who emerged from the West.

Unlike the series between the Bullets and Celtics, the Western Conference finals was low scoring and ugly. Golden State took game one on their home floor as Barry outdueled Bob "Butterbean" Love, thirty-eight to thirty-seven. Chicago took a nail-biter in game two, squeaking out a one-point win at home, thanks to a boneheaded play by the normally cerebral Rick Barry. With just a few seconds on the game clock, the Warriors had the ball, clinging to a one-point lead. All they had to do was hold the ball and they would win. But Barry inexplicably took a shot and missed. Barry's gaffe allowed the Bulls to tie up the game in regulation and win in overtime. After trading victories in games three, four, and five, the Bulls moved to within one win from taking the best-of-seven series.

Twenty-thousand screaming fans packed into Chicago Stadium on May 11, 1975, anticipating a Bulls victory and—finally—an NBA finals appearance. The atmosphere was electric and almost as wild as when Led Zepplin played that arena four months earlier and blew spectators' minds with their new hit song "Kashmir." At the end of the first quarter of game six, Bulls fans had reason to cheer as they clung to a seven-point lead. But Golden State's bench, easily the deepest in the league, helped the Warriors fight ahead in the second quarter, and at halftime the score was close: Golden State 46, Chicago 38. Now it was the Bulls' turn to rally, and "the crowd was louder than ever," Chicago guard Jerry Sloan remembered. Ironically, the difference maker in the fourth quarter was center Clifford Ray, dealt from Chicago to Golden State for Nate Thurmond just months earlier. Thurmond was held scoreless in game six, but Ray blocked three shots and played excellent defense to help the Warriors close out a fourteen-point win, sending the series to a decisive seventh game. "We felt that we not only let ourselves down and saw a golden opportunity slip away," said Sloan, "but that we let down the entire city of Chicago."[18]

Dick Motta was furious. If Bob Love and Norm Van Lier had not held out and missed time early in the season, the Bulls would have started better than 3–7, and it would be them, not Golden State, headed home for game seven. Motta blamed his stars for the team's failure to secure home-court advantage, and though the Bulls staked out a seemingly insurmountable nineteen-point lead in the first half, they watched as the Warriors came back to win the game and the series. "That was the final hurrah of the Chicago Bulls as we knew them," Motta said later. A short-lived Bulls pseudo-dynasty, never resulting in any league titles or even a finals appearance, came to a close when Chicago lost the 1975 Western Conference finals. Not until a guard named Michael Jordan led the team to multiple title wins in the 1990s would Chicago again stand among the league's elite.[19]

Though the Bullets' victory over the Celtics was a mild surprise—Boston was, after all, the defending champion and winner of sixty regular-season games—the Warriors' elimination of the Bulls was a shock. It apparently even surprised management at the Oakland Coliseum, where an ice skating show had already booked the Warriors' usual home court. Forced to move their "home" games to the nearby San Francisco Cow Palace, the Warriors looked even more rinky-dink when league officials had to work around a karate championship taking place in the Cow Palace—*Enter the Dragon* apparently made thousands of American kids Bruce Lee fans. No matter the location of Bay Area home games, gamblers established the Bullets as three-to-one favorites to take the series. Surely the Golden State Warriors, a team with one superstar and a deep if unspectacular supporting cast, would be no problem for the Eastern Conference–champion Bullets.

As game one tipped off in Washington, fans witnessed a milestone event that passed relatively unheralded at the time. Both head coaches, the Bullets' K. C. Jones and Warriors' Al Attles, were African Americans, and the 1975 NBA finals marked the first time in a major American sports championship that both head coaches were black. Not until 2007 would this be repeated when Tony Dungy of the Indianapolis Colts and Lovie Smith of the Chicago Bears met in the Super Bowl; to date, major league baseball's World Series has never pitted two African American managers against one another. Clearly the 1975 finals were a landmark in civil rights activity. But Attles and Jones were apparently unfazed by the significance of the event. "It wasn't something we thought about," Attles said later. "I knew it wasn't on K. C.'s mind because we never mentioned it . . . the only thing we were concerned about was trying to beat each other."[20]

Golden State jumped out to a fourteen-point lead at halftime in game one of the finals and never looked back, earning a 101–95 win in front of a stunned Bullets crowd. Because of the scheduling snafu resulting from the Ice Capades and karate tournament, the Bullets suddenly faced a must-win two-game West Coast swing. Rick Barry took over game two, finishing with a game-high thirty-six points as the Warriors clung to a one-point lead with just six seconds remaining. The Bullets missed two potential game winners in the waning moments before time expired: the underdog Warriors were suddenly up two games to none. "We came back and won that ball game," Barry remembered, "and that was like the handwriting on the wall. They never recovered." A two-game deficit quickly became three in front of a raucous San Francisco crowd as Golden State's depth proved decisive; Barry led all scorers with thirty-eight points, but five other Warriors joined Barry in scoring double figures. As one exasperated Bullets player admitted, "they're plain out-hustling us. They're getting to the loose balls, to the rebounds, cutting off the easy baskets."[21]

Facing elimination, the Bullets returned to D.C., stunned. Oddsmakers had installed them as favorites, and they led by double figures in every game but were down three games to none. Game four looked like an opportunity for the Bullets to begin a seemingly impossible comeback; referees ejected Attles with his team down fourteen in the first quarter after the Warriors coach objected to Bullets forward Mike Riordan putting Barry in a headlock that would have made San Francisco wrestling legends Pat Patterson and Ray Stevens proud. Even without their coach, the Warriors roared back, just as they had so many times already in the postseason. Their pressing, full-court defense simply wore down Bullets guards, and Butch Beard scored the team's last seven points, including a pair of clutch free throws, to seal a 96–95 nail-biter for the visiting Warriors. "It has to be the greatest upset in the history of the NBA finals," Barry declared. No one challenged him.[22]

Unsurprisingly, sportswriters named Barry the finals MVP after the Golden State golden boy had averaged twenty-nine points, four rebounds, and five assists in the series. But the entire Warriors team really earned MVP honors, playing selfless team basketball with contributions from each man on the roster. Even eleventh-man Bill Bridges chipped in, playing tough defense on Elvin Hayes to force the "Big E" to work extra hard to score. "This is a Cinderella team," Bridges said after the season. Barry had to agree. "This has been a fantasy year," he said, "it's a team that cares for each other and these have been the most beautiful individuals I've ever been associated with." "Everyone," he continued, "got a chance to contribute and did." Years later, Barry still talked lovingly of that team. "It was about a group of young men who were willing to put their egos aside," Barry said in a recent interview. "It was like a family." Attles, who became only the second African American head coach to win an NBA title (the first was, of course, Bill Russell), insisted that "we had good players. But we didn't have five of them. We had twelve of them."[23]

Sister Sledge had not yet released their 1979 hit "We Are Family," but one can imagine it a fitting anthem for the '75 Warriors, just as it became synonymous with Willie Stargell and baseball's late-seventies Pittsburgh Pirates. "I like the Warriors. They are a good team," Walt Frazier, star of the early-seventies Knicks teams, said at the time. "They remind me of the way we used to play." It can't be said any better. The Warriors were a good team: maybe even a great team. But they are rarely mentioned among the greatest champions of all time. In part, that stems from their short-lived success. They did not create a dynasty in the Bay Area and never won another title. But perhaps more importantly, many of the best basketball players in the world did not even play in the NBA. One, in particular, gained great notoriety for his actions in the increasingly popular ABA, where the doctor was always in.[24]

Statistics for 1974–1975

Eastern Conference	W	L	Western Conference	W	L
Atlantic Division			*Midwest Division*		
Boston Celtics	60	22	Chicago Bulls	47	35
Buffalo Braves	49	33	Kansas City–Omaha Kings	44	38
New York Knicks	40	42	Detroit Pistons	40	42
Philadelphia 76ers	34	48	Milwaukee Bucks	38	44
Central Division			*Pacific Division*		
Washington Bullets	60	22	Golden State Warriors	48	34
Houston Rockets	41	41	Seattle SuperSonics	43	39
Cleveland Cavaliers	40	42	Portland Trail Blazers	38	44
Atlanta Hawks	31	51	Phoenix Suns	32	50

New Orleans Jazz	23	59	Los Angeles Lakers	30	52

Playoffs

Eastern Conference First Round	Houston d. New York (2–1)
Western Conference First Round	Seattle d. Detroit (2–1)
Eastern Conference Semifinals	Boston d. Houston (4–1)
	Washington d. Buffalo (4–3)
Western Conference Semifinals	Chicago d. KC–Omaha (4–2)
	Golden State d. Seattle (4–2)
Eastern Conference Finals	Washington d. Boston (4–2)
Western Conference Finals	Golden State d. Chicago (4–3)
NBA Finals	Golden State d. Washington (4–0)

All-NBA Teams

First Team

F—Rick Barry (Golden State)

F—Elvin Hayes (Washington)

C—Bob McAdoo (Buffalo)

G—Walt Frazier (New York)

G—Nate "Tiny" Archibald (KC–Omaha)

Second Team

F—Spencer Haywood (Seattle)

F—John Havlicek (Boston)

C—Dave Cowens (Boston)

G—Jo Jo White (Boston)

G—Phil Chenier (Washington)

League Leaders

Points per Game (34.5)

Rebounds per Game (14.8)

Assists per Game (8.0)

Steals per Game (2.9)

Blocks per Game (3.3)

Bob McAdoo (Buffalo)

Wes Unseld (Washington)

Kevin Porter (Washington)

Rick Barry (Golden State)

Kareem Abdul-Jabbar (Milwaukee)

| Most Valuable Player | Bob McAdoo (Buffalo) |
| Rookie of the Year | Keith Wilkes (Golden State) |

Time-Out

The Doctor

He was friendly, but very quiet, trying to feel the situation out. For a
while, he just sat and watched. Then he came in to play and I was
guarding him. He started going around me—hell, jumping over me.
The kid did things I had never seen before.[1] —George Irvine

A murmur softly rippled through the 15,000 fans packed inside Denver's McNichols Arena as Julius Erving scooped up a red-, white-, and
blue-striped basketball and held it in one enormous hand. Erving wore
a blue jersey with "ABA All-Star" and the number 32 printed on his
chest; he was a hoops-playing Superman. Short blue shorts, white socks
pulled up to mid-calf, and an immaculate pair of white Converse Pro
sneakers completed the ensemble. Starting at one foul line, Erving
jogged downcourt toward the opposite basket, pacing out seven enormous steps. Fans strained to watch Erving, now standing three quarters
of the court away from his target. After a short pause and a deep breath,
Erving accelerated downcourt, his long strides quickly covering the
distance. Erving reached the foul line and leapt, huge Afro waving in
the mile-high stillness as he took flight fifteen feet from the rim. He
extended one long arm and floated through the air before powerfully
slamming the striped basketball through the hoop. The crowd erupted,
unable to believe what they had just seen.

Erving's famous dunk took place during halftime of the 1976 American Basketball Association (ABA) All-Star game as part of the first-ever slam dunk contest. Even before Erving took flight, he was an American sports icon, albeit one that fans rarely had the opportunity to see in person or even on television. For the previous half-decade, Erving almost single-handedly kept the ABA afloat amid rumors of its imminent demise. But even in early 1976, at the height of his powers, Erving existed in relative obscurity, often playing in half-filled arenas against teams in danger of folding.

Erving was used to flying under the radar. He grew up on Long Island and at an early age became a regular on the playground courts common to New York City. His mother and siblings called him June— short for Junior—and even as a child he was always running and jumping, leaping down flights of stairs or across paved lots. In the projects of Long Island, Erving honed his game, playing basketball and football until streetlights came on and mothers called their children home for dinner. One afternoon while playing football with friends, Erving went up to catch a pass but fell forward, shredding his knee on shards of broken glass. There was blood everywhere and June and his friends were terrified. Erving hopped across the street and up the stairs to his family's apartment, where his mother tried to clean the wound. But there was just too much blood. She took her son to the doctor and the physician diagnosed Julius with severe knee damage including several ligaments sliced clean through by the sharp glass. For three months, June hobbled around in a cast, forced to watch his friends play rather than running and jumping alongside them. While watching from his apartment window, Erving made a promise to himself: someday he would run even faster and jump even higher than he had before his injury. And he did. Erving became one of the best athletes in his class and the star of the Roosevelt High basketball team.

Erving graduated from Roosevelt as a six-foot-three forward and was not heavily recruited by powerhouse programs like UCLA, North Carolina, or Kentucky. Instead, Erving ended up at Massachusetts, where he became a star. In just two seasons (freshmen were still barred from the varsity squad), Erving averaged an astounding twenty-six points and twenty rebounds per game. In both seasons, his Minutemen won regular-season league titles and spots in the National Invitational Tournament (NIT) but never earned a bid to the more prestigious and media-driven NCAA tournament. Despite his on-court brilliance as a college student-athlete, few fans outside the northeast heard of Erving or were able to watch him play.

Summers spent at home from UMass meant basketball on the asphalt of New York City playgrounds. Despite playing for years on city courts while growing up, he had never visited the famous Holcombe Rucker Playground at 155th Street and Eighth Avenue. Finally, in 1969, Erving played at Rucker, squaring off against several New York Knicks prepping for their historic title run. "That day," one playground player recalled, "Julius found out how good he was." At the time, Rucker used a hype man to pump up the crowd by announcing big plays on a loudspeaker and giving the players ludicrous nicknames. Earl Monroe was "the Pearl" or "Black Jesus," Earl Manigault, "the Goat" (Greatest of All-Time), and Joe Hammond, "the Destroyer." But no one captured the attention of the Rucker faithful like Erving. Desperate for a handle to capture Erving's game, the announcer tried out "the Claw," "Black Moses," "Magic," and "Little Hawk" (after Connie "the Hawk" Hawkins, another New York City playground star). But Erving, who had gained a nickname in high school when a buddy told Julius that "you got more moves than Dr. Carter has liver pills," instructed the announcer to "just call me the Doctor."[2]

The nickname stuck, as did his reputation for brilliance at Rucker where—as the hype man continually reminded fans—the doctor was always operating on fools. One playground referee vividly remembered an experience calling a game involving Erving. "The first time Julius touched the ball, three defensive players converged on him," he said. "Suddenly, Julius just makes a sweeping move along the baseline, glides past all three of them, elevates, and, with his left hand, throws down a tremendous dunk." Soon the rooftops and trees around Rucker filled with spectators when the Doctor was playing; everyone wanted a story to tell their kids and grandkids about the unbelievable Julius Erving. The tales grew taller in their retellings—of Erving dunking from several feet behind the free throw line, of scoring fifty, sixty, or even seventy points in a single game, and of jumping over defenders to attack the basket with abandon. Regardless of their accuracy, these stories mattered. "Dr. J" resonated with fans on the playground and helped (along with Pete Axthelm's amazing book *The City Game*, published in 1970) legitimize that style of play as he soared higher and higher toward a pro career.[3]

In 1971, after his junior season at UMass and following a summer spent dominating at Rucker, the twenty-one-year-old Erving left school early to join the ABA's Virginia Squires. Rookie "Dr. J" took the league by storm, averaging twenty-seven points and nearly sixteen rebounds per game en route to winning All-ABA second team and All-Rookie first team honors. Only the arrival of enormous Kentucky Colonels center Artis Gilmore—voted both rookie of the year and most valuable player—kept Erving from walking away with more hardware after his freshman campaign. Erving hoped to cash in on his brilliant rookie season and tried to renegotiate his $75,000 annual salary. But not only did Squires owner Earl Foreman refuse, but Erving's paychecks also began to bounce. "Dr. J" threatened to jump leagues unless the financial issues were resolved, and his agent sent feelers to the Atlanta Hawks about possibly bringing Erving to the NBA. Paychecks kept bouncing, so Erving signed with Atlanta, more than doubling his Squires salary. But soon after signing with the Hawks—who envisioned pairing "Dr. J" with "Pistol Pete" Maravich to create undoubtedly the league's most exciting duo—the Milwaukee Bucks selected Erving in the first round of the draft. Suddenly lawsuits began flying both between leagues and between teams within leagues as the Squires, Bucks, and Hawks all claimed rights to Erving. "Dr. J" was caught squarely in the middle, a pawn in the interleague war. Within weeks, Erving went from teaming with Maravich in Atlanta for exhibition games, to preparing to suit up next to Kareem Abdul-Jabbar in Milwaukee, to finally rejoining the Squires after a federal appeals court determined he was legally bound to the ABA. Regardless of the outcome of the case, it was clear Erving was not long for the Squires. "I don't think my contract with Virginia is fair," Erving told *Sports Illustrated* that winter. "I have proven myself and I don't think I'm being paid the market value for the type of player I think I am."[4]

If Erving thought he was good, fans almost worshipped the great "Dr. J." Erving drew comparisons to a young Elgin Baylor, particularly in his ability to gracefully float in midair while contorting his body to make difficult shots seem effortless. Even Baylor himself admitted Erving could be the best forward to ever play the game. Yet Erving, ever humble, said "that's kinda heavy." Regardless, the brilliance of Dr. J was undeniable. In his second ABA season, Erving led the league in scoring, pouring in almost thirty-two points per night along with more than twelve rebounds. Despite the play of Erving and that of a toothpick-thin rookie guard named George "the Iceman" Gervin, Virginia floundered, losing to the powerful Kentucky Colonels (led by the towering inside duo of Artis Gilmore and Dan Issel) in the playoffs. Although his team made the postseason, Squires owner Earl Foreman lost hundreds of thousands of dollars that year, and with his star player again making noise about a pay raise and garnering interest from several NBA squads, Foreman decided to sell off certain assets to maintain control of his team. Recouping his losses without alienating his fellow owners was a tricky proposition. Fortunately, New York Nets owner Roy Boe jumped at the chance to add a star, particular of the homegrown variety like Erving. After all, Boe needed to fill the Nets brand-new stadium, the Nassau Coliseum. Getting Erving to the Big Apple was no easy feat and involved four teams across two competing leagues. The ABA's Nets paid the NBA's Hawks $500,000, of which the Hawks transferred half, as well as two second-round draft picks, to the Milwaukee Bucks. The Nets also paid the Squires a cool $1 million for Erving's ABA rights, sending two players to Virginia to complete the trade. All told, the Nets paid $1.75 million—plus a five-year, $2 million guaranteed contract—to get the Doctor in New York's trademark red and blue. "I'm making an investment," Boe explained, "figuring with Julius Erving on our side, we're going to win."[5]

Wins were hard to come by, at least at first, for Dr. J and the Nets. The team started slowly, dropping ten of their first fourteen games, including one to the lowly Wilt Chamberlain–coached San Diego Conquistadors. But a closed-door team meeting turned around their season as new head coach Kevin Loughery (who left Philadelphia after suffering through their record-setting seventy-three-loss season) made it clear Erving would be the focal point of the offense. Loughery replaced veteran players around Erving with a pair of youngsters who made the Nets a much more exciting and explosive team, comfortable playing at Dr. J's speed. John Williamson—the self-appointed "Super John"—was a stocky, cocksure shooting guard from New Mexico State who averaged more than fourteen points per game as a rookie while Larry Kenon—dubbed "Special K" after rejecting "Doctor K"—mimicked Erving as a high-flying forward. Kenon, from Memphis University, led the team in rebounding with more than eleven per game despite his skinny six-foot-nine frame. But the real difference maker for the Nets during the 1973–1974 season came via a midseason trade with Kentucky in the form of a Burt Reynolds lookalike named Wendell.[6]

Wendell Ladner was a hoops vagabond, playing for his fifth team in four seasons by the time he arrived in New York. Ladner was also a real character, known equally well for his off-court vanity and on-court hustle. Off the floor, the six-foot-five Ladner oozed machismo, constantly combing his hair (even during practice) and grooming his stylish mustache. While with the Kentucky Colonels, Ladner posed provocatively for a poster in which he lay on a locker room bench wearing only his team-issued shorts and holding a red, white, and blue basketball. The Mississippi-born Ladner was also a favorite of the ladies, and Erving, who rented Ladner a condo, had many stories about his teammates' nocturnal habits. But it was Ladner's on-court ability that really helped the Nets. Despite earning All-Star nods in his first two ABA seasons, Ladner was best cast as a role player who could inject defensive toughness and energy into a lifeless squad or, at bare minimum, throw elbows at or undercut opponents who were making too many shots. Ladner's toughness proved indispensable for the more finesse and offensive-minded Nets, who went 22–9 with Ladner in New York.

With Williamson, Kenon, and Ladner all contributing in their own ways, "Dr. J" led the Nets into the 1974 ABA playoffs. In the opening round, Erving's Nets met the overmatched Squires—who had sold George Gervin to the San Antonio Spurs in another cost-cutting measure—and prevailed in just five games. The Nets then faced off against Kentucky, who had knocked Erving and the Squires out of the playoffs a year earlier. This time, Dr. J gained the upper hand against Gilmore and company, sweeping the Colonels to earn a meeting against the Utah Stars for the ABA title. The Stars began life as the Anaheim Amigos, one of the original eleven ABA teams, but lasted just one season there before relocating and becoming the Los Angeles Stars. After two years in L.A., the Stars headed east to Salt Lake City but kept the moniker. During the 1973–1974 season, now in their fourth season, the Stars were the best team in the ABA's Western Division thanks to ABA stalwarts Willie Wise and Jimmy Jones and league-jumper Zelmo Beaty. But the Nets were too much in the ABA finals, besting the Stars in five games to give Dr. J his first championship ring.

Unsurprisingly, Erving earned playoff MVP honors, matching his well-deserved regular-season MVP award. Around this time, Dr. J began attracting more mainstream media attention as well. Endorsement deals with Converse, Spalding, Dr. Pepper, and ChapStick netted Erving as much money as did his basketball exploits, and the resulting commercials undoubtedly reached more viewers than did ABA broadcasts. Soon Erving was rubbing elbows with celebrities like Bill Cosby and Miles Davis in swanky New York City hot spots.

In 1975, Erving slowly emerged from the fog that had kept his amazing skills under the radar of the national media. That February, he played perhaps his greatest individual game in the ABA when, against the San Diego Conquistadors, he netted a career-best sixty-three points to go along with twenty-five rebounds. A few weeks later, the teams met again and Erving managed fifty-one points on just twenty-three shots. The scariest part for opponents? Dr. J was still only twenty-five years old and getting better every day.

During the 1974–1975 season, Erving repeated as ABA MVP (sharing the honor this time with Indiana Pacers muscle-bound forward George McGinnis) but could not lead his Nets past the plucky Spirits of St. Louis, whose cast of characters was as entertaining as any professional basketball roster before or since. Behind the efforts of St. Louis guards "Goo" Kennedy and "Fly" Williams, and rookie big men Maurice Lucas and Marvin "Bad News" Barnes, the Spirits knocked out the defending champs. Even more tragically for Nets fans, Wendell Ladner died that off-season when a commercial airplane bound for New York City crashed, taking the lives of 112 of the 124 people onboard, including the happy-go-lucky playboy from Mississippi.

Merger talks between the ABA and NBA distracted teams from both leagues during the 1975–1976 season. The Nets and Denver Nuggets tried to jump to the NBA, but the price tag was too steep—reportedly more than $6 million per team—and they remained yoked to a dying league. The Memphis Sounds (or was it the Tams? Or the Pros? It was hard to keep track) relocated to Baltimore as the Claws and then folded. The San Diego Sails (formerly the Chamberlain-coached Conquistadors) lasted less than a dozen games before closing their doors, while the once-proud Utah Stars stopped play just sixteen games into the season. The league scrambled to fill open dates, rerouting Erving's Nets from Salt Lake City to San Antonio and Indianapolis, where they played the Spurs and Pacers a dozen times each to complete the convoluted schedule.

Without Baltimore, San Diego, or Utah, the ABA included just seven teams. Sure, league officials worried about the long-term feasibility of the ABA. But more pressingly, they wondered what to do about their All-Star game plans. In the past, the best from the Eastern Division squared off against the top players from the Western Division. Now there were no divisions. So for their All-Star game, the ABA arranged for the league's best team to meet a squad comprised of the top players representing the other six franchises. Fortunately, with the game already scheduled for Denver, the Nuggets posted the league's best record, setting up a contest between the hometown team and the best-players-from-the-other-six-teams team. A sellout crowd of 15,021 came to watch a pregame concert starring Glen Campbell and Charlie Rich; many even stayed for the game. The Nuggets jumped out to an early lead over the All-Stars and led by one point after two quarters. But it was the halftime festivities that gained national attention (finally) for a league on its last legs.

Nuggets general manager and ABA financial director Carl Scheer desperately wanted the league and his organization to come out of All-Star weekend looking first class. After all, merger talks were still in the works. Scheer decided that, in addition to the pregame concert, the event needed more basketball-related entertainment to draw in fans. One ABA official recommended a slam dunk contest. The other representatives quickly agreed, but none of them really knew what that meant. "There had never been a dunking contest before, or at least none of us knew of one," remembered the league's PR man. "We had no idea about rules or anything like that. So we simply made it up as we went along."[7]

League officials chose five men (all of whom were already All-Stars and would be in Denver) to participate in the inaugural slam dunk contest. They included Erving's former teammates "Special K" Larry Kenon and "the Iceman" George Gervin, along with longtime Erving nemesis Artis Gilmore, Nuggets rookie guard David Thompson, and Erving himself. "Everybody was pumped up about the contest," recalled Denver center Dan Issel. "They told us that we didn't have to stay around during halftime, that we could go into the dressing room, but everyone stayed on the court and we sat on the floor." Players were just as engaged as the fans. "When a guy would make a good dunk," Issel said, "you'd see the other players cheering, giving each other high fives. It was like we all were back on the playground, watching this shootout to see who really was the master of the dunk." Players and fans both had plenty to cheer about. Early in the contest, Gervin threw down a beautiful windmill jam, whipping his long right arm all the way from his thigh to above his head in a quick motion ending with the ball thrown powerfully through the hoop. Gilmore's dunks looked like he was trying to tear down the basket, while Thompson brought the home crowd to its feet with a rim-rattling slam in which he spun 360 degrees in midair before throwing the ball through the rim. But it was Erving who captured the imagination of basketball fans that night after letting loose with his foul-line dunk. Unsurprisingly, Erving won the contest, earning him $1,000 and a new stereo system. Despite Erving besting Thompson, Denver fans still went home happy as the Nuggets came from behind in the fourth quarter of the All-Star game to pull out a last-minute win.[8]

The 1975–1976 season, the ABA's last, ended perfectly: with Dr. J on top. Erving's Nets finished second in the league behind Denver and appeared poised for a title run. New York's first-round opponents—the San Antonio Spurs—had other ideas, however. San Antonio, led by Gervin and Kenon (dealt by the Nets to the Spurs before the season) stretched New York to seven intense games, including a bench-clearing brawl in game four resulting in thrown punches and bloodied noses but remarkably no ejections. Against the Spurs, Erving averaged better than thirty-two points per game, outdueling his former teammate Gervin (who, in a losing effort, still managed a twenty-seven-point average) to set up a highly anticipated matchup against Denver for the ABA title.

The Nuggets were a deep and talented team, starting a frontline that included Issel, Thompson, and Bobby Jones (a six-foot-nine forward regarded as one of the league's top defenders). Erving scored forty-five points in the first game of the series and forty-eight in the second as his Nets jumped out to a 3–2 series lead as they returned to New York for game six. Had it been in the NBA rather than the ABA, the sixth game of the 1976 finals would rank as an all-time classic. Thompson led all scorers with forty-two points while Issel chipped in thirty (along with twenty rebounds). Late in the third quarter, the Nuggets held a twenty-two-point lead that, if it held, would stretch the series to a deciding seventh game—in Denver, no less. But the Nets roared back in front of a rowdy Nassau Coliseum crowd as Erving switched onto Thompson defensively to try and slow the Nuggets star. It worked. Nets guard "Super John" Williamson scored sixteen fourth-quarter points and Erving finished with thirty-one to lead the Nets to a heart-stopping, come-from-behind 112–106 victory to win the game, the series, and the very last ABA title.

Fittingly, the game six classic was the final game in ABA history and showcased the best the league had to offer: high-scoring, up-tempo basketball played at a high level with stars on both sides. The Nets and Nuggets each boasted a cast of NBA-caliber players, from the deep Denver frontcourt to the Nets' high-scoring tandem of Williamson and Erving. In the summer of 1976, the ABA and NBA finally merged, and Erving, for the first time, ascended to a national stage. But he was a star long before donning an NBA uniform. From the playgrounds of New York City to the pinnacle of a renegade league, "Dr. J" Julius Erving transformed professional basketball, bringing a high-flying, fan friendly, exciting style to the game.

"Dr. J" Julius Erving thunderously dunks over New Jersey Nets forward Jan van Breda Kolff.

"Pistol Pete" Maravich looks to put the moves on New York Knicks defender
Butch Beard.

Kareem Abdul-Jabbar shoots his patented skyhook over a helpless John Gianelli.

Rick Barry shoots one of his patented underhanded free throws. He led the **NBA** in free-throw percentage six times in ten **NBA** seasons.

Darryl Dawkins teaches Boston Celtics legend John Havlicek how he earned the nickname "Chocolate Thunder."

John Havlicek remains the only player in NBA history to record more than 25,000 points, 8,000 rebounds, and 6,000 assists in his career.

Moses Malone won the 1979 MVP award after averaging twenty-five points and
eighteen rebounds per game for the Houston Rockets.

Bob McAdoo of the Buffalo Braves fights Spencer Haywood for a rebound. In 1976, the two would become teammates—the "saviors" of the down-and-out Knicks.

Portland Trail Blazers center Bill Walton in an all-too-familiar pose: sitting on the bench watching his teammates play.

Nate "Tiny" Archibald, closely guarded by Walt "Clyde" Frazier.

Powerful Baltimore Bullets center Wes Unseld lays the ball into the basket against "the Kangaroo Kid" Billy Cunningham of the Philadelphia 76ers.

George "Iceman" Gervin of the San Antonio Spurs pulls down the easy rebound while future Hall of Fame coach Phil Jackson is blocked from the action.

7

1975 TO 1976

Two weeks before the NBA season tipped off, Chevy Chase welcomed late-night television viewers to a new show airing on NBC, announcing, "live from New York, it's Saturday night!" *Saturday Night Live* featured comedians such as John Belushi, Jane Curtin, Dan Akroyd, and, host of the pilot episode, George Carlin, who used his appearance to discuss the differences between two popular American sports. "Baseball is played on a diamond, in a park. The baseball park! Football is played on a gridiron, in a stadium," Carlin said. "In football, you wear a helmet; in baseball you wear a cap." Carlin failed to mention basketball in his monologue (played in an arena without helmet or cap), but his oversight is understandable. After all, NBC taped *Saturday Night Live* in Rockefeller Center, a mere mile from Madison Square Garden, where the once-mighty Knicks had fallen on hard times.

Reeling from the retirements of Dave DeBusschere, Jerry Lucas, and Willis Reed the previous spring, New York decided to buy big-name talent, sacrificing the future to win immediately. One target was Indiana Pacers star George McGinnis. In the 1970s, the prototypical power forward could muscle inside for rebounds, score over smaller opponents near the basket, and drive past slower defenders to finish with rim-rattling slam dunks. Only three pro players fit that bill: McGinnis and NBA standouts Spencer Haywood and Elvin Hayes. McGinnis, nicknamed "Baby Bull," carried a muscular 235 pounds on his six-foot-eight frame, and Knicks fans salivated at the thought of McGinnis playing in the Garden. But many obstacles blocked the way.

For one, he had a contract with the Pacers; more troublingly, the Philadelphia 76ers, not the Knicks, held McGinnis's NBA rights. Philly and
New York initially agreed to a handshake deal sending Earl "the Pearl"
Monroe and cash to the 76ers for McGinnis. But after his MVP-winning
season, the Sixers reconsidered. "When the Knicks came to us," recalled the Sixers general manager, "we told them no. We want McGinnis in Philadelphia. We aren't going to trade, deal or sell George." The
Knicks ignored the warning and signed McGinnis anyway, inking the
Pacers star to a six-year $2.4 million deal even as McGinnis sued the
NBA, claiming the draft process constituted an illegal monopoly. Philadelphia also filed a grievance with the NBA league office and, after the
courts decided the litigation in favor of the league, new commissioner
Larry O'Brien sided with the Sixers. Against his wishes, McGinnis went
to Philly and the Knicks were left empty-handed.[1]

Ten days after losing out on McGinnis, the Knicks whiffed again—
this time on three-time NBA MVP Kareem Abdul-Jabbar. Abdul-Jabbar wanted out of Milwaukee. That was no secret. Trade rumors swirled
around Kareem during the 1974–1975 season because although Abdul-
Jabbar liked playing for the Bucks, he hated living in Milwaukee. Milwaukee's front office tried to convince Abdul-Jabbar to stay, but in
March 1975, Kareem publicly expressed his dissatisfaction. "I don't
have any friends or family here," Abdul-Jabbar said. "The things I relate
to don't happen to be in this city to any meaningful degree." His admission put the Bucks in a tight spot, forcing Milwaukee to trade the best
player in the game at the peak of his career.[2]

Abdul-Jabbar held a trump card; a no-trade clause in his contract
allowed him to void any deal. Kareem and his advisers recommended
Milwaukee trade him to either New York (his boyhood home), Washington, D.C. (where he owned a house), or Los Angeles. The Knicks
tried desperately to land Kareem, offering the Bucks their choice of
players, picks, or cash. Not good enough. "The Knicks told us we could
have anybody on the team," said Bucks general manager Wayne Embry.
"But we didn't want anybody they already had. We wanted to rebuild
with younger players." The Bullets, too, lacked the young players or
draft picks Milwaukee wanted. But the Lakers? Unlike the Knicks and
Bullets, two veteran teams, LA's roster had been completely overhauled
and now featured multiple top-level prospects and potentially high draft
picks.[3]

Milwaukee and L.A., trying to be coy, negotiated in secret; representatives from both teams boarded airplanes and met in Denver, finalizing the deal in the United Airlines Red Carpet Club. In the end, the Lakers surrendered two young players already on their roster (center Elmore Smith and guard Brian Winters) along with two first-round draft choices (netting the Bucks Dave Meyers and Junior Bridgeman). Los Angeles owner Jack Kent Cooke also signed Abdul-Jabbar to a five-year, $3.1 million contract extension, once again making him the NBA's highest paid player.

Growing increasingly desperate, the Knicks (now without McGinnis *or* Abdul-Jabbar) sent out feelers to thirty-nine-year-old Wilt Chamberlain. Knicks team president Mike Burke admitted that contacting Chamberlain reeked of desperation but still went ahead with talks to bring "the Dipper" to the Big Apple. Burke and general manager Eddie Donovan flew to Los Angeles and even had a number 13 Knicks jersey made up for Wilt, just in case. "We felt confident," Burke said, "but first I wanted to talk to Wilt to see if he really wanted to play as a Knick or just to draw some big money."[4]

Waiting to board their flight to LAX, Burke and Donovan received a phone call from Bill Russell, the coach and general manager of the Seattle SuperSonics, gauging Knicks interest in disgruntled superstar Spencer Haywood. "Russell and I were no longer close," Haywood later recalled. "I was trying hard not to look like his bobo . . . he was more aloof with me. . . . It was like being rejected by your father." Russell and Sam Schulman, the Sonics owner, met Burke and Donovan in LA and over several cups of coffee discussed a potential deal that might finally give the Knicks their superstar. At the same time, the planned meeting with Chamberlain fell through because Wilt was apparently still in Hawaii playing volleyball. So Schulman, Russell, Burke, and Donovan came to an agreement. The Knicks would trade a first-round pick and $1.5 million to Seattle and the Sonics would send New York their savior.[5]

News of the deal energized New York fans and players. Haywood's "talents are obvious," said forward Bill Bradley. "The thing is that when we talk about winning, we can talk about it right now. We don't have to keep kidding ourselves." Walt Frazier agreed. "Spencer will generate excitement," he said, "and that's what it's all about in New York. You don't get a year to rebuild if you are the New York Knicks." For his part,

Haywood embraced the challenge of revitalizing the once-mighty Knicks. A reporter asked Haywood about being the Knicks' savior; he just grinned and answered, "then I'll save." But for all his bravado, Haywood failed to save the Knicks. Sure, he averaged twenty points and eleven rebounds per game, but New York still finished 38–44, their second straight losing season. Knicks fans remained restless. If Haywood was not the answer, who was?[6]

New York's roster turnover was only one of many big changes taking place in the summer of 1975. In June, the NBA named a replacement for outgoing league commissioner Walter Kennedy. Leading up to the announcement, the frontrunner appeared to be thirty-four-year-old African American deputy commissioner Simon Gourdine. If appointed, Gourdine would have been the first black commissioner in any major American sport, which, as of 2016, has yet to happen. Instead of Gourdine, owners tapped Larry O'Brien, a politician with no basketball background, to the post. Gourdine was gracious in defeat and soldiered on, serving in his capacity as deputy commissioner until 1981 and then returning as the NBA players union counsel in the 1990s. "I don't think I was passed over because I'm black," Gourdine said at the time. "O'Brien is a very talented guy and the NBA needs a cool, dispassionate thinker to handle the critical issues." But in 1975, the nation was struggling with increasingly militant black activism, and its players seemed to be ever more willing to challenge authority. As hockey star Derek Sanderson said, "when the country changed, the athlete didn't stay crew cut. The athlete didn't stay where sports told him to stay." Maybe even more poignantly, Kareem Abdul-Jabbar remembered that "black athletes were aware of exactly what time it was in America." And so the hiring of O'Brien over Gourdine in a sport becoming increasingly populated by black athletes certainly raised some eyebrows.[7]

Commissioner O'Brien was not unqualified; he just brought an outsider's perspective to the job. In 1960, he managed John F. Kennedy's successful campaign for the presidency; he served as a cabinet member during the LBJ administration; and, as the chairman of the Democratic National Committee, had his office in the Watergate Hotel famously burglarized in 1972. Team owners hoped his extensive political and legal background could help shepherd them through the sticky legal situations precipitated by the botched McGinnis signing, the Abdul-

Jabbar trade, the pending Oscar Robertson lawsuit, and the potential merger with the rival ABA.

Fortunately, O'Brien's arrival coincided with the revival of basketball in Los Angeles. Kareem Abdul-Jabbar's arrival made the Lakers prohibitive favorites for the NBA title in 1976, despite having posted the second-worst record in the league a season earlier. As Lakers owner Jack Kent Cooke admitted, "we expect to win a championship." Abdul-Jabbar was even better than advertised, earning his fourth MVP award (in just seven professional seasons) after averaging almost twenty-eight points, five assists, and a league-best seventeen rebounds and four blocked shots per game. The problem was that his teammates, much like those he left in Milwaukee, simply were not a good enough supporting cast to propel the team to the top. Opponents could double- or even triple-team Abdul-Jabbar with impunity, daring his teammates to beat them. Most teams just pounded on Kareem, fouling and frustrating him and forcing his teammates to beat them. Ironically, the Lakers' solution to their lack of interior toughness was sitting on their bench, waiting his turn. Kermit Washington, the team's 1973 first-round pick, played in just thirty-six games during the 1975–1976 season and scored barely three points per contest. But in the coming seasons, Kermit would provide tough rebounding and scoring punch for Kareem and the Lakers.[8]

The 1975–1976 Lakers were also a hairy bunch of guys. In fact, a group of modern journalists known as Freedarko anointed the squad the "hairiest team" of the decade thanks to shaggy-headed Pat Riley and Gail Goodrich alongside big-haired and mustachioed Kareem Abdul-Jabbar, Corky Calhoun, and Lucius Allen. Voluminous Afros, in particular, became important league-wide fashion statements. In the sixties, the Afro symbolized black pride and African American civil rights struggles, but by the seventies, it had moved firmly into the American mainstream. Wes Unseld was one of the first NBA players to wear an Afro, sporting a tight 'fro when he arrived in the league in 1968. During the seventies, Unseld's mane grew in volume (inversely relative to his "leaping" ability). Although he was the NBA MVP for the 1968–1969 season, Unseld was upstaged in the best-hair category by a pair of ABA imports: "Doctor J" Julius Erving and "Dr. Dunk" Darnell Hillman. Erving was the greatest player in ABA history. He also sported an exceptional Afro, which flew back when he threw down thunderous slam dunks. Hillman was not nearly as good as Erving, but he might have been the star of the barber shop; his Afro rivaled any in the sports world, even New York Yankees outfielder Oscar Gamble, who had to carefully set his ball cap atop the mushroom cloud growing from his dome. Late in the decade, other NBA players followed suit, such as Artis Gilmore, another ABA transplant, who measured nearly eight feet tall with his large Afro when he joined the Bulls in 1976.[9]

Hirsute or hairless, many NBA players in the seventies were fashion conscious; during the decade, their style choices changed dramatically. Bell-bottoms, polyester fabrics, and chest hair? In. Mod, tailor-made suits and "Beatles-esque" mop-top hairstyles? Out. Young African American men in particular adopted the funky James Brown look—high-heeled boots, leather jackets, silk print shirts, gold chains, and tight slacks. Even the coaches got in on the style game. Larry Brown sported a pair of overalls on the sidelines, whereas Dr. Jack Ramsay preferred garish plaid pants. But Golden State Warriors coach Al Attles had them all beat, sporting *Super Fly* polyester leisure suits and wide-collared silk print shirts as he pushed his team to the 1975 title.

Attles's Warriors clearly expected to successfully defend their championship and remained the deepest team in the league with nine players who averaged at least fifteen minutes of playing time per game. But their undisputed star was still Rick Barry, even after he spent the off-season deciding whether or not to retire and become a broadcaster. Convinced to return, Barry earned the most All-Star votes of any player in the league and first-team All-NBA recognition while one again pacing the league in free throw percentage (shooting underhanded, of course). Barry was also the only significant contributor on the Warriors team with white skin, leading starting center Clifford Ray to dub the team "the Golden Prince and his Black Knights."[10]

Although the prince and his knights were clearly the best team in the Pacific (and maybe in the entire league), the Seattle SuperSonics were rapidly closing the gap. Coach Bill Russell, who doubled as the team's general manager, shook up the roster in the off-season, sending Haywood to New York and oft-injured guard Archie Clark to Detroit, picking up two first-round draft picks and a couple million dollars in the process. Russell rebuilt his team around gigantic second-year center Tom "the Needle" Burleson and the exciting guard tandem of Donald "Slick" Watts (a bald-headed, sweatband-wearing, brash point guard who led the league in assists—8.1—and steals—3.18) and "Downtown" Freddie Brown, an All-Star who led the team in scoring. For the second straight season, Seattle won forty-three games but definitely seemed to be headed in the right direction under their Hall of Fame coach.

Three hours south of Seattle down Interstate 5, the Portland Trail Blazers stagnated. Portland followed a thirty-eight-win season with a thirty-seven win season, finishing almost exactly in the middle of the NBA in both points scored and points allowed. Much of the fault for the Blazers' inability to improve was laid at the feet (literally) of under-achieving big man Bill Walton. Walton missed almost half the season with foot and back problems, and rumors circulated around the league that the injury-prone Walton might never be fully healthy. He was also an off-court distraction whose personal distaste for the U.S. govern-ment made fans and the media question his patriotism. But when Wal-ton was healthy enough to play, Blazers fans could generally overlook these faults. After all, Walton was a basketball savant: an excellent scor-er, passer, defender, and rebounder. In his absence, the Blazers once again reverted to the (Sidney) Wicks and (Geoff) Petrie show. And once again, the quarrelsome twosome responded with excellent individual statistics (nineteen points and nine rebounds for Wicks and nineteen points and five assists from Petrie) but few wins. By the end of the season, questions abounded in Rip City. Could Walton ever be the best player on a title team? And could Petrie and/or Wicks be a part of that success? Fortunately for Blazers fans, these questions would be an-swered definitively (yes and no, respectively) in a few short months.

Before the 1976 season, one national publication predicted that "it's hard to see how the Suns can escape the cellar" in arguably the league's best division. Somewhat miraculously, Phoenix finished above last place, winning forty-two games despite trading away their leading scor-er, Charlie Scott, to the Boston Celtics. In return for Scott, the Suns picked up Paul Westphal, who became a star in the Arizona desert, more than doubling his scoring average to a team-leading twenty points per game. Westphal played ambidextrously, scoring on daring drives to the hoop and finishing with either hand. But Westphal was not the only important new addition in Phoenix, as the Suns drafted Alvan Adams from Oklahoma, where Phoenix head coach John McLeod had recruit-ed Adams to play four years earlier. Adams and Westphal immediately demonstrated great chemistry as Adams, who relied on a feathery outside jump shot and deft passing ability to overcome his undersized six-foot-nine frame, seemed to know exactly where his high-scoring teammate was on the floor at all times. MacLeod also used his Oklahoma connection in trading for veteran Garfield Heard, another former Sooner, who helped turn the season around. The Suns started the year 18–27 before picking up Heard and finishing strong to make the playoffs.

Adams took home rookie of the year honors in 1976, although, in accepting the trophy, even he acknowledged how much he benefitted from a few top draft choices signing with ABA teams. "I'd like to thank Coach John MacLeod," Adams began, "my teammates for making me look so good," he continued, "and, mostly, David Thompson for going to the ABA." Adams also earned a spot on the 1976 All-Star team as a rookie, his only appearance in the game. In the history of the NBA, only five players (Don Sunderlage and Ray Felix in 1954, Luke Jackson in 1965, and Bill Cartwright in 1980) earned that distinction. [11]

In many ways, then, Adams was a one-year wonder, a fad. Appropriately enough, the winter and spring of the 1975–1976 season was a popular time for such fads. That December, two of the most popular gifts under Christmas trees were the mood ring and the pet rock. For a cool $45 (or less for a knockoff), you could wear a piece of jewelry revealing your inner feelings. There were certainly NBA players who might have benefited from this increased self-awareness. Rick Barry's mood ring? Black. He rarely seemed at ease. Lloyd "All World" Free's? Definitely blue. Free was relaxed and calm, almost to a fault. And John "Hondo" Havlicek's? Green. Because Hondo seemed even to bleed Celtics green. The pet rock demonstrated an even greater level of marketing genius. It was, as the name implies, a rock—but this rock (retail price, just $4) came with a custom cardboard box and a thirty-two-page training manual. If you put on your mood ring and played with your pet rock while listening to "Disco Duck" by Rick Dees and His Cast of Idiots (maybe *the* ultimate one-hit wonder of the seventies) and watching Alvan Adams's Suns on television, you would have been in fad heaven.

While the Suns and the rest of the NBA's Pacific Division was strong from top to bottom, the Midwest was definitely the league's weakest as Milwaukee (38–44) and Detroit (36–46) both made the playoffs despite sub-.500 records. The most pleasant surprise in the Midwest was the Milwaukee Bucks. After trading away Kareem Abdul-Jabbar for pennies on the dollar, most Bucks fans expected the team to struggle. But the players acquired from Los Angeles helped Milwaukee to become one of the best young teams in the league. New center Elmore Smith finished second in the league in blocked shots (behind only Kareem), tossing back more than three per game; guard Brian Winters, the crown jewel of the Lakers trade, earned an All-Star berth with his eighteen point-per-game average; and rookies Dave Meyers and Junior Bridgeman each turned in strong first seasons. But it was veteran Bob Dandridge who was the real star, upping his scoring average to more than twenty-one points per game. Apparently, Milwaukee fans thought highly of their team; they stuffed All-Star ballot boxes to give Winters a starting assignment in the game and to make Dandridge, Smith, Meyers, and point guard Jim Price among the top three at their respective positions, ahead of far superior players. The Bucks were not a franchise in decline but were on the rise; amazingly, they won just as many games in the first year of the post–Abdul-Jabbar era as they had in his final season wearing Bucks green.

The Bucks probably exceeded expectations, but the other three teams in the Midwest definitely disappointed. The Detroit Pistons, expected to compete for the division title with Kareem out of Milwaukee, managed just thirty wins; the newly renamed Kansas City Kings (who played just a handful of games in Nebraska and dropped the hyphenated Omaha) fell to 31–51, despite the continued brilliance of point guard Tiny Archibald (24.8 points and 7.9 assists per game); and the reigning division winners from Chicago plummeted during the 1975–1976 season, winning twenty-three fewer games than they had the year before.

After falling to Golden State in the 1975 Western Conference finals, Bulls general manager and head coach Dick Motta blamed preseason holdouts Bob Love and Norm Van Lier for their postseason loss. "I would like in the worst way to get rid of Love and Van Lier," Motta groused, calling Love "the greediest player in the league." Unsurprisingly, Love and Van Lier were equally unhappy with Motta. Van Lier gamely played through his frustrations, but Love became a distraction. "Chicago is racist," Love said. "I don't get respect. I don't get endorsements. The coach plays me like a mule, then he doesn't pay me what I'm worth. I'd love to get out of here and play somewhere else." Like Love, fellow forward Chet "the Jet" Walker wanted a new contract; unlike Love, he decided to retire when Bulls management refused to renegotiate. Losing Walker left a gaping hole in the Bulls offense. In the past, Walker could be counted on to go one-on-one and create a scoring opportunity for himself as the shot clock ticked down, but now, without Walker, the team struggled offensively, finishing dead last in the league in scoring. To make matters worse, Nate Thurmond, acquired from the Warriors to be the final piece of a championship-winning team, was a disappointment. In November, the Bulls all but gave Thurmond to Cleveland. Poor team chemistry, retirements, and injuries decimated the Bulls, who dropped like a stone to the bottom of the Midwest.[12]

Thurmond left Chicago (a perennial contender) for Cleveland (a laughingstock). The Cavaliers, now in their sixth season, had never posted a winning record and appeared destined for another middle-of-the-road finish during the 1975–1976 season. But then, seemingly out of nowhere, the Cavs won forty-nine games and took home their first division title. Cleveland started slowly, opening the season 6–11. Then they traded for Thurmond. Click. Nate scored only five points a game as a backup center, but he became the heart and soul of the Cavs. Teammate Jim Chones remembered that "when we got Nate we were off to the races." In fact, Thurmond was so beloved in his short tenure in Cleveland that he became the first Cavalier to have his jersey retired by the team.[13]

Thurmond might have been the spiritual leader of the team, but the strength of the Cavaliers was its balance and depth; seven players averaged double figures in points, and ten played at least fifteen minutes per game. Starting guards Jim Cleamons, Bobby "Bingo" Smith, and Dick Snyder all stood between six-three and six-five and were castoffs acquired by the Cavs for a song. Forward Jim Brewer looked like a bust in his first two pro seasons after being drafted second overall in 1973, but he became a double-double machine, averaging eleven each of points and rebounds during the 1975–1976 season. Center Jim Chones was also a reclamation project, having jumped to the ABA in the middle of his junior year at Marquette (with his team undefeated and ranked second in the NCAA at the time). Chones underachieved in the ABA after signing a much-maligned $1 million contract and was cut by the ABA's Carolina Cougars before catching on with Cleveland. Off the bench, the Cavaliers featured two legitimate scoring threats: former top draft picks Campy Russell and Austin Carr. Carr, long considered a star in waiting, eased into what would become his customary role over the last six years of his career: an instant scorer with knee injuries that limited his minutes and mobility. Russell, meanwhile, was on the upswing and drew comparisons to former Bulls great Chet Walker for his one-on-one scoring ability. Bringing Russell and Carr off the bench meant the Cavaliers always had the ability to score with opponents. But it was their defense that really made the Cavs contenders as they finished second in the league (trailing only Chicago) in points allowed per game.

Finishing behind Cleveland in the Central Division was the defending conference champion Washington Bullets. After losing to the underdog Warriors in the '75 finals, Bullets management decided to go into win-now mode, trading young point guard Kevin Porter (who clashed with head coach K. C. Jones and many of his teammates) for steady veteran Dave Bing, a six-time All-Star and Washington, D.C., native. The thirty-two-year-old Bing was solid if unspectacular in his first year with the Bullets, averaging sixteen points and six assists per game and winning the All-Star game MVP award. But the team's real strength remained veteran big men Elvin Hayes and Wes Unseld. Hayes once again scored better than twenty points per game, and Unseld led the league in field goal percentage (56 percent) and (unofficially) in throwing pinpoint outlet passes and delivering intimidating scowls. Despite the team's solid starting five, their offense struggled (dropping from the top third to the bottom third in scoring), and they won just forty-eight games, a dozen fewer than the year before.

The Houston Rockets were stuck in a rut: good enough to avoid a high draft pick, but not good enough to seriously contend for the title. For the second straight year, Houston finished right around .500 (40–42 following a 41–41 season), and the team's top players remained the pint-sized but pugnacious Calvin "the Pocket Rocket" Murphy and the blue-collar Rudy Tomjanovich. From his point guard spot, Murphy set a league record, since broken, by connecting on fifty-eight straight free throws and finished second in the league from the charity stripe (90.7 percent). Flanking Murphy, Tomjanovich played like a young Dave DeBusschere, battling for rebounds and scrapping on defense, though Rudy T was a better scorer. In fact, Hall of Famer Hal Greer called Tomjanovich "one of the greatest pure shooters of all time" and the second-best bank shooter ever, behind only Celtics legend Sam Jones.

Rudy T and the Pocket Rocket were a very good duo, but they alone could not carry Houston deep into the playoffs.[14]

Behind the Cavaliers, Bullets, and Rockets in the Central Division were two teams linked by more than geography. The New Orleans Jazz and Atlanta Hawks were both southern cities in a predominantly northern league but were more closely associated because of the 1974 trade sending "Pistol Pete" Maravich from Atlanta to New Orleans.

Maravich entered his second season in New Orleans determined to prove to his critics that he could put team success above individual statistics. When he reported to training camp, he barely resembled the man who entered the league as a skinny youngster from LSU. Gone were the floppy gray socks, the number 44 jersey, and the droopy mustache. The new Pistol Pete was clean shaven and wore number 7 (and the single word "Pistol") on his gaudy, Mardi Gras–inspired purple, green, and gold Jazz jersey. Whether due to the number change or maybe in spite of it, the 1975–1976 season was certainly memorable for Maravich and his Jazz teammates. They played their home games in the cavernous Louisiana Superdome, which could seat more than 50,000. Pete and the Jazz began to fill it. In one early November game against the Lakers, a record 26,611 fans piled into the Superdome despite monsoon-like rain that doubtlessly kept some at home. In fact, the rain almost derailed Maravich, and the team had to send a boat to his home to ferry him to the arena. Ever the showman, Pistol Pete dropped in thirty points that night to lead the Jazz to victory. The crowds continued to grow and Maravich continued to entertain. On the season, Pistol Pete averaged twenty-six points, five rebounds, and five assists, earning him a spot on the All-NBA first team. Yet Pete remained an enigma. As one biographer recalled of Maravich, "he seemed a man of contrary impulses—a flamboyant player on the court but guardedly private off the court; a vegetarian who espoused the virtues of alfalfa sprouts and whole-grain bread but continued drinking to excess." On the court, Maravich clearly needed help: a better supporting cast would have enabled the Jazz to win more than thirty-eight games. But off the court, Maravich also needed help; he was a troubled young man struggling with alcoholism and the pressure of being one of the country's most recognizable athletes.[15]

The team that dealt Maravich—and who everyone outside New Orleans agreed had ripped off the Jazz—struggled mightily. Atlanta counted on using the draft picks acquired from New Orleans on one of two players: North Carolina State guard David "Skywalker" Thompson, a high-flying six-foot-four phenom who was a three-time All-American and two-time national player of the year, or Marvin "the Human Eraser" Webster, a seven footer from Morgan State who averaged—yes, averaged—twenty-one points, twenty-two rebounds, and eight blocked shots per game in leading the tiny Baltimore school to a Division II title.

Thompson and Webster were can't-miss prospects, and the Hawks drafted both. Atlanta selected Thompson with the first overall pick (acquired from the Jazz) and Webster with the third (their own pick) in the 1975 collegiate draft. But the Hawks were unable to sign either of them. Atlanta was a rebuilding team, and Thompson refused to be the savior of the franchise, explaining that "I had seen how they skewered Pete Maravich there." The Hawks also struggled to meet payroll and still faced heavy fines levied by the NBA when the team illegally signed Julius Erving a few seasons earlier. "They needed me and Webster to generate high ticket sales to help the franchise out of its dire financial straits," Thompson said. "But because they were low on cash, they could not afford us." Both players ultimately signed instead with the ABA's Denver Nuggets, leaving the Hawks with little to show for the Maravich deal. "It was," one journalist wrote, "the greatest disaster in Atlanta since the Union soldiers marched through." Scrambling to fill out their roster and boost attendance, the Hawks traded for aging Connie "the Hawk" Hawkins to play alongside young star forward John Drew and veteran guard "Sweet" Lou Hudson. Even with Hawkins, Drew, and Hudson, the Hawks struggled, finishing with the second-worst record (29–53) and the lowest average attendance (just over 5,500 per game) in the league.[16]

As Hawks fans stayed away, Philadelphia 76ers backers had much to celebrate. During the 1973–1974 season, they set an NBA record with seventy-three losses and finished at the bottom of the Atlantic Division. Two years later, they posted a winning record (46–36) and finished second in the Atlantic. Unsurprisingly, the arrival of strongman George McGinnis (the Knicks' loss was Philly's gain, after all) helped tremendously. He put up unbelievable statistics in his first NBA season (23 points per game, 12.6 rebounds per game, 4.7 assists per game), and journalists named him to the All-NBA first team; some even mentioned him as a potential MVP candidate.

Coming out of high school, McGinnis had turned down two hundred football scholarship offers to attend Indiana and play basketball for Lou Watson (in his last season before being replaced by a young Bobby Knight). Even in college, he was almost unguardable. "He was like a man among boys," Dick McGuire, a New York Knicks scout recalled, and one NBA general manager at the time quipped that, "George has muscles in places where other guys don't even have places." McGinnis shined at Indiana, averaging thirty points and fifteen rebounds per game and left after his sophomore year. "I went to college to play basketball, not to be a doctor or lawyer," McGinnis said. "When my class graduated from college, I already had two years of [professional basketball] experience and a little money." He starred for the Indiana Pacers for four seasons (winning two championship rings) before agreeing to a huge contract with Philadelphia—his backup choice after a deal with the Knicks fell through. Despite McGinnis's flaws (as *Boston Globe* reporter Bob Ryan wrote, "he still must be pulled from games at some very interesting moments because of his lack of basketball common sense"), many NBA insiders—maybe even a majority—preferred McGinnis to "Dr. J" Julius Erving. Although unbelievable today, it was a real debate then. As one former ABA coach recalled, "there were serious arguments in the ABA about who was better—McGinnis or Julius Erving. That was the kind of talent a young McGinnis had." McGinnis was bigger and stronger with two healthy knees; Dr. J was a proven commodity, but the "Baby Bull" probably had greater potential.[17]

Tied with the Sixers for second place in the Atlantic were the high-scoring Buffalo Braves. Under head coach Dr. Jack Ramsay, Buffalo boasted the second-best offense in the league as reigning MVP Bob McAdoo once again led the NBA in scoring (31.1 points per game) and twice tallied at least fifty. But Buffalo's flashy point guard Ernie Di-Gregorio struggled. In 1974, sportswriters named Ernie D as their rookie of the year; two years later he was a forgotten benchwarmer. The Braves were an up-and-coming team but were no longer the surefire title contenders they had been in 1974.

Buffalo's blueprint was the Atlantic Division champion Boston Celtics, whose roster revolved around three stars: Dave Cowens, John Havlicek, and Jo Jo White. But before the season, Celtics president Red Auerbach added a wild card, sending backup Paul Westphal to Phoenix for enigmatic guard Charlie Scott. Scott, an All-Star performer in both the NBA and ABA, seemed to be everything the Celtics were not. Boston relied on pressure defense, an up-tempo offensive attack, and selfless ball movement; Scott preferred to freelance and play one-on-one (or one-on-five, if he was really feeling it). "Charlie's going to learn our style of play," one teammate promised. "If he doesn't he's going to end up in a hospital." Scott was undeniably talented. But could he coexist with White in the Boston backcourt? At first, the answer was no. "The disdain [White] held for Scott carried over to their Celtic partnership," one journalist wrote. "The two guards spent the first half of the 1975–1976 season fighting for control of the ball and for turf." Predictably, Boston struggled out of the gate and, after seventeen games, stood at 10–7. But they soon found their rhythm, rattling off a nine-game winning streak, and never looked back. As it turned out, even Scott fell into line, in part because of the team's veteran leadership.[18]

In a February game against Houston, for example, Cowens set an important tone. The fiery redhead drove to the basket but was called for charging when he bumped into Mike Newlin. Stunned by the call, Cowens took off like a shot, head down, and dropped his shoulder into an unsuspecting Newlin, knocking the Rockets guard to the ground. Cowens turned to a nearby referee and barked, "Now that's a fucking foul." With Cowens playing like an angry junkyard dog, Havlicek running around like someone much younger than his thirty-five years, Paul Silas sweeping the boards, and both Scott and White streaking downcourt for easy layups, Boston won a league-high fifty-four games.[19]

In 1976, the playoffs included ten teams—five per conference—and featured exciting games from start to finish. In one opening-round, best-of-three series, the Philadelphia 76ers and Buffalo Braves came down to overtime in a winner-take-all game three. With just over thirty seconds remaining in the extra period and with the Braves clinging to a three-point lead, Sixers guard Fred Carter missed an off-balance shot. Steve Mix, who had thrown a punch at a Braves player earlier in the game but somehow avoided ejection, tipped in the errant shot to pull the Sixers within a single point. Seventeen seconds remained on the clock and the Sixers fouled Bob McAdoo, who approached the line. As he squared for his first shot, a female Sixers fan ran down to the court and shook the basket support—security was somewhat lax—and the crowd grew louder and louder, willing McAdoo to miss. He didn't. His

two free throws gave the Braves a three-point lead and the Sixers—
unable to score a three-point field goal, as it was not yet a part of the
NBA—fell by one, sending Buffalo to a semifinals meeting with the
Celtics. In the West, Milwaukee and Detroit also went to a third game
in their opening-round series. The Pistons overcame a late seven-point
deficit and led by one with less than a minute remaining. With a chance
to take the lead, the Bucks' inbounds pass was intercepted and the
Pistons survived, winning by three to earn a shot at the defending
champion Golden State Warriors.

Three of the four second-round matchups lacked drama: Boston,
Golden State, and Phoenix each won their respective series in six
games. But there was plenty of drama in the Eastern Conference semifinal between Cleveland and Washington, the so-called Miracle of
Richfield.

Most fans and sportswriters saw the Cavaliers as underdogs against
the more experienced Bullets. But Washington was not about to overlook the upstarts from Cleveland. "Sure I think they can win," Wes
Unseld said. "Cleveland is like the old Knicks. They shoot from outside,
run their plays well and don't let you fast break." After one game,
though, Unseld's statement looked foolish: the Cavs lost at home by five
in front of a team-record 19,994 fans. But the Cavaliers were resilient.
In game two, Cleveland earned a one-point win after guard Bingo
Smith drained a twenty-two footer as time expired. Game three was not
as close; the Cavs won by a dozen, much to the delight of the new-
record 21,061 fans in attendance. Despite losing game four in Washington, Cleveland fans were becoming fanatical about their Cavs. Game
five took place in front of, yes, a new record crowd packed into Richfield Coliseum. With just seconds remaining, Dick Snyder inbounded
the ball to Bingo Smith, the hero of game two, for another potential
game winner. This time, Bingo shot an air ball. But six-foot-tall guard
Jim Cleamons slipped behind the Bullets defenders, snatched the rebound, and scored on a twisting layup to give the Cavaliers another
exhilarating win. After the game, one Cleveland reporter wrote that
"Cavalier basketball is becoming a religious experience," deciding that
instead of counting the crowd by attendance, "they should measure it in
decibels." After dropping game six—in overtime, of course—in Washington, the teams returned to Cleveland for the decisive seventh game
in one of the most thrilling series in league history.[20]

April 1976 was a busy month. Two college dropouts (both named Steve—Jobs and Wozniak) started a computer company that they called Apple, and three hundred miles down Interstate 5 in Los Angeles, Chicago Cubs centerfielder Rick Monday saved an American flag from being burned by two protestors in the grass of Dodger Stadium. Journalists praised Monday's patriotism, particularly since Americans were prepping for a celebration of the American bicentennial. People around the country draped buildings and mailboxes in red, white, and blue bunting and painted fire hydrants to look like heroes of the revolutionary era. Some probably decorated while dancing to the latest pop hit, Johnnie Taylor's "Disco Lady," which encouraged listeners to "shake it up, shake it down, move it in, move it out."

In Cleveland and Washington, hoops fans were far more interested in the decisive seventh game of their hard-fought series than in, say, the newest *Sports Illustrated* swimsuit edition featuring twins Yvette and Yvonne Sylvander. Hal Lebovitz, a well-known Cleveland sportswriter, wrote before game seven that "the two teams have played so well, somehow it seems unfair that one has to lose tonight." Two hours before tip-off, 21,564 Cavaliers die-hards (another record) packed into Richfield Coliseum, rocking the arena and relentlessly booing their new archenemies from Washington. In the Bullets' locker room, Coach K. C. Jones had a player steady the chalkboard, which was shaking with the crowd noise. In the '70s, before the Internet or even cable television, fans from around the country following the series called into the local newspaper requesting score updates, while thousands more strained to hear longtime Cavaliers announcer Joe Tait call what would become perhaps the greatest game in team history.[21]

Unsurprisingly, game seven was close throughout and, with just seconds left, the score was tied at eighty-five. The hometown Cavaliers had the basketball with a chance to win in regulation, and Cleveland guard Dick Snyder massaged the ball, guarded by the lumbering Bullets center Wes Unseld. Hoping to get around the titanic Washington big man, Snyder took a dribble but found himself face-to-face with Phil Chenier, arguably the Bullets' best defender. In desperation, Snyder threw up a high-arching shot from about six feet away. "It wasn't the sweetest shot," Snyder later admitted. His coach agreed. "Just the Good Lord and Dick Snyder knew what was going to happen when Snyder got the ball," Coach Bill Fitch quipped. "And for a time, only the Good Lord knew." Miraculously, the ball banked off the backboard and dropped through the net, giving the Cavaliers a two-point lead with just four seconds left on the clock. Chenier missed a desperation eighteen footer as time expired, and Cleveland fans rushed the court. The "Miracle of Richfield" had made converts of the mass of Clevelanders pouring onto the floor. "It was unreal," remembered Cavaliers guard Austin Carr. "It was like a flood. . . . I'll never forget the noise." Fans tore down the baskets and spilled into the city streets, cars honking and fists pumping. "The Washington series," one Cleveland sportswriter decided, "was the greatest sporting event I will ever see in my life."[22]

Despite the Cavaliers' resilience in outlasting the Bullets, their Cinderella season came to an abrupt end against the powerful Celtics in the Eastern Conference finals; Boston won in six. In the Western Conference finals, the heavily favored Golden State Warriors and underdog Phoenix Suns matched up for the right to play the Celtics for the NBA title. Golden State and Phoenix split the first six games, including a double-overtime thriller in game four, won by the Suns. Even stretched to a seventh game, the Warriors, defending their title, remained the favorites. But in game seven, Golden State star forward Rick Barry came unhinged and likely cost his team the conference title. In the first few minutes of the game, Phoenix guard Ricky Sobers jumped Barry and punched him, the fight spilling into the stands where fans "literally pulled [Suns forward Curtis Perry] over the press table and pummeled him in the back." But it was Barry, watching the replay during halftime and recognizing that his teammates had not come to his aid, whose play suffered the most. In the second half, Barry went into what sportswriter Bill Simmons called "an elaborate game of 'eff you'" with his teammates, daring "the Black Knights" to save the season for the "Golden Prince." Final score: Phoenix 94, Golden State 86. "We deserved to lose," Barry complained afterward, arguing that "I never touched the ball sometimes. It was a total breakdown. Ridiculous." Coach Al Attles was diplomatic in defeat, agreeing that his team had not played hard, but refusing to single out Barry. Regardless of why the Warriors lost, their game seven collapse sent the "Sunderella" Suns to the finals, where their forty-two wins ranked among the lowest for any conference champion ever. "The Warriors had depth, speed, defense, poise, togetherness, experience and Rick Barry," one journalist wrote. "When the Suns upended them, the basketball-speaking world was speech-less."[23]

On paper, the Boston–Phoenix finals matchup seemed completely lopsided. Twelve championship banners hung from the rafters of the historic Boston Garden, including one from 1974, just two years earlier; the Suns had no banners. In fact, they had managed only three winning years in their eight NBA seasons. Following that script, Boston easily won games one and two to take a commanding 2–0 series lead. But Phoenix answered with wins in games three and four (which Boston coach Tommy Heinsohn blamed on poor officiating) to send the series back to Boston for the pivotal fifth game.

Game five of the 1976 finals is on the short list of the greatest games in NBA history. Midway through the first quarter, though, it looked like just another Celtics rout: Boston led 32–12. By halftime, the Suns had shaved the lead to fifteen, and after intermission their defense dominated, holding the high-scoring Celtics to just thirty-four second-half points. In the final moments, with the score knotted at ninety-five, Suns forward Curtis Perry missed two free throws, and Havlicek, playing with torn fascia in his right foot, also clanged a pair. As time expired in regulation, Celtics forward Paul Silas signaled for a time-out but referee Richie Powers intentionally ignored him. Powers knew Boston was out of timeouts and that assessing them a technical foul for the infraction could decide the game at the free throw line. Phoenix's coaching staff was irate and could not believe the no-call. In fact, assistant coach Al Bianchi never forgave Powers and later had a championship ring made for himself with the personalized message "Fuck you, Richie Powers" inscribed on it to remind him of game five. Given another chance, the Celtics managed to draw the game into overtime as midnight neared in Boston.[24]

The first overtime ended in a tie and with fifteen seconds left in the second extra period, the Celtics clung to a three-point lead. Boston fans rocked the arena with chants of "we're number one." But two quick baskets put the Suns back on top. With no time-outs remaining (this time, Silas did not signal for an illegal one), the Celtics worked the ball to Havlicek, who threw in an off-balance fifteen footer that seemed to seal Boston's win. Fans poured on the floor, assaulting Suns players and even referee Powers, who wrestled his attacker to the ground as players tried to pull the two apart. Finally, Powers disentangled himself from the crowd and security helped clear the court.

One second remained on the clock. It seemed a mere formality; Phoenix had to inbound the ball from the baseline opposite their basket, ninety-four feet away. But Suns star Paul Westphal, who became an accomplished coach in the early 1990s with the team, realized his squad still had a chance. He convinced coach John MacLeod to call a timeout, which the Suns did not have, and take the assessed technical foul. By rule, the Suns would receive the ball at midcourt, giving them a far better chance at a last-second basket. MacLeod agreed. Jo Jo White made the free throw from the assessed technical to put the Celtics back up by two. Security and fans edged closer to the court and Powers had to push them back to clear the floor for the final second of play. Boston coach Tom Heinsohn inserted six-eight Jim Ard to defend the inbounder, forward Curtis Perry. Suns players tried to set a screen to free Westphal for the last shot, but Ard was jumping up and down, waving his hands, and Perry could not find an opening. As a last resort, and with his five allotted seconds to inbound the ball ticking away, Perry threw the basketball to Gar Heard. Heard was a terrible shooter—one writer joked that Heard was known to "shoot air balls from five feet"—and the Celtics were happy to let Heard try a desperation twenty footer. Heard caught the pass, turned toward the basket, and let fly a high-arching shot just over the outstretched hand of Don Nelson. Heard's shot hit the rim and bounced through the net. Boston fans deflated: the game was headed to a third overtime tied at 112. Three of the five Celtics starters had already fouled out, leaving White and the hobbled Havlicek with a menagerie of unlikely reserves representing the team's best chance to win the game.[25]

Remarkably, benchwarmer Glenn McDonald (who played in just nine more games in his career after the '76 finals) scored eight points to lead Boston in the third overtime. Final score: Boston 128, Phoenix 126. Time elapsed: three hours, eight minutes. Rick Barry, hired by CBS to provide color commentary for the series, perhaps best summed up the collective sentiment of fans watching game five, declaring it "the most exciting basketball game I've ever seen."[26]

After the exhilarating fifth game, game six proved anticlimactic. Although it was close until midway through the fourth quarter, a Boston win was never really in doubt, and the Celtics, by virtue of their 87–80 victory, claimed the 1976 NBA finals four games to two as the clock struck midnight for the Sunderella Suns. "We were no fairy tale," insisted Phoenix's Curtis Perry. "We were for real." Whether or not the Suns could become an annual contender was up in the air in the spring of 1976, as was the potential for the aging Celtics to repeat. But what was not in doubt was that the league was about to undergo a serious transformation. In fact, the 1976 finals became the last before the long-awaited merger shook the league to its core.[27]

Statistics for 1975–1976

Eastern Conference	W	L	Western Conference	W	L
Atlantic Division			*Midwest Division*		
Boston Celtics	54	28	Milwaukee Bucks	38	44
Philadelphia 76ers	46	36	Detroit Pistons	36	46
Buffalo Braves	46	36	Kansas City Kings	31	51
New York Knicks	38	44	Chicago Bulls	24	58
Central Division			*Pacific Division*		
Cleveland Cavaliers	49	33	Golden State Warriors	59	23
Washington Bullets	48	34	Seattle SuperSonics	43	39
Houston Rockets	40	42	Phoenix Suns	42	40
New Orleans Jazz	38	44	Los Angeles Lakers	40	42
Atlanta Hawks	29	53	Portland Trail Blazers	37	45

Playoffs

Eastern Conference First Round	Buffalo d. Philadelphia (2–1)
Western Conference First Round	Detroit d. Milwaukee (2–1)
Eastern Conference Semifinals	Boston d. Buffalo (4–2)
	Cleveland d. Washington (4–3)
Western Conference Semifinals	Golden State d. Detroit (4–2)
	Phoenix d. Seattle (4–2)
Eastern Conference Finals	Boston d. Cleveland (4–2)
Western Conference Finals	Phoenix d. Golden State (4–3)
NBA Finals	Boston d. Phoenix (4–2)

All-NBA Teams

First Team	Second Team
F—Rick Barry (Golden State)	F—Elvin Hayes (Washington)
F—George McGinnis (Philadelphia)	F—John Havlicek (Boston)
C—Kareem Abdul-Jabbar (Los Angeles)	C—Dave Cowens (Boston)
G—Pete Maravich (New Orleans)	G—Randy Smith (Buffalo)
G—Nate "Tiny" Archibald (Kansas City)	G—Phil Smith (Golden State)

League Leaders

Points per Game (31.1)	Bob McAdoo (Buffalo)
Rebounds per Game (16.9)	Kareem Abdul-Jabbar (Los Angeles)
Assists per Game (8.1)	Slick Watts (Seattle)
Steals per Game (3.2)	Slick Watts (Seattle)
Blocks per Game (4.1)	Kareem Abdul-Jabbar (Los Angeles)
Most Valuable Player	Kareem Abdul-Jabbar (Los Angeles)
Rookie of the Year	Alvan Adams (Phoenix)

Time-Out

The Merger

We had no plan. None. We wanted to start a second basketball league and force the NBA to merge with us. That was a goal. But a plan? We had none. We went by the seat of our pants and made it up as we went along. If a rule didn't fit with something we wanted to do, we just changed it or ignored it. If someone had an idea, no matter how lame-brained, usually someone tried it.[1] —Dick Tinkham, owner of the ABA's Indiana Pacers

In the summer of 1976, people across the nation prepared for the two-hundredth anniversary of American independence by hanging red, white, and blue bunting from their homes and painting fire hydrants to look like Revolutionary War soldiers. They also flocked to movie theaters that summer to watch Robert Redford and Dustin Hoffman in the political thriller, *All the President's Men*, and jammed to the Sylvers' catchy disco hit "Boogie Fever."

But for basketball fans, the summer took on added importance. Instead of the usual arguments about favorite players and teams, hot stove discussions revolved around a long-anticipated business deal. After a decade of litigation, the war between the National Basketball Association (NBA) and the American Basketball Association (ABA) came to an end. The ABA-NBA merger both transformed the on-court product of pro basketball by emphasizing a more athletic style of play and revolutionized the business of the sport as young men began to enter the pro ranks before graduating from college and used their collective bargaining power to gain the right of free agency.

The ABA began as the brainchild of Buena Park, California, mayor Dennis Murphy. In the mid-sixties, Murphy tried to join the American Football League, an upstart organization competing with the mighty National Football League. But Murphy got in too late, and before he could secure funding, the football leagues merged, earning AFL owners millions of dollars in the process. So Murphy (who later dreamed up the World Hockey Association and World Team Tennis circuit) switched to plan B: pro basketball. Why basketball? "I saw that the NBA had twelve [teams]," Murphy said. "It seemed like there should be more teams. Why? I don't know. What the hell, it was worth a shot."[2]

In January 1967, the NFL's Green Bay Packers defeated the AFL's Kansas City Chiefs in the very first Super Bowl. But for Dennis Murphy, it was already basketball season. He and ABA commissioner George Mikan (a legendary center for the old Minneapolis Lakers) were hard at work, trying to identify potential franchise owners for their new league. By midyear, Murphy and Mikan managed to cobble together a league with eleven teams geographically spread from New Jersey to California. With a commissioner, owners, and teams in place, a new problem emerged: who was going to play?

Early ABA rosters featured players plucked from basketball's minor leagues, a homegrown college star or two, and a handful of men blacklisted from the NBA—including the league's first MVP, Connie "the Hawk" Hawkins. Some teams even held open tryouts, giving hundreds of weekend warriors a shot at pro ball.

To force a merger, though, the ABA desperately needed established stars. And to make that happen, the league needed to steal talented players from the NBA. Unfortunately for ABA owners, few veteran players were willing to bet on the new league at the risk of being blackballed by the NBA. Of course that didn't stop ABA owners from dreaming. In 1967, the owners met in secret and drafted NBA players to their rosters. "We were deluding ourselves into thinking that all these NBA guys would jump leagues," Pacers owner Dick Tinkham said. "Of course it didn't take long for reality to set in."[3]

In fact, only one NBA star jumped to the ABA in its first season: San Francisco Warriors forward Rick Barry. To sign Barry, the Oakland

Oaks made an offer Barry could hardly refuse: a promise to play for his college coach (and father-in-law) Bruce Hale and a three-year, $225,000 contract (nearly double his NBA salary). Although his deal with the Warriors was up for renewal, Barry was bound to the team through basketball's reserve clause. If Barry wanted to play for another team, he would have to sit out an entire season—his "option year." Warriors owner Franklin Mieuli sued both the Oaks and Barry, arguing that the reserve clause bound Barry to the Warriors for one year after the expiration of his contract. In essence, pro basketball owners—along with their counterparts in Major League Baseball and the National Football League—used the reserve clause to keep a player in perpetuity. Barring a trade, there was almost no way for a player to switch teams. This kept salaries artificially low, since athletes could not sell their services on the open market. Barry and his lawyers countersued, arguing that the reserve clause violated the Sherman Antitrust Act. The NBA, they charged, was a monopoly.

In 1922, the Supreme Court gave Major League Baseball an antitrust exemption, but pro basketball had no such legal protection. Rick Barry was a pioneer, paving the way for free agency in American pro sports by challenging team owners. But the media portrayed Barry as something else entirely: a money-hungry and selfish prima donna. Ultimately, a San Francisco judge agreed (although maybe not with the prima donna bit) and ruled in favor of the Warriors. Barry had to sit out an entire season before joining the Oaks in the fall of 1968.

With their one proven star sidelined, ABA owners had to be creative to entice fans to their games. The Miami Floridians hired "bikini girls," clad in skimpy swimwear; the Denver Rockets held "halter top night," providing free attendance to appropriately attired ladies; and the Kentucky Colonels once featured a halftime exhibition game between Playboy playmates and a team of local celebrities. The Colonels also signed Penny Ann Early, a young woman who gained national media attention after Churchill Downs refused to allow her to work as a jockey. Early checked into one regular-season game against the Los Angeles Stars wearing a miniskirt and turtleneck sweater. She threw an inbounds pass and then the team called time-out to hustle her back to the bench. Although brief, her appearance in the game made Penny Ann Early the only woman to ever play in a regular-season NBA or ABA contest.

The league's most famous gimmick, though, was the brainchild of Commissioner Mikan, who had poor vision. Soon the red, white, and blue striped basketball, which was easier for Mikan to see, became synonymous with the ABA. If a player released his shot with a good backspin, the red, white, and blue colors created a beautiful blur. League officials attempted to patent the ball, but found that color schemes could not be copyrighted. And though sporting goods manufacturers churned out millions of the red, white, and blue basketballs, the ABA did not receive a dime.

The patriotically colored basketball was a spectacular gimmick, but more lasting was the ABA's adoption of the three-point line. For a league trying to establish a unique identity, the three pointer was an exciting addition. Three-point field goals had been tried in earlier leagues—most notably the short-lived American Basketball League of the early sixties—but for most ABA players, it was a completely new (and exhilarating) experience. "The three-point shot helped make our league special," one ABA vet said, "but you had to be careful, because it could be addicting." During the first ABA season, several players became addicted: one hoisted twenty-six three-pointers in a single game, and the league-leader launched 461, nearly six per outing. In fact, many teams employed a specialist whose only job was to stand behind the line and shoot the ball if it was passed to him. Today, the three pointer is an accepted part of the game. In 1967, the idea was revolutionary.[4]

Even as the ABA promoted its uniqueness, team owners remained focused on merging with the NBA. "There is going to be a merger," Carolina Cougars owner Jim Gardner promised in 1969. "Under no circumstances can a merger not come true. It's just a question of when." Merger talks continued even as the ABA gained a reputation for being more hip: an outlaw league full of oversized personalities. The ABA was just cooler than the NBA, featuring colorful players like Marvin "Bad News" Barnes. Barnes was as crazy off the court as he was successful on it: averaging better than twenty-four points per game while regularly ranking among the league leaders in rebounds. Yet he was often maddeningly disinterested, like the time he arrived late to the arena, scarfed down a bag of fast food, and then scored fifty. The quintessential Marvin Barnes story occurred when "Bad News" played for the short-lived Spirits of St. Louis. "Making airplanes just about killed Marvin," then-Spirits announcer Bob Costas remembered. "Once he got the itinerary for that trip [St. Louis to Kentucky] and noticed that the flight was exactly one hour. Because of the change of time zones, our return flight would leave Louisville at 8:00 AM and arrive in St. Louis at 7:59. Marvin looked at that and announced, 'I ain't goin' on no time machine. I ain't takin' no flight that takes me back in time.'"[5]

On April 16, 1970, when Barnes was still in high school, a group of NBA players filed a class-action antitrust lawsuit in New York District Court on behalf of the National Basketball Players Association (NBPA). There were fourteen co-plaintiffs, one per NBA team, but the lawsuit took the name of union president (and Milwaukee Bucks All-Star guard) Oscar Robertson. Across the United States, trade union activism had peaked in the 1950s and 1960s, and during this era, Bob Cousy, then the NBA's top player, organized a player's union. In the decade following the creation of the NBPA, the union improved players' pension funds, insurance benefits, and minimum salaries. But in filing the Robertson suit, the association made a much bigger play: attacking the reserve clause itself. Their arguments mirrored those made by Rick Barry three years earlier—the reserve clause restricted fair trade, and a merger between the NBA and ABA would constitute an illegal monopoly.

Just three months earlier, Curt Flood had filed a similar suit against Major League Baseball, comparing baseball's reserve clause to chattel slavery. But while Flood lost his case and divided baseball players who lacked free agency until December 1975, the Robertson suit unified NBA athletes. "The players couldn't care less whether there is one league, or two, or a dozen, and they couldn't care less if they're playing against the Los Angeles Lakers or the Denver Rockets," Robertson explained. "All the players care about," he added, "is their rights as American citizens to be able to negotiate freely for their services." The Robertson suit did not prevent the merger from taking place, but it did provide a near-insurmountable obstacle. For a merger to occur, either the Supreme Court would have to rule in favor of the owners, or the players would have to drop their lawsuit.[6]

While the two leagues settled into an uneasy détente, the ABA used two new tactics to improve their league: hardship cases and the Dolgoff Plan. In the early 1970s, the NBA only allowed players four or more years removed from high school to enter the league. There were no such restrictions in the ABA. In fact, ABA owners decided they could morally justify signing underage athletes by targeting players who needed to earn money for their families and calling them hardship cases. Spencer Haywood became the league's first hardship case when he signed with the Denver Rockets as a twenty year old in 1969, but Haywood was soon followed by a score of fellow hardshippers such as George McGinnis and Artis Gilmore. Even using the hardship rule, the ABA had to convince talented players to join their less-established league. Owners often did so by offering exorbitant contracts through a financial scheme known as the Dolgoff Plan. Under the Dolgoff Plan, teams extended compensation over a long period of time by paying annual annuities spread out over decades. So a contract reported as a four-year, $1 million deal might actually pay out only a quarter of that over the four years and then the rest after the player turned forty. The Dolgoff Plan allowed ABA owners to offer enormous sums of money without bankrupting themselves in the process. But players and agents fixated on the total payout and leveraged ABA deals to sign NBA contracts, where the money was not deferred. In just two seasons, median NBA player salaries increased more than 50 percent; in 1969, the average was $35,000 and in 1971, $55,000.

As salaries escalated and hardship cases like Haywood emerged as superstars, basketball fans began debating whether the ABA's best could compete with NBA stars. To pick up a few bucks in the off-season, a team of NBA All-Stars battled ABA All-Stars in the Houston Astrodome in May 1971. To ensure an even playing field, the first half of this historic game was conducted under NBA rules, and the second under ABA guidelines (including both a red, white, and blue ball and the three-point shot). Final score: NBA 125, ABA 100. NBA players, expected to dominate, made excuses for the close game. Oscar Robertson said his team competed "only hard enough to win," while John Havlicek claimed the game meant more to ABA players: "they had nothing to lose."[7]

A few months later, ABA and NBA owners agreed to a series of interleague exhibition games, hoping to attract some fans to otherwise meaningless preseason games. The first game, held in Dallas, pitted the NBA's Milwaukee Bucks against the ABA's Dallas Chaparrals. The reigning NBA champion Bucks won—by just three points—over a Dallas team that finished with a .500 record. Although the NBA dominated this first exhibition season, winning fourteen of the twenty-two interleague games, the ABA eventually came to hold its own and in fact dominated the last three years of interleague play. In 1973, the ABA went 15–10; in 1974, 16–7; and in 1975, the final year of the exhibitions, they finished 31–17, giving them a 79–76 overall record in the five-year series.

Between 1970 and 1975, merger talks progressed slowly. Although the U.S. Senate Antitrust Subcommittee approved the merger in September 1972, NBA owners backed out when faced with the specter of free agency and the end of the reserve clause. "The NBA didn't like the changes," said Pacers owner Dick Tinkham, "so it was back to square one. We went back to suing each other and trying to bankrupt each other to sign players, and no one was making any money. Now and then," Tinkham recalled, "we'd have more merger meetings, then we'd break up and declare war on each other." This was a difficult time for both leagues. The NBA had a national television deal, but ratings dropped as traditional powerhouse teams in New York and Los Angeles struggled to replace retired superstar players such as Jerry West, Elgin Baylor, Wilt Chamberlain, and Willis Reed. The ABA had young, elite talent like Spencer Haywood, Artis Gilmore, George McGinnis, and Julius Erving, but lacked a TV deal, limiting their national exposure.[8]

This stasis continued until September 1975, when two ABA teams, the Denver Nuggets and New York Nets, broke rank and tried to negotiate a separate deal with the NBA. The Nuggets and Nets were two of the best teams in the ABA. More importantly, each featured an exceptionally marketable star: Denver guard David "Skywalker" Thompson, a high-flying rookie sensation who led his North Carolina State Wolfpack to the 1974 NCAA title, and New York forward "Dr. J" Julius Erving, the reigning league MVP known far and wide for his voluminous Afro and rim-rattling dunks. CBS, which broadcast NBA games at the time, understood better than anyone the media potential of a merged league including the Nets and Nuggets and offered a $5 million contract if the two sides could come to an agreement. "We would like to see certain ABA teams in the NBA," said CBS president Bob Wussler. "I think it would be better TV production if the Denver Nuggets, with David Thompson, and New York Nets, with Julius Erving, were in the NBA structure." Wussler was less worried about antitrust legislation than he was about creating a media presence, citing a 28 percent drop in ratings for NBA games the previous season. "I think the problem with our

ratings," Wussler explained, "was that the superstars weren't super
enough and the super teams didn't play up to expectation. I think the
NBA needs new faces, but the ABA in itself is not that strong to warrant
a TV contract." With threats of lawsuits looming and with the NBA
divided over whether or not to accept an additional team in New York
City, the Nets and Nuggets remained in the ABA. Although Thompson
later claimed "the joining of the two leagues was purely and completely
born out of basic economics," basketball owners certainly realized how
important "Skywalker" and "Dr. J" were to merger talks in 1975 and
1976.[9]

This not-so-subtle nudge from CBS brought the players union representatives and team owners back to the bargaining table, and in February 1976 the two sides settled the Robertson suit out of court. Most
importantly, NBA owners agreed to remove the antiquated reserve
clause. In short, as Oscar Robertson himself later explained, "we had
brought free agency to basketball."[10]

With the Robertson suit resolved, ABA and NBA owners finally
hammered out a merger agreement. Unfortunately for ABA fans, their
league had very little to bargain with by the summer of 1976. Sure, they
still featured some of the world's most exciting basketball players, but
only seven teams remained after three dropped out early in the season.
Although the NBA was more stable, they too were desperate for a
merger. As Knicks owner Mike Burke explained, "it was time to take off
or land, because we were out of runway."[11]

Under the terms of the merger agreement, four ABA teams joined
the NBA: the Denver Nuggets, Indiana Pacers, New York Nets, and
San Antonio Spurs. Each paid a $3.2 million entrance fee and received
no television money from the league until 1980. Additionally, the Nets
had to pay a $4.8 million indemnity for intruding into the Knicks terri-
tory. The ABA four would keep their own players, but the remaining
ABA talent would be made available in a special dispersal draft. It was a
steep price to pay to join the NBA; nothing like the instant millions
Dennis Murphy foresaw when he formed the league nearly a decade
earlier.

The Nuggets, Pacers, Nets, and Spurs all struggled financially to
varying degrees in the coming seasons. The defending ABA-champion
Nets had to sell Julius Erving, their star player and top gate attraction,
to remain solvent, while the Nuggets traded for big-name talent to

increase ticket sales (their primary source of income without the TV money). But the lowest point for these four occurred in the summer of 1977, when the Indiana Pacers held a telethon to sell season tickets after team owners failed to meet payroll.

Despite the misfortunes of their colleagues, two ABA ownership groups made a mint on the deal—by not joining the NBA at all. In exchange for folding his team, Kentucky Colonels owner John Y. Brown received $3.3 million. Three years later, he owned the Boston Celtics, drafted Larry Bird, became the governor of Kentucky, and married former Miss America Phyllis George. Not a bad year for Mr. Brown.

Spirits of St. Louis owners Danny and Ozzy Silna, on the other hand, made life far more difficult for their NBA counterparts. After hours of intense negotiations, the Silna brothers agreed to a deal paying them $2.2 million up front plus a percentage of NBA television revenue in perpetuity. Yes, in perpetuity. In the 1970s, this deal (figured as four-seventh of a full revenue share of TV money) amounted to roughly $500,000 per year. But by the early 2000s, NBA owners were annually writing the Silnas a $20 million check. Finally, in January 2014, the two sides agreed to end their longstanding (and incredibly one-sided) partnership. The Silnas received a $500 million one-time payment from the league and a smaller portion of the annual revenue. Danny and Ozzy Silna only owned the Spirits of St. Louis for two years, yet earned almost a billion dollars over four decades for their stubbornness.

In the coming decades, the NBA-ABA merger would have a far-reaching impact. The game changed aesthetically after the merger as teams began moving away from the traditional model favoring a dominant center to one featuring athletic wing players like Erving, Thompson, and Spurs superstar "Iceman" George Gervin. As Knicks guard Walt Frazier explained, "the NBA was ripe for some changes . . . the transition to a speed, showtime-type of game really took off."[12]

In the long run, the most significant outcome of the merger took place off the court, as it reconfigured the relationship between teams and players. Baseball owners recoiled at the efforts of Curt Flood, Andy Messersmith, and Dave McNally in fighting the reserve clause (and, in fact, locked players out of spring training in 1976). In the NBA a similar shift took place—power transferred from owners to players as the open market determined player compensation. Labor disputes did occur in the late '70s and early '80s in pro basketball, but NBA players and owners avoided a labor stoppage until the 1995 lockout.

When NBA players originally filed the Robertson suit in 1970, their greatest fear was that a merger between the rival leagues would drive down salaries. In fact, they agreed to drop their suit only because owners guaranteed the end of the reserve clause. But player fears that a merger would negatively affect salaries proved unfounded. Yes, minimum player salaries plateaued in this era of national stagflation and average salaries climbed at only a relatively constant rate, but top stars commanded more and more money each season. Television revenue generated by big-name talent certainly helped as media exposure made star players increasingly valuable to team owners. In 1968, Wilt Chamberlain (or Bill Russell) was the highest-paid player in the league at approximately $200,000 per season; ten years later, David Thompson pulled down four times that, and by the early 1980s, even marginal players made more than Chamberlain had at his peak. These salary increases relied heavily on the ability of players to use free agency as a negotiating tactic. Unhappy athletes could threaten to sign elsewhere or demand a trade.

On paper, the league was sometimes laughable: teams relocated and changed names so regularly that it became difficult to keep track of whether the squad located in Memphis was referred to as the Pros, the Tams (*Tennessee-Arkansas-Mississippi*), or the Sounds. Yet the ABA was a cult sensation; it was cool and underground, its players legendary for their transience. Few fans had actually *seen* "Dr. J," "Bad News," or "Skywalker" play, but as they dribbled their red, white, and blue striped basketballs and hoisted long-distance jump shots worth three points a pop, they were nevertheless participating in a basketball revolution. Fittingly, the greatest ABA star of them all, Julius Erving, perhaps sums up the influence of the ABA best. "Every night I watch an NBA game I see the ABA," Erving said. "When you watch the up-tempo game and the three-point shot and much of what the strategy employed is, it is definitely an ABA game. There is no question about it. You see the flair. You see the innovation." The NBA today is more popular than ever, reaching a global audience and featuring a generation of high-profile stars, many of whom make just as much off the court as on. But the league would not be where it is today without the ABA and the 1976 merger. Not too shabby for a league without a plan. [13]

8

1976 TO 1977

A capacity crowd of 10,938 fans packed into tiny Milwaukee Arena in February 1977 to witness a historic event. For the first time ever, former ABA stars would play alongside their NBA counterparts in an All-Star game as teammates rather than opponents. This time, instead of league against league, players split into West versus East. Representing the Western Conference, high-flying Denver Nuggets guard David "Skywalker" Thompson paired with Los Angeles Lakers king of the skyhook, Kareem Abdul-Jabbar. For the East, Julius Erving finally got his chance to (legally) play alongside Pete Maravich without a $25,000 fine when "Pistol Pete" fired passes to "Dr. J."

Unlike modern All-Star games, where defense is frowned upon and passing strongly discouraged, the players genuinely wanted to win in 1977. "I took it seriously," Suns guard Paul Westphal said. "And I think most guys did back then." The game was a thriller, and with sixteen seconds left on the clock the East had the ball, down by one point. Maravich received the inbounds pass and worked off a screen set by Bob McAdoo, trying to drive to the basket or dish the ball to Erving for a last-second game winner. But Westphal had other ideas, tipping the ball away as the clock ran out, preserving an exciting 125–124 win for the West.[1]

The All-Star game was just the tip of the iceberg. The 1976–1977 NBA season was the most exciting of the decade, bar none. Adding four ABA teams immediately transformed the league, providing both an influx of talent and finally laying to rest tired arguments about ABA inferiority. Although none of the ABA four made the Finals, former ABA players took leading roles in the playoffs and earned almost half the spots in the All-Star game. There was even a dunk contest—the NBA's first.

In the mid-seventies, the best player in the ABA (and maybe the best in the entire world) was New York Nets forward "Dr. J" Julius Erving. Joining the NBA, though, stretched Nets owner Roy Boe to the breaking point, and he had to sell his star to stay in business. And so, on October 20, 1976, just two days before the start of the regular season and mere weeks after presidential candidate Jimmy Carter famously admitted in *Playboy* magazine to "lusting in his heart," Boe sold Erving to the Philadelphia 76ers for a cool $3 million. Erving also received a six-year, $3.2 million contract from Philadelphia, earning him a second nickname: "the Six Million Dollar Man," a reference to the television program featuring Lee Majors as Steve Austin, a bionic astronaut turned secret agent. And just like the hit TV show, suspense and action dominated Erving's contract talks; even after the sides came to an agreement, the deal still required the approval of league commissioner Larry O'Brien. Sixers fans waited with bated breath, well aware that O'Brien's counterpart in Major League Baseball, Bowie Kuhn, had overturned the sales of Vida Blue, Rollie Fingers, and Joe Rudi from the penny-pinching Oakland Athletics just months earlier. When O'Brien finally okayed the deal a few days later, fans in the City of Brotherly Love could hardly believe their luck. Even the players were stunned. "Me and the Doctor together?" Sixers star forward George McGinnis gushed. "Oh my God!"[2]

Thanks to McGinnis and Erving, sportswriters were quick to anoint the Sixers as the team to beat in 1976–1977. But Philly was not just a two-trick pony. In fact, the 76ers featured an incredibly talented and diverse cast of colorful characters, and all of them wore uniforms designed specifically in honor of America's bicentennial birthday. The Sixers blue road kits were especially cool, with stars running up the sides of both the jersey and the short shorts, best set off (of course) by a pair of high white socks striped blue or red at the top.

Backing up the Sixers regulars (McGinnis, Erving, guards Henry Bibby and Doug Collins, and center Caldwell Jones) was an even more eclectic lot—a bench unit calling themselves the Bomb Squad. Reserve forward Steve Mix was always on the lookout for a fight, and Joe Bryant, nicknamed "Jellybean," welcomed a son named Kobe just two years later. Relieving Jones at center was second-year man Darryl Dawkins, a six-foot-eleven, 250-pound man-child nicknamed "Chocolate Thunder" by pop star Stevie Wonder. "He could be the next Wilt," Lakers forward Kermit Washington decided after the two met. "He put an arm on me and I felt like a flea pinned by an elephant." In 1976, Dawkins jumped directly from high school to the NBA, the final first-round choice to do so until Kevin Garnett two decades later. Dawkins struggled as a rookie and remained a backup as the Sixers made a run for the title. But when he did play, Dawkins, who claimed to hail from the planet Lovetron, provided great copy for Sixers beat writers, giving each of his dunks its own sobriquet: including the "Rim Wrecker," "Goal-rilla," and "Yo-Mama."[3]

The outside yin to Dawkins's inside yang was sassy guard Lloyd Free. Free, who called himself "All-World" and later legally changed his name to "World B. Free," considered himself basketball's answer to Muhammad Ali. Free was a six-foot-two guard with half of an Afro (bald in the front with long, frizzy hair in the back) and a mouth constantly in motion. On the court, Free was a gunner specializing in thirty-foot "moon" shots, fluctuating between "spectacularly accurate or embarrassingly inconsistent." "Free is as physically gifted as any guard who has ever played the game," admitted the *Boston Globe*'s Bob Ryan. But, as Ryan explained, "the nuances of the game totally escape him." In short, Free was both perfect for the Sixers, and a fitting symbol of the seventies. Journalist Tom Wolfe coined the phrase "The 'Me' Decade" in an August 1976 edition of *New York* magazine. In his article, Wolfe rambled about the narcissism of Americans and the "greatest age of individualism in American history!" In the NBA, few players flaunted their individualism better than Free. Sportswriters dismissed "All-World" as a one-dimensional scorer but, as Julius Erving said with a chuckle, "that is one fantastic dimension."[4]

Philadelphia featured undeniable talent and larger-than-life personalities, even if they failed to give off the underdog vibe that made Philly's favorite son, Rocky Balboa, an Academy Award winner in 1977. Instead, as one sportswriter predicted, "the most difficult thing the Sixers will have to withstand this year is the various, competing demands of ego among their deep, talented young players." They were a dream team who finished with the second-highest win total in the league and seemed to be peaking at playoff time. The success of the 1976–1977 Sixers even wiped away memories of their nine-win team a few years earlier as Doctor J, Baby Bull, All-World, Jellybean, and Chocolate Thunder seemed a lock to bring a title to the City of Brotherly Love.[5]

While Sixers fans celebrated their sudden good fortune, Dr. J's former team, the New York Nets, did not fare well in his absence. With Erving, the team won the 1976 ABA title and expected to compete for the NBA championship after the merger. Without Erving, they were a laughingstock. CBS, planning to air the Nets' opening night game against the Golden State Warriors, cancelled the broadcast, citing a sudden lack of star power and fan interest. It was far from the lowest point of the season. Electric guard Nate "Tiny" Archibald—acquired from Kansas City for the high price of guard Brian Taylor and two first-round draft picks—was left without a running mate in Erving's absence and blew out a knee, costing him most of the season. New York then jettisoned its highest scorer, guard "Super" John Williamson, to the Indiana Pacers for Afro-wearing dunk specialist Darnell Hillman. Nets fans could only hope that Archibald might recover his All-Star form and that Hillman would become more than just an exciting player to watch dunk in pregame warmups. Not that anyone saw his dunks, of course; the Nets finished twentieth (out of twenty-two teams) in attendance on the season, drawing fewer than eight thousand fans per game to Nassau Coliseum.

Between the 50–31 Sixers and 22–60 Nets in the Atlantic Division, three perennial contenders fought for relevance. The Boston Celtics were the defending champions. But Bill Russell and company had won eleven rings in thirteen seasons for Beantown during the fifties and sixties, and the pressure to repeat was tremendous. It showed in their off-season personnel decisions. A year after turning malcontent Charlie Scott into an integral part of a title-winning team, the Celtics paid $500,000 to Portland for Sidney Wicks, another talented enigma. For his part, Wicks promised to fall in line. "The Celtics, like UCLA, have a winning tradition," Wicks said. "It's easy to play under those conditions." The Wicks experiment might have worked if not for another deal decimating team morale. Shortly after signing Wicks, the Celtics lost forward Paul Silas when a clerical error allowed the thirteen-year veteran to become a free agent. Rather than let Silas leave without compensation, Celtics president Red Auerbach hastily engineered a three-team trade sending Silas to the Denver Nuggets for Detroit Pistons forward Curtis Rowe, Wicks's teammate at UCLA.[6]

Trading Silas, a locker room leader, for Rowe, another potential problem child, infuriated center Dave Cowens. "Pay [Silas] the fucking money, and we'll win another championship!" Cowens screamed at Auerbach. Cowens took the loss of Silas especially hard, and went on an unpaid leave of absence, setting no timetable for his return. The big redhead even spent a day driving a Boston cab. "I just wanted to see what it's like," Cowens explained. "I really wanted to show my buddy around Boston and thought it'd be a cool way and we'd have some fun. We picked up a few fares. We took some long routes around the city. And no one recognized me." But his sabbatical was about more than just joyriding with a friend. "I just lost my enthusiasm for the game," Cowens said. "I don't want to spoil the Celtics and I don't want to take their money if I'm not earning it. I just quit my job, that's all. What's wrong with that? Other guys do it every day. Nobody makes a big thing out of them." Team officials and fans certainly made it a big thing, although Auerbach insisted that doctors found no sign of depression. Cowens returned to the team in January, but despite having six players who averaged double figures in scoring (led by Jo Jo White's 19.6 points per game), the Celtics clearly missed Silas's veteran leadership and toughness, finishing second in their division with forty-four wins.[7]

Like Celtics followers, New York Knicks fans wanted an instant title contender. In 1976 the team picked up Spencer Haywood after whiffing on Kareem Abdul-Jabbar, George McGinnis, and Wilt Chamberlain. Before the '77 season, the Nets—who owed the Knicks $4.8 million for moving into their territory—offered up Julius Erving in return for waiving this payment. Inexplicably, the Knicks refused, arguing that they needed the cash to pay the high salaries already owed Haywood, Walt Frazier, and Earl Monroe. But after a slow start to the season, they did an about-face, buying superstar center Bob McAdoo from the Buffalo Braves for $2.5 million.

McAdoo became, in the words of one journalist, "the Knicks' next store-bought Messiah" and his agent demanded a contract commensurate with a lesser deity: five years for $2.5 million—just a little less than what Dr. J earned in Philadelphia. Knicks officials feared that such a large, long-term guaranteed contract would allow McAdoo to become complacent, but they were more afraid to lose him. Agreeing to McAdoo's contract demand gave the Knicks former All-Stars at every position: the Rolls-Royce Backcourt of Earl "the Pearl" Monroe and Walt "Clyde" Frazier along with McAdoo, Spencer Haywood (limited to just thirty-one games because of injuries), and Bill Bradley. In 1979, Bradley would become the junior U.S. senator from New Jersey and, at age thirty-five, one of the youngest congressmen in American history. He held the seat for almost two decades before making an unsuccessful run for the presidency in 2000. But during the 1976–1977 season, Bradley scored barely four points per game and teams ignored him on offense, daring him to shoot. The lone bright spot for New York fans, who celebrated a Yankees' World Series win a few months after the end of the Knicks' sad season, was the emergence of second-round pick Lonnie Shelton, a bull-strong forward providing much-needed scoring and rebounding. At 40–42, the Knicks, despite being a strong team on paper, disappointed, facing a future full of high-priced contracts doled out to underachieving veterans.[8]

The fall of the New York Knicks also proved disastrous to television ratings, the lifeblood of the NBA in the 1970s. Television viewing skyrocketed in the sixties and, in 1964, the NBA signed their first TV deal with ABC to broadcast a handful of games (including the finals). Five years later, the sides extended their contract, netting the NBA a relatively paltry $3 million per season (far less than the $16.5 million earned by Major League Baseball or the $22 million doled out to the National Football League). At first, ABC's coverage was shoddy and the league looked second rate. But ABC Sports president Roone Arledge worked tirelessly to improve the product. "Arledge had not been a basketball fan," historian David Halberstam explained, "but he was quickly impressed by the beauty of the game." Arledge made an important decision in covering basketball. Rather than focus on team rivalries, he promoted individual matchups: Bill Bradley against John Havlicek and Willis Reed facing Dave Cowens, rather than Knicks versus Celtics.[9]

Despite Arledge's efforts, the NBA wanted a better deal, something comparable to the MLB and NFL packages, when their deal came up for renewal in 1973. The league also demanded that ABC air NBA games on Saturday afternoons, interfering with the network's lucrative college football lineup. ABC refused and the NBA jumped to CBS for the 1973–1974 season, despite admonitions by Celtics president Red

Auerbach to remain loyal. "You don't really think a man like Roone Arledge is going to take this lying down, do you?" Auerbach asked his fellow owners. Arledge did not, in fact, take it lying down and set out to crush the NBA with new head-to-head original programming. NBA ratings plummeted, dropping 20 percent in its first season on CBS and continuing to free fall for most of the decade. One journalist disappointed in the network coverage of the league wrote that CBS "present[ed] the pros as a bunch of guys running more or less aimlessly around the court in shiny underwear."[10]

In 1976, because of these declining ratings, CBS shifted their Sunday afternoon basketball offerings away from national matchups in favor of regional games. Rather than watching a Los Angeles–New York game, viewers in the Midwest might instead catch the Nuggets and Bulls or Houston and Kansas City. To promote the games, CBS switched its lead-in from *Superstars*, a hilariously horrible show in which Joe Frazier almost drowned in a 1973 episode, to *Challenge of the Sexes*, which similarly flopped; surprisingly few Americans wanted to tune into a tennis match between *Charlie's Angels* actress Farrah Fawcett and comedian Bill Cosby.

In the early seventies, the Buffalo Braves looked like a surefire bet to win an NBA title during the decade with a trio of players—Ernie DiGregorio, Randy Smith, and Bob McAdoo—who could pass, score, rebound, and defend as well as any threesome in the league. But a knee injury cost DiGregorio much of his quickness, and McAdoo grew disillusioned with a lack of national media coverage and found himself traded to New York. Making matters worse, owner Paul Snyder openly threatened to move the team to Toronto or Florida and issued an ultimatum: unless fans purchased 5,000 season tickets for 1976–1977, the Braves were gone. After Buffalo got a restraining order against Snyder, he sold the team to John Y. Brown, former owner of the ABA's Kentucky Colonels. Brown immediately made his mark on the franchise, spearheading the move to send McAdoo to the Big Apple. "I felt McAdoo was a selfish player," Brown said, "and totally unrealistic in his financial demands."[11]

Dealing a former MVP to a division rival was not the only move Brown made when he took over the Braves. In the nine months from June 1976 to February of the following year, Buffalo made no less than nine major trades involving thirteen players and six draft picks (all under three different head coaches). One of the trades netted the Braves Moses Malone. After just two games in Buffalo, though, the Braves rerouted Moses to Houston. Without Malone or McAdoo on the team, the Braves turned to first-year forward Adrian Dantley, selected sixth overall out of Notre Dame, to anchor their frontcourt. A starting frontcourt of Dantley, McAdoo, and Malone might have been one for the ages, but by season's end only Dantey remained a Brave. At six-foot-five, Dantley stood four or five inches shorter than most power forwards in the NBA. But his slick pump fakes allowed Dantley to use his chiseled body more effectively than any other player in the league. Above all, Dantley was a master at drawing fouls, finishing fifth in the league in free throw attempts (almost eight per game) and earning rookie of the year honors thanks to a twenty-point scoring average. Even with (or perhaps because of) the tremendous roster shakeup, Buffalo (30–52) dropped to fourth place in the Atlantic, and rumors began to swirl that Brown wanted to move the team to Louisville, where he was eyeing a run for Kentucky's governorship in 1978.

Benefitting the most from the Braves' roster overhaul were the Central Division–winning Houston Rockets, who added Moses Malone to an already solid roster including John Lucas (the top pick in the 1976 draft), Calvin "the Pocket Rocket" Murphy, and perennial All-Star forward Rudy Tomjanovich. With a 49–33 finish, Houston won the first division title in franchise history and seemed to be on the cusp of competing for an NBA title.

As in Houston, a new acquisition for New Orleans transformed the future of the franchise. In August 1976, the Summer Olympic Games in Montreal came to an end with Romanian Nadia Comăneci capturing the hearts of gymnastics fans with her eye-popping perfect 10. Also that month, the Chicago White Sox took the field wearing Bermuda shorts (a first and, thankfully, a last in pro baseball) while the duet "Don't Go Breaking My Heart," featuring Elton John and Kiki Dee shot to the top of the Billboard pop charts. Flying under the radar, except to die-hard basketball fans, was the Jazz's signing of free agent guard Gail Goodrich from the Lakers. Goodrich was unspectacular but was an excellent scorer who the Jazz hoped would fit well next to Pistol Pete Maravich in the New Orleans backcourt. Under the terms of the settlement of the Robertson suit in 1976, the Jazz had to send Los Angeles a compensation package consisting of players, draft picks, or cash.

   After hours of negotiating and trying to avoid involving Commissioner O'Brien (who opposed free agency and almost certainly would have
decided against New Orleans), the two sides came to an agreement. In
exchange for the thirty-three-year-old guard, the Jazz sent the Lakers
two first-round picks (in 1977 and 1979) and agreed to swap first round-
ers in 1978. Signing Goodrich ultimately cost the Jazz two Hall of Famers: Moses Malone (given up for the 1977 first-round pick) and Earvin
"Magic" Johnson (selected by LA with the 1979 Jazz choice). Even
without the benefit of foresight, sportswriters at the time panned the
deal. "Hopes were high," one journalist wrote, "expectations great,
compensation to Los Angeles outrageous." In their first game together,
Goodrich and Maravich combined for fifty-three points in a Jazz win.
But when Goodrich suffered a season-ending Achilles injury in January,
the team sputtered. All told, their big free agent pickup played in less
than half the team's games and averaged less than thirteen points as the
35–47 Jazz remained near the bottom of the league.[12]
   In the midst of this turmoil, Maravich turned in perhaps his best
season as a pro, leading the league in scoring (31.1 points per game) and
earning All-NBA first team. But on two nights in late winter, Maravich
truly made his mark on the NBA. On February 25, 1977, New Orleans
hosted the Knicks, exhausted after playing an overtime game the night
before in Atlanta. Maravich came out on fire and, by the time he fouled
out with a little over a minute left in the game, had scored sixty-eight
points, the most in an NBA game since Wilt equaled the feat a decade
earlier. "It was a beautiful thing to watch for the fans here," Knicks
coach Red Holzman admitted. "We didn't play well, but he was phenomenal." Maravich shot twenty-six of forty-three from the field (remember, there was still no three-point line) and sixteen of nineteen
from the free throw line, setting a scoring record for guards that stood
until "Jellybean" Bryant's son Kobe tallied eighty-one (against Jimmie
Walker's kid, Jalen Rose) nearly thirty years later. Less than a month
after his sixty-eight-point outburst, Maravich turned in another memorable game. On March 18, a car crash injured five of Pete's teammates,
forcing the Jazz to suit up only seven players against the Suns. That
night, Maravich tallied an amazing 51 of his team's 104 points to will the
short-handed Jazz to a four-point win. In the spring of '77, Pete was, as
one biographer recalled, "the best player in basketball, in a state of high

harmony with the game." Sadly, Maravich's best season was wasted on a team that could do no better than thirty-five wins.[13]

Despite their struggles, Jazz fans could at least point to the depths plumbed by the Atlanta Hawks as proof of their own mediocrity. After swinging and missing on David Thompson and Marvin Webster in the 1975 draft, the Hawks watched helplessly as the Nuggets (who signed both Thompson and Webster) made the ABA finals. Now in the same league as the Nuggets, the Hawks dealt for Trail Blazers sharpshooter Geoff Petrie, giving up a selection in the dispersal draft that netted Portland powerful forward Maurice Lucas. Unfortunately for Hawks fans, Petrie reinjured his chronically ailing left knee and never played a game for Atlanta, or for anyone else in the NBA, and retired at the ripe old age of twenty-eight. Without Petrie (or Thompson, or Webster), the Hawks finished near the bottom of the league in every offensive category and eked out just thirty-one wins.

In Denver, Hawks draftees Thompson and Webster soared and the Nuggets captured the Midwest Division title with a 50–32 record. Guard David Thompson, known as "Skywalker" for his aerobatic exploits—including a tremendous forty-four-inch vertical leap that allowed him to attack the basket and finish with rim-rattling dunks—was the team's best player. Skywalker paired perfectly with center Dan Issel, a self-described "short, slow, white center with an eighth-grade head fake"; a capable outside shooter who pulled opposing centers away from the hoop, giving Thompson more room to operate. Although rarely mentioned as one of the league's all-time greats, Issel retired in 1985 as the fourth-highest scorer in pro basketball history (27,482 points), behind only Kareem Abdul-Jabbar, Wilt Chamberlain, and Julius Erving.[14]

Denver boasted enviable depth along their front line as well. Forward Bobby Jones was probably the best defensive player in the league and was a tremendous athlete with leaping ability that, in the words of journalist Woody Paige, allowed him to go "up where no other white man has ever been." Paul Silas, picked up from the Boston Celtics after a contract snafu, provided toughness and a winning attitude as a reserve forward, and Marvin "the Human Eraser" Webster, in just his second season, looked like a diamond in the rough, playing limited minutes but demonstrating an uncanny knack for blocking shots. The Nuggets also benefitted from the fact that most NBA players had never played in

Denver and were unfamiliar with the thin air of the Mile High City; the team boasted a gaudy 36–5 home record in front of the league's biggest crowds. Adding to their psychological advantage, the Nuggets supplied oxygen tanks to visiting teams. Regardless of their mind games or rowdy fans, Denver's success proved that the four former ABA teams were for real and that their league had been the equal (or at least the near-equal) of the NBA in every way.[15]

The Nuggets surged, but another ex-ABA team within the division struggled. "On paper, we're the weakest team comin' in," Indiana Pacers coach Bobby "Slick" Leonard conceded, "maybe even weaker than the paper." Leonard's Pacers were once the darlings of the ABA and winners of three league titles. But by the summer of 1976, the team had fallen on hard times owing to several key retirements (including former star Roger Brown) and the financial cost of the merger. The face of the franchise became point guard Don Buse, who led the league in both assists (8.5 per game) and steals (3.47 per game). Writing for *Basketball Digest*, Indianapolis sportswriter Bill Benner called Buse "the kind of player every team would like to have," celebrating his undeniable "court smarts." Also, as the Pacers media guide explained, "Don is a bachelor who enjoys hunting and fishing. He spends his summer relaxing, drinking a little beer and playing a whole lot of softball." No wonder he was a fan favorite. On the court, Buse flew around like a man possessed, caroming off the floor and opposing players alike as the undisputed leader of the 36–46 Pacers.[16]

If not for the merger, the Detroit Pistons might well have claimed their first division title since 1956, when they still played home games in Fort Wayne, Indiana. Instead, the Pistons settled for second in the Midwest and a rare playoff appearance. All-Star Bob Lanier remained among the league's elite centers, scoring better than twenty-five points per game and anchoring the team's defense. But the most interesting Piston, at least from a personality standpoint, was newcomer Marvin "Bad News" Barnes. Unsurprisingly, Barnes started his tenure in the Motor City by holding out for more money, eventually signing a seven-year, $2.1 million deal. In the ABA, Barnes earned a reputation as a flamboyant free spirit; a rep carried over to the NBA. "He's a nice guy, a sweet guy," one opposing owner explained. "He's just totally unreliable. He's probably in the top five players in basketball, talentwise. In terms of value to a team," the owner continued, "he's probably in the bottom 10 percent." On the floor, Barnes played like a young Spencer Haywood: a six-foot-eight forward with a soft shooting touch and unbelievable feel for the game. "On the court I'm a superstar," Barnes proclaimed. "Nobody comes to play like I do." But off the court? Well, even Barnes admitted he had his flaws. "I'm not what you call your regular NBA apple-pie-and-ice-cream guy," he said. "I'm the bad guy." Weeks after ending his holdout, the bad guy violated probation by carrying a concealed weapon in the Detroit airport. His lawyers requested community service, but the judge sentenced him to a year in jail. Barnes played in fifty-three games as he awaited his prison term but was a disappointment on the court as well, and maybe more than any other player in the seventies, "Bad News" Barnes wasted considerable talent and disappointed at every turn.[17]

After years of fielding good-but-not-great teams, the Chicago Bulls bottomed out during the 1975–1976 season, finishing a league-worst 24–58. If there was a silver lining, their last-place effort did give them the chance to select seven-foot-two, 240-pound Artis Gilmore in the ABA dispersal draft. Chicago originally drafted Gilmore in 1971 and envisioned him as the perfect complement to their core of Bob Love, Chet Walker, Jerry Sloan, and Norm Van Lier. Gilmore signed instead with the Kentucky Colonels and helped lead them to the 1975 ABA title. After the Colonels folded, Chicago paid $1 million to select the former Jacksonville star, locking him into a multiyear deal worth about $450,000 annually. But there was a problem: Gilmore did not want to play in Chicago. He despised the weather and the Bulls offense in which the center acted as a playmaker rather than a primary scoring option. Despite his reservations, Gilmore instantly became one of the top two or three centers in the league, and fans eagerly anticipated his battles against Kareem Abdul-Jabbar. "Abdul-Jabbar vs. Gilmore may not be as jarring a matchup as Chamberlain vs. Russell," one journalist wrote, "but it's not over yet. It should get better with age." The comparison was fitting. Abdul-Jabbar played a more finesse game (à la Bill Russell), whereas Gilmore dominated with his size and strength (as had Chamberlain). As Gilmore explained, "when I dunk, I try to make the ball stick to the floor." Gilmore and the Bulls started slowly in his first season in the Windy City, losing all ten of their games in November. But a late season stretch in which they won twenty of their last twenty-four games (known in Chicago as the "Miracle on Madison Street") helped the Bulls to an unlikely playoff berth as Gilmore emerged as an Afroed superstar.[18]

After a promising thirty-eight-win season in 1975–1976 (their first without Kareem Abdul-Jabbar), the Milwaukee Bucks (30–52) took a step backwards in 1976–1977. Milwaukee planned to build around the four players acquired in the Abdul-Jabbar deal: All-Star shooting guard Brian Winters, forwards Dave Meyers and Junior Bridgeman, and center Elmore Smith. But only Winters and Bridgeman lived up to expectations, posting solid numbers (19.3 points per game for Winters and 14.4 for Bridgeman) while Meyers struggled with injuries and Smith was traded to the Cavs. Sensing the Bucks were headed in the wrong direction, the team fired Larry Costello and replaced him with Don Nelson, a former Celtics player who preferred a more fast-breaking, up-tempo style. This was Nelson's first coaching gig in a career that would span more than three decades and four franchises, resulting in an NBA-record 1,335 victories and a spot in the Naismith Memorial Basketball Hall of Fame.

Top to bottom, the Pacific Division was the best in basketball, and the defending Western Conference–champion Phoenix Suns, for example, finished dead last. In Phoenix, for the first time in league history, twin brothers played on the same team (ironically, the Suns would suit up the second set—Marcus and Markieff Morris—in February 2013). Dick and Tom Van Arsdale entered the NBA together in 1965: Dick with the Knicks and Tom with the Pistons. "Tom couldn't stand the separation," the brothers remembered. "It was traumatic for him," and he decided to quit the team to attend law school. But Dick would have none of it, telling his twin to "get his ass back to Detroit." More than a decade later, the brothers reunited with the Suns. Over their careers, the Van Arsdales accumulated remarkably similar statistics. Dick averaged sixteen points per game; Tom fifteen. Both made first-team All-Rookie in 1965, and each suited up for three All-Star games. In fact, when Dick made the 1969 All-Star squad, he tried to convince Tom to play for him in the second half. Tom refused. Dick tried the switch again in their last game together in Phoenix. Again, Tom said no. As they neared retirement, the Van Arsdale duo provided little more than a heartwarming story. Dick managed just 7.7 points per game, while Tom chipped in 5.8—or at least we think so. After all, Dick may have actually convinced Tom to switch jerseys once or twice in there.[19]

Seattle had no family reunions to brighten up the SuperSonics' rather dreary season. Coach Bill Russell was in his fourth year with the team, but by the end of the season, it was clear that the Russell era was drawing to a close. Before the last away game, the team held a practice in which, for fun, Russell—now forty-three—showed up in sneakers and swatted away shots by Slick Watts, Nick Weatherspoon, and rookie guard Dennis Johnson. "Did Russell know that they grumbled about his alleged greatness," Russell biographer Aram Goudsouzian asked rhetorically. "Was he proving something?" After his defensive display, Russell grabbed a ball and dunked it, "cackling his way off the court. He had enough, he said." In one autobiography, Russell admitted that "we were on the brink of contention except for one problem—and the problem was me." Having entirely rebuilt the roster and unloaded several bloated contracts while picking up numerous draft picks, the Sonics now boasted a young, deep core with talent at every position. True, center Tom Burleson (nicknamed "the Needle" for his resemblance to the tall, thin Seattle landmark) regressed somewhat during the 1976–1977 season, dropping from sixteen to ten points per game. But the guard trio of Watts, Johnson, and "Downtown" Freddie Brown was among the league's best. Watts finished second in the NBA in assists and third in steals (after leading the league in both during the 1975–1976 season); Brown bombed in rainbow shots from long range and led the team with seventeen points per game; and Johnson was an exceptional athlete who could guard anyone on the court. But, once again, the team finished near the bottom of the division and Coach Russell questioned his own desire to continue. "When I came here four years ago," Russell said, "the franchise was in a mess and I wanted to turn it into a team that didn't need me. Maybe," he admitted, "I've succeeded."[20]

Atop the competitive Pacific were the 52–30 Los Angeles Lakers. Having traded away four starting-caliber players for Abdul-Jabbar in the summer of 1975, the Lakers were still filling in gaps. But Kareem once again reminded fans why he was the best player in the game, winning his fifth MVP award and leading the league in blocked shots (4.1 per game) and field goal percentage, connecting on nearly 58 percent of his attempts. Oh, and he also found time to participate in the NBA's first slam dunk contest.

Kareem did not win the contest. Neither did fan favorites like "Dr. J" Julius Erving or David "Skywalker" Thompson (who lost three times before CBS, desperate for star power, allowed him to be removed from what was billed as a single-elimination tournament). Instead, the finalists were then–Pacers center Darnell "Dr. Dunk" Hillman and Larry McNeill, no longer even on an NBA roster by the time the taped special aired during the playoffs. Clearly not the spectacle of the 1976 ABA contest in Denver, fan interest in the event was so low that the league shelved the slam dunk contest until 1984, when it became a staple of All-Star weekend and the site of legendary showdowns between Michael Jordan, Dominique Wilkens, and Spud Webb.

His dunk contest fizzle notwithstanding, Abdul-Jabbar had a tremendous season. But he was no longer a one-man team. Despite losing Gail Goodrich to the New Orleans Jazz, the Lakers thrived under new head coach and longtime Lakers great Jerry West, whose appointment to the bench marked the end of a series of unlikely events. After he retired in 1974, West sued team owner Jack Kent Cooke over a contract dispute; West wanted to be paid the same amount he earned as a player while Cooke hoped to cut his salary. To resolve the suit, Cooke promoted West to head coach and paid him more money. For his part, West possessed one of the greatest basketball minds in the league and proved particularly innovative by hiring two full-time coaches to sit alongside him on the bench. Most other teams had just one bench assistant, freeing others to watch game film or travel to scout upcoming opponents. The trio of Jerry West, offensive coach Stan Albeck, and defensive specialist Jack McCloskey deftly blended the talents of Abdul-Jabbar with those of emerging power forward Kermit Washington. Washington languished on the bench for most of his first three years in LA before begging Pete Newell for help. Newell eventually turned his workouts with Washington into a permanent career and over the decades his celebrated "Big Man Camp" would attract players like Shaquille O'Neal, Hakeem Olajuwon, and Bill Walton. By the fall of 1976, Washington's hard work had paid off as Newell's star pupil averaged a career-high nine points and nine rebounds per night, providing a powerful inside presence next to Abdul-Jabbar, something the goggle-wearing big man had lacked for most of his career.

The Lakers' closest competitors in the Pacific were the suddenly relevant Portland Trail Blazers. Since selecting UCLA center Bill Walton first overall in 1974, Portland fans had expected the big redhead to lead them to an NBA title. But Walton lost most of his first two seasons to injuries and fans began to question his commitment to his team, his sport—and his nation. When Walton called for the rejection of the U.S. government and his lawyer likened his existence to servitude (calling Walton's $400,000 annual contract "legal slavery"), Blazers fans had enough. "He's been pampered all his life," complained one. "If a guy wants to sniff wildflowers instead of playing, OK, but he shouldn't take $2.5 million to do it." Walton's vegetarian, counterculture lifestyle also did not jibe with life in the American Northwest. Local sportswriters penned columns raising the possibility that Walton was faking injuries and making anti-government statements as a way to get out of Portland. In an effort to salvage Walton's career, new head coach Dr. Jack Ramsay decided to completely overhaul the roster, building around his multitalented but brittle big man. Between 1971 and 1976, Blazers teams had counted on the inside-outside scoring ability of Sidney Wicks and Geoff Petrie, both rookies of the year and multiyear NBA All-Stars. In the summer of '76, the Blazers traded both; Petrie went to Atlanta in exchange for the right to select Maurice Lucas in the ABA dispersal draft, and Wicks ended up in Boston for cash.[21]

Miraculously, the team gelled almost immediately without Wicks and Petrie in the lineup. Larry Bird, later Walton's teammate in Boston, called the 1976–1977 Blazers "the epitome of basketball," praising them for their selfless play. "Teamwork is preached so much," said Portland guard Lionel Hollins, "that when one of us turns an ankle, we all limp." Years later, Walton admitted a particular fondness for this team. "We played so well together and understood exactly what had to be done to win. We became," he said, "what Ramsay believed the game of basketball should be: fast breaks, teamwork, ball movement and pressure defense." Ramsay compared his team's offense to "a ballet, a graceful sweep and flow of patterned movement, counterpointed by daring and imaginative flights of solitary brilliance." Offensively, the team revolved around Walton. His willingness and ability to pass was unheard of for a seven footer, as was his deadly fifteen-foot jump shot. Often, Hollins initiated the offense by passing the ball to Walton at the high post, where he could find cutting guards or dump the ball inside to Lucas, the team's leading scorer.[22]

In his first NBA season, the six-foot-eight Lucas provided toughness on both ends of the floor, protecting the more finesse Walton in much the same way Kermit Washington complemented Kareem Abdul-Jabbar. Lucas was an on-court enforcer, a "bad boy" who filled the role a decade before the late-eighties Pistons laid claim to the title. "I don't look for a fight," Lucas insisted, although he added "I don't want to be known as a nice guy." In fact, Lucas was already a well-known pugilist before ever suiting up for the Blazers. In 1973, while playing for the United States in the World University Games, a fight broke out between players from the United States and Cuba, leading rowdy fans on both sides to rush the court. Lucas, remembered then-teammate David Thompson, "single-handedly [took] on the Cuban weightlifters and boxers who spilled out of the stands. . . . He fended off every single one of them." Then, as a rookie with the ABA's Spirits of St. Louis, Lucas kayoed seven-foot-two Artis Gilmore. "After punching Gilmore," remembered his coach, "Lucas was ready to take on everyone else in the league and no one wanted any part of Maurice Lucas." Yet for all of his toughness, Lucas was also a fine basketball player who took pressure off Walton both on offense and defense.[23]

Rather than rely on one or two ball-dominant players (i.e., Petrie and Wicks), the new-look Blazers moved the ball quickly from side to side, working for the best shot possible. Unsurprisingly, Portland finished near the top of the league in every offensive statistical category. But they also played dogged defense, forcing opponents to drive toward Walton, who led the league in both rebounding (14.4 per game) and blocked shots (3.25). With their enviable depth, the Blazers could press opponents up and down the floor, creating turnovers just like the Celtics of old. Opponents fortunate enough to break the press still had to penetrate Portland's stout half-court defense, and, if they missed, Walton's long outlet passes often resulted in easy layups for his teammates. During the regular season, the Blazers were streaky, dropping five straight in February only to win six in a row to end the year. Fittingly, in their last regular season game, Portland destroyed the division-winning Lakers, 145–116. The Western Conference was wide open, but no one was hotter than the Blazers by the spring of '77.

The playoffs looked like a four-team race; bettors heavily favored the Sixers in the East and either the Trail Blazers, Lakers, or Nuggets in the West. Following the merger, the playoffs had grown again, including six teams from each conference (rather than five) with division winners earning first-round byes.

Regardless of the seeding, this would be unlike any other postseason in league history, since all but two of the league's twenty-six referees went on strike at the end of the regular season. Only Richie Powers and Earl Strom remained loyal, joined by a collection of strikebreakers recruited from the college ranks. "The officials were seeking the right to collective bargaining," Strom explained, "an arbitration clause, life insurance . . . increases in salary and expenses, and an increase in playoff pay." In a league struggling to gain national attention, the referee strike was a major blow. On-court play would doubtlessly suffer and the relationship between the NBA and CBS was already strained; television magnates rightfully feared that fans would tune out the inferior product. They were right.[24]

With replacement refs calling the action, the conference semifinals came down to matchups between Boston and Philly; Houston and Washington; Portland and Denver; and Los Angeles and Golden State. In the East, the Sixers eked out a seven-game victory over the over-matched Celtics while the Rockets shot by the Bullets in six, including an overtime thriller dominated by Moses Malone. That night, Malone collected thirty-one points and twenty-six rebounds (including fifteen offensive boards) to overcome a thirty-seven-point outburst by Bullets guard Phil Chenier. Predictably, the Western Conference semis were similarly tight; Lucas, Walton, and the Blazers ousted David "Skywalker" Thompson, Dan Issel, and the Nuggets in six games while Abdul-Jabbar's Lakers took seven to get past the pesky Warriors.

The 1977 NBA Final Four looked ultracompetitive and fans settled in for long series between the Sixers and Rockets and the Lakers and Blazers. They were sorely disappointed. With the referee strike settled (referee pay more than quadrupled, from $150 per playoff game to at least $750 for late-round games) the Sixers polished off the Rockets in six games, holding off a furious Houston rally to earn a trip to the finals, while the Blazers swept the Lakers. In game three of that series, Walton made fans stand up and take notice when he threw down a thunderous dunk through Abdul-Jabbar. On television, legendary Portland announcer Bill Schonely screamed "Walton over Jabbar!" following his call with "Oh, baby, he's fouled!"[25]

As Walton and the Trail Blazers rolled through the playoffs, Portland witnessed a wave of unrestrained enthusiasm known as "Blazermania." Fans cheered on their favorite Blazers, their demigods clad in black, red, and white short shorts. It became almost a religion. Walton, Lucas, guard Lionel Hollins, and the rest flew into the Portland airport at 3:00 AM after ousting Los Angeles, and thousands of Blazermaniacs met them at the gate. One young woman, slurring her speech, asked her boyfriend, "How great would it be to be a Blazer right now?" Leaning against the wall for support, her paramour sagely replied, "I got news for you. I *am* a Blazer. God damn it, we're all Blazers." Coach Ramsay was at a loss for words at the outpouring of enthusiasm. "I've never seen anything like it," Ramsay said. "I got all choked up."[26]

Conference championship wins by the Blazers and Sixers set up an incredibly important finals matchup full of interesting storylines and subplots. "Everybody knew the series would be one of contrasts," wrote *Sports Illustrated*'s Curry Kirkpatrick; "Blazer calculation vs. 76er creativity; Portland discipline vs. Philly anarchy." It was playground ball against the old school: black against white. Sure, the Trail Blazers had black players, four of their top eight were African American, in fact, but the perception was that they played "white" basketball, more disciplined and more teamwork based than the perceived "black" playground style preferred by the Sixers—who, to be fair, regularly played two white players. "Philadelphia," said David Halberstam, "because of its modified schoolyard play, its one-on-one style, had been cast by the media, by fans, by other coaches, as the bad guys." The Sixers also had a reputation for being all sizzle and no steak; a group of ball-hogging, me-first, stat-watching egotists. "Erving and McGinnis went together like cream cheese and scrapple," insisted Kirkpatrick. "They could not get along, much less play alongside each other. Neither man could coexist with [Lloyd] Free, who monopolized the ball and was known to start shooting before the concluding notes of the national anthem." Even McGinnis recalled, "we had a George play, a Doug Collins play, a Julius Erving play, and a play for Lloyd Free. You had your play," he said, "and you could wait around until your turn came around again."[27]

Unfortunately for 76ers fans, the finals quickly turned into the Doctor J show as his outspoken supporting cast all but disappeared. McGinnis was slowed by a deep muscle pull in his groin, requiring cortisone shots to deaden the pain. As a result, Big George played abysmally, connecting on less than 40 percent of his field goal attempts and just over 50 percent of his free throws (after shooting 46 percent and 68 percent respectively during the regular season). Sportswriters slaughtered McGinnis for disappearing in the finals. "George [McGinnis] took more off the table than any 'superstar' ever," wrote Bill Simmons in his 2009 *Book of Basketball*. "You can't believe how much McGinnis secretly sucked until you watch his stink bomb in the '77 finals."[28]

McGinnis bombed, with free shots under 30 percent from the field, and scored less than half his regular season total, and Portland fans became increasingly excited about the possibility of the city's first major sports title. Although Blazermania was evident even before game one (a Sixers win), a fight that broke out during game two set the tone for the rest of the series. Late in the fourth quarter, with the Sixers up by twenty, Blazers guard Herm Gilliam drove the lane and took a short shot, which huge Philly center Darryl Dawkins contested. Gilliam missed and Dawkins aggressively went after the rebound, pulling Portland's Bobby Gross, along with the ball, to the floor in the process. Gross popped up and began pointing at Dawkins, cursing at the much taller man. Several Sixers grabbed Gross and held him back and the situation looked to be under control. Then, inexplicably, Dawkins charged at Gross and took a wild swing, connecting instead with his teammate Doug Collins, who required four stitches after the game to close the cut. Dawkins backpedaled away from the action—right into Maurice Lucas, who stunned the 250-pound "Chocolate Thunder" with a forearm strike to the back of his neck that would have made pro wrestler Chief Jay Strongbow proud. Dawkins stumbled and then whipped around, leading to an unintentionally hilarious moment in which both muscle-bound enforcers put up their dukes as if bareknuckle boxing. Dawkins juked and jived, doing his best Muhammad Ali impression before Lucas threw three quick jabs in succession, none of which connected. Both benches cleared, fans spilled onto the court, and Julius Erving sat down on the floor, apparently disinterested in the whole affair. It took several minutes for Philly's finest to clear fans and players off the court and restore order. The referees (real ones, not the replacement refs relegated to the opening rounds) tossed both Dawkins and Lucas, and the game ended a few minutes later: Sixers 107, Blazers 89. In his rage, Dawkins destroyed the home locker room, caving in a toilet stall and smashing a wall fan. NBA officials levied $2,500 fines to Dawkins and Lucas, although neither was suspended. Looking back, the fight was a turning point in the series: the time the Blazers, considered the "softer" of the teams, stood up for themselves.

Before tip-off in game three, Lucas walked over to the Philadelphia bench and shook hands with Dawkins, letting fans and players from both teams know there were no hard feelings; it was time to focus on basketball. The Blazers demolished the Sixers in games three and four in Portland, with Bobby Gross blanketing Julius Erving as Walton, Lucas, and Hollins provided the offensive fireworks to tie the series at two games apiece. Game five, in Philadelphia, also went to Portland (Blazers 110, Sixers 104), as Gross scored a team-high twenty-five points to send the series back to Oregon, where the Blazers hoped to finish off the Sixers at home.

Bedlam reigned in Portland before game six. Businesses closed early and fans crowded around TV sets to watch a potential series-clinching win. Television ratings showed that 96 percent—yes, 96 percent—of Oregonians watching TV tuned in to game six. The streets of Portland flooded with fans even before the Blazers survived with a 109–107 win. As George McGinnis's last-second game-tying shot went awry, radio listeners could barely hear Bill Schonley scream, "the game is over! The game is over!" above the roar of the crowd. Although CBS immediately switched to coverage of the Kemper Open golf tournament, deliriously happy Portland fans celebrated long into the night, honking their car horns to the staccato beat of "we're number one."

Portland's mayor declared the day after the game-six win "Trail Blazer Day" and hosted a celebration for the team, drawing upward of 250,000 fans downtown—the largest public gathering in the state's history. A parade stretched along the city streets, and as one Blazermaniac remembered, "the people were reaching out to touch and grab the conquering heroes as if they were gods." The tallest of the gods, Bill Walton, rode his bicycle to the festivities, only to have it stolen. So when Walton took his turn on the microphone to address the crowd at the victory celebration, he asked if "whoever took my bike [could] please bring it back. It's the only one I have," adding that "if anyone out there has any more beer, please pass it up here." Supplied with a cold brew, though still lacking his bike, Walton poured part of the beer on Portland's mayor. No one cared. Blazermania was in full bloom.[29]

The 1976–1977 Blazers, like so many teams before them, looked certain to create a lasting dynasty. After all, they had all the requirements: a dominant center, a deep and talented core of young players, an inside scoring threat, an exuberant fan base, and a well-respected coach. Yet as was often the case in the '70s, the Blazers dynasty was short-lived, and by the end of the '78 season, there would be a new team hoisting the championship trophy.

Statistics for 1976–1977

Eastern Conference	W	L	Western Conference	W	L
Atlantic Division			*Midwest Division*		
Philadelphia 76ers	50	32	Denver Nuggets	50	32
Boston Celtics	44	38	Detroit Pistons	44	38
New York Knicks	40	42	Chicago Bulls	44	38
Buffalo Braves	30	52	Kansas City Kings	40	42
New York Nets	22	60	Indiana Pacers	36	46
			Milwaukee Bucks	30	52
Central Division			*Pacific Division*		
Houston Rockets	49	33	Los Angeles Lakers	53	29
Washington Bullets	48	34	Portland Trail Blazers	49	33
San Antonio Spurs	44	38	Golden State Warriors	46	36
Cleveland Cavaliers	43	39	Seattle SuperSonics	40	42
New Orleans Jazz	35	47	Phoenix Suns	34	48
Atlanta Hawks	31	51			

Playoffs

Eastern Conference First Round	Boston d. San Antonio (2–0)
	Washington d. Cleveland (2–1)
Western Conference First Round	Golden State d. Detroit (2–1)
	Portland d. Chicago (2–1)
Eastern Conference Semifinals	Houston d. Washington (4–2)
	Philadelphia d. Boston (4–3)
Western Conference Semifinals	Los Angeles d. Golden State (4–3)
	Portland d. Denver (4–2)
Eastern Conference Finals	Philadelphia d. Houston (4–2)
Western Conference Finals	Portland d. Los Angeles (4–0)
NBA Finals	Portland d. Philadelphia (4–2)

All-NBA Teams

First Team	Second Team
F—Elvin Hayes (Washington)	F—Julius Erving (Philadelphia)
F—David Thompson (Denver)	F—George McGinnis (Philadelphia)
C—Kareem Abdul-Jabbar (Los Angeles)	C—Bill Walton (Portland)
G—Pete Maravich (New Orleans)	G—George Gervin (San Antonio)
G—Paul Westphal (Phoenix)	G—Jo Jo White (Boston)

League Leaders

Points per Game (31.1)	Pete Maravich (New Orleans)
Rebounds per Game (14.4)	Bill Walton (Portland)
Assists per Game (8.5)	Don Buse (Indiana)
Steals per Game (3.5)	Don Buse (Indiana)
Blocks per Game (3.2)	Bill Walton (Portland)
Most Valuable Player	Kareem Abdul-Jabbar (Los Angeles)
Rookie of the Year	Adrian Dantley (Buffalo)

9

1977 TO 1978

On December 9, 1977, the Houston Rockets visited the Fabulous
Forum of Inglewood to play the Los Angeles Lakers. Both had designs
on an NBA title, but each sat several games under .500 at that moment.
At halftime, the score was tied at fifty-five. Ho hum. Just another game
in a long NBA season. But moments into the second half, Rockets
center Kevin Kunnert and Lakers forward Kermit Washington got tan-
gled up near midcourt. "We were used to fights," remembered one
Rockets beat writer. "Back then, fights broke out in the NBA every
night. When Kermit and Kunnert squared off, your first response was
'Oh look, another stupid NBA fight, what else is new?'" Players from
both teams hurried over to break up their teammates; the Lakers' Kareem Abdul-Jabbar held back Kunnert while the Rockets' Rudy Tomjanovich sprinted at Washington. In his peripheral vision, Washington
sensed movement. In one fluid motion, he turned and swung a powerful fist at the approaching blur.[1]

"I grew up in the streets," Washington later explained. "You learn
there that if you're in a fight and someone is coming up from behind
you, you swing first and ask questions later." Washington's right hand
connected squarely with Tomjanovich's jaw and the Rockets forward
dropped like a stone. Abdul-Jabbar compared the sound of Tomjanovich's head hitting the court to "a watermelon [that] had been dropped
on a concrete floor," and one Lakers assistant called it simply "the
greatest punch in the history of mankind." Tomjanovich unsteadily tried
to stand, insistent that he remain in the game despite an aching head

and an oddly bitter taste in his mouth. Fortunately, the team doctor convinced Rudy to leave for a local emergency room where the physicians on call were amazed he had even survived, comparing his injuries to those sustained by someone thrown through the windshield of a car traveling at fifty miles per hour. Tomjanovich suffered a fractured skull, cracked eye socket, serious damage to his tear ducts, and other facial disfigurements; the bitterness he tasted was spinal fluid leaking from his brain.[2]

By the winter of 1977, the image of the powerful and violent black man was well-established in the American mainstream. Blaxploitation films like 1971's *Shaft* (and its less-celebrated sequels, *Shaft's Big Score* and *Shaft in Africa*) popularized the concept of tough black dudes sticking it to "the man." This aggressiveness was reflected in American sports as well. The seventies were a golden age for professional boxing, highlighted by title bouts featuring Muhammad Ali, Joe Frazier, and George Foreman. But not only pro pugilists found ways to release pent-up aggression; fights also broke out in the National Football League, in Major League Baseball, and of course in the National Hockey League with regularity. Like many of these sports, basketball had a history of on-court enforcers whose primary role was to protect star teammates. "You need a rugged, we're-not-going-to-take-any-nonsense personality on a team," explained one coach. "It's important for your team to let it be known that you will not be pushed around, will not be intimidated." Left unsaid, most of these enforcers were African American, reinforcing cultural stereotypes of violent black masculinity. For someone like Julius Erving, thunderously dunking on an opponent might validate his virility. For others like Kermit Washington, it might require throwing a punch to defend a teammate.[3]

NBA violence peaked in the late seventies; officials documented forty-one fights during the 1976–1977 season alone, including the famous Maurice Lucas versus Darryl Dawkins dustup in game two of the finals. The league tried to legislate against aggressiveness by penalizing players both for "excessive and/or vigorous swinging of the elbows" and for fighting, fining would-be brawlers $10,000. But even as the NBA worked to curtail violence, the sports media praised basketball's tough guys. Weeks before Washington's famous punch, *Sports Illustrated* published an article titled "Nobody, but Nobody, Is Going to Hurt My Teammates," celebrating six NBA enforcers: Bob Lanier, Calvin Murphy, Dennis Awtrey, Dawkins, Lucas, and—of course—Kermit Washington.

Murphy was the short guy on the list, a diminutive five-nine, 165-pound All-Star guard for the Rockets who was a Golden Gloves boxer as a teenager and who as a pro bragged that he had "been in seventeen full-fledged fights during eight years in the league and had never lost." Murphy once picked a fight with six-foot-eight Sidney Wicks, overcoming the size difference by grabbing Wicks's Afro and punching him into submission. Lucas started fights with Artis Gilmore and Julius Erving as an ABA rookie; Dawkins was more poet than fighter before mixing it up with Lucas; and Lanier, another tall and powerful black athlete, kayoed an opponent in his second year in the NBA and word got around not to mess with "Dobber." Awtrey, the only white player to make the list, comes across in the *SI* article as a mischievous rascal possessing the "off-court demeanor of a puppy, and his blue eyes twinkle innocently when he says, 'Why would I hit a guy for no reason?'" In contrast to the overtly violent nature attributed to the black athletes on the list, *Sports Illustrated* basically described Awtrey as an overgrown Dennis the Menace.[4]

Like many of the league's other enforcers, Washington was a powerfully built African American with a well-deserved reputation for violence, having been involved in numerous brawls in his short career. Initially, Washington struggled to find a niche in the NBA, averaging just 3.8 points and 3.3 rebounds per game as a rookie. After two more disappointing seasons spent watching more than playing, he convinced celebrated big man coach Pete Newell to help him improve. It worked. Early in the 1977–1978 season, Washington was averaging career highs in points (11.5 per game) and rebounds (11.2) and even had a chance to make the All-Star team. But the stigma of being an enforcer weighed heavily on him. "I'm not a policeman," he insisted in the *SI* article. "I'm not a fighter . . . some of us don't have the talent of the Dr. J's and the Kareem Abdul-Jabbars, so we have to do our jobs the best way we can. I'm just an aggressive guy trying to survive."[5]

Although *Sports Illustrated* left him off their list, Abdul-Jabbar, Washington's L.A. teammate, got into a fight early in the season, sucker punching Milwaukee Bucks rookie center Kent Benson (the first overall pick in the draft), breaking both Benson's jaw and his own right hand in the process. Kareem insisted Benson threw an elbow to start the fight and was livid when the white rookie escaped suspension. "Typical NBA justice," Abdul-Jabbar wrote, "discipline the nigger." Commissioner Larry O'Brien avoided discussing race but was very outspoken about violence after the Abdul-Jabbar event. "Every player in the NBA is on notice that I oppose fighting during games, no matter what the provocation," O'Brien said. "I will use all the powers of my office to prevent violence within the NBA."[6]

Fast-forward to December 10, 1977, the day after Washington dropped Tomjanovich with "the punch." O'Brien and the NBA suddenly faced a public relations nightmare: a powerfully built African American player nearly killed a popular white player on a basketball court in front of thousands of spectators and television viewers. The commissioner fined Washington $10,000 and suspended him without pay for sixty days, the longest suspension handed down for an on-court action in the history of the league. O'Brien's decision stunned Washington. "Most teams probably won't have anything to do with me," Kermit complained. "I may never play again."[7]

Media reports painted Washington as a dark-skinned villain. The *New York Times* printed an editorial denouncing NBA violence, and CBS anchor Walter Cronkite discussed the league's response to on-court physicality. But it was NBC's popular *Saturday Night Live* television program that really exploited the situation. On its regular "Weekend Update" segment, Garrett Morris, an African American comedian, claimed that once again the media was casting African American men as violent thugs. Video of Washington punching Tomjanovich played over and over as Morris tried to humorously justify the violence; "we blacks get blamed for everything!" Morris insisted. "The brother barely touched him." Pause. "Maybe we need a different angle."[8]

"The punch" marked a low point for professional basketball in the 1970s. Just months after the NBA celebrated a successful merger with the ABA and the selfless team play of the title-winning Portland Trail Blazers, the league was suddenly shrouded in controversy. Future commissioner David Stern, then working as NBA legal counsel, called this the NBA's "dark days" and admitted Washington's punch "appeared to symbolize everything people were saying about us": that the league was too violent and too black. Washington served his suspension and was traded by Los Angeles; without Rudy T, Houston plummeted down the standings.[9]

The 1977–1978 season was chaotic for everyone, not just the Lakers and Rockets. It also marked the first full-fledged summer of free agency, and a number of talented players switched teams: the Warriors lost Jamaal Wilkes to the Lakers and Gus Williams to the SuperSonics; Bobby Dandridge went from the Bucks to the Bullets; and Leonard "Truck" Robinson took his powerful rebounding to the improving Jazz. It was also an exciting season on the court as fans witnessed a record-breaking race for the scoring title and the retirement of an all-time great, even as a dark cloud hung over the future of the sport.

For the first five months of the season, the Portland Trail Blazers seemed a lock to repeat as NBA champions, starting the year 50–10 to take a commanding lead in the Pacific Division. Along with All-Star players Maurice Lucas, Lionel Hollins, and Bill Walton, Portland boasted the best fans in the league. Self-proclaimed "Blazermaniacs" filled not only each of the 12,666 seats in Memorial Coliseum, but also packed into a 3,000-seat movie theater across the street to watch games on closed-circuit television. The Blazers were rollin'. But in the season's sixty-first game, the unthinkable happened; Walton, who had a history of chronic leg and back problems, fractured his foot. The good news? He could probably return in time for the playoffs. The bad news? Once again Walton faced hard questions about his fragile health. Predictably, the team sputtered in the absence of the league MVP (dropping fourteen of their last twenty-two), but remained the favorites in the West— as long as Walton could suit up in the postseason.

Unlike Portland, the Seattle SuperSonics came out of the gates slowly, starting 5–17 under rookie head coach Bob Hopkins, Bill Russell's replacement on the sidelines. Little more than a month into the season, Seattle owner Sam Schulman fired Hopkins, replacing him with Lenny Wilkens. Wilkens immediately turned the team around, changing the starting lineup and juggling playing time on a deep, superstar-less team. The Sonics responded with a hot streak, winning six straight and forty-two of their last sixty. "You always expect a little surge after a coaching change," Wilkens admitted, "but this is too many wins to be a little surge."[10]

Seattle's backcourt fueled the turnaround; free agent signee Gus Williams (the team leader in scoring with 18.1 points per game) paired with "Downtown" Freddie Brown and Dennis Johnson to create a formidable trio. Brown was a veteran sharpshooter, bombing in rainbow jump shots from, well, downtown, while Johnson was a long-armed defensive stopper nicknamed "Airplane" for his amazing leaping ability.

The Sonics also boasted frontcourt depth, mixing talented youth with experienced vets. Paul Silas, picked up with Marvin Webster in a preseason trade with Denver, was in his fourteenth NBA season and, at age thirty-four, could hardly leave his feet for a rebound. Even ground-bound, though, Silas was a perfect on- and off-court leader for the young Sonics squad, setting hard screens, providing interior toughness, and serving as an off-court mentor. Like Silas, John Johnson had bounced around (making two All-Star teams) before landing in Seattle. Johnson was the consummate facilitator and perhaps the league's first "point forward," regularly initiating the offense despite standing six-foot-seven. The two youngsters in the Sonics frontcourt were Webster, a seven footer nicknamed "the Human Eraser" for his shot-blocking ability, and six-eleven rookie Jack Sikma, whose blonde locks seemed better suited to a Lego figure than a pro athlete.

Most NBA fans assumed the Lakers could challenge Portland for the top spot in the Pacific Division. After all, Kareem Abdul-Jabbar was the reigning MVP and Kermit Washington was his perfect foil, a muscular forward who excelled at rebounding and on defense. Without Abdul-Jabbar, out for the first quarter of the season with a broken hand, and Washington, suspended and then traded after just twenty-five games, the team crumbled. Even before those losses, the Lakers struggled with continuity, trying to integrate several new players into the rotation. "I wasn't sure why they had made so many changes to a team that won fifty-three games," Washington said later. "The year before, every guy knew his role and had been happy with it," he explained. "With all the new players, it just seemed as if we were never on the same page." Two of the biggest acquisitions were smooth forward Jamaal "Silk" Wilkes, signed away from Golden State as a free agent, and veteran guard "Sweet" Lou Hudson, picked up in a trade with the Atlanta Hawks. The team also dealt for former rookie of the year Ernie DiGregorio, but coach Jerry West complained so emphatically about the ex-Buffalo star's shortcomings that Lakers owner Jack Kent Cooke cut him midway through the season. DiGregorio was expendable, at least in part be-cause of the rise of unheralded rookie point guard Norm Nixon. Nixon, selected late in the first round of the draft, excelled as a floor general for the Lakers, earning All-Rookie honors after scoring almost fourteen points and a handing out a team-high seven assists per game.[11]

Nixon was a steal with the twenty-second pick of the 1977 draft. But more importantly, that draft signaled a league-wide shift away from dominant big men and toward more athletic scorers. The Milwaukee Bucks took Indiana center Kent Benson first overall, envisioning him as "another Dave Cowens or Bill Walton"—a talented white-skinned, fundamentally sound inside player who would have probably been an All-Star in the fifties or sixties. But by selecting Benson, the Bucks passed on three tremendously athletic wing players, all of whom had considerably better careers. Fortunately the Bucks had three first-round picks and selected UCLA forward Marques Johnson third. *Sports Illustrated*'s Curry Kirkpatrick called Johnson "the golden strongboy out of UCLA," a fitting description for a thunder-dunking highflier who drew comparisons to a young Elgin Baylor or Gus "Honeycomb" Johnson. Marques Johnson led all rookies in rebounding (10.6) and finished third in scoring (19.5), but despite his all-around brilliance, Marques was not quite as good as two other forwards selected in the draft. Picking fifth, the Phoenix Suns chose North Carolina's Walter Davis. Davis won the rookie of the year award as a whip-thin six-foot-six swingman with a soft shooting touch (especially from eight or nine feet out) and an uncanny understanding of the game that drew comparisons to a young John Havlicek. The third major contributor from the '77 rookie class was New Jersey (formerly New York) Nets forward Bernard King. Davis, Johnson, and King were the cream of the crop of a strong NBA draft—Kirkpatrick acknowledged that, "hyperbole aside, Walter Davis, Bernard King and Marques Johnson may be the best athletes ever to come into the same professional sport at the same time at the same position"[12]

King twice made the Associated Press All-American team at the University of Tennessee but slipped to the Nets at pick number seven because of off-court concerns: he was arrested five times in Knoxville during an eighteen-month span for violations ranging from loitering to larceny. Despite his off-court problems (and there were many, even after he turned pro), King was a prodigy on the court. Ray Mears, King's coach at Tennessee, called Bernard "the quickest basketball player I've seen around in all the time I've been involved in the game." King was not only quick, he was also exceptionally strong, able to score almost at will on sweeping drives to the basket. Against smaller defenders, the six-foot-six King bulled his way to the basket. "When he got the ball and faced you up," future Hall of Famer Chris Mullin explained, "he was in charge." Yet questions remained about King's attitude. In one game as a rookie, King threw the ball at Pistons center Bob Lanier, inciting a bench-clearing brawl that ended with King and Lanier spilling into the stands and onto spectators.[13]

The '77 draft was memorable beyond the selections of All-Stars Davis, Johnson, and King. For one, it was the final one held via telephone. After three decades, league officials finally acknowledged the logistical nightmare of a twenty-two team, four-hour conference call resulting in a $1,500 phone bill. The eight-round draft also featured some memorable selections. With their first three picks, the Bulls selected Tate Armstrong, Mike Glenn, and Steve Sheppard; sportswriters dubbed it the "Astronaut Draft" after their outer space–exploring namesakes Neil Armstrong, John Glenn, and Alan Shepard. In the seventh round, the Kings drafted gold medal decathlete Bruce Jenner, who last played in high school. As it turned out, Jenner would be far more involved in the NBA decades later when his stepdaughters Kim and Khloé Kardashian married pro players.

Two picks ahead of Jenner, the Jazz selected another Olympian, Lusia "Lucy" Harris, who played on the first U.S. women's Olympic team in 1976, leading them to a silver medal. With that pick, the 137th overall, the Jazz also became the first team in NBA history to "officially" draft a woman. Seven years earlier, San Francisco Warriors owner Franklin Mieuli chose Denise Long in the thirteenth round, hoping to form an all-women's basketball league around the high-scoring Long (who averaged more than sixty points per game playing six-on-six basketball for her Iowa high school team). But commissioner Walter Kennedy voided the choice and Long became an unofficial draftee. Now, in '76, just four years after Congress passed Title IX of the Education Amendments protecting Americans from gender-based discrimination, the Jazz were allowed to keep their choice, although, as general manager Frank Layden quipped, "it turned out she was pregnant, so we'd really drafted two people." Harris never played for New Orleans—or for any NBA team, for that matter—but she did spend a season in the short-lived Women's Professional Basketball League and in 1992 became one of just two women then enshrined in the Naismith Memorial Basketball Hall of Fame.[14]

Drafting Harris gained the Jazz a lot of mainstream media attention but very few wins. In Denver, the Nuggets lacked publicity, but won far more than New Orleans and hoped to build upon their 52–30 record from 1976–1977. Before the 1977–1978 season, the Nuggets made a pair of blockbuster trades, sending Paul Silas and Marvin Webster to Seattle and receiving veteran point guard Brian Taylor from Kansas City. Taylor was a six-foot-two, two-time ABA All-Star, an accomplished long-distance shooter, and a whiz at stealing the basketball from opposing guards. "He possessed excellent speed," David Thompson remembered of his teammate, "had good height, could really shoot, and was as good a defender at the guard position as there was in the league." With Taylor running the show, the Nuggets utilized what Coach Larry Brown called their "passing game," a freestyle offense (not unlike the much-heralded triangle offense installed by Phil Jackson and Tex Winter in Chicago in the 1980s), taking advantage of the outside shooting ability of both Taylor and center Dan Issel. Their ability to stretch the floor allowed Thompson to attack the basket at will, and only Adrian Dantley made more free throws than Thompson in the 1977–1978 season. After forty games, with the Nuggets on a nine-game winning streak and, at 27–13, boasting the third-best record in the league, Taylor suddenly left the team and declared himself a free agent, citing an unpaid $50,000 bonus owed him by the Nuggets.[15]

Without Taylor, even more responsibility fell to David "Skywalker" Thompson. As a collegian, Thompson led North Carolina State to the 1974 NCAA championship, breaking a streak of seven straight titles by UCLA dating to the Lew Alcindor era. He was also a three-time All-American and back-to-back national player of the year. From 1967 to 1976, the NCAA outlawed the slam dunk (the so-called Alcindor Rule), but Thompson and teammate Monte Towe perfected the alley-oop pass and shot, resulting in numerous above-the-rim layups for the high-flying Skywalker. Opponents and teammates alike raved about Thompson; Dick Vitale called him "Baryshnikov in shorts, a ballerina of basketball"; Bill Walton remembered Thompson as "the single greatest college player whom I ever played against," calling him "Michael Jordan, Kobe Bryant, Tracy McGrady and LeBron James rolled into one." Walton might have exaggerated, but others saw a little bit of Julius Erving in Thompson's game, although they had far different styles. Dr. J was taller (six-feet-seven-inches tall) and floated to the rim while waving the ball around in one gigantic hand, whereas Skywalker was an explosive dynamo packed into a six-foot-four frame with hands too small to even palm the basketball. "There's no one in the league who can stop him," said one Nuggets teammate. "He can score on anyone." The biggest news out of Denver, though, was the contract extension Thompson signed during the season. Fearing that teams like the Knicks or Lakers would throw huge deals at Thompson if he hit the free agent market in the summer of '78, the Nuggets agreed to a massive five-year, $4 million contract, making "Skywalker" the highest-paid player in NBA history.[16]

Today, salaries are popular fodder for NBA fans discussing their favorite teams, leading to endless debates about which players are worth "maximum" salaries and which are not. Prior to the salary cap, introduced in 1984 and set at a strict $3.6 million per squad, there was no spending limit, leading to intense bidding wars between teams and leagues for top talent. During the seventies, the average player salary rose from $35,000 per year, requiring all but the top-paid guys to find off-season second jobs, to $142,000. By 1980 few if any players relied on off-season work to make ends meet.

Rising salaries created conflict in both the locker room and between players and management. "In the NBA, respect is measured by the figures on a player's contract, plain and simple," said Oscar Robertson. In the sixties, an informal pecking order dictated player salaries: Wilt Chamberlain, Bill Russell (reportedly paid $1 more per year than Chamberlain), Robertson, and Jerry West made the most money, while perennial All-Stars like Rick Barry, John Havlicek, and Dave DeBusschere earned slightly less. And so on down the line all the way to the lowest-paid benchwarmers. ABA owners inverted this pyramid, signing unproven rookies to huge deals in an effort to keep potential superstars from the NBA. To keep pace, NBA teams had to artificially increase salaries, and by mid-decade, "big money and superstars made camaraderie more difficult. It was hard," Pulitzer Prize–winning author David Halberstam explained, "for a player making $60,000 a year to pal around with one making $500,000." Financial disparities sparked jealousy among players. Star athletes, Halberstam wrote, developed both "an exaggerated impression of their own worth and a distorted sense of why they were actually playing the game." Making matters worse, fewer players entered the league with a college degree, and many came from low-income backgrounds. Some dealt poorly with their newfound wealth, wasting it on wine, women, and song (or, more appropriately for the era, pot, groupies, and disco records), leading to shortened or wasted careers.[17]

Thompson's contract marked a pivotal moment in NBA history—a shift in power from owners to players. But it did not come without a cost. With dwindling attendance and a drop in television ratings, some owners simply could not afford their high-priced stars and were forced to sell their teams or consider bankruptcy. Financial problems forced the Indiana Pacers to that brink, and in the summer of 1977, the team sold talented players, cut team personnel, and held a telethon. Yes, a telethon. Indiana's owners announced that summer a need to sell 8,000 season tickets to remain solvent; by the end of June, they were only halfway to their goal. So the team convinced a local TV station to air a "Save the Pacers" telethon. For more than sixteen hours on July 3 and 4, the Pacers filled the airwaves with local bands and state celebrities (including Indiana Hoosiers coach Bobby Knight) while players and volunteers worked the phones. Even former Pacers forward George McGinnis bought a few tickets and taped a segment to promote the team. Thanks to the telethon, the Pacers sold the necessary tickets. Despite the success, however, Indiana continued to cut costs, trading away leading scorer Billy Knight and fan favorite Don Buse, receiving guard Ricky Sobers (from Phoenix) and reigning rookie of the year Adrian Dantley (from Buffalo) in return. Dantley lasted only a few weeks in Indiana blue and gold before the team shipped him to the Lakers for rookie center James Edwards (and cash, of course). Pacers fans held out hope, however, that their on-court mediocrity would translate into a high draft pick. One player that Hoosiers knew quite well—and who was expected to declare his eligibility for the 1978 draft—was Indiana State forward Larry Bird.

Predictably, no Pacers made the All-Star team; far more surprisingly, neither did Kareem Abdul-Jabbar. In fact, 1978 marked the only time in his twenty-year career Kareem was not named to the team. In his place, the West started Bill Walton at center who, in his one and only All-Star appearance (he sat out the 1977 game with an injury), scored fifteen points and pulled down ten rebounds. But it was not enough: the

East won 133–125. On a team full of stars, including Dave Cowens, John Havlicek, and Julius Erving, the hero for the East was reserve guard Randy Smith of the Buffalo Braves, who came off the bench to score twenty-seven points, earning the All-Star MVP award.

In the regular season, Smith led the Braves to a fourth-place finish in the Atlantic, a distant twenty-eight games behind the division-winning Philadelphia 76ers. Before the season, the Sixers public relations team promoted their star-studded squad using the slogan "We owe you one," in reference to making but not winning the 1977 finals. In addition to a new catchphrase, they also had a new coach. Gene Shue was out, and legendary Sixers forward Billy Cunningham was in. Cunningham promised to play a faster-paced style to take full advantage of the team's myriad offensive weapons. It worked. Philadelphia led the league in scoring (114.7 points per game) and went 55–27 during the regular season behind "Dr. J" Julius Erving and the "Baby Bull" George McGinnis, the best forward tandem in the league. Erving started in the All-Star game, made All-NBA first team, and led the team in scoring (20.6 points per game) while McGinnis scored nearly as often (20.3 points per game) and pulled down a team-high 10.4 rebounds per game. The Sixers also returned "the Bomb Squad"—arguably the best bench in the league—and were once again the clear favorites to represent the Eastern Conference in the NBA finals.

Compared to Philadelphia, the rest of the Atlantic Division struggled. The New York Knicks won forty-three games, good for second place, but should have been better. During the off-season, they signed free agent Jim Cleamons from the Cavaliers, and as compensation the Knicks sent legendary guard Walt "Clyde" Frazier to Cleveland. Frazier was stunned and blamed his former teammate and new Knicks coach Willis Reed for the trade. "When the trade came," Frazier wrote in his 1988 autobiography, "Willis never said a word. He still hasn't."[18]

Once the season began, Coach Reed had far more pressing concerns than a disgruntled ex-teammate. After all, he had to somehow convince a team full of ball-dominant superstars to sacrifice individual statistics for team success. Fortunately for Reed, veteran guard Earl "the Pearl" Monroe, playing on two surgically repaired knees, discovered the fountain of youth, emerging "like a retired magician" near season's end with a series of twenty- and thirty-point scoring nights reminiscent of the team's glory days. But while teammate Bob McAdoo also remained a force on offense, averaging 26.5 points and 12.8 rebounds per game, Spencer Haywood remained an enigma. Haywood flashed moments of brilliance, including a thirty-seven-point outburst against Indiana, but dealt with a lot of personal problems. Before his big game against the Pacers, Haywood met with Coach Reed. "I had to straighten out a couple of things," Haywood said. "I was sort of unhappy with myself and my playing time." During the season, Haywood also met the super-model Iman, marrying her after a whirlwind five-month courtship. Off-court distractions definitely affected Haywood's on-court performance, and more often than not Coach Reed benched Haywood in favor of second-year forward Lonnie Shelton, a team-first player willing to do the dirty work.[19]

Like the Knicks, the Boston Celtics (32–50) were a talented bunch struggling with continuity. Sure, their roster included seven former All-Stars: Dave Bing, Dave Cowens, John Havlicek, Curtis Rowe, Charlie Scott, Jo Jo White, and Sidney Wicks. But they were frustratingly inconsistent, defeating the defending champion Trail Blazers in Portland and then losing six straight games at home. In an attempt to shake up the roster, Boston traded Scott to Los Angeles for Kermit Washington and signed Ernie DiGregorio after the Lakers cut him. Neither move helped. As the team struggled, Rowe and Wicks, in particular, became locker room cancers. Quizzed about the lack of team success, Rowe responded, "hey man, there's no Ws and Ls on the pay check." Wicks, Rowe's buddy from their days at UCLA, played the worst basketball of his career, setting career lows in every statistical category. *Boston Globe* sportswriter Bob Ryan decided Wicks, in Portland, was "a high-scoring loser. In Boston," Ryan wrote, "he has merely been a loser."[20]

More troubling even than the team's on-court mediocrity was the racial turmoil plaguing Boston throughout the late seventies. Desegregation in city school districts turned into violent public protests after Boston began busing nearly a quarter of its 87,000 public school students across the city to fulfill racial quotas. Many white Bostonians openly opposed the busing initiative and protested, sometimes violently, about its effect on their children. The lasting image of the riots, a photograph titled "The Soiling of Old Glory," depicts a young white man menacingly thrusting the point of an American flag toward an African American attorney.

Boston sports, likewise, had a long history of problems with race. In the '50s and '60s, Bill Russell was overshadowed by white hockey player Bobby Orr and white baseball players Ted Williams and Carl Yastrzemski, despite the eleven championship titles he brought to Beantown. The racial problems persisted and perhaps even intensified in the late seventies. "Plain and simple, black people didn't like the Celtics," Celtics forward Cedric "Cornbread" Maxwell explained. "They were too white—or at least that's how they were presented." New York filmmaker Spike Lee, a die-hard Knicks fan, agreed. "To me," Lee said, "the Celtics represent white supremacy." Bob McAdoo recalled that Boston was "a place that destroyed black careers. It was," he decided, "a graveyard for blacks." In the 1960s, the Celtics broke racial stereotypes by regularly playing four, or even five, African American players at a time. By the late seventies, though, even Red Auerbach, the architect of those teams, faced accusations of racism after releasing longtime coach Tom Heinsohn. Auerbach blamed Heinsohn's failures not on any of his own shortcomings, but instead on the Celtics players, most of whom were African American. "I was hoping," Auerbach said, "these monkeys could turn it around." Whether the statement was intentionally racist or not, by the early eighties the Celtics were the whitest team in an increasingly black league.[21]

As dreary as the Celtics season was, it was made a little brighter by celebrations of retiring Boston legend John "Hondo" Havlicek. As Havlicek made his last circuit of the league, many opponents presented the future Hall of Famer with lavish gifts. In Oakland, the Golden State Warriors gave him a solid gold money clip; Denver paid for John and his wife Beth to take a well-deserved vacation; Seattle ponied up an outboard motor; and, not to be outdone, Philadelphia gave the Havliceks a basket including everything "from scrapple to a Liberty Bell." Even the league kicked in for Hondo's farewell tour, writing him a check for $925, equal to the amount he paid in fines over his sixteen-year career. As Boston's season mercifully neared its end, the team went all out to celebrate Havlicek's achievements. On April 9, 1978, Hondo showed up in a rented tuxedo and left with a motor home given to him by the Celtics front office.[22]

Havlicek is easily overlooked when listing the best players in NBA history, perhaps because no single part of his game defined him. "John's never had a definite profile like Bill Russell or Cousy," teammate Dave

Cowens explained. "He's played all these games without being recognized." Havlicek had played in more games and taken more shots than any player in the history of the league, appearing in thirteen straight All-Star games and winning eight championship rings with two distinctly different squads: six with the Bill Russell/Sam Jones Celtics and two alongside Cowens and Jo Jo White. Hondo is still the only player in league history to record more than 25,000 points, 8,000 rebounds, and 6,000 assists, and he excelled in big games. His defense in the 1965 conference finals, memorialized in Johnny Most's famous call of "*Havlicek stole the ball!*" and his wrong-footed shot in the second overtime of the greatest game ever played (game five of the 1976 finals) were two of the most memorable moments in NBA history. Fittingly, Hondo ended his career with a remarkable twenty-nine-point performance in leading Boston over the Buffalo Braves as the crowd in the Boston Garden gave him a standing ovation lasting for several minutes.[23]

On the very day of Havlicek's retirement ceremony, April 9, 1978, San Antonio Spurs forward George "the Iceman" Gervin and Denver Nuggets guard David "Skywalker" Thompson battled for the league scoring title. Going into the season's final game, Gervin held a slight advantage—26.78 to 26.57 points per game. Thompson's Nuggets faced the Pistons in a rather meaningless matchup; Detroit, playing its final game in Cobo Hall before moving to the spacious Pontiac Silverdome, was not playoff bound, and Denver was already locked into the second seed in the West. But Thompson had something to play for, and the 4,000 fans who showed up that day witnessed history. No camera crews were on hand because Havlicek's retirement made for far better copy. But after an NBA-record thirty-two-point first quarter in which Thompson connected on thirteen of fourteen shots from the field and all six of his free throw attempts, news quickly spread that the Skywalker was doing something special in the Motor City. Brent Musberger, covering the Celtics-Braves game, cut into the telecast to update fans about Thompson's climbing point totals. "I was definitely in the zone," Thompson said. "I felt like Superman on steroids. There wasn't a shot I put up that I didn't think, as soon as it left my hands, would go anywhere but in the hoop." Thompson went into halftime having scored fifty-three points and was on pace to break one hundred, Wilt Chamberlain's legendary single-game scoring record. In the second half, Detroit double- and even triple-teamed Thompson in a desperate attempt to keep him in double digits. They succeeded. He scored seventy-three, then the highest total recorded by a guard and the third-highest mark for any player (Chamberlain also once tallied seventy-eight). With his outburst, Thompson moved into first place in the scoring race, and "the Iceman" George Gervin needed at least fifty-eight points to regain the title.[24]

"The Iceman" was a thin wisp of a man, standing six-foot-eight and weighing 180 pounds dripping wet. Gervin grew up in Detroit and earned a scholarship to Long Beach State, then coached by the legendary Jerry Tarkanian. But the culture shock was too much and Gervin transferred to Eastern Michigan, a small school just thirty miles west of Detroit. In his only collegiate season, 1971–1972, Gervin averaged nearly thirty points a game to lead his Eagles to the NCAA Division II Final Four against eventual champion Roanoke College. During the game against Roanoke, Gervin punched an opposing player; he was promptly suspended and then kicked off the team.

After bouncing around a few semipro leagues, Gervin caught on with the ABA's Virginia Squires, where teammate Fatty Taylor dubbed him "the Iceman" because Gervin was "always cool." After a trade sent him to the San Antonio Spurs, Gervin gained another nickname, J. J., because of his physical resemblance to Jimmie Walker's character on the hit TV show *Good Times*. In San Antonio, Gervin became a star. "Gervin was to San Antonio what Babe Ruth was to New York," Spurs owner Angelo Drossos explained. "He was the symbol of basketball in this town." Gervin's specialty was the finger-roll shot, flipping the ball underhanded from as far as ten or twelve feet from the basket. "He can get his shot off from anywhere," said Julius Erving. "He's taking the finger roll and using it almost like Kareem uses the skyhook; it's a shot he can get in traffic whenever he wants." Opposing teams tried to slow down Gervin by playing him physically, grabbing and pushing the rail-thin "Iceman" to throw off his rhythm. But by the spring of 1978, Gervin was used to such tactics. "The man is just toying with the whole NBA," teammate George Karl said. Gervin agreed: "whereas I ain't too fast, here to there my gig is zigzaggin'."[25]

On April 9, Gervin watched helplessly as the scoring title seemed to slip from his grasp. He knew he needed at least fifty-eight points to overtake Thompson, but his Spurs faced the Jazz, a decent defensive team. "The Iceman" torched them. He scored twenty in the first quar-

ter and then topped Thompson's hours-old record by dropping in thirty-three in the second, also giving him fifty-three at the half. He needed
only five points after halftime to pass Thompson, though the Jazz
wanted none of it. "We were going to George exclusively," Spurs coach
Doug Moe remembered, "and the Jazz were trying to stop him exclu-
sively and it was something to watch." Gervin managed only ten points
in the second half, but it was more than enough. He finished the game
with sixty-three points, the highest total of his career and the fourth-
highest total in the entire decade.[26]

Surrendering sixty-three points to George Gervin on the season's
last day was a fitting end to a forgettable year for the cellar-dwelling
Jazz. Alongside superstar guard "Pistol Pete" Maravich, New Orleans
featured free agent signee Leonard "Truck" Robinson, a bruising six-
foot-seven forward with a badass Afro. For the first time in his career,
Pistol Pete shared the court with a dominant big man. It was short-
lived. In late January, while playing perhaps the best basketball of his
career, Pistol Pete blew out his knee. At the time, the Jazz were above
.500; after the injury, they dropped eight straight and finished 39–43.
Robinson was the team's lone bright spot, leading the league in rebounding (15.7 per game) and earning a spot on the All-NBA first team.
Gail Goodrich, whom the Jazz had overpaid to leave Los Angeles as a
free agent a season earlier, stayed healthy but was not the superstar
New Orleans expected when they surrendered multiple first-round
choices as compensation for him, and "Stumpy" retired after the following season. On the whole, the 1977–1978 season was disappointing for
Jazz fans, and there were whispers that the team might not be long for
the Crescent City.

Unlike in New Orleans, there was little chance of the Cleveland
Cavaliers, Atlanta Hawks, or Houston Rockets leaving their respective
cities. There was also little chance of any of them competing for an
NBA title. Despite adding a big-name gate attraction in Walt Frazier,
Cleveland struggled to regain the magic of the 1976 "Miracle of Richfield" Cavaliers. Frazier was uncomfortable in Cleveland. "The Cavaliers never accepted me," he said, "because to them, I was New York, I
was always an outsider on that team." Not only was Frazier closely
associated with the Knicks, but he was also a step or two slower than in
his heyday. "He's thirty-two going on forty," complained head coach
Bill Fitch. "Looking at Frazier puts me to sleep." The league was chang-

ing and Frazier simply could not keep up with the new generation of younger, faster guards and new rules limiting hand checking. In Houston, the Rockets bottomed out after the Rudy Tomjanovich injury, losing five straight games even as Moses Malone emerged as a dominant offensive force, finishing second in the league in rebounding (15 rebounds per game) and upping his scoring average from 13.5 to 19.4 points per game. Malone was clearly a star in the making. So too was Hawks forward John Drew, although unlike Malone, Drew was surrounded by a crew of castoffs made worse by a meddling owner. According to the rumor mill, Ted Turner was looking to sell the team and he began cutting costs, releasing starting guard Kenny Charles after learning that the Hawks owed Charles half a million dollars over the next five seasons. Despite the turmoil, Atlanta was one of the NBA's feel-good stories, playing hard-nosed defense for coach of the year Hubie Brown and scrapping their way to a 41–41 record.[27]

Based on the regular season, there was little reason to expect the Washington Bullets to seriously contend for an NBA title after nearly a decade of near-misses. Sure, the duo of Wes Unseld and Elvin Hayes still ranked among the most consistent inside tandems in the league. But both were on the wrong side of thirty and had their limitations: Unseld could barely jump and his offense consisted of setting bone-crushing picks and hurling pinpoint outlet passes, while Hayes had a reputation as a coach killer and as a player who disappeared in big moments. In fact, Hayes expected to be traded after struggling in the 1977 playoffs. "For myself and for my nerves," Hayes told the *Washington Post*, "maybe another place will be better for me." Whether Hayes backed away from this statement or whether the Bullets simply found no takers for an enigmatic thirty-two-year-old forward, Hayes remained in a snazzy red-, white-, and blue-striped Bullets uniform. Paired with Hayes at forward was another player with a reputation for selfishness: free agent signee Bobby Dandridge, who scored nineteen points per game in Coach Dick Motta's offensive system (which required high-scoring forwards). Even after making the playoffs with a 44–38 record, few NBA fans outside D.C. predicted that the Bullets would still be playing into June or that Motta would make the phrase "It ain't over until the fat lady sings" a part of the American lexicon.[28]

There were two clear favorites heading into the playoffs: the Philadelphia 76ers in the East and the Portland Trail Blazers in the West.

After missing the end of the regular season because of foot injuries, Blazers center Bill Walton desperately wanted to play in the postseason. Against Seattle in his first game back, he looked like the Walton of old, scoring seventeen points and pulling down sixteen rebounds. Before game two, Walton felt some discomfort and the Blazers team doctor recommended shooting Xylocaine, a numbing agent, into his foot. Somewhat reluctantly, Walton agreed. It was a decision he came to regret, and he eventually sued the physician for malpractice. During the game, the pain returned and Walton took himself out. X-rays showed he had a broken foot. Again. The Blazers won game two, but with Walton sidelined, Seattle took out Portland in six games. With the Blazers eliminated, the Nuggets became the prohibitive favorites in the West and made the conference finals by beating the Bucks in a back-and-forth series that ended with David "Skywalker" Thompson exploding for thirty-seven in the decisive seventh game.

"Skywalker"—no relation to Luke, the hero of the 1977 film *Star Wars*—played his heart out against the SuperSonics in the Western Conference finals. Fans anticipated a tightly contested series and, as expected, it was competitive. But Denver, still without Brian Taylor (who never returned after leaving the team in midseason), could not overcome the three-guard rotation of "Downtown" Freddie Brown, Dennis Johnson, and Gus Williams unleashed by Seattle, and the Sonics eliminated Thompson and the Nuggets in six games.

In the East, the 76ers swept the Knicks to earn a spot in the conference finals while the Bullets had a far more difficult time getting past the high-scoring Spurs, winning the series in six hard-fought games. Game six, though, might have been the most bizarre of the entire playoffs. First, an airline lost the luggage of Spurs guard Mike Gale, who, lacking a backup Spurs kit, resorted to wearing a Washington road uniform turned inside out. Then, in the third quarter, the lights went out, delaying the game for several minutes before power could be restored. Maybe most bizarrely, at least for the majority of NBA fans who expected the Spurs to prevail, the final score was San Antonio 100, Washington 103. The Bullets were headed to the conference finals.

Philadelphia had stars at every position (even on their bench); the Bullets countered with solid veterans and role players. But shockingly, it was the Bullets who started quickly in the series, downing the high-flying Sixers in an exhilarating overtime game one, despite Wes Unseld limping around on an injured ankle. George McGinnis continued his run of poor playoff performances dating to the previous spring, and head coach Billy Cunningham sat his muscle-bound star for much of the second half of game two. "It was no slap at George," Cunningham explained in his postgame remarks. "This is the playoffs. We're here to win." But McGinnis loudly and publicly disagreed. "I don't want to sound like a crybaby," McGinnis said, "but Billy never played me sixteen, eighteen minutes at a time. Steve [Mix] played great, but if I had stayed in there, there's no doubt I would have been better." Mix had twenty-two points in the Sixers' game-two win, but it was McGinnis who led the team in scoring in their game three loss in Washington. After the Bullets won game four to take a commanding 3–1 series lead, Elvin Hayes took a shot at McGinnis as well. "I don't think Cunningham has much confidence in McGinnis," Hayes said. "When the tough time comes, he puts in Mix. They can't hide George out there." McGinnis lashed out at Hayes. "If he thinks I'm the choker," McGinnis said, "he ought to check out his own playoff record." [29]

Whether or not he won the war of words, Hayes certainly won the on-court battle. He was brilliant in the series and his trademark turnaround jump shot was nearly unstoppable. Every time he made a basket, the home crowd erupted into frenzied calls of "EEEEEEEE." Despite Hayes's brilliance, the Bullets' lead was not safe against the talented Sixers, who earned a critical game five win, sending the series back to Washington. In the sixth game, the score seesawed and, with just twelve seconds remaining, the teams were tied. Hayes missed a long jump shot that fell into the hands of teammate Charles Johnson. Johnson threw up a desperation eighteen footer, but he too barely grazed the rim. The ball bounced right to Unseld, still favoring a sprained right ankle, who jumped just high enough to tip it in. The Sixers, with one last shot, inbounded the ball to Lloyd Free, who, rather than pass off to Julius Erving or George McGinnis, decided to try and tie the game on his own, hoisting a long jump shot that not only missed, but also resulted in an offensive foul call on the self-proclaimed "All-World." The game was over and the Bullets continued their Cinderella run, moving into the NBA finals despite being underdogs in nearly every series.

The championship matchup between the Washington Bullets and Seattle SuperSonics was as unlikely as any in NBA history. Both teams failed to win their own divisions and finished third and fourth in their respective conferences; both also lacked a bona fide superstar or dominant center. Yet in the spring of 1978, the Sonics and Bullets battled in a grueling seven-game series that would go down as one of the most exciting of all time, even though few people outside Washington (D.C. or the state) cared.

Momentum shifted back and forth for the first six games of the finals. Seattle won game one at home, 106–102, thanks to the offensive firepower of sharpshooting guard "Downtown" Freddie Brown, who scored sixteen points in the final nine minutes of the game with his team trailing by double digits. Returning to D.C. for games two and three, the Bullets faced continual reminders of their lack of franchise success in finals appearances. In their two previous trips (1971 and 1975), the Bullets had been swept. Now they were already down one game to none. Washington won game two, but the Sonics took game three, returning to Seattle for game four, up 2–1. With the Seattle Coliseum booked, 39,457 fans (an NBA finals record that stood for more than a decade) packed into the spacious Kingdome, where they witnessed an overtime classic in which Bullets reserve Charles Johnson took over in the extra period to even the series at two games apiece. Johnson was living out a real-life fairy tale. Despite starting at guard for the title-winning 1974–1975 Warriors, Golden State cut Johnson midway through the 1977–1978 season. After Phil Chenier went down with back problems, the Bullets signed Johnson to a ten-day contract expecting to release him a week or two later. But by late May, with Chenier still sidelined, Johnson had become an invaluable reserve, filling in capably at both point guard and shooting guard for the surging Bullets.

Despite Johnson's resolve, Seattle won game five. Two days later, Washington staved off elimination by winning game six in D.C., sending the series back to Seattle for a decisive seventh game.

Before game seven, reporters peppered Bullets coach Dick Motta with questions about his team's chances of winning the series against the favored Sonics. His reply, "The opera isn't over 'til the fat lady sings," popularized (if not coined) a now-common phrase. Soon Motta's slogan was plastered on T-shirts around D.C., making the Bullets a suddenly hip team in the nation's football-crazed capital.[30]

Motta's rallying cry took some of the pressure off his team heading into the winner-take-all game seven, but Bullets players knew what was at stake. "I remember flying out to Seattle," Elvin Hayes recalled years later, "thinking about all the things I had gone through all the years that I had played in the NBA. All of that was coming down to one game, a championship game." Hayes was determined to shed the loser label following him since his Houston Cougars lost to Lew Alcindor and the powerful UCLA Bruins a decade earlier in the NCAA tournament. But gaining personal redemption was not in the cards for Washington's "Big E," as Hayes scored only twelve points and fouled out early in the fourth quarter of game seven. Fortunately, his teammates came through in the clutch. Bobby Dandridge and Charles Johnson each scored nineteen points while Seattle's high-powered guard trio struggled. Brown dropped twenty-one, but Gus Williams—like Hayes—managed just twelve points before fouling out, and Dennis Johnson—after a magnificent first six games—disappeared entirely, missing all fourteen of his shots from the field. Even so, the Sonics remained within four points late in the game and forced a Washington miss. Players from both teams chased down the rebound, but the ball bounced right through the legs of Marvin Webster and into the waiting hands of Bullets reserve center (and future L.A. Lakers exec) Mitch Kupchak. Kupchak scored and was fouled, converting a three-point play to extend the lead to seven. Two Wes Unseld free throws sealed the game—and the series—for the Bullets.[31]

Unseld earned the finals MVP award despite a mediocre stat line, averaging nine points, twelve rebounds, and four assists per game. But, as Hayes said, "Wes never need no stats." He simply fueled the Bullets' will to win and refused to let them lose. Nils Lofgren, later a member of Bruce Springsteen's E Street Band, was a huge Bullets fan then living in D.C. Inspired by his team's run to the championship, Lofgren composed and performed a song titled "Bullets Fever," which became a local cult classic. The lyrics are priceless, including lines like "C. J., Tom and Larry are fast as light. Kevin, Bobby and Elvin they shoot out of sight!" along with a catchy refrain repeating the phrase "Bullets fever."[32]

After game seven, Coach Motta pulled on a T-shirt emblazoned with his personal slogan, "The opera isn't over 'til the fat lady sings," and reveled in a beer-soaked locker room celebration. Charles Johnson sat contemplatively apart from his teammates, slowly sipping from a bottle of beer in a quiet corner, letting it all soak in. He finally took questions from the throng of media waiting to hear from this rags-to-riches hero. "This is more emotional than my championship with the Warriors," Johnson said. "I was naïve and young as far as basketball was concerned then. I didn't know what it was to be a world champion." Interviewed in the postgame revelry, Elvin Hayes wore a huge grin. "They can say whatever they want," Hayes said of his many critics, "but they gotta say one thing: E's a world champion. He wears a ring."[33]

Today, championship-winning teams expect an invitation to the White House for a photo op with the president. In the 1970s, few teams had that honor. But in June 1978, President Jimmy Carter invited the Bullets to the White House. Despite being a native Georgian and die-hard Atlanta Hawks fan, Carter recognized the goodwill to be won by posing for photographs and meeting with the D.C.–based NBA champs. "I am very proud of the Bullets," Carter said in his brief re-marks to the team, "although I really wish they could have won without beating Atlanta." Bullets owner Abe Pollin handed Carter a t-shirt pro-claiming "The opera isn't over 'til the fat lady sings!" and Coach Motta presented the president with a basketball. Carter dribbled a few times and then lobbed a pass to Charles Johnson before being whisked away to another meeting. Carter spent just a couple of minutes with the Bullets, but he was a busy man that summer as news concerning a toxic waste dump near Love Canal, New York, was turning the site into a national catastrophe.[34]

Many people associated with pro basketball were not as impressed as President Carter with Washington's win. One NBA coach sneered that the Bullets won only "because *somebody's* got to win." *Sports Illustrat-ed* writer John Papanek even argued that "the collapse of the Philadel-phia 76ers, and injuries to Bill Walton and other Portland Trail Blazers, tainted the Bullets' win." And modern sportswriter Bill Simmons claims the Bullets "stumbled into the trophy only because Bill Walton's broken foot opened the door for every pseudo-contender." Yet despite these reasonable claims, it was the Bullets who pushed through that door, defeating all comers and besting three teams with far better regular-season records to win their first league title. The fat lady had sung and Washington had its NBA title at long last.[35]

Serious questions still remained. Could the league survive the nega-tive publicity garnered by the Kermit Washington punch? What about rumors of drug use in the league? Was it as widespread as was being reported? And could the NBA turn around plummeting television ratings? For the time being, at least, as the hit disco single released by the Bee Gees in midseason reminded Americans, the league was "Stayin' Alive."

Statistics for 1977–1978

Eastern Conference	W	L	Western Conference	W	L
Atlantic Division			*Midwest Division*		
Philadelphia 76ers	55	27	Denver Nuggets	48	34
New York Knicks	43	39	Milwaukee Bucks	44	38
Boston Celtics	32	50	Chicago Bulls	40	42
Buffalo Braves	27	55	Detroit Pistons	38	44
New Jersey Nets	24	58	Kansas City Kings	31	51
			Indiana Pacers	31	51
Central Division			*Pacific Division*		
San Antonio Spurs	52	30	Portland Trail Blazers	58	24
Washington Bullets	44	38	Phoenix Suns	49	33
Cleveland Cavaliers	43	39	Seattle SuperSonics	47	35
Atlanta Hawks	41	41	Los Angeles Lakers	45	37
New Orleans Jazz	39	43	Golden State Warriors	43	39
Houston Rockets	28	54			

Playoffs

Eastern Conference First Round	New York d. Cleveland (2–0)
	Washington d. Atlanta (2–0)
Western Conference First Round	Milwaukee d. Phoenix (2–0)
	Seattle d. Los Angeles (2–1)
Eastern Conference Semifinals	Philadelphia d. New York (4–0)
	Washington d. San Antonio (4–2)
Western Conference Semifinals	Denver d. Milwaukee (4–3)
	Seattle d. Portland (4–2)
Eastern Conference Finals	Washington d. Philadelphia (4–2)
Western Conference Finals	Seattle d. Denver (4–2)

NBA Finals   Washington d. Seattle (4–3)

All-NBA Teams

First Team   **Second Team**

F—Julius Erving (Philadelphia)   F—Walter Davis (Phoenix)

F—Leonard "Truck" Robinson   F—Maurice Lucas (Portland)
(New Orleans)

C—Bill Walton (Portland)   C—Kareem Abdul-Jabbar (Los
                                    Angeles)

G—George Gervin (San Antonio)   G—Pete Maravich (New
                                    Orleans)

G—David Thompson (Denver)   G—Paul Westphal (Phoenix)

League Leaders

Points per Game (27.2)   George Gervin (San Antonio)

Rebounds per Game (15.7)   Truck Robinson (New Orleans)

Assists per Game (10.2)   Kevin Porter (Detroit/New Jersey)

Steals per Game (2.7)   Ron Lee (Phoenix)

Blocks per Game (3.4)   George Johnson (New Jersey)

Most Valuable Player   Bill Walton (Portland)

Rookie of the Year   Walter Davis (Phoenix)

10

1978 TO 1979

On November 28, 1977, a new issue of *Sports Illustrated* featuring the headline "College Basketball's Secret Weapon" hit newsstands. Its iconic cover showed two cheerleaders, hunched over with index fingers raised to their lips in a shushing gesture, in front of Indiana State forward Larry Bird. Thanks to that magazine issue and an All-American season on the hardwood, Bird did not remain a secret for long and, in the summer of '78, had a difficult decision to make. Should he return to Indiana State for his senior season? Or should he forego his final year of eligibility and enter the NBA draft?

Born and raised in French Lick, Indiana, Bird initially signed to play collegiately at Indiana University but dropped out before suiting up for the Hoosiers because of homesickness and disagreements with fiery head coach Bobby Knight. A year later, he enrolled at Indiana State and after two seasons as a Sycamore became eligible for the 1978 NBA draft. Picking first, the Indiana Pacers desperately wanted the hometown hero. Coach Bob "Slick" Leonard met with Bird several times to drink beer and discuss the possibility of Bird suiting up for the Pacers. But Bird held two trump cards: he still retained one season of college eligibility, and NBA rules allowed him to wait a full calendar year after the draft before signing. Indiana was in a tough spot. If Bird returned to college or refused to sign with the Pacers, he could enter the 1979 draft and the team would have nothing to show for the number-one pick. "After several conversations with Larry," Leonard said, "he convinced me that he was going to return to college for another year." Already having lost forward Dan Roundfield as a free agent, Leonard and the Pacers decided not to gamble on Bird. After a proposed trade with the Philadelphia 76ers fell through that would have returned former Pacers star George McGinnis to Indiana, the team agreed to send the pick to Portland.[1]

Now armed with the number-one pick, Portland tried to convince Bird to join All-Stars Bill Walton and Maurice Lucas in a devastating frontcourt. But Bird was not interested, complaining that Walton was "hurt all the time." Spurned by Bird, the Blazers took Minnesota center Mychal Thompson, the first foreign-born player selected first overall in draft history (and the father of future "Splash Brother" Klay Thompson). The Kansas City Kings, drafting second and desperate for point guard help, tried to convince Michigan State star Earvin "Magic" Johnson to leave college early. But, like Bird, Johnson decided to return to school, and the Kings took North Carolina's Phil Ford, later named rookie of the year. Now selecting third, the Pacers chose Kentucky center Rick Robey; the New York Knicks followed with exciting guard Micheal Ray Richardson; and the Golden State Warriors drafted swingman Purvis Short fifth. Picking sixth, Boston was now on the clock.[2]

Celtics team president Red Auerbach punctuated important wins by puffing on a victory cigar. Bird falling to the Celtics in the 1978 draft might have made Auerbach light up a stogie for old times' sake. Unfortunately, the rest of the storied franchise was in shambles. After decades of excellence, Boston faced serious on- and off-court problems. Team owner Irv Levin, a film producer, wanted to relocate the franchise closer to his California home and threatened to move the Celtics to the West Coast. To keep the team in Boston, David Stern—then the league's legal counsel—arranged a complicated trade: Levin and Buffalo Braves owner John Y. Brown swapped *franchises*. Levin moved the Braves to San Diego, and Brown took over the Celtics. Without consulting Auerbach, the owners also agreed on a six-player trade: the newly christened San Diego Clippers received notorious malcontent Sidney Wicks along with Kermit Washington and Kevin Kunnert (both integral parts of "the Punch" in December 1977), while the Celtics acquired Marvin "Bad News" Barnes, Nate "Tiny" Archibald, Billy Knight, and a few draft picks. There was just one more issue to resolve. Which of the two Celtics first-round picks was headed to San Diego: Larry Bird or Freeman Williams (drafted two picks after Bird)? Brown let Levin choose. Levin's attorney recommended the Clippers pass on Bird, telling his client, "he's supposed to be slow and can't jump that well. My advice is to let them keep Bird." Levin agreed. "Everybody back east thinks I raped Boston and stole their best players," Levin boasted, "and I think I did too." But he soon found out otherwise. Freeman Williams lasted just five seasons in the NBA, and Larry Bird was transcendent. "I could've had him," Levin remembered wistfully, "and changed NBA history." Not even Bird, though, could have saved the 1978–1979 Celtics. As Larry led Indiana State to the NCAA title game, the team that drafted him faltered; the Sycamores won thirty-three times that season, four more than the Celtics in almost fifty fewer games.[3]

A subpar record was not the only problem in Boston. Owner John Y. Brown and President Red Auerbach struggled for power, and Red nearly left the Celtics for the hated Knicks rather than put up with a meddling owner. In July, Brown negotiated a trade with Indiana, sending a first-round pick to the Pacers for reserve guard Earl Tatum. Infuriated, Auerbach traded Tatum to the Pistons just three games into the season. Undeterred, Brown dealt longtime Celtic Jo Jo White to New York and in a separate trade landed Bob McAdoo from the Knicks in exchange for a whopping three first-round draft choices. "McAdoo's game was a complete contradiction to the Celtics tradition of ball movement and finding the open man," journalist Michael Connelly wrote in his 2008 book *Rebound!* Fans in Boston Garden took to chanting a catchy jingle every time McAdoo screwed up: "McAdoo; McAdon't; McAwill; McAwon't." Clearly McAdoo was not Boston's savior and in fact lasted only twenty games in Beantown. After the season, he signed a free agent contract with the Detroit Pistons, netting the Celtics two cornerstones of their championship-winning teams of the 1980s: Robert Parish and Kevin McHale.[4]

Much like the Celtics, the Knicks tried to recapture their glory years by trading away future draft picks and promising young players for short-term, well-known fixes. In 1975, New York dealt for Spencer Haywood, who memorably responded to a reporter's question about being the savior of the team with "then I'll save." The next season, it was Bob McAdoo, but he also failed to bring a title to the Big Apple. As longtime guard Earl "the Pearl" Monroe explained, "teams [used to] draft and trade to fill their needs. Now they draft and trade for names to fill their arenas." After years of adopting that strategy, the Knicks abruptly reversed course and began to build for the future. During the 1978–1979 season, they dealt both Haywood and McAdoo, replacing them with young players such as Marvin "the Human Eraser" Webster. After a stellar 1978 finals, Webster became the hottest free agent on the market, and the Knicks desperately wanted him, having missed out on big names like David Thompson, Kareem Abdul-Jabbar, and George McGinnis in the recent past. "We're going to make a big pitch for Webster," the Knicks president admitted. "We have our cap set for Webster." Webster and the Knicks eventually agreed on a five-year, $1.2 million deal, and promising forward Lonnie Shelton ended up in Seattle as free agent compensation. Even with Webster, New York managed just thirty-one wins as the short-lived experiment of pairing Webster, McAdoo, and Haywood failed to produce, and Monroe limped through his last pro season, surrendering playing time to recent first-round picks Ray Williams and Micheal Ray Richardson. Fortunately for Knicks fans, there was light at the end of the tunnel. Williams, Richardson, and Webster were young and athletic, giving New York a solid foundation to build a title contender. Plus, the team had three Celtics first-round picks headed their way thanks to the McAdoo trade. The future in the Big Apple seemed bright indeed.[5]

Sharing the Atlantic Division with the Celtics, Knicks, and New Jersey Nets (whose high scoring duo of "Super" John Williamson and Bernard King helped them to a 37–45 record despite a midseason cocaine charge for King), were the Philadelphia 76ers and Washington Bullets. Bullets coach Dick Motta led a veteran team featuring Wes Unseld, Elvin Hayes, Bob Dandridge, and a deep bench. When Motta's defending champs cruised to fifty-four wins—tops in the league—Celtics legend Sam Jones called them "the best team I've ever seen."[6]

Only Philly could challenge Washington in the Eastern Conference, though by the fall of 1978, some of the luster had worn off the so-called super team. Abrupt playoff exits the previous two seasons convinced management they needed to shake up their roster: "All-World" Lloyd Free went to San Diego and George McGinnis found himself in Denver, dealt for Bobby Jones. Both trades improved the Sixers. Jones was a better fit than McGinnis next to "Dr. J" Julius Erving, since most of his points came from timely cuts to the basket or from offensive rebounds. Dealing Free also helped—call it addition by subtraction—as rookie Maurice Cheeks stepped into a starting role. The second-round pick from West Texas State led the Sixers in assists (5.3 per game) despite being given little chance of even making the team in training camp. But not everything was rosy in the City of Brotherly Love. Most troublingly, superstar forward Julius Erving seemed to be regressing. "Dr. J is not the player we once knew," one NBA coach said. "The electricity isn't there." Still, Erving remained a consistent offensive threat, averaging better than twenty-three points per game on the season. The highlight of Erving's year, though, might have been his role in the cult classic film, *The Fish That Saved Pittsburgh*. In the movie Erving, playing a character named Moses Guthrie, stars for the fictional Pittsburgh Pythons, who sign a group of players all born under the astrological sign of Pisces (the "fish" in the film title). The plot is predictable. After a rough start, the Pythons' cast of misfits (including identical twins, a preacher, and a disc jockey) come together as a team. Come to think of it, this is exactly what happened for the late-seventies Sixers.[7]

The Fish That Saved Pittsburgh featured a huge cast of NBA players including Los Angeles Lakers Kareem Abdul-Jabbar, Norm Nixon, and Connie Hawkins. One star left out of the film, though, was Erving's former Virginia Squires teammate George "the Iceman" Gervin. Gervin led the league in scoring for the second straight season (29.6 points per game), although this time it was not nearly as close a race. During the 1977–1978 season, Gervin scored sixty-three points in his last game to pass David Thompson for the title. This year, he had a comfortable margin over runner-up Lloyd Free. But it was the return of point guard James Silas that made San Antonio a legitimate title contender. Silas was a star in the ABA: "he could accelerate, he could explode, he could shoot and he could jump over people," ex-Spurs coach Bob Bass remembered. During the 1975–1976 season, Silas averaged twenty-nine points and five assists, good enough for a spot on the All-ABA first team alongside Julius Erving and Artis Gilmore (and ahead of Gervin and David Thompson). Knee injuries wiped out much of his next two seasons, and NBA fans knew little about the man once known as "Captain Late" or "the Late Mr. Si" for his late-game heroics.[8]

San Antonio also boasted one of the league's best home-court advantages, rivaled only by Portland's Blazermaniacs. The Baseline Bums, a holdover from the Spurs' ABA days, sat in the rows directly above the visiting team's locker room. Once the game began, the Bums proceeded to "wave a gigantic Texas flag, chant obscenities at the officials and

occasionally spill beer on the opponents when they leave the court."
With the Bums cheering on their beloved Spurs, Silas running the team
as point guard, and Gervin and Larry "Special K" Kenon (an underrated
forward and perfect sidekick for Gervin) filling the wings on fast breaks,
San Antonio could blow by any team in the league—and they often did,
leading the NBA in scoring for the second time in three seasons with
119.3 points per game. Only a lack of prior postseason success scared
Spurs fans, since teams played more deliberately in the playoffs, and
San Antonio had yet to prove they could win playing at a slower pace.[9]

Gervin, Silas, and Kenon were not the only high-scoring trio from
Texas. The Houston Rockets featured Rick Barry, Rudy Tomjanovich,
and Moses Malone and scored the fifth-most points in the league while
leading the NBA in offensive efficiency. Barry was the newest Rocket,
signed by Houston as free agent insurance in case Tomjanovich could
not return from the injuries sustained from the punch delivered by
Kermit Washington a year earlier. Fortunately for Rockets fans, Rudy T
did return, and after missing most of the previous season, Tomjanovich
earned a spot on the All-Star team after averaging nineteen points and
almost eight rebounds per game while wearing a face mask eerily similar to the headgear worn by Leatherface in the 1974 horror film *The
Texas Chainsaw Massacre*.

Barry and Tomjanovich joined Malone, one of the NBA's top centers, to create a formidable front line. In just his third NBA season and
fifth as a pro, Malone continued his meteoric rise from high school
phenom to elite pro center, culminating in an MVP-winning season.
During the 1976–1977 season, as a NBA rookie, Malone played for
three teams and finished with averages of thirteen points and thirteen
rebounds per game. In his second season, he increased those numbers
to nineteen points and fifteen rebounds. And during the 1978–1979
season, Malone led the league in rebounding (17.6 per game) and finished in the top five in scoring (24.8 points per game), even though
head coach Tom Nissalke ran few plays for his young center. Instead,
Nissalke relied heavily on Malone's most amazing skill: offensive rebounding. Moses was blessed with good size at six-ten, 215 pounds, and
he was able to use his strength to push smaller players away from the
boards. But he also used unbelievably quick feet to put himself in a
perfect position to collect errant shots. "Most basketball fans see Moses," Kermit Washington said, "and they all think, look how tall he is.

What they don't see is the quickness. How can a man that big have feet like that? No one watching the game sees his feet. They're amazing. And the strength. Mo just wears you out."[10]

Malone was relentless in his pursuit of the basketball, ripping down missed shots with one hand and then bouncing right back up for the score. "Moses thinks that anything that hits the backboard is his," teammate Calvin Murphy explained. "He doesn't realize that there are nine other guys on the court." Darryl Dawkins, an inch taller and thirty pounds heavier than Malone, compared playing Moses to "trying to box out an octopus." Unsurprisingly, Malone's 587 offensive rebounds (more than seven per game) led all players during the 1978–1979 season and remains the top single-season mark in league history. Although the statistic was not recorded until after the merger, Malone is still the career leader in offensive rebounds, more than 2,400 ahead of Artis Gilmore, his nearest competitor.[11]

The Atlanta Hawks, Cleveland Cavaliers, and Detroit Pistons all finished behind both Malone's Rockets and Gervin's Spurs in the Central Division. Atlanta relied on forward John Drew and young center Wayne "Tree" Rollins, who finished third in the league in blocked shots, swatting away more than three per game. Cleveland was a team stuck in the past, their roster packed with aging veteran players including Walt "Clyde" Frazier, who was a shell of his former self; he played only fifteen total games during the 1978–1979 and 1979–1980 seasons before retiring as a Cavalier. Unsurprisingly, Cleveland's slow-paced style drew few fans out to the suburb of Richfield, where the Cavs played their home games, usually in front of sparse crowds.

Attendance also suffered in Detroit, where the cheers of Pistons fans were swallowed up in the cavernous Pontiac Silverdome. Pistons backers did, however, adore new head coach Dick Vitale. Today, Vitale is known more for his post-coaching career as an exuberant announcer, but he was equally energetic roaming the sidelines, exhorting his Pistons to work harder and riding referees about every missed call. During one game against Cleveland, Vitale threw such a fit that cops had to drag him—kicking and screaming—off the floor. Vitale had reason to be frustrated; his talented Pistons definitely underachieved. Point guard Kevin Porter set a league record with 1,099 assists (13.4 per game) and center Bob Lanier remained a reliable scorer from the low post whose hook shot was second to only Kareem Abdul-Jabbar's. Vitale promised

Pistons fans their team would play with "enthusiasm and excitement," but the stress of trying to motivate a dozen wealthy grown men for eighty-two games wore on the excitable coach. His players noticed. As Lanier said, "it's a sad thing watching him and watching the strain it's putting on him." Vitale lasted just a season and a half in Detroit, leaving the NBA for a broadcasting career. Long after fans forgot about his brief stint with the Pistons, Vitale's trademark phrases like "diaper dandy" and "dipsy-do-dunk-a-roo" became part of the American sports lexicon.[12]

Vitale's Pistons won only thirty games on the season. But that was four more than the New Orleans Jazz managed. Jazz owners expected to immediately compete for a title after trading for "Pistol Pete" Maravich in 1974. Moving into the Superdome for the 1975–1976 season caused attendance to spike, and they signed free agent guard Gail Goodrich in the hopes of creating a high-scoring backcourt. But when Maravich and Goodrich struggled with injuries (and attendance dipped), the blame, as usual, shifted to Pistol Pete. "Whenever things aren't going well," Maravich said, "they blame the white boy making the most money." In desperation, the Jazz traded away future draft choices for veterans Slick Watts and Spencer Haywood. For his part, Haywood loved the move to the Big Easy. As a jazz aficionado, he was in music heaven; as a basketball player, he had an opportunity to rebuild his career after failing to save the Knicks. Haywood played excellent basketball for the Jazz, contributing twenty-four points and nine rebounds from his forward position. But in April 1979, the team announced its biggest move to date. Citing lease issues in the spacious Superdome, team owners decided to pull the plug on their short-lived New Orleans experiment and relocate the team to Salt Lake City. Within months, the team moved to Utah, traded Haywood, released Maravich, and waved good-bye to the retiring Goodrich.[13]

Unlike the Jazz, the Kansas City Kings appeared to be on the rise. Instead of making splashy free agent signings or trading for big name players, the Kings worked to develop homegrown talent and, during the 1978–1979 season, all five starters were Kings' first-round picks. Wing players Scott Wedman (a 1974 top-ten pick) and Otis Birdsong (the number-two selection in 1977) combined for forty points per game, while rookie of the year Phil Ford (also drafted second overall) led the squad with 8.6 assists, fourth in the league. At season's end, Kansas City

(48–34) stood in the top ten in both offense and defense, and all five starters averaged double figures in points.

Kansas City won the Midwest Division by a single game over the Denver Nuggets, who were in win-now mode. After back-to-back division titles but early playoff exits, Denver orchestrated a pair of huge off-season deals that they hoped would put them over the top. First they traded for Charlie Scott, envisioning him as the point guard they lacked after Brian Taylor left the team a year earlier. Then they sent fan-favorite Bobby Jones (a two-time All-Defensive performer) to Philadelphia in exchange for high-scoring George McGinnis. Although not entirely self-serving (the Nuggets traded Jones, in part, because his asthma was made worse by the mile-high atmosphere in Denver), it was a lopsided deal. "Jones was a blue-collar, hardworking, team-oriented, outstanding player at both ends of the court," teammate David Thompson said. McGinnis, on the other hand, was a chain-smoking scoring machine who pulled a disappearing act on defense. Adding Scott and McGinnis also disrupted team chemistry. "The problem with our new high-profile additions," Thompson explained, "was their highly verbose natures. Our new Dynamic Duo was so outspoken that it dramatically changed the whole personality of the team." At times, the Nuggets looked invincible, reeling off six- and seven-game winning streaks in January and March. Other times, they struggled, dropping six straight in November. "We'd look unbeatable one night," Thompson said, "and like a rec-league team the next." Management continued to tinker, firing head coach Larry Brown in midseason and shipping McGinnis back to the Indiana Pacers as the team tried to rebuild on the fly, working to surround David Thompson (and his twenty-four points per game and $800,000 annual salary) with enough talent to take them to the next level.[14]

Trading for George McGinnis made little sense for the Indiana Pacers, except for reasons of nostalgia since the team had won ABA titles in both 1972 and 1973 with Big George on the court. But bad personnel decisions had become commonplace in Indiana. After passing on Larry Bird in the 1978 draft, the Pacers selected forward Rick Robey. A few months later, Robey went to Boston for another former Pacers great, Billy Knight. Knight and McGinnis played together briefly in Indiana before the merger, and now they were, as Peaches & Herb crooned in their 1978 hit song, "Reunited." But for Pacers fans, reunited did not feel so good. As Pulitzer Prize–winning author David Halberstam wrote, McGinnis was "an incomplete superstar of dazzling but limited abilities," while *Boston Globe* columnist Bob Ryan was blunt in his evaluation of Knight, "a finesse player on offense and a nonfactor in every other facet of his game. He didn't defend, he didn't pass, and he didn't appear to work up a sweat—ever." The Knight and McGinnis experiment proved an abject failure. Making matters worse, Alex English (dealt with a first-round pick to Denver for McGinnis) became a Hall of Famer, scoring more points than any other NBA player in the 1980s.[15]

Before signing with the Pacers, English played for the Milwaukee Bucks, who finished the 1978–1979 season with the same record as Indiana. The 1977 draft was supposed to give the Bucks three surefire stars. But only one panned out as Marques Johnson, picked third, made his first All-Star team and finished third in the league in scoring (25.6 points per game) during the 1978–1979 season. But former top pick Kent Benson was a bust, and eleventh overall selection Ernie Grunfeld settled in as a role player as the Bucks limped to thirty-eight wins.

Despite making questionable personnel decisions, both Indiana and Milwaukee finished above the down-on-their-luck Chicago Bulls. Before the season, the team said good-bye to Norm Van Lier and Tom Boerwinkle, the two remaining links to their early seventies mini-dynasty. They also waved farewell to a fictional player: Ken Reeves. Reeves served as the title character of the television program *The White Shadow*, and according to the show's story line, he blew out his knee playing for Chicago, forcing him to become the basketball coach of Carver High School in Los Angeles. The show resonated with American youth and also touched on topics pertinent to pro basketball. In one episode, Coach Reeves talks his star player, Warren Coolidge, out of skipping college to sign a pro contract; in another, Mario "Salami" Pettrino faces jail time for breaking an opponent's jaw during an on-court fight—shades of Kermit Washington and Rudy Tomjanovich.

With a primarily African American cast, *The White Shadow* looked unlike many other television shows in the 1970s. Issues of race permeated not only network TV, but the NBA as well. By 1979, more African Americans played in the league than ever before: that was a fact. But only the paying public could decide whether it was good or bad. One controversial letter to the editor printed in the pages of *Bas-ketball Digest* captures the stereotypical view of many white NBA fans.

> I question whether you will print this letter because this is a subject
> basketball writers, coaches and administrators choose to deny or ig-
> nore. However, if you really want to know why NBA attendance has
> dropped over the past few years, look at race. . . . The number of
> black players in the NBA continues to increase. If black fans identify
> with black players, that is considered to be normal. However, if white
> fans identify with who they can identify with, this is considered to be
> racism. More white players would be in the NBA if general managers
> would consider seriously nondramatic skills like teamwork, attitude
> and defense.

This issue of race became well-worn territory when critics explained the decline in popularity of the sport in the late seventies. As one unnamed league exec rhetorically asked, "How can you sell a black sport to a white public?" Cavaliers owner Ted Stepien, before purchasing the team in 1980, said "I need white people. . . . I think the Cavs have too many blacks." "You need a blend of white and black," Stepien ex-plained. "I think that draws, and I think that's a better team."[16]

The Bulls (the real team, not the one from which Ken Reeves re-tired) had a mix of white and black players, but they did not draw well and were not a good team. Chicago finished in the bottom third in attendance and ranked dead last in the league in scoring. Fortunately for Bulls fans, they did seem to have a plan: building around All-Star center Artis Gilmore. Gilmore connected on 57.5 percent of his shots from the field, good for fourth in the league, and averaged twenty-four points and thirteen rebounds per game. Amazingly, this was below his career average. Gilmore retired in 1987 having made 59.9 percent of his career field goal attempts, still an all-time record. During the 1978–1979 season, Gilmore got some help from rookie point guard Reggie Theus. Theus, the ninth pick in the draft, earned the nickname "Rush Street Reggie" for embracing Chicago's nightlife. Beloved off the court, Theus was maddeningly inconsistent on it. "Theus has the athlet-ic ability to do anything he wants to on a court," one journalist wrote, but he was "sensational one minute and outlandish the next." An acro-batic drive to the basket followed by a pass sailing ten rows into the stands became commonplace for Rush Street Reggie. Gilmore and

Theus led Chicago to a last-place finish in the Western Conference, earning them a shot (depending on the outcome of a coin flip) at the top overall pick in the 1979 draft, widely believed to be Michigan State sensation Earvin "Magic" Johnson.[17]

In 1975, the Golden State Warriors won the NBA title, and a year later the Phoenix Suns made an unlikely run to the finals. But by the fall of 1978, both teams looked drastically different. In the Bay Area, point guard John Lucas replaced Rick Barry as the face of the franchise. Lucas finished second in the league in assists and was also a multisport star who spent his off-seasons playing professional tennis. Lucas specialized in mixed doubles and received a lot of media attention for teaming with Renee Richards. Richards, formerly Richard Raskind, underwent sex reassignment surgery in 1975 and then attempted to play in the U.S. Open as a woman. The United States Tennis Association barred her from participating, but the New York Supreme Court overturned their decision and allowed her to play in the 1977 Open. Richards lost in the first round, but her pairing with Lucas in World TeamTennis was far more successful, and they went 28–1 as a duo. "We really freaked people out," Lucas joked, "a black and a transsexual! But we were good."[18]

Lucas's basketball partner, backcourt mate Phil Smith, was in his prime during the late seventies, a perfect complementary player who twice scored more than fifty points in a single game thanks to both a strong inside game and a reliable outside jump shot. Also for the Warriors, center Robert Parish emerged as a top-notch inside player and once recorded thirty points and thirty rebounds in a single game, a feat duplicated only twice in the three decades since (by Moses Malone and Kevin Love). But Parish seemed best suited to a complementary role; he was less a traditional, back-to-the-basket post player than a long-limbed athlete able to create scoring opportunities for himself with offensive rebounds and shots in transition.

Like Golden State, Phoenix counted on wing players to make the team go. Paul Westphal and Walter Davis each averaged nearly twenty-four points per game and made the All-Star team. After missing out on free agent forward Dan Roundfield (despite appearing on his doorstep at midnight on the first day of free agency), Phoenix general manager Jerry Colangelo added Leonard "Truck" Robinson from the New Orleans Jazz in a midseason deal. With Robinson and Davis starting at forward, 1976 rookie of the year Alvan Adams manning the pivot, and

Westphal pairing with All-Defensive point guard Don Buse in the back-court, the Suns starting five was as talented and versatile as any in the league. Regardless of whether or not they could win a title, the Suns, who won eight of their last ten regular-season games, served notice that they would make some noise in the playoffs.

Sandwiched between the Warriors and Suns in the Pacific Division were two franchises that would soon be intricately linked through big man Bill Walton. The Portland Trail Blazers, less than two seasons removed from the Blazermania title team, struggled with on- and off-court problems during the 1978–1979 season. Walton sat out the entire season with foot injuries and the team's two best remaining players, powerful forward Maurice Lucas and lead guard Lionel Hollins, grew increasingly disillusioned with their salaries and perceived lack of importance to the organization. Although the Blazers made the playoffs and finished with a winning record, they were in no way the team that had thoroughly revolutionized the game just eighteen months earlier.

The newly christened San Diego Clippers (formerly the Buffalo Braves) arrived in California with high hopes and a completely reshuffled roster. The new-look Clippers relied on the scoring prowess of guard Lloyd "All-World" Free, acquired for a future first-round pick from Philadelphia. "That is nothing," Coach Gene Shue said of the trade. "Lloyd is one of the most talented players in the league, and they just gave him away." In "giving away" Free, the Sixers landed a pick that ended up as the fourth overall selection in the loaded 1984 draft. For Lloyd Free, a high-scoring, enigmatic guard, the Sixers netted Auburn's "Round Mound of Rebound," Charles Barkley. Typical Clippers. But during the 1978–1979 season, Barkley was a short, fat high schooler and Free was an offensive force. All-World averaged 28.8 points per game, second in the league behind only Gervin from San Antonio. "Nobody can guard me," Free said, "I tried to guard myself once, but I couldn't do it. I'm unstoppable." Free also recognized the power of promotion. "People talk about winning," Free said, "but it's not really about winning. Times have changed. Today it's a show. People want to see that razzle-dazzle—guys taking crazy shots and hitting them." Garnering fan interest was equally as important as winning games, at least in Free's mind. "You have to have some jazz in the game, 'cause if you don't," Free warned, "people won't come out." Despite Free's razzle-dazzle, the Clippers finished near the bottom of the league in attendance.

Looking forward, the Clippers knew they needed a dominant center. Fortunately, one became available soon after the season ended; an oft-injured but undeniably talented big man would seek a change of scenery from the Pacific Northwest to sunny California, shaking up the basketball world.[19]

One hundred and twenty miles up the California coast from San Diego, the Los Angeles Lakers struggled, despite another MVP-worthy season from Kareem Abdul-Jabbar. Since arriving in 1975, Kareem's Lakers had no NBA titles and only once even reached the conference finals. In short, the Abdul-Jabbar experiment looked like a failure. During the 1978–1979 season, Abdul-Jabbar again ranked among the league leaders in points (23.8), rebounds (12.8), and blocked shots (4), but the Lakers offense sometimes relied too heavily on their goggle-wearing center. "We had twenty-two seconds to get Kareem his sky-hook," complained departed guard Charlie Scott. "If we couldn't, we had two seconds to try something else."[20]

In the off-season, Abdul-Jabbar appeared as airline pilot Roger Murdock in the film *Airplane!* In a hilarious scene (just one of many), Abdul-Jabbar, as Murdock, denies that he is Kareem Abdul-Jabbar. Finally, a kid named Joey goads Murdock to the breaking point. "I think you're the greatest, but my dad says you don't work hard enough on defense. And he says lots of times, you don't even run downcourt. And that you don't really try . . . except during the playoffs." Murdock, now breaking character, angrily responds, "The hell I don't! Listen, kid. I've been hearing that crap ever since I was at UCLA. I'm out there busting my buns every night. Tell your old man to drag Walton and Lanier up and down the court for forty-eight minutes!" Abdul-Jabbar's sense of humor in filming *Airplane!* shocked many NBA fans and sportswriters who had grown used to Kareem being sullen and moody; he showed moviegoers a lighter side.

The NBA's only airplane-themed team, the Seattle SuperSonics, lost in the 1978 finals to Wes Unseld, Elvin Hayes, and the Washington Bullets. They came into the 1978–1979 season with one goal in mind: winning the title. "The Sonics are a fine blend of experience . . . and youth . . . of jive and solidarity; of shooters, passers, rebounders and defenders," one journalist wrote. Seattle also featured an important new starting forward. When center Marvin Webster signed with the Knicks in the off-season, commissioner Larry O'Brien gave Seattle the choice

between perennial All-Star Bob McAdoo or second-year forward Lonnie Shelton as compensation. "McAdoo was the better player," coach
Lenny Wilkens admitted, "but Shelton was the better player for us."
Adding Shelton, described by Wilkens as "a grizzly bear, because he
could be mean and strong," allowed Jack Sikma to slide over to center.
Sikma, raised on a farm in central Illinois, earned the nickname "Banger" for his willingness to mix it up inside. With Sikma manning the
middle, the Sonics were not a classic NBA team; instead of a dominant,
back-to-the-basket center flanked by high-scoring forwards and pass-
first guards, the Sonics featured a balanced offensive attack led by the
high-scoring guard triumvirate of Gus Williams, Dennis Johnson, and
"Downtown" Freddie Brown. At forward, John Johnson led the team in
assists and regularly initiated the offense as a "point forward," while
Shelton played tough defense and set bone-crushing screens. Under
Coach Wilkens, Seattle became far and away the best defensive team in
the NBA, poised for a deep postseason run.[21]

In early 1979, as NBA teams made a final push for the playoffs, the
attention of basketball fans turned to March Madness and the college
game. The 1979 NCAA Tournament is the most famous in hoops history, culminating in a championship matchup between the undefeated
and top-seeded Indiana State Sycamores, led by Boston Celtics draftee
Larry Bird, and the second-seeded Michigan State Spartans, directed
by charismatic point guard Earvin "Magic" Johnson. Bird and Johnson
could not have been more different: the former grew up as a shy young
man in rural French Lick, Indiana, while the latter was brash and gre-
garious, one of ten Johnson children born and raised in Lansing, Michigan. Likewise, the Indiana State–Michigan State game was a battle of
opposites. "It was the matchup every college basketball fan longed to
see," Bird said. It was big school versus small school; David versus
Goliath; Bird versus Johnson; and white versus black. CBS's broadcast
drew a 24.1 Nielsen rating, the highest in college basketball history,
even though the game itself failed to live up to the hype. Bird shot
poorly, scoring just nineteen points on 7-for-21 shooting, and Johnson's
Spartans breezed to an easy 75–64 victory. College hoops fans celebrated the end of an amazing tournament. But for NBA fans, it was just the
beginning of a legendary rivalry that would transform their sport.[22]

With Johnson and the Spartans crowned as NCAA champs, the pro
circuit entered its postseason lacking a clear-cut favorite. Front-runners

Washington and Seattle faced long odds in returning to the finals; the last championship rematch took place six years earlier in 1973 when Willis Reed led the Knicks over Wilt Chamberlain and the Lakers. But Sonics and Bullets players remained confident. "Don't be fooling yourself," said Seattle guard "Downtown" Freddie Brown, "you know it all boils down to us against Washington one more time." For their part, the Sonics advanced with relative ease, defeating the Lakers in five games to set up a Western Conference finals matchup against the surging Suns. But the Bullets had a far more difficult road, matching up in the Eastern Conference semifinals against a young and hungry Atlanta Hawks team.[23]

Washington featured a deep, experienced roster with multiple All-Stars, while Atlanta trotted out the NBA's youngest team, relying on a player (John Drew) who was in and out of rehab for cocaine addiction just a few years later. Realizing his team's disadvantage, Hawks coach Hubie Brown ramped into high gear. Known for his hands-on approach, Brown drove his charges even harder. "Our people," Brown said, "have to be subservient to my goals. That's it." Brown also erupted at even small mistakes made by his players. "Everybody in the NBA is soft to begin with," Brown explained. "They come here spoiled. They've been the star in high school and college and they are soft. It's my job to harden them." He rigidly called specific sets on each offensive and defensive possession and outlawed improvisational one-on-one play. Although Brown is probably best remembered as a longtime broadcaster (and earned a spot in the Hall of Fame for his contributions to the game), his coaching gave the 1978–1979 Hawks an edge; they were not intimidated by the defending world champions. Knotted at three games apiece, game seven of the Hawks-Bullets series was a classic. President Jimmy Carter watched intently from the stands and skillfully dodged questions about whether he rooted for his hometown Hawks or the D.C.–based Bullets when interviewed at halftime. As the president cheered, the two teams traded the lead back and forth until, in the fourth quarter, the Bullets pulled away, emerging with a 100–94 victory.[24]

Dispatching the Hawks and their meticulously patterned offense meant the Bullets had to face the free-wheeling, high-octane attack of the Spurs in the next round. San Antonio came out hot, winning three of the first four from Washington to take firm control of the Eastern

Conference finals. Only the 1968 Celtics and 1970 Lakers had come back to win a seven-game series after trailing 3–1, but the Bullets shot back, winning the next two games to force an unlikely seventh game in front of a raucous crowd in the sold-out Capital Centre. Spurs star George "the Iceman" Gervin scored forty-two points to lead all scorers in game seven but was shut down in the fourth quarter by the Bullets' Bobby Dandridge. As the Iceman cooled off, Washington began to drive the ball to the basket and draw fouls, clawing back from a ten-point fourth-quarter deficit to take a two-point lead with under a minute remaining. Clock ticking toward zero, the Spurs put the ball into the hands of guard James Silas, known as "Captain Late" for his last-minute heroics dating to his days in the ABA. Silas again came through in the clutch as his soft jumper tied the game at 105. Back on offense, Washington worked the ball to Dandridge, who drove past Spurs forward Larry Kenon and knocked down a jump shot that gave him thirty-seven points on the night. After a Spurs timeout, Silas drove the lane, hoping to draw a foul or make a shot, sending the game into overtime. But Elvin Hayes left his man to help on defense and blocked Silas's attempt. The Bullets hung on, winning the game and the series by the closest of margins, 107–105. San Antonio coach Doug Moe ripped officials in his postgame interview. "They wanted to give the game to the Bullets," he charged, "and they did. Up until the last two minutes they called a great game, but after that we got screwed." Whether or not officiating played a role in the outcome of the game, Washington was headed back to the NBA finals where, perhaps, Coach Motta might make that fat lady sing once more.[25]

Just one day before the classic Spurs-Bullets game seven, the Sonics and Suns engaged in their own seventh game for the right to advance out of the Western Conference. Nearly 38,000 screaming fans packed the spacious Kingdome to cheer on their beloved Sonics, who traded punches with the Suns like heavyweight fighters for the first three quarters. A late Seattle run gave them a twelve-point lead midway through the fourth, but Phoenix came roaring back as Walter Davis scored fourteen of his team-high twenty-six points in the fourth quarter. With just four seconds left, Paul Westphal stole an errant inbounds pass and scored to cut the lead to two. Westphal was also fouled on the play, giving him one additional free throw. Standing at the charity stripe, Westphal must have thought back to game six of the 1976 finals when he convinced his coach to call a time-out and risk the assessed technical foul in order to give Phoenix the ball at midcourt. Now, Westphal intentionally missed his free throw attempt, hoping a Suns player could pull down the rebound and score quickly to tie the game. This time Westphal's strategy backfired. Sonics center Jack Sikma grabbed the rebound—his game-high eleventh—and converted two free throws to ice the game and give Seattle a harrowing 4–3 series win.

The 1979 NBA finals between the Washington Bullets and Seattle SuperSonics marked both a rematch of the thrilling '78 series and a contest of the league's two most physical teams. The Bullets sent out bruising center Wes Unseld, powerful forward Elvin Hayes, and reserve man Mitch Kupchak in the frontcourt, while the Sonics countered with Jack "Banger" Sikma, grizzly bear–strong forward Lonnie Shelton, and savvy veteran Paul Silas. "This series is going to be a physical one," Silas predicted. "The team that controls the boards will be able to control the game." As expected with two closely matched teams, game one came down to the final seconds. But surprisingly it was the guards and not the celebrated big men who decided the game's outcome. With the game on the line, Bullets reserve guard Larry Wright drove to the basket and missed a potential game winner. But referee Ed Rush called a foul on Sonics guard Dennis Johnson, giving Wright three chances to make two free throws (another relic of the '70s), any of which would win the game. He missed the first and the hometown Washington fans grew silent, suddenly nervous he might miss the next two as well. Wright took a deep breath and stepped up to the line. His second shot swished through the net. Bullets fans were ecstatic. Sonics fans were livid. "What did Dennis Johnson do to him?" demanded Seattle owner Sam Schulman. "I just saw the replay and he went right up for the shot with Wright. I didn't see any contact." Johnson was angry and sarcastic afterward. "I must have fouled, because the referee said so and they won the game," Johnson said, adding that "I'm not saying anything about the referees because you pay for it dearly."[26]

Motivated by Rush's miscall, Johnson took over the series on the defensive end. In game two, DJ and the Sonics held the Bullets to just eighty-two points, their lowest output of the season. Washington coach Dick Motta accused the Sonics of playing a zone defense, then illegal in the NBA. "Motta said we zoned," Johnson said, "but we didn't get caught." Three days later, Seattle won game three to take a 2–1 lead in the best-of-seven series. The Sonics also controlled game four but missed several chances to win the game in regulation and Washington forced overtime. In the extra period, little-used former star Phil Chenier pulled the Bullets to within two, but Johnson preserved the win by blocking a potentially game-tying shot and the Sonics prevailed, 114–112. At halftime of game five, the hometown Bullets held a 51–43 lead and looked like they might extend the series. But Johnson and Gus Williams would have none of it, leading a furious comeback. Final score: Seattle 97, Washington 93. The Sonics celebrated the franchise's first (and, to date, only) NBA title.[27]

The combination of Williams and Johnson was electric in the '79 finals, drawing comparisons to the "Rolls Royce Backcourt" of Walt Frazier and Earl Monroe of the old Knicks. Together, DJ and Gus eviscerated the Bullets, combining for more than half of Seattle's points in the five-game series. But in naming the finals MVP, there was really only one choice: Johnson averaged twenty-two points, six rebounds, six assists, two steals, and two blocks, more than making up for his 0-for-14 performance in 1978's game seven. But numbers alone cannot describe his impact on both ends of the court. Although prone to moodiness and sulkiness that eventually resulted in a nasty contract dispute, Johnson, when engaged, was among the best players in the NBA, especially on defense where his long arms and almost supernatural quickness caused fits for opposing guards. In the 1979 finals he was on and the Bullets backcourt had no chance.

As usual, sportswriters clamored to anoint another apparent dynasty-in-the-making. But before the champagne had dried on their garish gold and green uniforms, Silas shot down any talk of a repeat. "I'm beginning to think there are no such things as dynasties anymore," the sage veteran said. "The structure of the league and the game has changed so much. Sometimes I think that the team that survives the 100-game marathon has the best chance at winning it all." History was on the side of Silas: back-to-back titles were a near impossibility—the last squad to repeat was the '69 Celtics with Bill Russell—and eight different franchises claimed titles in the seventies.[28]

What Silas could not have known was that the league was on the verge of a great transition stemming (fittingly) from the outcome of a flipped coin. One coin flip delivered Lew Alcindor to Milwaukee in 1969; another would send Alcindor (now known as Kareem Abdul-

Jabbar) a legendary running mate, Michigan State star Earvin "Magic" Johnson. In the fall of 1979, Larry Bird and Magic Johnson suited up for the Celtics and Lakers respectively, and almost overnight the balance of power in the league shifted. No longer would Washington, Seattle, San Antonio, or Phoenix rule the roost. Instead, Boston and LA were about to embark on an epic struggle defining the decade of decadence.

Statistics for 1978–1979

Eastern Conference	W	L	Western Conference	W	L
Atlantic Division			*Midwest Division*		
Washington Bullets	54	28	Kansas City Kings	48	34
Philadelphia 76ers	47	35	Denver Nuggets	47	35
New Jersey Nets	37	45	Milwaukee Bucks	38	44
New York Knicks	31	51	Indiana Pacers	38	44
Boston Celtics	29	53	Chicago Bulls	31	51
Central Division			*Pacific Division*		
San Antonio Spurs	48	34	Seattle SuperSonics	52	30
Houston Rockets	47	35	Phoenix Suns	50	32
Atlanta Hawks	46	36	Los Angeles Lakers	47	35
Detroit Pistons	30	52	Portland Trail Blazers	45	37
Cleveland Cavaliers	30	52	San Diego Clippers	43	39
New Orleans Jazz	26	56	Golden State Warriors	38	44

Playoffs

Eastern Conference First Round	Atlanta d. Houston (2–0)
	Philadelphia d. New Jersey (2–0)
Western Conference First Round	Los Angeles d. Denver (2–1)
	Phoenix d. Portland (2–1)
Eastern Conference Semifinals	San Antonio d. Philadelphia (4–3)
	Washington d. Atlanta (4–3)
Western Conference Semifinals	Phoenix d. Kansas City (4–1)
	Seattle d. Los Angeles (4–1)
Eastern Conference Finals	Washington d. San Antonio (4–3)

Western Conference Finals	Seattle d. Phoenix (4–3)
NBA Finals	Seattle d. Washington (4–1)

All-NBA Teams

First Team	Second Team
F—Marques Johnson (Milwaukee)	F—Walter Davis (Phoenix)
F—Elvin Hayes (Washington)	F—Bob Dandridge (Washington)
C—Moses Malone (Houston)	C—Kareem Abdul-Jabbar (Los Angeles)
G—George Gervin (San Antonio)	G—Phil Ford (Kansas City)
G—Paul Westphal (Phoenix)	G—Lloyd Free (San Diego)

League Leaders

Points per Game (29.6)	George Gervin (San Antonio)
Rebounds per Game (17.6)	Moses Malone (Houston)
Assists per Game (13.45)	Kevin Porter (Detroit)
Steals per Game (2.5)	M. L. Carr (Detroit)
Blocks per Game (4.0)	Kareem Abdul-Jabbar (Los Angeles)
Most Valuable Player	Moses Malone (Houston)
Rookie of the Year	Phil Ford (Kansas City)

POSTGAME
The Eighties

Earvin "Magic" Johnson made his NBA debut for the Los Angeles Lakers against the San Diego Clippers on October 12, 1979, nearly seven months after leading Michigan State to the NCAA title. Johnson was nervous, admitting as much to Brent Musberger in a pregame interview. Magic tripped over his pants during warmups, missed his first two shots from the field, and was called for traveling as San Diego jumped out to an early lead. But Johnson rallied, helping the Lakers claw to within a single point of the Clippers as time ticked away. Lakers coach Jack McKinney called for a time-out and diagrammed a last-second play designed to free up Johnson near the hoop. San Diego defended the play well, and, instead, the ball went to Kareem Abdul-Jabbar at the foul line. Kareem caught it and in one smooth motion pivoted, launching a feathery soft skyhook. The ball swished through the net, giving the Lakers a buzzer-beating 103–102 win. For Abdul-Jabbar, it was just an early season win and as usual Kareem was subdued in his postgame interview. But for Johnson it was so much more. Even as Kareem's hook shot settled through the net, Magic was running over to embrace the veteran center in a bear hug. Musberger praised Magic's youthful exuberance. "He looks like he just won the NCAA championship!" Musberger laughed. Johnson's grin stretched from ear to ear, his enthusiasm infectious.[1]

On the opposite coast, fellow rookie Larry Bird of the Boston Celtics watched on television as Johnson celebrated the Lakers' opening night win. Bird's debut had been less auspicious as he scored fourteen points in helping Boston to a 114–105 win over the Houston Rockets.

In the 1980s, these two precocious rookies became synonymous with professional basketball. During that decade, Johnson's Lakers met Bird's Celtics just three times in the NBA finals, but it seemed like they always battled for the title. Los Angeles won NBA championships in 1980, 1982, 1985, 1987, and 1988; Boston won rings in 1981, 1984, and 1986. For basketball fans, Bird and Johnson were linked by more than just team success. Both stood around six-foot-nine, although Johnson was a point guard and a better passer, while Bird played forward and possessed a more reliable outside shot. Both rebounded well for their positions and neither was known as a defensive stopper. Each won three MVP awards and fans selected them to twelve All-Star games apiece. Chronic back injuries shortened Bird's career, while Johnson abruptly retired in 1991 after revealing he was HIV positive. Bird hung up his sneakers for good in 1992, but Johnson returned to the Lakers for a short stint in January 1996, reinventing himself as a bulked-up power forward before re-retiring later that spring. In 1998, voters named Bird to the Naismith Basketball Hall of Fame; four years later, he gave the induction speech for Johnson when Magic joined him in Springfield.

Larry Legend and the Magic Man arrived in a league struggling with racial problems, illicit drug use, and viewer apathy. "Professional basketball was going to light up America," Curry Kirkpatrick wrote in a 1978 *Sports Illustrated* feature. "It was going to make us forget football, not to mention old, dull baseball and *Charlie's Angels*, too. Professional basketball," Kirkpatrick quipped, "was going to replace politics, ice cream, sex and the church." As Kirkpatrick recognized, the league was facing a serious image crisis. "Sponsors were flocking out of the NBA," legal counsel David Stern recalled, "because it was perceived as a bunch of high-salaried, drug-sniffing black guys." In 1984, NBA owners named Stern the league's commissioner. In his thirty subsequent years in the role, Stern faced many problems—referees accused of point shaving, the "Malice in the Palace," Dennis Rodman—but through it all, he was adamant that the late seventies were the NBA's "dark days."[2]

During the late seventies and early eighties, recreational drug use was endemic. In 1980, a *Los Angeles Times* investigation charged 75 percent of NBA players with using drugs. For many, the drug of choice was cocaine, a so-called drug without a downside. Unlike alcohol or marijuana, which dulled the senses, coke increased alertness. It was chic both in the entertainment industry (Richard Pryor set himself on fire after freebasing cocaine during the making of the film *Bustin' Loose* in 1980) and in the sports world.[3]

"We were the converts to the Church of Cocaine," Spencer Haywood wrote in his 1992 autobiography. "We were the high priests of Cool. Hallelujah." Haywood ranked among the most well-known drug users in the game, having picked up the habit when he arrived in New York in 1975. "Freebasing was a game," Haywood said. "I hid behind the coke." In 1979, Haywood landed in L.A., feeding his addiction. "I wasn't the only Laker doing coke," Haywood said. "I got high at least once with eight other players." Some players used cocaine recreationally, but Haywood became addicted, mixing cocaine and heroin with alcohol and Quaaludes to stabilize the high. Cocaine ruined Haywood's career, but he was far from the only star to abuse drugs. Marvin "Bad News" Barnes allegedly snorted cocaine during a game while sitting on the bench, his head hidden under a towel. David "Skywalker" Thompson first used coke to deal with the "physical and mental exhaustion" of the 1976 ABA playoffs. Within a few years, Thompson—like Haywood—was hooked. "I used cocaine as my escape," Thompson recalled, although he refused to admit his problem to himself or others until 1983, by which point the surefire Hall of Famer was a shell of his former self. The list goes on and on. Walter Davis, John Drew, Bernard King, John Lucas, and Micheal Ray Richardson (to name but a few) threw away promising careers by abusing cocaine, marijuana, alcohol, or narcotics in the late seventies and early eighties. In 1983, paralleling President Ronald Reagan's national initiative promoting drug awareness, the NBA created a Drug Education Prevention Committee.[4]

As the nation and the league waged a war on drugs, Magic Johnson and Larry Bird gained much-needed goodwill for the NBA as superstar players (one black, one white, and both, as far as we know, drug free) playing in major markets. Within weeks of their NBA debuts, Bird and Magic established themselves as stars; Johnson lit up the Nuggets for thirty-one points, eight rebounds, and six assists in an early November game, and a week later Bird achieved his first career triple-double, tallying twenty-three points, nineteen rebounds, and ten assists against the Pistons. "Some nights," Bird said, "the game just seems really easy."[5]

Johnson and the Lakers met Bird and the Celtics for the first time on December 28, 1979. For NBA fans, it was a late Christmas gift, and a crowd of 17,505 packed into the Forum, L.A.'s first sellout in more than a year. Television ratings revealed more Americans tuned in to that regular-season contest than to any NBA finals game during the 1970s, even though the game itself was a stinker. Los Angeles blew out Boston, and Bird scored only sixteen points, calling the hype "stupid." "The NBA has got to do it and get publicity," Bird admitted. But, he reminded reporters, "I just come to play. I ain't going to go out of my way to do no commercials for the NBA or nothing like that." More tactfully, Johnson called it a "special game," adding "I'm enjoying doing what I do."[6]

By season's end, Bird helped the Celtics to a then-record thirty-two game improvement in the standings, and Boston's sixty-one wins led the league, earning them the top spot in the playoffs. Bird also won acclaim as the league's rookie of the year, leading all first-year players in scoring and rebounding (21.3 points and 10.4 rebounds per game) while handing out 4.5 assists per contest.

But it was Johnson who had the more—ahem—magical season in 1979–1980. His Lakers finished 60–22, bolstered by the arrival of Spencer Haywood. Haywood never achieved the superstardom many predicted when he jumped to the Seattle SuperSonics in 1971, but (when sober) he remained a productive player and a perfect fit next to Abdul-Jabbar. The Lakers were rolling before a midseason bicycle accident derailed Jack McKinney's promising coaching career. Assistant Paul Westhead took over, and several players, including Haywood, clashed with the new boss. Unsurprisingly, Haywood turned to drugs and even passed out at a practice. When Haywood admitted his problem to Westhead, he was thrown off the team. By his own admission, Haywood did eighteen hits of crack that night and planned to have Westhead killed by cutting the brakes on his car. Fortunately, Haywood's mother intervened and he never followed through on his plan. Unfortunately, his career was all but over. Haywood played overseas in Italy and returned for a cup of coffee with the Washington Bullets before calling it quits for good in 1983.

After Westhead dismissed him from the team, Haywood had to watch the 1980 finals on television. And like most Americans tuned into the CBS broadcast, he must have been awed by the performance of the Lakers rookie guard. Magic Johnson ramped up his game in the postseason, increasing his numbers across the board, averaging a remarkable eighteen points, ten rebounds, and nine assists. Most memorably, with Kareem Abdul-Jabbar sidelined, Johnson jumped center in game six of the finals against the Philadelphia 76ers (who had knocked Bird and the Celtics out a round earlier). Johnson played all five positions that night and scored a career-high forty-two points in leading the Lakers to a 123–107 win, giving Los Angeles its first championship since the fabled '72 team. Kareem and Magic, without Haywood, paired up for nine more seasons in L.A. as Lakers general manager Jerry West put together four more title-winning teams. Kareem retired in 1989, hanging up his goggles as a nineteen-time All-Star, six-time most valuable player, and the leading scorer in NBA history, scoring 38,387 points over an amazing twenty-year career.

The 1979–1980 Lakers added Haywood to give them a veteran presence for their title run. That season, the Celtics made a similar move, signing "Pistol Pete" Maravich. In 1979, the New Orleans Jazz relocated to Salt Lake City, keeping their nickname despite the dissonance between it and their new home. Maravich resisted, and the newly christened Utah Jazz waived their former star, allowing Pistol Pete to sign with the Celtics. For the first time in his ten-year career, Pete played a supporting role, passing the "Great White Hope" torch to new teammate Larry Bird. Although he flashed moments of brilliance, Pete wore two heavy knee braces and could no longer score as he once did. After clashing with Coach Bill Fitch, Maravich considered retirement. To talk Maravich out of quitting, the Celtics sent veteran center Dave Cowens to meet with Maravich. Instead, Pistol Pete convinced the big redhead to join him in retirement. "The two men were kindred spirits who loved to play the game," one historian explained. But the game was no longer fun for them. Cowens sat out two years, returning for a forgettable stint with the 1982–1983 Milwaukee Bucks before turning to coaching. But for Pistol Pete, game five of the 1980 Eastern Conference finals was his last in the NBA. Without basketball in his life, Maravich became a recluse and his search for meaning eventually led him to become a born-again Christian. Less than eight years after retiring from the NBA, Maravich collapsed while playing a game of pickup basketball at a church gym and died of an undiagnosed congenital heart defect. When the NBA announced its list of the fifty greatest basketball players of all time in 1996, only Maravich was no longer alive.[7]

The Utah Jazz (who considered taking on the name "Saints" in their move to Salt Lake City but decided that might make New Orleans fans even more angry) struggled mightily in the early eighties, winning fewer than thirty games in each of the first four seasons of the decade. Star forward Adrian Dantley twice won the scoring title (1980–1981 and 1983–1984), and following his second title, the Jazz used the sixteenth pick in the historic 1984 draft on diminutive guard John Stockton out of Gonzaga. The next year, they took a gamble on hulking Louisiana Tech forward Karl Malone. Stockton and Malone, coached by Jerry Sloan (the "Original Bull" himself) never won an NBA title, but they did lead the Jazz to nineteen straight playoff berths and multiple finals appearances.

The San Antonio Spurs became heated rivals with the Jazz once the Spurs moved to the Western Conference in 1980. George "the Iceman" Gervin remained one of the NBA's top point makers (twice leading the league in points per game in the eighties) and retired as the eighth-leading scorer in pro basketball history. Early in the decade, San Antonio made a title run, pairing Gervin with former Bulls star Artis Gilmore for a few seasons. But the duo never advanced beyond the Western Conference finals, and Gervin moved to the Chicago Bulls, where he retired in 1986 after a rather forgettable season caddying for second-year guard Michael Jordan. After Gervin left, San Antonio was mediocre for most of the eighties. During the 1988–1989 season, they finished 21–61 but won the NBA's draft lottery, allowing them to select David Robinson, the cornerstone of multiple title-winning teams stretching into the next millennium.

In 1978, Gervin famously dueled Denver Nuggets star David Thompson for the league scoring title. That year, Thompson signed the richest contract in NBA history, earning him $800,000 annually. Within a year, as pressure mounted for the highly paid "Skywalker" to lead Denver to a title, Thompson began using drugs more aggressively. "I was thoroughly addicted," Thompson later admitted, and "my drug usage began to affect even my play." His scoring output dipped from twenty-seven points per game in the 1977–1978 season to twenty-four and then twenty-one over the next two seasons. In 1982, Denver traded Thompson to Seattle and remade themselves as a record-setting offensive juggernaut under Coach Doug Moe, setting a single-game scoring record by tallying 184 points in a three-overtime win against the Pistons in 1983. Star center Dan Issel lasted with the Nuggets until 1985, when the thirty-seven-year-old, seven-time All-Star retired as the fourth-highest scorer in league history. Meanwhile, Thompson was reviving his once-promising career, finishing second in the voting for league's Comeback Player of the Year award after overcoming his cocaine and marijuana addictions. In 1983, Thompson earned an All-Star berth but, in March 1984, his career came to an abrupt end when he fell down the steps of New York's famed Studio 54 and blew out his knee. He retired before his thirtieth birthday.[8]

Seattle traded for Thompson because of internal dissent splitting the team apart almost immediately after they won the 1979 title. "The champagne bubbles hadn't even gone flat before the problems started," Coach Lenny Wilkens remembered. Finals MVP Dennis Johnson was woefully underpaid but locked into a long-term deal that Sonics management refused to renegotiate. So too was Johnson's running mate, Gus Williams. Williams and Johnson played well during the 1979–1980 season and Seattle went 56–26. But they lost to the Lakers in the Western Conference finals, and Williams sat out the entire 1980–1981 season in a contract dispute while Seattle traded DJ—after he earned All-NBA second-team and All-Defensive first-team honors—to the Suns for Paul Westphal. In 1983, Johnson moved again, this time to Boston, where he became an integral part of two championship squads. As a Celtic, the man once nicknamed "Airplane" for his tremendous physical gifts became a cerebral assassin, using his mind more than his body to frustrate opposing guards and run the high-octane Boston offense.[9]

Another player who earned a second chance as a cog in the mid-eighties Celtics machine was much-maligned center Bill Walton. After signing with the San Diego Clippers in 1979, Walton went corporate, trading tie-dyed shirts and bicycles for a Mercedes-Benz and $1,400 suits. "Maybe I didn't care so much about that before," Walton admitted at the time, "but people change." Despite his highbrow wardrobe, Walton still struggled with foot, ankle, and back problems, playing only fourteen games in his first four years combined in San Diego. Finally, after seven disappointing seasons, the Clippers traded Walton to Boston for a first-round pick and former finals MVP Cedric "Cornbread" Maxwell. Maxwell played just one season for new Clippers owner Donald Sterling, a realtor and lawyer who had recently purchased the team and relocated them to Los Angeles. In 1988, Sterling hired legendary Laker Elgin Baylor to serve as the team's vice president of basketball operations, but the team became the laughingstock of the league before revelations of racism finally forced Sterling out as the Clippers' owner in 2014.[10]

Freed from the Clippers, Walton enjoyed a career revival in Boston. He played just two seasons in Celtics green, but his performance on the 1985–1986 squad made them one of the greatest of all time. Able to play an amazing eighty games, the highest in his career, Walton earned the Sixth Man of the Year award backing up Robert Parish and Kevin McHale. With Parish, McHale, Walton, Bird, Dennis Johnson, and Danny Ainge (picked up as a second-round choice that was part of the famed franchise flip of 1978), the 1985–1986 Celtics won sixty-seven games and the NBA title.

Other than the Lakers, the Celtics' greatest adversary in the eighties was the Philadelphia 76ers. The Sixers' trade of George McGinnis to Denver in 1978 was a clear indication that they would go only as far as Julius "Dr. J" Erving could take them. In 1980, Philly beat Boston before losing to Los Angeles in the finals. The next spring, they jumped out to a commanding 3–1 lead in an Eastern Conference finals rematch against Boston, but the Celtics roared back and took the decisive seventh game in one of the most thrilling series in league history, closing out the contest with a Larry Bird sixteen footer. After falling to the Lakers again in the 1982 finals, Philly signed reigning MVP Moses Malone from the Houston Rockets and breezed to the 1983 title, winning sixty-five regular-season games and nearly accomplishing Malone's famed "fo' fo' fo'" prediction of sweeping the playoffs. Only the Milwaukee Bucks—who put together some very good seasons in the eighties themselves—managed to steal one from the Sixers that postseason. Thanks to an amazingly shortsighted trade with San Diego netting Philly the fourth overall pick in the loaded 1984 draft, the Sixers added Auburn power forward Charles Barkley, the self-proclaimed "Round Mound of Rebound." Even with Erving, Malone, and Barkley, the Sixers were unable to win another title. In 1986, they traded Malone to the Bullets, where he played for another rough-and-tumble former center: head coach Wes Unseld. The following season, Erving retired. Dr. J left the game as a sixteen-time All-Star, four-time MVP (three times in the ABA and once in the NBA), and only the third player in pro basketball history to top the 30,000 point plateau. Without Erving and Malone around, Barkley became the sole superstar in the City of Brotherly Love before moving to Phoenix in the nineties.

Early in the 1980s, many future coaching legends were gaining valuable on-the-job experience. Phil Jackson took a head coaching position in the Continental Basketball Association (CBA) before landing with the Chicago Bulls as an assistant in 1987. Two years later, Jackson replaced Doug Collins (the former Sixers guard) on the Bulls bench and led the team to six titles; he won four more with the Kobe Bryant–era Lakers to finish a single ring behind Bill Russell. Rudy Tomjanovich, after winning two rings himself while coaching the mid-nineties Houston Rockets, replaced Jackson in Los Angeles—ironically, the same franchise he had sued two decades earlier after suffering severe facial injuries at the hands of Lakers forward Kermit Washington. Rudy T could not win a title for Los Angeles, but Pat Riley certainly could. Riley, after a forgettable NBA career spent mostly as a reserve, took the Lakers job in 1982 after the team canned Paul Westhead. Riley led L.A. to four titles before leaving for the Big Apple. He spent four seasons in New York and then went to Miami, first as the head coach (winning the 2006 championship), and then as the executive who brought together Dwyane Wade, LeBron James, and Chris Bosh to create two more title-winning teams in South Beach. All told, Jackson, Riley, and Tomjanovich (all of whom played in the NBA in the '70s) combined for seventeen coaching titles spread over three decades.

Jackson, Riley, and Tomjanovich all coached the Lakers, one of four truly great franchises of the 1980s alongside the Celtics, Sixers, and Detroit Pistons. Detroit started the eighties much as they had ended the seventies: poorly. An ill-fated trade for aging superstar Bob McAdoo, pushed for by exuberant head coach Dick Vitale in 1979, created internal turmoil. Bob Lanier, the team's star center, resented McAdoo's attitude, and the two clashed both on and off the court. "The team situation is not good," McAdoo said. "We've got five rookies, two second-year players, a new coach and no hope of winning a championship." At one point, McAdoo allegedly informed team officials he was going to stay "injured" until they acquired a better point guard. Vitale was the first to go, fired in November 1979; three months later, Lanier followed him out the door, traded to Milwaukee, where he played on some very good Bucks teams. In early 1981, Detroit cut McAdoo, who latched on with the Lakers (his sixth team in six years) and reinvented himself—à la Bill Walton—as an excellent reserve on two champion-ship-winning teams. Shortly after McAdoo's exit, the Pistons selected Indiana University point guard Isiah Thomas in the '81 draft. Over the next several years, Pistons GM "Trader" Jack McCloskey made numer-ous savvy deals and draft choices bringing the team guard Joe Dumars, forwards Dennis Rodman, Mark Aguirre, and Rick Mahorn, and center Bill Laimbeer. McCloskey's "Bad Boy" Pistons won the NBA title in 1989 and repeated the next season to become the first champions of the 1990s.[11]

Detroit's greatest foes resided in New York and Chicago. At the dawn of the 1980s, the Knicks were in shambles. "The Knicks have tried just about every option open to a team with endless corporate millions behind it," wrote one journalist, "except exercising intelligence and pa-tience." In 1979, the team appeared on the cusp of something great, building around young center Marvin "the Human Eraser" Webster and guards Ray Williams and Micheal Ray Richardson. Unfortunately, Webster struggled with hepatitis (sidelining him for two full seasons), Williams left New York as a free agent, and drug problems derailed Richardson's career. In 1982, New York swapped Richardson for an-other troubled soul: Golden State forward Bernard King. King had a breakout 1984–1985 season, leading the league in scoring with more than thirty-two points per game, including an unforgettable sixty points on Christmas Day. But a career-threatening knee injury in 1985 again forced the Knicks into rebuilding mode. The gods finally smiled on Knicks fans when, in the first-ever NBA draft lottery (replacing the antiquated coin flip), New York earned the top slot, allowing them to draft Georgetown center Patrick Ewing. Ewing never led the Knicks to an NBA title, but New York once again became a basketball mecca after a decade spent chasing, and usually missing out on, superstar talent and on-court success.[12]

One reason the Knicks never won an NBA title in the eighties or nineties was a dynasty cultivated in Chicago: five times between 1989 and 1996, the Bulls eliminated the Knicks from the playoffs. New York was good, even great. But Chicago was better. In 1979–1980, Chicago went 30–52 despite the potent duo of guard "Rush Street" Reggie Theus and center Artis Gilmore. They improved to 45–37 the next season and both Theus and Gilmore earned All-Star nods. But then the team limped to a thirty-four-win campaign and the Bulls traded Gilmore to San Antonio. During the 1983–1984 season, Theus was also sent packing and the Bulls bottomed out, winning just twenty-seven games on the season. Fortunately, that gave the Bulls the third overall selection in the famed 1984 draft. Chicago general manager Rod Thorn considered trades that might have brought back Julius Erving or 1983 top overall choice Ralph Sampson but ultimately decided to stand pat. The Rockets, picking first after having tanked by playing over-the-hill big man Elvin Hayes in meaningless late-season games to get him 50,000 career minutes played, selected Akeem (later Hakeem) Olajuwon from the University of Houston. With the second pick, the Portland Trail Blazers chose oft-injured Kentucky center Sam Bowie.

Picking third, the Bulls took North Carolina guard Michael Jordan and never looked back. Jordan achieved tremendous personal success in his first few years in Chicago, winning rookie of the year honors and earning slots on the All-Star team every season. But his Bulls continued to struggle, finishing under .500 and cycling through three head coaches in Jordan's first three seasons. In the 1987 draft, the Bulls traded their own first-round choice (Olden Polynice) to Seattle for the number-five overall pick used on an unheralded forward out of tiny Central Arkansas named Scottie Pippen. The triumvirate of Jordan, Pippen, and Horace Grant (plucked with the tenth overall pick of the '87 draft) gave the Bulls their title-winning core. Under Phil Jackson, Chicago won an NBA title—the first in franchise history—in 1991 and then repeated the feat in '92, '93, '96, '97, and '98. Bird and Johnson could both lay claim to playing for the team of the eighties, but Jordan's Bulls were clearly the team of the nineties.

In the 1980s, Magic Johnson, Larry Bird, and, to a lesser extent, Michael Jordan, brought professional basketball unrivaled popularity. Fortunately, this coincided with the growth of cable television (more televised games meant more potential fans) and the appointment of David Stern as the NBA's commissioner. Looking back, it might be easy to cast the 1970s (as Stern does) as the league's "dark days." But none of the NBA's growth in the eighties would have been possible without the efforts of basketball's pioneers of the 1970s. Oscar Robertson challenged the NBA's monopoly and ultimately earned the abolition of the antiquated reserve clause. Rick Barry sat out for an entire season rather than play for less money. During the decade, player salaries skyrocketed, the three-point shot emerged as an offensive weapon (finally adopted by the NBA in 1979), and the ABA created the dunk contest, which later became a highlight of All-Star weekend as high fliers like Jordan and Atlanta Hawks star Dominique Wilkins battled for the title of league's best dunker. The NBA might not have lived up to expectations that it would surpass the NFL and MLB as the "sport of the seventies," but its players and teams transformed professional basketball in important ways. "In the 1970s," David Thompson once wrote, "basketball emerged from the Dark Ages into prime time."[13]

NOTES

PREGAME

1. William F. Russell, "I'm Not Involved Anymore," *Sports Illustrated*, August 4, 1969.
2. Quoted in Roland Lazenby, *The NBA Finals: A Fifty Year Celebration* (Lincolnwood, IL: Master's Press, 1996), 134.
3. Lazenby, *The NBA Finals*, 136.
4. Mal Florence, "Even Champ Celts Salute Loser West," *Sporting News*, May 17, 1969, 47.
5. Wilt Chamberlain, *Wilt: Just Like Any Other 7-Foot Black Millionaire Who Lives Next Door* (New York: Macmillan, 1973), 218; Jerry West and Jonathan Coleman, *West by West: My Charmed, Tormented Life* (New York: Little, Brown, 2011), 86.

I. 1969 TO 1970

1. From 1966, which marked the end of the territorial draft era, until 1984, when the league switched to the modern draft lottery system, the NBA determined the first pick in the collegiate draft by a coin flip between the worst team from each conference or division. League officials hoped this measure would help prevent squads from losing on purpose to secure the top overall selection.
2. Tex Maule, "Lew Turns Small Change to Big Bucks," *Sports Illustrated*, March 9, 1970.

3. Kareem Abdul-Jabbar and Peter Knobler, *Giant Steps* (New York: Bantam Books, 1983), 196, 197.

4. Don Brown, "Exclusive! The Coming Battle for Lew Alcindor," *Pro Basketball Almanac 1969* (New York: McFadden-Bartell, 1970), 12; Lew Alcindor and Jack Olsen, "A Year of Turmoil and Decision," *Sports Illustrated*, November 10, 1969.

5. Dave DeBusschere, *The Open Man: A Championship Diary*, ed. Paul D. Zimmerman and Dick Schaap (New York: Random House, 1970), 43–44; Bob Ryan, "Hank Finkel: Occupation, Bench Warmer," *Basketball Digest*, January 1976, 82.

6. Walt Frazier with Neil Offen, *Walt Frazier: One Magical Season and a Basketball Life* (New York: Times Books, 1988), 184; Jim O'Brien, "Muscles McGinnis a Deadly Shooter," *Sporting News*, February 24 1973, 3.

7. Terry Pluto, *Tall Tales: The Glory Years of the NBA* (Lincoln: University of Nebraska Press, 1992), 82.

8. Pete Axthelm, *The City Game: Basketball in New York from the World Champion Knicks to the World of the Playgrounds* (New York: Harper & Row, 1970), 46; Willis Reed, *A Will to Win: The Comeback Year* (Englewood Cliffs, NJ: Prentice-Hall, 1973), 9; Lazenby, *The NBA Finals*, 143; Phil Jackson, *Maverick: More Than a Game* (Chicago: Playboy Press, 1975), 6.

9. Walt Frazier and Ira Berkow, *Rockin' Steady: A Guide to Basketball and Cool* (New York: Warner Paperback Library, 1974), 14, 19–20, 216–22; "Burning Questions for Walt Frazier," http://espn.go.com/page2/s/questions/frazier.html (accessed October 10, 2014).

10. Jim Murray, "Murray's Best," *Sporting News*, February 12, 1972, 16.

11. "The Knicks Driving toward the Top," *Sport*, March 1970, 17–18. As Yago Colás demonstrates in his excellent book, *Ball Don't Lie: Myth, Genealogy, and Invention in the Cultures of Basketball* (Philadelphia: Temple University Press, 2016), much of the celebratory narrative that he dubs the "Myth of the Garden" was invented by sportswriters and the players themselves and results in a narrative of black masculinity being subjugated in the name of peaceful coexistence. However, as symbols of togetherness, these Knicks did provide a welcome respite from the social ills of the day.

12. "All-Star Lucas 'Didn't Fit into Royals' Style,'" *Sporting News*, November 8, 1969, 32; Oscar Robertson, *The Big O: My Life, My Times, My Game* (Emmaus, PA: Rodale Press, 2003), 228–29.

13. Frazier, *Walt Frazier*, 118; Robertson, *The Big O*, 227.

14. "Letters," *New York*, November 22, 1971, 6; William G. Mokray, ed., *Basketball's Best, 1970–1971* (Pleasantville, NY: Champion Sports Publishing, 1970), 27; Al Silverman, ed., *Pro Basketball Almanac 1970* (New York: Mcfadden-Bartell, 1969), 3, 6.

15. Roland Lazenby, *Jerry West: The Life and Legend of a Basketball Icon* (New York: Ballantine Books, 2009), 291; Frank Deford, "Merger, Madness and Maravich," *Sports Illustrated*, April 6, 1970.

16. Frank Deford, "Beware of the Hawks," *Sports Illustrated*, April 13, 1970.

17. David Wolf, *Foul! The Connie Hawkins Story* (New York: Holt, Rinehart, and Winston, 1972), 50.

18. Joe Gilmartin, "Connie Hawkins' Revolution in Arizona," *Basketball's All-Pro Annual 1971*, ed. Zander Hollander (New York: Popular Library, 1970), 29; Tex Maule, "A Coming-out Party for Lew and Connie," *Sports Illustrated*, October 6, 1969; Harry Klaff, ed., "Suns on Rise," *Countrywide Sports: Basketball Sports Special,* 1970, 37; Silverman, *Pro Basketball Almanac 1970*, 3; Wolf, *Foul!* 280; Robertson, *The Big O*, 206–7.

19. Wells Twombly, "Who'll Get Hayes? Pro Rush Near," *Sporting News*, February 24, 1968, 3.

20. DeBusschere, *The Open Man*, 240; Jerry West, "The Game I'll Never Forget," *Basketball Digest*, December 1973, 35–36; Frank Deford, "East Is Knicks but West Is West," *Sports Illustrated*, May 11, 1970.

21. Harvey Araton, *When the Garden Was Eden: Clyde, the Captain, Dollar Bill, and the Glory Days of the New York Knicks* (New York: HarperCollins, 2011), 140; Peter N. Carroll, *It Seemed Like Nothing Happened: America in the 1970s* (New Brunswick, NJ: Rutgers University Press, 2000), 21.

22. Araton, *When the Garden Was Eden*, 119.

23. DeBusschere, *Open Man*, 247–48; Frazier, *Walt Frazier*, 4; Sabin, *Basketball Stars of 1971*, 37.

24. Willis Reed with Phil Pepe, *A View from the Rim: Willis Reed on Basketball* (Philadelphia: Lippincott), 200.

25. Frazier, *Walt Frazier*, 243; Araton, *When the Garden Was Eden*, 160.

26. Sam Goldaper, "Demoralized and Tired," *New York Times*, May 9, 1970, 29; Wilt Chamberlain, *Wilt: Just Like Any Other 7-Foot Black Millionaire Who Lives Next Door* (New York: Macmillan, 1973), 236.

THE PISTOL

1. Bob Dylan, *Chronicles: Volume One* (New York: Simon and Schuster, 2004), 168.

2. Mark Kriegel, *Pistol: The Life of Pete Maravich* (New York: Free Press, 2007), 69, 74; Phil Berger, *Forever Showtime: The Checkered Life of Pistol Pete Maravich* (Dallas: Taylor, 1999), 56.

3. Kriegel, *Pistol*, 89.

4. Kriegel, *Pistol*, 64, 66.

5. Wayne Federman and Marshall Terrill with Jackie Maravich, *Maravich: The Authorized Biography of Pistol Pete* (Carol Stream, IL: Tyndale House, 2006), 25, 60; Kriegel, *Pistol*, 117.

6. Estimates vary widely as to how many more points Pete would have scored with the inclusion of a three-point line. One reporter for the *Baton Rouge State-Times* insisted that he would have averaged an additional 7.8 points per contest while Bryant Gumbel, interviewed for a documentary about Maravich that aired on CBS in 2001, estimated that he would have gained "ten or twelve more" points each game with the benefit of a three-point line.

7. Pete Maravich and Darrel Campbell, *Heir to a Dream* (Nashville: Thomas Nelson, 1987), 134.

8. Federman, Terrill, and Maravich, *Maravich*, 174; George Cunningham, "Pete Maravich: 'He's Going to Be Better,'" in *Pro Basketball Illustrated*, ed. Alan Goldfarb, 71–72 (New York: Complete Sports Publications, 1970), 26.

9. Frank Deford, "Merger, Madness and Maravich," *Sports Illustrated*, April 6, 1970.

10. Kriegel, *Pistol*, 189; Frank Deford, "The Hawks: Fouled up but Flourishing," *Sports Illustrated*, March 8, 1971.

11. Frank Hyland, "Pete Maravich: Will He Make It?" in *Pro Basketball Illustrated*, ed. Alan Goldfarb, 70–71 (New York: Complete Sports Publications, 1970), 30; Federman, Terrill, and Maravich, *Maravich*, 178; Kriegel, *Pistol*, 191.

12. Kriegel, *Pistol*, 195.

13. Berger, *Forever Showtime*, 137, 138; Federman, *Maravich*, 184; Kriegel, *Pistol*, 198.

14. Federman, *Maravich*, 184, 185; Berger, *Forever Showtime*, 144.

15. Berger, *Forever Showtime*, 140.

16. Peter Carry, "We Have a Slight Delay in Show Time," *Sports Illustrated*, October 26, 1970.

2. 1970 TO 1971

1. Terry Pluto, *Loose Balls: The Short, Wild Life of the American Basketball Association* (New York: Simon & Schuster, 1990), 193; Peter Carry, "We Have a Slight Delay in Show Time," *Sports Illustrated*, October 26, 1970.

2. Pluto, *Loose Balls*, 198.

3. Oscar Robertson, *The Big O: My Life, My Times, My Game* (Emmaus, PA: Rodale Press, 2003), 244–45.

4. For comparison, the league-average scoring was 112.4 points per game in 1970–1971 and 100 points per game in 2014–2015. "Kareem of the Crop," *Sports Illustrated*, October 16, 1972.

5. "Dick Motta Puts Emphasis on Discipline, Team Play," *Daily Herald* (Provo, UT), March 17, 1971, 7.

6. Chet Walker with Chris Messenger, *Long Time Coming: A Black Athlete's Coming-of-Age in America* (New York: Grove Press, 1995), 220; Bill Bradley, *Life on the Run* (New York: Quadrangle/New York Times, 1976), 53.

7. Frank Deford, "The Loop Has Gone Hoops-a-Daisy," *Sports Illustrated*, February 9, 1970.

8. Louis Sabin, *Basketball Stars of 1971* (New York: Pyramid Books, 1970), 9.

9. Spencer Haywood with Scott Ostler, *Spencer Haywood: The Rise, the Fall, the Recovery* (New York: Amistad, 1992), 17, 92, 94, 95.

10. Curry Kirkpatrick, "The Team That Went over the Hill," *Sports Illustrated*, April 15, 1968.

11. Bill Libby and Spencer Haywood, *Stand up for Something: The Spencer Haywood Story* (New York: Grosset and Dunlap, 1975), 58.

12. Pluto, *Loose Balls*, 207.

13. Haywood and Ostler, *Spencer Haywood*, 227; Libby and Haywood, *Stand Up*, 9.

14. Fred Ferretti, "TV: Are Racism and Bigotry Funny? CBS 'Family' Series May Shock Some," *New York Times*, January 12, 1971, 70.

15. Libby and Haywood, *Stand Up*, 8; Haywood and Ostler, *Spencer Haywood*, 125.

16. Associated Press, "Bulls Seek $600,000 Damages from Sonics in Protest of Haywood," *New York Times*, January 3, 1971.

17. "Haywood Case Is Intensified As Trail Blazers Protest Loss to Seattle," *New York Times*, January 4, 1971; Associated Press, "Royals List Haywood As 'No. 24—Ineligible,'" *New York Times*, January 10, 1971.

18. Peter Carry, "Geoff Who? And Mod Todd," *Sports Illustrated*, November 2, 1970.

19. Joe Menzer and Burt Graeff, *Cavs from Fitch to Fratello* (Champaign, IL: Sagamore Publishing, 1994), 6, 11, 14; Peter Carry, "A War Is over, and the Shooting Starts," *Sports Illustrated*, October 25, 1971.

20. Phil Berger, *Forever Showtime: The Checkered Life of Pistol Pete Maravich* (Dallas: Taylor Publishing, 1999), 142, 152; Phil Hirsch, ed. *Basketball Sports Stars of 1972* (Hewfred Publications, 1972), 13.

21. Mark Kriegel, *Pistol: The Life of Pete Maravich* (New York: Free Press, 2007), 197.

22. Mike Janofsky, "Jack Marin's Guide to the NBA Cities," *Complete Sports* 7, no. 4 (winter 1971): 58, 60; Mike Klingaman, "Catching up with . . . Jack Marin," *Baltimore Sun*, May 12, 2009, http://weblogs.baltimoresun.com/sports/thetoydepartment/2009/05/catching_up_with_jack_marin.html (accessed January 14, 2016).

23. Janofsky, "Jack Marin's Guide to the NBA Cities," 62.

24. Bob Ryan, *Celtics Pride: The Rebuilding of Boston's World Championship Basketball Team* (Boston: Little, Brown, 1975), 41; Phil Elderkin, "Bill Rode Bench," *Sporting News*, October 10, 1970, 54; Willis Reed, *A Will to Win: The Comeback Year* (Englewood Cliffs, NJ: Prentice-Hall, 1973), 121; Bob Gutkowski, "Dave Cowens: Man in Perpetual Motion," *Pro Basketball Illustrated*, 72–73 (New York: Complete Sports Publications, 1972), 71.

25. Peter Carry, "We Can Punch, We Can Dance," *Sports Illustrated*, April 12, 1971.

26. Harvey Araton, *When the Garden Was Eden: Clyde, the Captain, Dollar Bill, and the Glory Days of the New York Knicks* (New York: HarperCollins, 2001), 202; Leonard Koppett, "Bullets Eliminate Knicks 93–91," *New York Times*, April 20, 1971, 55.

27. Robertson, *The Big O*, 266; Terry Bledsoe, "Knicks Will Be Missed in Final Playoff," *Milwaukee Journal*, April 21, 1971, 2; Kareem Abdul-Jabbar and Peter Knobler, *Giant Steps* (New York: Bantam Books, 1983), 222; Bob Wolf, "Bullets Destined to Win? They Think So," *Milwaukee Journal*, April 21, 1971, 2.

28. Robertson, *The Big O*, 272.

29. Harry Klaff, *Countrywide Sports Basketball Sports Special*, December 1971, 9; Peter Carry, "The Best Team—Ever," *Sports Illustrated*, November 15, 1971.

3. 1971 TO 1972

1. In 1960–1961, Wilt Chamberlain averaged more than twenty-seven rebounds per game to lead the league and the following season scored better than fifty points per game to outpace Baylor and the rest of the NBA. Wilt Chamberlain, *Wilt: Just Like Any Other 7-Foot Black Millionaire Who Lives Next Door* (New York: Macmillan, 1973), 211.

2. "Pacific," *Sports Illustrated*, October 25, 1971.

3. Jerry Crowe, "That Iconic NBA Silhouette Can Be Traced Back to Him," *Los Angeles Times*, April 27, 2010.

4. Roland Lazenby, *Jerry West: The Life and Legend of a Basketball Icon* (New York: Ballantine Books, 2009), 282; Alan Goldfarb, ed., *Complete Sports* 7, no. 4 (winter 1971).

5. Martin Lader and Joe Carnicelli, eds., *Pro Basketball Guide 1970* (New York: Cord Communications, 1969), 72; Richard Levin, "Opinion: Wilt Chamberlain Should Stay Retired," *Basketball Digest*, April 1979, 6.

6. Chamberlain, *Wilt*, 222.

7. Phil Elderkin, "Plenty of Shooters," *Sporting News*, December 18, 1971, 37.

8. Peter Carry, "Getting up and Going after a Title," *Sports Illustrated*, December 13, 1971; Charley Rosen, *The Pivotal Season: How the 1971–72 Los Angeles Lakers Changed the NBA* (New York: St. Martin's Press, 2005), 99; Ron Thomas, *They Cleared the Lane: The NBA's Black Pioneers* (Lincoln: University of Nebraska Press, 2002), 191.

9. Lew Alcindor and Jack Olsen, "A Year of Turmoil and Decision," *Sports Illustrated*, November 10, 1969; Kareem Abdul-Jabbar and Peter Knobler, *Giant Steps* (New York: Bantam Books, 1983), 234–35; Chamberlain, *Wilt*, 232.

10. Neal Walk, as quoted in Rosen, *The Pivotal Season*, 88; Dick Motta with Jerry Jenkins, *Stuff It: The Story of Dick Motta, Toughest Little Coach in the NBA* (Radnor, PA: Chilton, 1975), 153; Phil Elderkin, "A Sleeper for Bullets?" *Sporting News*, June 24, 1972, 55.

11. Hal Bock and Ben Olan, *Basketball Stars of 1974* (New York: Pyramid Books, 1973), 29.

12. Bob Wischnia, "Charlie Scott: Color Him Controversial," *Basketball Digest*, February 1975, 37.

13. Oscar Robertson, *The Big O: My Life, My Times, My Game* (Emmaus, PA: Rodale Press, 2003), 174.

14. Bill Bradley, *Life on the Run* (New York: Quadrangle/New York Times, 1976), 27; Harvey Araton, *When the Garden Was Eden: Clyde, the Captain, Dollar Bill, and the Glory Days of the New York Knicks* (New York: HarperCollins, 2011), 240.

15. Lader and Martin, *Pro Basketball Guide 1972—Cord Sportfacts* (Waco, TX: Cord Communications, 1972), 86; Jerry Kirshenbaum, "Eeginnprst Ejrry Aclsu," *Sports Illustrated*, October 8, 1973.

16. Walt Frazier with Neil Offen, *Walt Frazier: One Magical Season and a Basketball Life* (New York: Times Books, 1988), 190–91; Araton, *When the Garden Was Eden*, 214.

17. Ben Osborne, ed., *Slamkicks: Basketball Sneakers That Changed the Game* (New York: Universal Publishing, 2013), 43.

18. Bobbito Garcia, *Where'd You Get Those? New York City's Sneaker Culture, 1960–1987* (New York: Testify Books, 2013), 18.

19. Walt Hazzard, Naismith Basketball Hall of Fame Archives, "NBA Press Releases," box 4 of 5; Gregory M. Lamb, "Buffalo's Randy Smith: Most Versatile Pro Athlete?" *Basketball Digest*, March 1976, 38.

20. Al Silverman, ed., *Pro Basketball Almanac 1972* (New York: Macfadden-Bartell, 1972), 15.

21. Associated Press, "Hawk Cager May Sit Out," *Spokane* (WA) *Daily Chronicle*, November 30, 1971.

22. Thomas Rogers, "Bucks Dethroned," *New York Times*, April 23, 1972.

23. Leonard Koppett, "Lakers Still Can't Believe What Knicks Did to Them: What Happened?" *New York Times*, April 28, 1972.

24. Roland Lazenby, *The NBA Finals: A Fifty Year Celebration* (Lincolnwood, IL: Master's Press, 1996), 161.

25. Rosen, *The Pivotal Season*, 278.

4. 1972 TO 1973

1. Terry Pluto, *Loose Balls: The Short, Wild Life of the American Basketball Association* (New York: Simon & Schuster, 1990), 482.

2. Charley Rosen, *Perfectly Awful: The Philadelphia 76ers' Horrendous and Hilarious 1972–1973 Season* (Lincoln: University of Nebraska Press, 2014), 23, 43.

3. Rosen, *Perfectly Awful*, 31.

4. Kerry D. Marshall, *Two of a Kind: The Tom and Dick Van Arsdale Story* (Indianapolis: Scott Publications, 1992), 125. Tanking, or putting out less-than-one's-best effort with the goal of improving one's draft order, is not a new concept. As early as 1971, national publications like *Sporting News* called out franchises trying out that practice. See, for example, Bob Wolf, "Antiquated Toss," *Sporting News*, January 30, 1971, 17.

5. "Three Clubs vs. One Kneecap," *Sports Illustrated*, October 16, 1972.

6. David Wolf, *Foul! The Connie Hawkins Story* (New York: Holt, Rinehart, and Winston, 1972), 290.

7. Willis Reed, *A Will to Win: The Comeback Year* (Englewood Cliffs, NJ: Prentice-Hall, 1973), 68.

8. Paul Attner, "Mike Riordan: Last of the Blue Collar Pros," *Basketball Digest*, April 1978, 82; Peter Gammons, "Mike Riordan: No Glamor, Just Class," *Basketball Digest*, April 1975, 70; Pete Axthelm, *The City Game: Basketball in New York from the World Champion Knicks to the World of the Playgrounds* (New York: Harper & Row, 1970), 102; Walt Frazier with Neil

Offen, *Walt Frazier: One Magical Season and a Basketball Life* (New York: Times Books, 1988), 159.

9. Jim O'Brien, "Is the Pressure Too Much for Elvin Hayes?" *Basketball Digest*, January 1975, 34; Peter Carry, "The Bullets Are High Caliber," *Sports Illustrated*, January 29, 1973.

10. Wayne Federman and Marshall Terrill with Jackie Maravich, *Maravich: The Authorized Biography of Pistol Pete* (Carol Stream, IL: Tyndale House, 2006), 216–17; Julius Erving with Karl Taro Greenfeld, *Dr. J: The Autobiography* (New York: HarperCollins, 2013), 225; Pluto, *Loose Balls*, 265.

11. "Royals to Leave Cincinnati," (Wilmington) *Star-News*, March 14, 1972.

12. Rosen, *Perfectly Awful*, 69; Hal Bock and Ben Olan, *Basketball Stars of 1974* (New York: Pyramid Books, 1973), 93.

13. *Basketball Weekly*, January 4, 1973.

14. Peter Carry, "It Hurts When They Aren't the Best," *Sports Illustrated*, March 5, 1973.

15. "Could Have Been, Now May Be," *Sports Illustrated*, November 27, 1972.

16. Jack McCallum, "Ahead of the Game," *Sports Illustrated*, April 15, 2002.

17. Murray Janoff, "War Heating Up as NBA Clubs Draft Three off ABA Rosters," *Sporting News*, April 29, 1972, 40; David Halberstam, *The Breaks of the Game* (New York: Alfred A. Knopf, 1981), 98.

18. Peter Carry, "You Might Say He Arrived in the Rick of Time," *Sports Illustrated*, November 19, 1973; Cameron Stauth, *The Franchise: Building a Winner with the World Champion Detroit Pistons, Basketball's Bad Boys* (New York: William Morrow, 1990), 42.

19. Bob Ryan, *Celtics Pride: The Rebuilding of Boston's World Championship Basketball Team* (Boston: Little, Brown, 1975), 194.

20. Harvey Araton, *When the Garden Was Eden: Clyde, the Captain, Dollar Bill, and the Glory Days of the New York Knicks* (New York: HarperCollins, 2011), 282.

21. Roland Lazenby, *The NBA Finals: A Fifty Year Celebration* (Lincolnwood, IL: Master's Press, 1996), 163.

22. Frazier and Offen, *Walt Frazier*, 248; Lazenby, *The NBA Finals*, 162; Araton, *When the Garden Was Eden*, 287.

5. 1973 TO 1974

1. Bob Logan, "NBA Owner's Report," *Basketball Weekly*, March 8, 1973.

2. Don Fair, "What Next for Spencer Haywood?" *Basketball Digest*, January 1974, 18, 22; Spencer Haywood with Scott Ostler, *Spencer Haywood: The Rise, the Fall, the Recovery* (New York: Amistad, 1992), 158.

3. Armand Schneider, "From Courtside," *Basketball Digest*, February 1974, 6; Peter Carry, "High but No Longer Mighty," *Sports Illustrated*, October 29, 1973.

4. "Milwaukee Has New Gusto and Detroit Is in Gear," *Sports Illustrated*, October 15, 1973.

5. "Who's Fat? Not Me Says Bucks' Big O," *Basketball Weekly*, December 19, 1973, 12; Jerry Conway, "Most Over-Rated Players in the NBA," *Basketball Digest*, January 1974, 29; Mal Florence, "The Big Men," *Basketball Digest*, November 1973, 48.

6. Zander Hollander, ed., *The Complete Handbook of Pro Basketball 1975* (New York: Signet, 1974), 17.

7. David W. Cowens, "John Havlicek: A Player's Player," *Basketball Digest*, November 1978, 72; Jim O'Brien, "Even a Hobbling Hondo Is Better Than None at All," *Basketball Digest*, June 1977, 88.

8. Curry Kirkpatrick, "It's the End of a Long, Long Run," *Sports Illustrated*, October 28, 1974; Bob Rubin, "Is Havlicek the World's Best Athlete?" *Pro Basketball Almanac 1970*, ed. Al Silverman (New York: Macfadden-Bartell, 1970), 11.

9. Jim Baker, "Buffalo's Bob McAdoo: The NBA's Top Scoring Machine," *Basketball Digest*, November 1975, 38, 42; Michael K. Herbert, "Additional Notes," *Basketball Digest*, April 1975, 12; Shawn Fury, *Rise and Fire: The Origins, Science, and Evolution of the Jump Shot—And How It Transformed Basketball Forever* (New York: Flatiron Books, 2016), 206.

10. Bert Rosenthal, "Ernie DiGregorio: Will the College Flash Be a Flash in the Pan Pro?" *Pro Basketball Sports Stars of 1974*, 7, no. 2 (winter 1972): 30.

11. Milt Northrop, "Buffalo Braves: The NBA's Team of the Future," *Basketball Digest*, April 1974, 48; Nick Curan, ed., *National Basketball Association Official Guide for 1974–75* (St. Louis: Sporting News, 1974), 41.

12. Peter Carry, "They're Centers of Attention," *Sports Illustrated*, May 13, 1974; Harvey Araton, *When the Garden Was Eden: Clyde, the Captain, Dollar Bill, and the Glory Days of the New York Knicks* (New York: HarperCollins, 2011), 78.

13. Bob Ryan, *Celtics Pride: The Rebuilding of Boston's World Championship Basketball Team* (Boston: Little, Brown, 1975), 234; Wayne Embry, *The Inside Game: Race, Power, and Politics in the NBA* (Akron, OH: University of Akron Press, 2004), 227.

14. John Havlicek and Bob Ryan, *Hondo: Celtic Man in Motion* (New York: Prentice Hall, 1977), 152; Hollander, *The Complete Handbook of Pro Basketball 1975*, 18.

15. Joe Fitzgerald, *That Championship Feeling: The Story of the Boston Celtics* (New York: Charles Scribner's Sons, 1975), 252; Carry, "They're Centers of Attention."

6. 1974 TO 1975

1. Bert Rosenthal, "The Imminent Decline and Fall of the New York Knicks," *Basketball News 1974–75 Pro Yearbook*, ed. Bob Rubin (New York: National Sports Publishing, 1974), 37.

2. Bob Logan, "Bucks Will Win," *Basketball Digest*, November 1974, 20; Larry Felser, "McAdoo Can Do It All, but Who's Watching?" *Sporting News*, January 11, 1975, 3.

3. Peter Finney, "The Showboat Moves to New Orleans," *Popular Sports All-Pro Basketball 1975*, ed. Zander Hollander (New York: Popular Library, 1975), 13; Pat Williams and Jerry B. Jenkins, *The Gingerbread Man: Pat Williams—Then and Now* (Philadelphia: A. J. Holman, 1974), 114; Bob Wolf, "Hawk Heist Had the Earmarks of Grand Larceny," *Sporting News*, June 8, 1974, 47.

4. Cord Communications Corporation, *Pro Basketball '75–'76* (New York: Pocket Books, 1975), 50.

5. UPI, "Maravich Accepts Trade to New Orleans Quintet," *New York Times*, May 4, 1974, 29.

6. John Kuenster, "From Courtside," *Basketball Digest*, December 1974, 6.

7. Kuenster, "From Courtside," 80; Kareem Abdul-Jabbar and Peter Knobler, *Giant Steps* (New York: Bantam Books, 1983), 269–70.

8. Terry Pluto, *Loose Balls: The Short, Wild Life of the American Basketball Association* (New York: Simon & Schuster, 1990), 223; Jim O'Brien, "ABA Draft Reveals Pickers' Lack of Homework," *Sporting News*, May 4, 1974, 45.

9. Neil Andersen, "What Bill Walton Means to the Trail Blazers," *Basketball Digest*, February 1975, 22, 24.

10. Gil Lyons, "Despite Setbacks, Spencer Haywood Is Reaching His Goals," *Basketball Digest*, February 1975, 55.

11. Pat Putnam and Jane Gross, "Centers of Interest," *Sports Illustrated*, October 28, 1974.

12. Steve Hershey and Darrell Simmons, "Inside the NBA," in *The Complete Handbook of Pro Basketball: 1980 Season*, ed. Zander Hollander (New York: Signet, 1979), 92.

13. Jamaal Wilkes, *Jamaal Wilkes: Memoirs of the Original Smooth As Silk* (Los Angeles: 88 Str8 Enterprises, 2015), 179.

14. Peter Carry, "Yes, Rick, There Is a Virginia," *Sports Illustrated*, August 24, 1970.

15. Bob Gutkowski, "Who's the Best Forward in the Game?" *Pro Basketball Illustrated 1974–75*, ed. Jim McNally (New York: Complete Sports Publications, 1974), 8.

16. Larry Bortstein, "How to Shoot Free Throws by Rick Barry," *Basketball Digest*, December 1977, 16.

17. Paul Attner, "How Rick Barry Changed Pro Basketball," *Basketball Digest*, April 1978, 26; Bill Simmons, *The Book of Basketball* (New York: Random House, 2009), 497, 265; Peter Vecsey, "Rick Barry: The Basketball Gypsy," *Pro Basketball Illustrated 1971–72*, ed. Alan Goldfarb (New York: Complete Sports Publications, 1970), 21.

18. "Jerry Sloan: My Most Memorabull Game," www.nba.com/bulls/history/sloan/750511.html (accessed April 27, 2015).

19. Roland Lazenby, *And Now, Your Chicago Bulls! A Thirty-Year Celebration* (Dallas: Taylor, 1995), 100.

20. Roland Lazenby, *The NBA Finals: A Fifty Year Celebration* (Lincolnwood, IL: Master's Press, 1996), 175.

21. Lazenby, *The NBA Finals*, 176.

22. Lazenby, *The NBA Finals*, 176, 177.

23. *Pro Basketball '75–76*, 129, 142; Neil Tarpley, "'Was Like a Family': Rick Barry Led Golden State to 1975 NBA Title," *Eureka* (CA) *Times Standard*, April 7, 2013; Bert Rosenthal, "Al Attles Recalls: The Game I'll Never Forget," *Basketball Digest*, June 1978, 45.

24. Art Spander, "Why the Golden State Warriors Are Even Stronger This Year," *Basketball Digest*, March 1976, 24.

THE DOCTOR

1. Terry Pluto, *Loose Balls: The Short, Wild Life of the American Basketball Association* (New York: Simon & Schuster, 1990), 226.

2. Marty Bell, *The Legend of Dr. J* (New York: Coward, McCann and Geoghegan, 1975), 15, 58; Julius Erving with Karl Taro Greenfeld, *Dr. J: The Autobiography* (New York: HarperCollins, 2013), 82.

3. Vincent M. Mallozzi, *Asphalt Gods: An Oral History of the Rucker Tournament* (New York: Doubleday, 2003), 112.

4. Peter Carry, "The Net-Ripping, Backboard-Shaking, Mind-Blowing Dr. J," *Sports Illustrated*, December 11, 1972.

5. Jim O'Brien, "Julius Erving: The Nets' One-Man Franchise," *Basketball Digest*, December 1973, 18; Bell, *The Legend of Dr. J*, 24.

6. Chamberlain intended to serve as a player-coach for the Conquistadors (nicknamed the Q's). But Los Angeles Lakers owner Jack Kent Cooke managed a legal injunction against such an action, forcing Chamberlain to make his last official appearance on a professional basketball sideline as a mildly interested coach for a mediocre ABA squad.

7. Pluto, *Loose Balls*, 26.

8. Pluto, *Loose Balls*, 27.

7. 1975 TO 1976

1. Pat Putnam, "Score a Basket for Brotherly Love," *Sports Illustrated*, June 23, 1975.

2. Thomas Bonk, "June 16, 1975: A Banner Day for Lakers: Kareem Takes His Post," *Los Angeles Times*, December 25, 1987, 1.

3. Cord Communications Corporation, *Pro Basketball '75–'76* (New York: Pocket Books, 1975), 24.

4. Pat Putnam, "The Fortune Cookie Smiled," *Sports Illustrated*, November 3, 1975.

5. Spencer Haywood with Scott Ostler, *Spencer Haywood: The Rise, the Fall, the Recovery* (New York: Amistad, 1992), 166.

6. Putnam, "The Fortune Cookie"; Bill Libby and Spencer Haywood, *Stand up for Something: The Spencer Haywood Story* (New York: Grosset and Dunlap, 1975), 282.

7. *Pro Basketball '75–'76*, 171; *Fields of Fire: Sport in the 60's* (Home Box Office, 1995).

8. Phil Elderkin, "Basketball's Biggest Trade: Kareem Is a Laker," *Basketball Digest*, November 1975, 12.

9. Bethlehem Shoals and Jacob Weinstein, *Freedarko Presents: The Undisputed Guide to Pro Basketball History* (New York: Bloomsbury, 2010), 98.

10. Frank Deford, "Everybody Gets into the Act," *Sports Illustrated*, February 16, 1976.

11. Robert W. Creamer, ed. "They Said It," *Sports Illustrated*, May 24, 1976.

12. Bob Wolf, "Bulls' Coach Fires Salvos at Love and Van Lier," *Sporting News*, October 25, 1975, 30; Curry Kirkpatrick, "Choice Seats at the Bull Ring," *Sports Illustrated*, February 2, 1976.

13. Joe Menzer and Burt Graeff, *Cavs from Fitch to Fratello* (Champaign, IL: Sagamore Publishing, 1994), 45.

14. George White, "Tomjanovich . . . A Rocket Always on Target," *Sporting News*, January 29, 1977, 3.

15. Phil Berger, *Forever Showtime: The Checkered Life of Pistol Pete Maravich* (Dallas: Taylor, 1999), 198.

16. David Thompson with Sean Stormes and Marshall Terrill, *David Thompson: Skywalker* (Sports Publishing, 2003), 145; Bruce Weber, *All-Pro Basketball Stars 1976* (New York: Scholastic Book Services, 1976), 81.

17. Hal Bock and Ben Olan, *Basketball Stars of 1974* (New York: Pyramid Books, 1973); Julius Erving with Karl Taro Greenfeld, *Dr. J: The Autobiography* (New York: HarperCollins, 2013), 302; Jeff Meyers, "Basketball's Big Jump: George McGinnis Is a 76er," *Basketball Digest*, November 1975, 62; Bob Ryan, "76ers: Traveling Circus," *Basketball Weekly*, January 6, 1977; Terry Pluto, *Loose Balls: The Short, Wild Life of the American Basketball Association* (New York: Simon & Schuster, 1990), 198.

18. Pat Putnam and Curry Kirkpatrick, "Atlantic: Can a Scott Be a Celt?" *Sports Illustrated*, October 27, 1975; Michael P. Connelly, *Rebound! Basketball, Busing, Larry Bird, and the Rebirth of Boston* (New York: Voyageur Press, 2010), 138.

19. David Halberstam, *The Breaks of the Game* (New York: Alfred A. Knopf, 1981), 322.

20. Curry Kirkpatrick, "At Long Last It's Crunchtime," *Sports Illustrated*, April 19, 1976; Jonathan Knight, *Classic Cavs: The 50 Greatest Games in Cleveland Cavaliers History* (Kent, OH: Kent State University Press, 2009), 197.

21. Knight, *Classic Cavs*, 197.

22. Knight, *Classic Cavs*, 199; Menzer and Graeff, *Cavs*, 47.

23. Kerry D. Marshall, *Two of a Kind: The Tom and Dick Van Arsdale Story* (Indianapolis: Scott Publications, 1992), 142; Bill Simmons, *The Book of Basketball* (New York: Random House, 2009), 21; Curry Kirkpatrick, "Have the Suns Risen in the West? Yes," *Sports Illustrated*, May 24, 1976; Joe Gilmartin, "Why Phoenix Was No Fluke," *Basketball Digest*, November 1976, 43.

24. Connelly, *Rebound!* 131.

25. Ken Denlinger, "But Game Five Was Basketball's Highpoint," *Basketball Digest*, November 1976, 40.

26. Roland Lazenby, *The NBA Finals: A Fifty Year Celebration* (Lincolnwood, IL: Master's Press, 1996), 180.

27. Barry McDermott, "Call Them Champs Again," *Sports Illustrated*, June 14, 1976.

THE MERGER

1. Terry Pluto, *Loose Balls: The Short, Wild Life of the American Basketball Association* (New York: Simon & Schuster, 1990), 17.
2. Pluto, *Loose Balls*, 5.
3. Pluto, *Loose Balls*, 48–49.
4. Pluto, *Loose Balls*, 72.
5. Martin Lader and Joe Carnicelli, eds., *Pro Basketball Guide 1970* (New York: Cord Communications, 1969), 90; Pluto, *Loose Balls*, 379.
6. Oscar Robertson, "Our Livelihood . . . Our Future," *Pro Basketball Guide 1973*, ed. Martin Lader and Joe Carnicelli (Cord Sportfacts, 1972), 35.
7. Vito Stellino, ed., *Sports All Stars 1972 Pro Basketball* (New York: Maco Publishing, 1971), 28.
8. Pluto, *Loose Balls*, 482.
9. Sam Goldaper, "NBA Gets Merger 'Spur,'" *New York Times*, May 25, 1976, 54; David Thompson with Sean Stormes and Marshall Terrill, *David Thompson: Skywalker* (Sports Publishing, 2003), 172.
10. Oscar Robertson, *The Big O: My Life, My Times, My Game* (Emmaus, PA: Rodale Press, 2003), 314.
11. Bob Logan, "How the ABA and NBA Merged," *Basketball Digest*, November 1976, 49, 53.
12. Walt Frazier with Neil Offen, *Walt Frazier: One Magical Season and a Basketball Life* (New York: Times Books, 1988), 95.
13. Quoted in Yago Colás, *Ball Don't Lie: Myth, Genealogy, and Invention in the Cultures of Basketball* (Philadelphia: Temple University Press, 2016), 85.

8. 1976 TO 1977

1. Stefan Bondy, "In 1977 NBA All-Star Game, Paul Westphal Was Really the Best," *New York Daily News*, February 12, 2015.
2. Curry Kirkpatrick, "The Dr. Doubled His Fee," *Sports Illustrated*, November 1, 1976.
3. David Halberstam, *The Breaks of the Game* (New York: Alfred A. Knopf, 1981), 305.

4. Charles Rosen, *God, Man, and Basketball Jones: The Thinking Fan's Guide to Professional Basketball* (New York: Holt, Rinehart and Winston, 1979), 86; Bob Ryan, "76ers Traveling Circus," *Basketball Weekly*, January 6, 1977; Julius Erving with Karl Taro Greenfeld, *Dr. J: The Autobiography* (New York: HarperCollins, 2013), 318.

5. Bill Livingston, "The Fans Love Dr. J., but . . . George McGinnis Is the Power of the 76ers," *Basketball Digest*, February 1977, 26.

6. Michael Herbert, "From Courtside," *Basketball Digest*, March 1977, 11.

7. Michael P. Connelly, *Rebound! Basketball, Busing, Larry Bird, and the Rebirth of Boston* (New York: Voyageur Press, 2010), 158; Lynn Hoppes, "Dave Cowens Talks about His Days As Cab Driver," ESPN Page Two, http://espn.go.com/espn/page2/index?id=5285963 (accessed June 12, 2015); John Papanek, "The Fire Was Gone and So He Quit," *Sports Illustrated*, November 22, 1976.

8. Rosen, *God, Man, and Basketball Jones*, 133.

9. Halberstam, *Breaks of the Game*, 215.

10. Halberstam, *Breaks of the Game*, 218; William Leggett, "Basketfuls of Information," *Sports Illustrated*, February 9, 1976.

11. Milt Northrop, "What's Happening in Buffalo?" *Basketball Digest*, February 1978, 34.

12. Ron Brocato, "Gail Goodrich Wants to Finish What He Started Last Year," *Basketball Digest*, January 1978, 71.

13. "Maravich: 68 in Rout of the Knicks," *New York Times*, February 26, 1977, 34; Mark Kriegel, *Pistol: The Life of Pete Maravich* (New York: Free Press, 2007), 257.

14. Dan Issel with Buddy Martin, *Parting Shots* (Chicago: Contemporary Books, 1985), 41.

15. Woodrow Paige Jr., "Denver: Hotbed of Pro Basketball," *Basketball Digest*, February 1977, 34.

16. Curry Kirkpatrick, Pat Putnam, and John Papanek, "Midwest Division," *Sports Illustrated*, October 25, 1976; Bill Benner, "The Kind of Player Every Team Would Like to Have," *Basketball Digest*, April 1977, 82.

17. Tony Kornheiser, "'I'm the Bad Guy,' Barnes Says, and Many Agree," *New York Times*, November 28, 1976, 197.

18. Richard Levin, "Kareem Abdul-Jabbar vs. Artis Gilmore: Pro Basketball's Biggest Matchup," *Basketball Digest*, May 1977, 23; John Papanek, "Strutting Their Stuffs," *Sports Illustrated*, February 9, 1976.

19. Kerry D. Marshall, *Two of a Kind: The Tom and Dick Van Arsdale Story* (Indianapolis: Scott Publications, 1992), 77, 112.

20. Aram Goudsouzian, *King of the Court: Bill Russell and the Basketball Revolution* (Berkeley: University of California Press, 2010), 265; Bill Russell

and Taylor Branch, *Second Wind: The Memoirs of an Opinionated Man* (New York: Random House, 1979), 257; Joe Gilmartin, "Sonic Slick Wants Super Money," *Sporting News*, March 12, 1977, 6.

21. Rick Telander, "Bill Walton Won't You Please Play Ball?" *Sports Illustrated*, January 27, 1975.

22. Larry Bird with Jackie MacMullan, *Bird Watching: On Playing and Coaching the Game I Love* (New York: Warner Books, 1999), 291; Curry Kirkpatrick, "A Fever Called Blazermania," *Sports Illustrated*, October 31, 1977; Bill Walton with Gene Wojciechowski, *Nothing but Net: Just Give Me the Ball and Get out of the Way* (New York: Hyperion, 1994), 74; Matt Love, ed., *Red Hot and Rollin': A Retrospection of the Portland Trail Blazers' 1976–77 Championship Season* (Pacific City, OR: Nestucca Spit Press, 2007), 19.

23. Rel Bochat, "Maurice Lucas: Mr. Muscle of the Portland Trail Blazers," *Basketball Digest*, November 1977, 41; Bob Robinson, "Maurice Lucas: Basketball's Most Powerful Forward," *Basketball Digest*, November 1977, 41; David Thompson with Sean Stormes and Marshall Terrill, *David Thompson: Skywalker* (Sports Publishing, 2003), 60; Terry Pluto, *Loose Balls: The Short, Wild Life of the American Basketball Association* (New York: Simon & Schuster, 1990), 434.

24. Earl Strom with Blaine Johnson, *Calling the Shots: My Five Decades in the NBA* (New York: Simon & Schuster, 1990), 181.

25. Love, *Red Hot and Rollin'*, 111.

26. Larry Colton, *Idol Time: Profile in Blazermania* (Forest Grove, OR: Timber Press, 1978), 10, 11.

27. Curry Kirkpatrick, "There's No Place Like Home Court," *Sports Illustrated*, June 6, 1977; Halberstam, *Breaks of the Game*, 27; Curry Kirkpatrick, "Good, But Why Not the Best?" *Sports Illustrated*, March 21, 1977; Bob Wolf, "Nuggets' Midwest Rivals Look to Be Overmatched," *Sporting News*, October 14, 1978, 10.

28. Bill Simmons, *The Book of Basketball* (New York: Random House, 2009), 120.

29. Colton, *Idol Time*, 41; Love, *Red Hot and Rollin'*, 113.

9. 1977 TO 1978

1. John Feinstein, *The Punch: One Night, Two Lives, and the Fight That Changed Basketball Forever* (New York: Hachette, 2002), 19.

2. Feinstein, *The Punch*, 18; Kareem Abdul-Jabbar and Peter Knobler, *Giant Steps* (New York: Bantam Books, 1983), 287; Bill Simmons, *The Book of Basketball* (New York: Random House, 2009), 142.

3. John Papanek, "Nobody, but Nobody, Is Going to Hurt My Team-mates," *Sports Illustrated*, October 31, 1977.

4. Papanek, "Nobody."

5. Papanek, "Nobody."

6. Abdul-Jabbar, *Giant Steps*, 286; "Fracture, Fine for Jabbar," *Sporting News*, November 5, 1977, 50.

7. Curry Kirkpatrick, "Shattered and Shaken," *Sports Illustrated*, January 2, 1978.

8. Feinstein, *The Punch*, 87.

9. Feinstein, *The Punch*, 30, 11.

10. John Papanek, "Add Super to the Sonics," *Sports Illustrated*, January 9, 1978.

11. Feinstein, *The Punch*, 184.

12. Zander Hollander, *The Complete Handbook of Pro Basketball: 1980 Season* (New York: Signet, 1979), 237; Curry Kirkpatrick, "It's Whoooosh! Boom! Whoop! Time," *Sports Illustrated*, February 20, 1978.

13. Nick Curan, ed., *National Basketball Association Official Guide for 1977–78* (St. Louis: Sporting News, 1977), 98; "Unstoppable: Bernard King," NBATV, aired September 4, 2013.

14. Filip Bondy, *Tip-Off: How the 1984 Draft Changed Basketball Forever* (Cambridge, MA: Da Capo Press, 2007), 161.

15. David Thompson with Sean Stormes and Marshall Terrill, *David Thompson: Skywalker* (Sports Publishing, 2003), 186.

16. Thompson, *David Thompson*, 269, vii; Mike Madigan, "Thompson So Brilliant Nuggets Grow Uneasy," *Sporting News*, March 18, 1978, 3.

17. Oscar Robertson, *The Big O: My Life, My Times, My Game* (Emmaus, PA: Rodale Press, 2003), 224; David Halberstam, *The Breaks of the Game* (New York: Alfred A. Knopf, 1981), 13, 144.

18. Walt Frazier with Neil Offen, *Walt Frazier: One Magical Season and a Basketball Life* (New York: Times Books, 1988), 50.

19. Mike Lupica, "Earl Monroe: The Magic Show Is Back," *Basketball Digest*, March 1977, 18; Sam Goldaper, "Knicks Top Pacers: Haywood Scores 37," *New York Times*, February 10, 1978, B5.

20. Dan Shaughnessy, *Ever Green: The Boston Celtics, A History in the Words of Their Players, Coaches, Fans, and Foes, from 1946 to the Present* (New York: St. Martin's Press, 1990), 163; Bob Ryan, "Rebuilding the Celtics," *Basketball Digest*, April 1978, 18.

21. Larry Bird and Earvin "Magic" Johnson with Jackie MacMullan, *When the Game Was Ours* (New York: Houghton Mifflin, 2009), 106; Harvey Araton and Filip Bond, *The Selling of the Green: The Financial Rise and Moral Decline of the Boston Celtics* (New York: HarperCollins, 1992), xi, 38; Jeff Pearlman, *Showtime: Magic, Kareem, Riley, and the Los Angeles Lakers Dynasty of the 1980s* (New York: Gotham Books, 2014), 232.

22. John Powers, *The Short Season: A Boston Celtics Diary 1977–1978* (New York: Harper & Row, 1979), 208.

23. Curry Kirkpatrick, "It's the End of a Long, Long Run," *Sports Illustrated*, April 10, 1978.

24. Thompson, *David Thompson*, 189.

25. Terry Pluto, *Loose Balls: The Short, Wild Life of the American Basketball Association* (New York: Simon & Schuster, 1990), 356, 357; Julius Erving with Karl Taro Greenfeld, *Dr. J: The Autobiography* (New York: HarperCollins, 2013), 230; Curry Kirkpatrick, "Iceman Cometh and Scoreth," *Sports Illustrated*, March 6, 1978.

26. Sam Goldaper, "Thompson Gets 73, Gervin Gets Title," *New York Times*, April 10, 1978, C7.

27. Walt Frazier with Dan Markowitz, *The Game within the Game* (New York: Hyperion, 2006), 83; Curry Kirkpatrick, "Why Is This Man Eating Popcorn?" *Sports Illustrated*, April 17, 1978.

28. David DuPree, "Bing Upset at Motta's Clean Bill," *Washington Post*, May 13, 1977, C1.

29. John Papanek, "Another Chapter in the Philadelphia Story," *Sports Illustrated*, May 15, 1978.

30. Tony Kornheiser, "Unseld a Bullet with Impact," *New York Times*, June 5, 1978, C6.

31. Roland Lazenby, *The NBA Finals: A Fifty Year Celebration* (Lincolnwood, IL: Master's Press, 1996), 194.

32. Curry Kirkpatrick, "Whatever Happens It'll Be Washington," *Sports Illustrated*, June 5, 1978.

33. Dave Anderson, "C. J., As in Calmly Jubilant," *New York Times*, June 9, 1978, A20; John Papanek, "They're First, at Long Last," *Sports Illustrated*, June 19, 1978.

34. John Papanek, "They're First, at Long Last."

35. Charles Rosen, *God, Man and Basketball Jones: The Thinking Fan's Guide to Professional Basketball* (New York: Holt, Rinehart and Winston, 1979), 142; Curry Kirkpatrick, "Heavens, What a Year Ahead!" *Sports Illustrated*, October 16, 1978; Simmons, *Book of Basketball*, 421.

10. 1978 TO 1979

1. Tom Keating, "The Rebuilding of the Indiana Pacers," *Basketball Digest*, December 1978, 49.

2. Larry Bird and Earvin "Magic" Johnson with Jackie MacMullan, *When the Game Was Ours* (New York: Houghton Mifflin, 2009), 34.

3. Michael P. Connelly, *Rebound! Basketball, Busing, Larry Bird, and the Rebirth of Boston* (New York: Voyageur Press, 2010), 176–77; Charles Rosen, *God, Man and Basketball Jones: The Thinking Fan's Guide to Professional Basketball* (New York: Holt, Rinehart and Winston, 1979), 135; Harvey Araton and Filip Bond, *The Selling of the Green: The Financial Rise and Moral Decline of the Boston Celtics* (New York: HarperCollins, 1992), 108.

4. Connelly, *Rebound!* 191.

5. Associated Press, "Copy DeBusschere in Haywood's Plan," *Bangor* (ME) *Daily News*, October 24, 1975, 17; Sam Goldaper, "Draft Leaves the Knicks Still Searching," *New York Times*, June 11, 1978, S10.

6. Steve Hershey, "Washington's Bullets: The Best Team of the '70s?" *Basketball Digest*, December 1979, 39.

7. Curry Kirkpatrick, "Hey, What's up with the Doc?" *Sports Illustrated*, March 26, 1979.

8. John Papanek, "He Surely Is the Spur of the Moment," *Sports Illustrated*, February 5, 1979.

9. Randy Harvey, "George Gervin: San Antonio's Sensational Scorer," *Basketball Digest*, December 1978, 21.

10. David Halberstam, *The Breaks of the Game* (New York: Alfred A. Knopf, 1981), 194.

11. *Baltimore Afro-American*, March 15, 1977, 13; "Notes, Quotes & Comments," *Basketball Digest*, June 1979, 19.

12. "Notes, Quotes & Comments," *Basketball Digest*, February 1979, 14.

13. *Basketball Digest*, January 1979, 68.

14. David Thompson with Sean Stormes and Marshall Terrill, *David Thompson: Skywalker* (Champaign, IL: Sports Publishing, 2003), 197, 199.

15. Halberstam, *Breaks*, 243; Bob Ryan, *Scribe: My Life in Sports* (New York: Bloomsbury, 2014), 93.

16. "The Fans Speak Out," *Basketball Digest*, May 1979, 12–13; John Papanek, "There's an Ill Wind Blowing for the NBA," *Sports Illustrated*, February 26, 1979; John Matthew Smith, "'Gifts That God Didn't Give': White Hopes, Basketball, and the Legend of Larry Bird," *Massachusetts Historical Review* 13 (2011): 6.

17. Zander Hollander, ed., *The Complete Handbook of Pro Basketball: 1980 Season* (New York: Signet, 1979), 256; Paul Attner, "The New Breed of NBA Guard," *Basketball Digest*, May 1979, 46.

18. Glenn Dickey, "Lucas Makes Warriors Forget Barry," *Sporting News*.

19. John Papanek, "Born Free and Living up to His Name," *Sports Illustrated*, January 22, 1979; Joe Hamelin, "Lloyd Free: Even His Critics Admit He's All-World," *Basketball Digest*, June 1979, 37.

20. "Notes, Quotes & Comments," *Basketball Digest*, March 1979, 16.

21. Curry Kirkpatrick, "The Sonics Keep Their Garde Up," *Sports Illustrated*, November 13, 1978; Lenny Wilkens with Terry Pluto, *Unguarded: My Forty Years Surviving in the NBA* (New York: Simon and Schuster, 2000), 177.

22. Bird, Johnson, and MacMullan, *When the Game Was Ours*, 29.

23. Roland Lazenby, *The NBA Finals: A Fifty Year Celebration* (Lincolnwood, IL: Master's Press, 1996), 196.

24. "'It's Okay if You're a Machine': Inside Hubie Brown's Brutal Philosophy," *Atlanta Journal & Constitution*, December 9, 1979. Reprinted on deadspin.com.

25. Sam Goldaper, "Bullets Beat Spurs, Reach Finals," *New York Times*, May 19, 1979, 17.

26. Sam Goldaper, "NBA Final Series Has a Familiar Cast," *New York Times*, May 20, 1979, S10; Sam Goldaper, "Bullets Win in Disputed Finish, 99–97," *New York Times*, May 21, 1979, C1.

27. Sam Goldaper, "Sonics Tie Series, Top Bullets, 92–82," *New York Times*, May 25, 1979, A19.

28. "Sonics Put Together the Right Chemistry," *New York Times*, June 3, 1979, S5.

POSTGAME

1. Jeff Pearlman, *Showtime: Magic, Kareem, Riley, and the Los Angeles Lakers Dynasty of the 1980s* (New York: Gotham Books, 2014), 67.

2. Curry Kirkpatrick, "Heavens, What a Year Ahead!" *Sports Illustrated*, October 16, 1978; David J. Leonard, *After Artest: The NBA and the Assault on Blackness* (Albany: State University of New York Press, 2012), 9, 30.

3. Matthew Schneider-Mayerson, "'Too Black': Race in the 'Dark Ages' of the National Basketball Association," *The International Journal of Sport & Society* 1, no. 1 (2010): 227.

4. Spencer Haywood with Scott Ostler, *Spencer Haywood: The Rise, the Fall, the Recovery* (New York: Amistad, 1992), 33, 190, 192–93; David Thomp-

son with Sean Stormes and Marshall Terrill, *David Thompson: Skywalker* (Champaign, IL: Sports Publishing, 2003), 218.

5. Larry Bird and Earvin "Magic" Johnson with Jackie MacMullan, *When the Game Was Ours* (New York: Houghton Mifflin, 2009), 79.

6. Malcolm Moran, "Bird-Magic Meeting Fails to Ignite Match," *New York Times*, December 30, 1979, S13.

7. Michael P. Connelly, *Rebound! Basketball, Busing, Larry Bird, and the Rebirth of Boston* (New York: Voyageur Press, 2010), 245.

8. Thompson, Stormes, and Terrill, *David Thompson*, 204.

9. Lenny Wilkens with Terry Pluto, *Unguarded: My Forty Years Surviving in the NBA* (New York: Simon and Schuster, 2000), 186.

10. John Papanek, "Climbing to the Top Again," *Sports Illustrated*, October 15, 1979.

11. Charlie Vincent, "Big Egos Are Showing—And Pistons Pay the Price," *Sporting News*, December 22, 1979, 29.

12. "Atlantic Division," *Sports Illustrated*, October 15, 1979.

13. Thompson, Stormes, and Terrill, *David Thompson*, 267.

SELECT BIBLIOGRAPHY

BOOKS

Abdul-Aziz, Zaid. *Darkness to Sunlight: The Life-Changing Journey of Zaid Abdul-Aziz ("Don Smith")* (Seattle: Sunlight Publishing, 2006).

Abdul-Jabbar, Kareem, and Peter Knobler. *Giant Steps* (New York: Bantam Books, 1983).

Abrams, Brett L., and Raphael Mazzone. *The Bullets, the Wizards and Washington D.C. Basketball* (Lanham, MD: Scarecrow Press, 2013).

Addy, Steve. *The Detroit Pistons: Four Decades of Motor City Memories* (Saginaw, MI: Sports Publishing, 1997).

Araton, Harvey. *When the Garden Was Eden: Clyde, the Captain, Dollar Bill, and the Glory Days of the New York Knicks* (New York: HarperCollins, 2011).

Araton, Harvey, and Filip Bond. *The Selling of the Green: The Financial Rise and Moral Decline of the Boston Celtics* (New York: HarperCollins, 1992).

Axthelm, Pete. *The City Game: Basketball in New York from the World Champion Knicks to the World of the Playgrounds* (New York: Harper & Row, 1970).

Barry, Rick. *Pro Basketball '75–76.* (New York: Pocket Books, 1975).

Barry, Rick, with Bill Libby. *Confessions of a Basketball Gypsy: The Rick Barry Story* (New York: Dell, 1972).

Batchelor, Bob, ed. *Basketball in America: From the Playgrounds to Jordan's Game and Beyond* (New York: Haworth Press, 2005).

Bell, Marty. *The Legend of Dr. J* (New York: Coward, McCann and Geoghegan, 1975).

Berger, Phil. *Forever Showtime: The Checkered Life of Pistol Pete Maravich* (Dallas: Taylor, 1999).

———. *Miracle on 33rd Street: The New York Knickerbockers' Championship Season* (New York: Simon and Schuster, 1970).

Bird, Larry, with Bob Ryan. *Drive: The Story of My Life* (New York: Bantam Books, 1989).

Bird, Larry, and Earvin "Magic" Johnson, with Jackie MacMullan. *When the Game Was Ours* (New York: Houghton Mifflin, 2009).

Bird, Larry, with Jackie MacMullan. *Bird Watching: On Playing and Coaching the Game I Love* (New York: Warner Books, 1999).

Bock, Hal, and Ben Olan. *Basketball Stars of 1974* (New York: Pyramid Books, 1973).

Bodanza, Mark C. *Make It Count: The Life and Times of Basketball Great JoJo White* (Bloomington, IN: iUniverse, 2012).

Bondy, Filip. *Tip-Off: How the 1984 Draft Changed Basketball Forever* (Cambridge, MA: Da Capo Press, 2007).

Bonner, Mike. *Collecting Basketball Cards: A Complete Guide with Prices* (San Jose: ToExcel, 1999).

Boyd, Todd. *Young, Black, Rich, and Famous* (Lincoln: University of Nebraska Press, 2003).

Boyd, Todd, and Kenneth L. Shropshire, eds. *Basketball Jones: America above the Rim* (New York: New York University Press, 2000).

Bradley, Bill. *Life on the Run* (New York: Quadrangle/New York Times, 1976).

Bradley, Robert D. *Compendium of Professional Basketball* (Tempe: Xaler Press, 1999).

———. *The Basketball Draft Fact Book: A History of Professional Basketball's College Drafts* (Lanham, MD: Scarecrow Press, 2013).

Carroll, Peter N. *It Seemed Like Nothing Happened: America in the 1970s* (New Brunswick, NJ: Rutgers University Press, 2000).

Chamberlain, Wilt. *A View from Above* (New York: Villard Books, 1991).

———. *Wilt: Just Like Any Other 7-Foot Black Millionaire Who Lives Next Door* (New York: Macmillan, 1973).

Cherry, Robert Allen. *Wilt: Larger Than Life* (Chicago: Triumph Books, 2004).

Colás, Yago. *Ball Don't Lie: Myth, Genealogy, and Invention in the Cultures of Basketball* (Philadelphia: Temple University Press, 2016).

Cole, Lewis. *A Loose Game: The Sport and Business of Basketball* (Indianapolis: Bobbs-Merrill, 1978).

Colton, Larry. *Idol Time: Profile in Blazermania* (Forest Grove, OR: Timber Press, 1978).

Compu-Scout System. *Computerized Pro-Rated NBA-ABA Players' Guide* (New York: Stadia Sports Publishing, 1973).

Connelly, Michael P. *Rebound! Basketball, Busing, Larry Bird, and the Rebirth of Boston* (New York: Voyageur Press, 2010).

Dawkins, Darryl, with George Wirt. *Chocolate Thunder: The In-Your-Face, All-over-the-Place, Death-Defyin', Memorizin', Slam-Jam Adventures of Double-D* (Chicago: Contemporary Books, 1986).

DeBusschere, Dave. *The Open Man: A Championship Diary*, ed. Paul D. Zimmerman and Dick Schaap (New York: Random House, 1970).

Embry, Wayne. *The Inside Game: Race, Power, and Politics in the NBA* (Akron, OH: University of Akron Press, 2004).

Erving, Julius, with Karl Taro Greenfeld. *Dr. J: The Autobiography* (New York: HarperCollins, 2013).

Farred, Grant. *Phantom Calls: Race and the Globalization of the NBA* (Chicago: Prickly Paradigm Press, 2006).

Federman, Wayne, and Marshall Terrill, with Jackie Maravich. *Maravich: The Authorized Biography of Pistol Pete* (Carol Stream, IL: Tyndale House, 2006).

Feinstein, John. *The Punch: One Night, Two Lives, and the Fight That Changed Basketball Forever* (New York: Hachette, 2002).

Fitzgerald, Joe. *That Championship Feeling: The Story of the Boston Celtics* (New York: Charles Scribner's Sons, 1975).

Forney, Craig A. *The Holy Trinity of American Sports: Civil Religion in Football, Baseball, and Basketball* (Macon, GA: Mercer University Press, 2007).

Frazier, Walt, with Dan Markowitz. *The Game within the Game* (New York: Hyperion, 2006).

Frazier, Walt, and Ira Berkow. *Rockin' Steady: A Guide to Basketball and Cool* (New York: Warner Paperback Library, 1974).

Frazier, Walt, with Neil Offen. *Walt Frazier: One Magical Season and a Basketball Life* (New York: Times Books, 1988).

Friedman, Lester D. *American Cinema of the 1970s: Themes and Variations* (New Brunswick, NJ: Rutgers University Press, 2007).

Frum, David. *How We Got Here: The 70's, the Decade That Brought You Modern Life (For Better or Worse)* (New York: Basic Books, 2000).

Fury, Shawn. *Rise and Fire: The Origins, Science, and Evolution of the Jump Shot—And How It Transformed Basketball Forever* (New York: Flatiron Books, 2016).

Garcia, Bobbito. *Where'd You Get Those? New York City's Sneaker Culture: 1960–1987* (New York: Testify Books, 2013).

Gentile, Derek. *Smooth Moves: Juking, Jamming, Hooking & Slamming, Basketball's Plays, Players, Action & Style* (New York: Black Dog & Leventhal Publishers, 2003).

George, Nelson. *Elevating the Game: Black Men and Basketball* (New York: HarperCollins, 1992).

Goudsouzian, Aram. *King of the Court: Bill Russell and the Basketball Revolution* (Berkeley: University of California Press, 2010).

Halberstam, David. *The Breaks of the Game* (New York: Alfred A. Knopf, 1981).

Havlicek, John, and Bob Ryan. *Hondo: Celtic Man in Motion* (New York: Prentice-Hall, 1977).

Hayes, Elvin, and Bill Gilbert. *They Call Me "The Big E"* (Englewood Cliffs, NJ, Prentice-Hall, 1978).

Haywood, Spencer, with Scott Ostler. *Spencer Haywood: The Rise, the Fall, the Recovery* (New York: Amistad, 1992).

Heinsohn, Tommy, with Leonard Lewin. *Heinsohn, Don't You Ever Smile? The Life and Times of Tommy Heinsohn and the Boston Celtics* (New York: Doubleday, 1976).

Herald, Jacqueline. *Fashions of a Decade: The 1970s* (New York: Infobase Publishing, 2007).

Hollander, Zander, ed. *The Complete Handbook of Pro Basketball 1975* (New York: Signet, 1974).

———. *The Complete Handbook of Pro Basketball 1976* (New York: Signet, 1975).

———. *The Complete Handbook of Pro Basketball: 1980* (New York: Signet, 1979).

Holzman, Red, and Harvey Frommer. *Holzman on Hoops: The Man Who Led the Knicks through Two World Championships Tells It Like It Was* (Dallas: Taylor, 1991).

Issel, Dan, with Buddy Martin. *Parting Shots* (Chicago: Contemporary Books, 1985).

Jackson, Phil. *Maverick: More Than a Game* (Chicago: Playboy Press, 1975).

Johnson, Blaire. *What's Happening?! A Revealing Journey through the World of Professional Basketball* (Englewood Cliffs, NJ: Prentice-Hall, 1978).

Johnson, Earvin "Magic," with William Novak. *My Life* (New York: Random House, 1992).

Keteyian, Aram, Harvey Araton, and Martin F. Dardis. *Money Players: Days and Nights Inside the New NBA* (New York: Pocket Books, 1997).

Klein, David. *Rookie: The World of the NBA* (Chicago: Cowles, 1971).

Knight, Jonathan. *Classic Cavs: The 50 Greatest Games in Cleveland Cavaliers History* (Kent, OH: Kent State University Press, 2009).

Kriegel, Mark. *Pistol: The Life of Pete Maravich* (New York: Free Press, 2007).

Lane, Jeffrey. *Under the Boards: The Cultural Revolution in Basketball* (Lincoln: University of Nebraska Press, 2007).

Lazenby, Roland. *And Now, Your Chicago Bulls! A Thirty-Year Celebration* (Dallas: Taylor, 1995).

———. *Jerry West: The Life and Legend of a Basketball Icon* (New York: Ballantine Books, 2009).

———. *The Lakers: A Basketball Journey* (New York: St. Martin's Press, 1993).

———. *The NBA Finals: A Fifty Year Celebration* (Lincolnwood, IL: Master's Press, 1996).

Leonard, David J. *After Artest: The NBA and the Assault on Blackness* (Albany: State University of New York Press, 2012).

Lewis, Thabiti. *Ballers of the New School: Race and Sports in America* (Chicago: Third World Press, 2010).

Libby, Bill, and Spencer Haywood. *Stand up for Something: The Spencer Haywood Story* (New York: Grosset and Dunlap, 1975).

Logan, Bob. *The Bulls and Chicago: A Stormy Affair* (Chicago: Follett, 1975).

Love, Matt, ed. *Red Hot and Rollin': A Retrospection of the Portland Trail Blazers' 1976–77 Championship Season* (Pacific City, OR: Nestucca Spit Press, 2007).

Love, Robert Earl, with Mel Watkins. *The Bob Love Story: If It's Gonna Be, It's Up to Me.* (Lincolnwood, IL: Contemporary Books, 2000).

Lynch, Wayne. *Season of the 76ers: The Story of Wilt Chamberlain and the 1967 NBA Champion Philadelphia 76ers* (New York: Thomas Dunne Books, 2002).

Mallozzi, Vincent M. *Asphalt Gods: An Oral History of the Rucker Tournament* (New York: Doubleday, 2003).

———. *Doc: The Rise and Rise of Julius Erving* (Hoboken: John Wiley & Sons, 2010).

Maravich, Pete, and Darrel Campbell. *Heir to a Dream* (Nashville: Thomas Nelson, 1987).

Marshall, Kerry D. *Two of a Kind: The Tom and Dick Van Arsdale Story* (Indianapolis: Scott Publications, 1992).

McPhee, John. *A Sense of Where You Are: A Profile of William Warren Bradley* (New York: Farrar, Straus and Giroux, 1965).

Menzer, Joe, and Burt Graeff. *Cavs from Fitch to Fratello* (Champaign, IL: Sagamore Publishing, 1994).

Miller, Patrick, and David K. Wiggins, eds. *Sport and the Color Line: Black Athletes and Race Relations in Twentieth-Century America* (New York: Routledge, 2004).

Motta, Dick, with Jerry Jenkins. *Stuff It: The Story of Dick Motta, Toughest Little Coach in the NBA* (Radnor, PA: Chilton, 1975).

Nelson, Murry. *Abe Saperstein and the American Basketball League, 1960–63: The Upstarts Who Shot for Three and Lost to the NBA* (Jefferson, NC: McFarland, 2013).

Osborne, Ben, ed. *Slamkicks: Basketball Sneakers That Changed the Game* (New York: Universal Publishing, 2013).

Pearlman, Jeff. *Showtime: Magic, Kareem, Riley, and the Los Angeles Lakers Dynasty of the 1980s* (New York: Gotham Books, 2014).

Pluto, Terry. *Loose Balls: The Short, Wild Life of the American Basketball Association* (New York: Simon & Schuster, 1990).

———. *Tall Tales: The Glory Years of the NBA* (Lincoln: University of Nebraska Press, 1992).

Pomerantz, Gary. *Wilt, 1962: The Night of 100 Points and the Dawn of a New Era* (New York: Crown, 2005).

Powell, Shaun. *Souled Out? How Blacks Are Winning and Losing in Sports* (Champaign, IL: Human Kinetics, 2008).

Powers, John. *The Short Season: A Boston Celtics Diary 1977–1978* (New York: Harper & Row, 1979).

Powers, Richie, with Mark Mulvoy. *Overtime! An Uninhibited Account of a Referee's Life in the NBA* (New York: David McKay, 1975).

Rader, Benjamin G. *In Its Own Image: How Television Has Transformed Sports* (New York: Free Press, 1984).

Rappoport, Ken. *The Little League That Could: A History of the American Football League* (Lanham, MD: Taylor Trade, 2010).

Reed, Willis. *A Will to Win: The Comeback Year* (Englewood Cliffs, NJ: Prentice-Hall, 1973).

Reed, Willis, with Phil Pepe. *A View from the Rim: Willis Reed on Basketball* (Philadelphia: Lippincott, 1971).

Richmond, Peter. *Phil Jackson: Lord of the Rings* (New York: Blue Rider Press, 2013).

Robertson, Oscar. *The Big O: My Life, My Times, My Game* (Emmaus, PA: Rodale Press, 2003).

Rosen, Charles. *God, Man and Basketball Jones: The Thinking Fan's Guide to Professional Basketball* (New York: Holt, Rinehart and Winston, 1979).

Rosen, Charley. *Perfectly Awful: The Philadelphia 76ers' Horrendous and Hilarious 1972–1973 Season* (Lincoln: University of Nebraska Press, 2014).

———. *The Pivotal Season: How the 1971–72 Los Angeles Lakers Changed the NBA* (New York: St. Martin's Press, 2005).

Russell, Bill. *Red and Me: My Coach, My Lifelong Friend* (New York: HarperCollins, 2009).

Russell, Bill, and Taylor Branch. *Second Wind: The Memoirs of an Opinionated Man* (New York: Random House, 1979).

Ryan, Bob. *Celtics Pride: The Rebuilding of Boston's World Championship Basketball Team* (Boston: Little, Brown, 1975).

———. *Scribe: My Life in Sports* (New York: Bloomsbury, 2014).

Sabin, Louis. *Basketball Stars of 1971* (New York: Pyramid Books, 1970).

————. *Basketball Stars of 1972* (New York: Pyramid Books, 1971).

Sagert, Kelly Boyer. *The 1970s* (Westport, CT: Greenwood Press, 2007).

Shaughnessy, Dan. *Ever Green: The Boston Celtics, a History in the Words of Their Players, Coaches, Fans, and Foes, from 1946 to the Present* (New York: St. Martin's Press, 1990).

Shoals, Bethlehem, and Jacob Weinstein. *Freedarko Presents: The Undisputed Guide to Pro Basketball History* (New York: Bloomsbury, 2010).

Simmons, Bill. *The Book of Basketball* (New York: Random House, 2009).

Skinner, Tina, *Fashionable Clothing from the Sears Catalog: Mid-1970s* (Altglen, PA: Schiffer Publishing, 1999).

Smith, John Matthew. *The Sons of Westwood: John Wooden, UCLA, and the Dynasty That Changed College Basketball* (Urbana: University of Illinois Press, 2013).

Stainback, Barry. *Basketball Stars of 1968* (New York: Pyramid Books, 1967).

Stauth, Cameron. *The Franchise: Building a Winner with the World Champion Detroit Pistons, Basketball's Bad Boys* (New York: William Morrow, 1990).

Steele, Valerie. *Fifty Years of Fashion: New Look to Now* (New Haven, CT: Yale University Press, 1997).

Strom, Earl, with Blaine Johnson. *Calling the Shots: My Five Decades in the NBA* (New York: Simon & Schuster, 1990).

Surdam, David George. *The Rise of the National Basketball Association* (Urbana: University of Illinois Press, 2012).

Thomas, Ron. *They Cleared the Lane: The NBA's Black Pioneers* (Lincoln: University of Nebraska Press, 2002).

Thompson, David, with Sean Stormes and Marshall Terrill. *David Thompson: Skywalker* (Champaign, IL: Sports Publishing, 2003).

Van Arsdale, Tom, and Dick Van Arsdale, with Joel H. Cohen. *Our Basketball Lives* (New York: G. P. Putnam's Sons, 1973).

Walker, Chet, with Chris Messenger. *Long Time Coming: A Black Athlete's Coming-of-Age in America* (New York: Grove Press, 1995).

Walton, Bill, with Gene Wojciechowski. *Nothing but Net: Just Give Me the Ball and Get out of the Way* (New York: Hyperion, 1994).

Weber, Bruce. *All-Pro Basketball Stars 1976* (New York: Scholastic Book Services, 1976).

Wendel, Tim. *Buffalo, Home of the Braves* (Traverse City, MI: Sun Bear Press, 2009).

West, Jerry, and Bill Libby. *Mr. Clutch: The Jerry West Story* (Englewood Hills, NJ: Prentice-Hall, 1969).

West, Jerry, and Jonathan Coleman. *West by West: My Charmed, Tormented Life* (New York: Little, Brown, 2011).

Whalen, Thomas J. *Dynasty's End: Bill Russell and the 1968–69 World Champion Boston Celtics* (Boston: Northeastern University Press, 2004).

Wiggins, David K. *Glory Bound: Black Athletes in White America* (Syracuse: Syracuse University Press, 1997).

Wilkens, Lenny, with Terry Pluto. *Unguarded: My Forty Years Surviving in the NBA* (New York: Simon and Schuster, 2000).

Wilkes, Jamaal. *Jamaal Wilkes: Memoirs of the Original Smooth As Silk* (Los Angeles: 88 Str8 Enterprises, 2015).

Williams, Pat, and Jerry B. Jenkins. *The Gingerbread Man: Pat Williams—Then and Now* (Philadelphia: A. J. Holman, 1974).

Wolf, David. *Foul! The Connie Hawkins Story* (New York: Holt, Rinehart, and Winston, 1972).

Zirin, Dave. *A People's History of Sports in the United States: 250 Years of Politics, Protest, People, and Play* (New York: New Press, 2008).

UNPUBLISHED THESIS

Sarmento, Mario R. "The NBA on Network Television: A Historical Analysis." MA thesis, University of Florida, 1998.

FILMS

Doucette, Eddie. *Countdown to a Dream*. www.youtube.com/watch?v=nEgfomjJVZE. Accessed December 2, 2014.
Roy, George. *Pistol Pete: The Life and Times of Pete Maravich* (Sheridan, WY: Black Canyon Productions, 2001).
Touched by Gold: The History-Making Story of the 1971–1972 NBA Champion Los Angeles Lakers (New York: Bombo Sports & Entertainment, 2012).

NEWSPAPERS AND MAGAZINES

Action Sports Basketball
Basketball
Basketball Digest
Basketball News
Basketball News 1973–74 Pro Yearbook
Basketball Sports Stars
Basketball Weekly
Basketball's All-Pro Annual
Basketball's Best
Complete Sports
The Complete Televiewer's Guide to Pro Basketball
Countrywide Sports
Fast Break
National Basketball Association Official Guide
New York Times
Popular Sports All-Pro Basketball
Pro Basketball Almanac
Pro Basketball Guide
Pro Basketball Illustrated
Pro Basketball Sports Stars
SPORT
The Sporting News
Sports All Stars
Sports All Stars Pro Basketball
Sports Illustrated
Sports Review Basketball
Sports Review's Basketball
Victory Sports Series

INDEX

ABOUT THE AUTHOR

Adam J. Criblez is assistant professor of history at Southeast Missouri State University. His first book, *Parading Patriotism: Independence Days in the Urban Midwest, 1826–1876* (2013) won several regional history awards. He lives in Cape Girardeau, Missouri, with his wife and three daughters.